Managing Ethics in Business Organizations

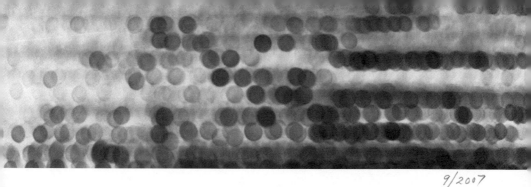

9/2007

Managing Ethics in Business Organizations

SOCIAL SCIENTIFIC PERSPECTIVES

Linda Klebe Treviño
Gary R. Weaver

STANFORD BUSINESS BOOKS
An imprint of STANFORD UNIVERSITY PRESS

Stanford University Press
Stanford, California

Printed in the United States of America
on acid-free, archival-quality paper.

Special discounts for bulk quantities of Stanford Business Books are
available to corporations, professional associations, and other organizations. For details and discount information, contact the special sales
department of Stanford University Press.

Library of Congress Cataloging-in-Publication Data

Treviño, Linda Klebe
    Managing ethics in organizations : a social scientific perspective on
    business ethics / Linda Klebe Treviño, Gary R. Weaver.
        p.   cm.
    ISBN 0-8047-4376-2
        1. Business ethics. I. Weaver, Gary R. (Gary Richard). 1952–
    II. Title.
    HF5387 .T735 2003
    174'.4 — dc21   2002011480

Original Printing 2003

Last figure below indicates year of this printing:
12   11   10   09   08   07   06   05   04   03

Typeset by BookMatters in 11/14 Filosofia

Table of Contents

Preface

Our discussions of ethics in organizations began in late 1990. These early discussions—focusing on different approaches to understanding ethics in organizations and culminating in an article that is now Chapter 1 of this book—developed into a productive research partnership, generating theoretical frameworks and empirical studies about the various factors that influence ethical and unethical behavior in organizations. Now, about a decade later, we think it wise to "take stock" of our research on organizational ethics by bringing together a number of original journal articles with additional chapters written specifically for this volume. Our hope is that, by doing so, we can serve the study of business ethics in multiple ways. First, we have used this opportunity to draw connections between aspects of our work that have always been obvious to us but perhaps have not been apparent to others. Second, this book also affords an opportunity for us to comment on the overall state of business ethics research, both its prospects and opportunities for the future and its current difficulties and deficiencies. Finally, and pragmatically, this book brings together a collection of articles originally published in very diverse outlets, in a form that we hope will be more accessible to scholars, practitioners, and students concerned with ethics in organizations. Our overall goal is to convey the results of a research program that we hope has added substantially to the understanding of ethics in organizations.

In Part I, we focus on metatheoretical issues related to business ethics as a field of study, and we explain how our joint work—which has been mostly in the empirical arena—fits into that broader framework. In Part II, we take on the role of organizational sociologists who study the influences on the development of organizational structures and practices aimed at fostering ethical behavior in organizations. We present the results of a major empirical research project that outlines these influences. In Part III, we function more as organizational social psychologists who are interested in understanding how individual differences, issues, and organizational characteristics influence individual ethical decision making and behavior in organizations. We present the results of multiple empirical research projects that help to flesh out these influences. Finally, Part IV offers two chapters written for this volume. The first outlines a host of methodological issues that face those conducting research in the area of business ethics. The final chapter provides our thoughts on the future of business ethics research, including outlining a number of open questions that remain.

We would like to thank those who have supported us and collaborated with us, as follows:

Linda Treviño: I would like to begin by thanking my mentors, who supported my dissertation work at Texas A & M University, particularly Stuart Youngblood, Richard Woodman, Don Hellriegel, and Mary Zey (then in the sociology department). These mentors supported a dissertation on ethical decision making in organizations at a time when that was not a widely accepted topic of study in organizational behavior. I also would like to thank my supportive family and network of friends, my exceptional colleagues at Penn State, and the doctoral students with whom I have worked on research related to ethics and justice in organizations: Gail Ball, Kenneth Butterfield, Kelly Mollica, Michael Brown, and, of course, Gary Weaver. I reserve special thanks for my husband and best friend, Dan, who supports my work and my very being in every way.

Gary Weaver: As someone who once wrote a Ph.D. dissertation on philosophical issues in the explanation of human action, but who then actually became a practitioner of empirical social science, I have encountered the challenges and tensions described in Parts I and IV first hand. Thus, I owe special thanks to those social science scholars who aided and abetted my interdisciplinary endeavor, sometimes by offering help and encouragement, other times by adapting to philosophical idiosyncrasies. Obviously, this group includes Linda Treviño, but also prominently includes Penn State colleagues Phil Cochran, Denny Gioia, and Martin Kilduff. Jim Weber and Tom Donaldson also have been valued sources of encouragement at various times, although they may not realize it. Empathy seems a likely source of sensitivity to ethical issues in business, and so in my own case I also owe thanks to my late father, Drew Weaver, for giving me an insider's perspective on less-than-kindly dealings in the corporate world (he being the victim, not perpetrator). In light of his experiences, he also warned me, "Never work for a bank." I did not, but now I warn my children, "Never get two Ph.D. degrees." So I offer my deepest gratitude to my long-suffering, good-humored, and unconditionally supportive family: wife June, children Evan and Priscilla, mother Lillian, and in-laws Louise and the late Robert Heistand.

Both authors: We both thank colleagues who have contributed to the work reported here as well as related projects over the years. Co-authors who have contributed to the work in this book include Dennis Gioia, Philip Cochran (both of Penn State), Ken Butterfield (Washington State University), Donald McCabe (Rutgers University), Barbara Toffler and David Gibson (both formerly of Arthur Andersen LLP). We also acknowledge the Stanford University Press editorial team and the organizations that have supported various parts of the research presented in this book: the Ethics in Business Research Fund of the American Institute of Certified Public Accountants, the former Ethics and Responsible Business Practices Services group at Arthur Andersen LLP, and the University of Delaware's General University Research Fund. Final preparation of the book, including work on chapters not previously published, was supported by a grant from the College of Business and Economics at the University of Delaware.

Managing Ethics in Business Organizations

Introduction: Business Ethics as a Field of Inquiry

Business ethics is quite old as a topic of individual and societal concern, but it is relatively new as a topic of social scientific scrutiny. Ancient writers, such as Aristotle and Cicero, made numerous observations on and evaluations of the ethical propriety of commercial practices, such as interest rates and the pricing of goods. Other ancient sources offer strictures on the ways commerce is to be conducted (for example, by the standards of ancient Israel, business contracts were to be made at the gate of a city, that is, in full public view). Scholastic writers of the late Middle Ages (for example, Aquinas) likewise sometimes addressed the proper conduct of business, as did their immediate successors in Reformation-era Europe (for example, Luther, Calvin). Enlightenment and post-Enlightenment era philosophy contributed many still-active frameworks for analyzing ethical issues in business and commerce, for example, Locke's positions on the appropriation of property and accumulation of wealth, Kant's categorical imperative, and Bentham's and Mill's utilitarianisms. Twentieth-century writers have continued to develop these earlier perspectives (for example, in a renewal and adaptation of Aristotelian virtue ethics or in business-specific reformulations of Kantian theory) and also have contributed new perspectives variously rooted in contemporary pragmatism, naturalism, and assorted post-modernisms.

The late twentieth century was, relatively speaking, a booming time for business ethics. The years since World War II saw a growing range of ethically relevant business activities and issues gain prominence in the United States and other Western economies. The 1950s saw the American electric equipment industry stirred by a massive price-fixing and antitrust scandal involving some of the most well-known and respected names in American business. Countercultural and environmental movements of the 1960s and 1970s, inspired in part by ethical questions about established institutions (for example, the Vietnam war protests and the Nixon-era Watergate scandal) kept attention on questions of the ethical behavior of large organizations and institutions. Defense-industry contracting fraud and bribery scandals, along with insider-trading securities frauds and dubious practices of corporate "raiders" and junk bond financiers, brought more attention to business ethics in the 1970s and 1980s. At least some of these events and practices generated new legal mandates for American business. For example, the Foreign Corrupt Practices Act (1977) outlawed payments by American businesses to foreign officials and a 1986 revision gave new life to the long-moribund False Claims Act of 1863 (originally enacted to deal with defense contracting fraud during the Civil War) by extending it to protect persons who "blow the whistle" on fraudulent financial transactions with the federal government.

Missing from much early and recent attention to business ethics, however, is systematic attention to the psychological, social psychological, and sociological context within which ethical and unethical human behavior occurs in business organizations. Complex organizations have become the venue within which the bulk of business activity takes place, and those organizations can have many different influences on the ethics of their members. The ethical stances of these organizations in turn reflect myriad influences arising both internally and externally. For example, it may have seemed like conventional wisdom in the business world of the early 1990s for executives at Sears, Roebuck & Company to boost productivity by putting auto repair shop employees on commission and quota-based incentive systems. Repair shop employees, however, responded to those organizational influences by lying to customers and performing unneeded repairs. This occurred within the context of an external environment in which relevant government agencies were anxious to prove their effectiveness and created an incendiary situation that soon tarnished the company name and led to much lost business.

Consequently, important as it is to engage in the normative study of what is, and is not, ethically proper in business, it is just as important to understand the organizational and institutional context within which ethical issues, awareness, and behavior are situated. There is at least some precedent for doing so within business ethics scholarship itself. Adam Smith's pioneering writings in the eighteenth century provide a good example. Smith's approach to questions of proper behavior in the commercial world invokes explicit normative judgments about how individual and collective actions contribute to or detract from societal welfare; but those judgments are rooted in a particular understanding of the psychological and sociological aspects of ethical behavior. Moreover, they are relatively complex portraits of human behavior. Most readers probably are familiar with how Smith, in *The Wealth of Nations* (originally published in 1776), posits self-interest as a key motivation for behavior and proceeds to draw out positive social consequences of self-interested behavior; but Smith also recognizes the potential negative impacts of self-interested behavior and the economic system it generates. For example, he laments the working-class stultification likely to be generated by ever-increasing specialization of labor and the probability that businesses will collude so as to thwart market-based restraints on their self-interest. This raises an important question: If Smith was not naively oblivious to the potential negatives of a market economy driven by self-interest, how could he propose such a system so forcefully? Part of the answer lies in the fact that Smith's normative claims and proposals reflect a particular understanding of moral psychology, an understanding explicated earlier in Smith's *Theory of Moral Sentiments* (1759). There Smith addresses persons' capacity to be sympathetic toward the predicaments of others and posits that this natural sense of sympathy attendant to interpersonal relations is the basis for the "impartial spectator" (what we might call one's conscience) by which we judge and guide our own actions. In short, the moral psychology provides the basis for thinking that excesses of self-interest possible in unfettered markets might be held in check much of the time.

Our point here is neither to defend nor criticize Smith but to offer him as an example of how theorizing about issues of business ethics need not be strictly normative in focus but also can (and should) incorporate attention to psychological and sociological issues. Although contemporary psychological and sociological theories differ from Smith's, the propriety of his approach remains: effective thinking about business ethics requires attention to both normative and social scientific issues.

Despite the importance of social scientific inquiry to a full understanding of ethics in organizations, until recently, most social scientific scholarship and managerial writing about business has avoided questions of ethics—either normative or empirical. There are, of course, some notable exceptions. For example, Chester Barnard's 1938 classic of management theory, *The Functions of the Executive*, forthrightly addressed questions of managerial responsibility, focusing primarily on intraorganizational processes. Barnard argued that one of the tasks of management theorizing was to distinguish an executive's responsibility to further the "objective purpose" of the organization from the executive's own self-interested purposes. One can criticize Barnard for reifying the subjective purposes of executives into the "objective purpose" of the organization, but one cannot deny that his effort to develop a theoretical understanding of formal organizations addressed both normative and descriptive issues. From an extraorganizational perspective, Adolf Berle and Gardiner Means' *The Modern Corporation and Private Property* (1933) similarly considered questions of executive responsibility mixed with economic and sociological analysis, considering how public policy and corporate governance might be used to discipline an increasingly autonomous class of corporate executives.

For much of the twentieth century, however, social science–oriented scholarship largely left questions of business ethics unaddressed, leaving the subject to be considered, if at all, in primarily normative works (for example, Sharp and Fox's *Business Ethics: Studies in Fair Competition*, 1937) or managerial guidebooks (for example, Heermance's *Codes of Ethics*, 1924). Even today, the bulk of writing on business ethics is normative, rooted in humanities disciplines, such as philosophy or, to a lesser extent, religion. For example, most articles appearing in recent years in *Business Ethics Quarterly* and the *Journal of Business Ethics* are philosophical and normative in orientation.

Raymond Baumhart's 1961 *Harvard Business Review* article, "How ethical are businessmen?" followed in 1968 by his *An Honest Profit: What Businessmen Say About Ethics in Business*, sometimes is credited as being the first modern empirical research on business ethics. It is instructive to consider what Baumhart, and others soon to follow, did and did not do. Baumhart's interviews with and questionnaire answers from managers form the basis for an interesting and informative portrait of business managers' values and attitudes toward ethical questions. This portrait, along with those soon to follow from other researchers, grounds their questions and interpretive frameworks more in the surface-level categories of the managerial world than in the more abstract categories of theoretical psychology, sociology, and economics. As attention to business ethics grew through the 1960s and 1970s, more empirical studies of ethical practices in business appeared (for example, Chatov 1980; White and Montgomery 1980), but typically these were descriptive and largely atheoretical. Although one could find studies reporting the number of companies with codes of ethics (for example), empirical research on the actual behavioral impact of codes (based on psychological theory) or on the reasons why codes are adopted (based on sociological theory) mostly were absent.

Thus, empirical study of business ethics in the 1960s and 1970s focused largely on identifying managers' own values and on describing or recommending basic formal elements of organizations that might help managers deal with ethical issues (for example, codes of ethics). As business ethics grew as a matter of popular concern through the 1980s and early 1990s, however, a new range of social scientific research addressed specific questions. Much theoretical and empirical research began to address questions of individual ethical decision making, the influences on it, and its behavioral outcomes (for example, Hegarty and Sims 1978, 1979). Additional research focused on other individually oriented, intraorganizational issues, in particular questions of organizational justice and its outcomes (for example, Ball, Treviño and Sims 1994; Greenberg 1990; Treviño and Ball 1992) and whistle blowing by employees (for example, Miceli and Near 1992). A different strain of research, focused more on extraorganizational issues, later began to address corporations' responses to societal expectations for responsible behavior, even to the point of trying to assess the impact of socially responsible corporate behavior on financial performance (for example, Waddock and Graves 1997).

The foregoing topics represent a rather narrow set of issues in business ethics and also embody a split between intraorganizational and extraorganizational phenomena. Relatively absent through the 1980s and early 1990s, for example, are studies that cross the boundary between intraorganizational and extraorganizational processes and influences. Many of the extant individual-level studies in this period focused on individual differences (such as gender, age, education) as predictors of ethical decision making or behavior but did not address the role of organizational context. Likewise, studies of organizations' responses to external pressures did not necessarily take into account the role of managerial agency in determining responses to those pressures (Cochran and Nigh 1987; Staw and Szwajkowski 1975). Yet wide-ranging empirical studies of business ethics are important, if for no other reason than to see that public policy initiatives achieve their intended outcomes and avoid unintended consequences. For example, under guidelines introduced by the United States Sentencing Commission in 1991, U.S. law now gives substantial incentives—in the form of reduced penalties attached to violations of the law—to organizations that proactively implement various initiatives intended to foster ethical and legal behavior by employees. Yet, until recently, the effectiveness of the proposed initiatives, and their appropriateness across multiple kinds of organizations, has not received the kind of systematic, theoretically informed empirical study that should drive such an important government policy initiative.

In some ways, the absence of research on these issues should not be surprising. Business ethics is a sensitive topic for most managers and for most organizations, with the potential for embarrassment (at least) or civil and criminal legal exposure (at worst). So it is often hard to find organizations and managers willing to participate in empirical research. This fact may explain the predominance of studies of individual ethical decision making and values in much of the extant body of business ethics research because such research more easily can be done in a less threatening laboratory setting (often using student subjects). Even that kind of controlled, laboratory research, however, can be afflicted with a range of methodological doubts. Student subjects, for example, may disguise or misrepresent their actual beliefs, attitudes, and intentions for the sake of not appearing to violate social norms of good behavior. Thus, empirical business ethics research confronts methodological difficulties avoided by many other venues of organizational inquiry, difficulties that nevertheless are easily noted by diligent gatekeepers of the scholarly publishing process. So the methodological issues of the field make it a relatively high-risk venue from the standpoint of a scholar's academic career advancement.

Also missing from most business ethics research has been careful attention to the relationship between normative and social scientific understandings of business ethics—relationships embraced by early writers such as Smith but largely ignored by most social scientific students of business ethics in the 1980s and 1990s. Donaldson and Preston (1995) have argued that questions and theories of business ethics and social responsibilities can be understood as either descriptive (that is, answering questions about what businesses or managers do vis-à-vis ethics), instrumental (that is, answering questions about how to achieve a particular end) or normative (that is, answering questions about what ought to be done, or what ends ought to be pursued). Most humanities-based scholars of business ethics find themselves focused on the last of these questions, whereas social science—based scholars are focused on one or both of the first two; but little crossover has occurred. One might say that the attitude of normative and social scientific business ethics scholars toward each others' work often has been like the attitude of most citizens toward the sewer system: "They know it is there, they assume that it works, and they question the good sense of anyone who goes poking around in it" (an analogy borrowed from McClelland (1975, 18), who used it to describe economists' attitudes toward metatheory).

What follows in this book is the result of a decade's work by the authors—individually, jointly, and with others—aimed both at broadening the range of theoretically informed empirical research on business ethics and at dealing with the underlying questions of the nature of business ethics research (methodologically and in terms of the normative—empirical relationship). Portions of the work are adapted from previously published articles, and other portions of the work are new.

Figure I.1 provides an overview of the work, with the different parts of the book labeled in the figure. Part I of the book acknowledges the normative foundation of business ethics scholarship and addresses the ever-present metatheoretical questions involved in doing empirical research about normative issues. Chapter 1, "*Business* Ethics/Business *Ethics*: One Field or Two?" explains the range of methodological, conceptual, and institutional boundaries that too easily separate normative and empirical theorists from each other. Chapter 2, "Normative and Empirical Business Ethics," moves from the fact of normative/empirical distinctions to examine different rationales for and approaches to maintaining or removing those distinctions. The 1990s saw a number of papers published on questions of inte-

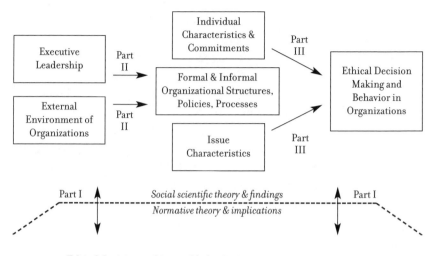

FIGURE I.1. Ethical decision making and behavior in organizations

grating normative and empirical inquiry in business ethics, including our own. Chapter 3, "Perspectives, Possibilities, and Motives for Integration" provides a postscript to that decade of theorizing. In it, we provide our own perspective for how to think about the relationship of normative and empirical scholarship, one that holds both in tension as bracketed perspectives on a more complex phenomenon. We also offer our own assessment of recent efforts at integration, and consider why the issue is likely never to cease vexing business ethics research.

Part II of the book addresses organization-level issues, in particular by describing, and then explaining, the factors that influence the increasing institutionalization of formal systems designed to manage ethics in organizations. Chapter 4, "Has Business Ethics Come of Age?" provides a summary of the state of organizational ethics initiatives in the 1990s. Interesting as that may be in itself, however, it is important to consider what influences organizations to engage in particular activities and to do so from a perspective informed by organization theory and organizational behavior (that is, extraorganizational and intraorganizational influences). Chapters 5 and 6 ("Corporate Ethics Programs as Control Systems" and "Integrated and De-coupled Corporate Social Performance") do just that. Chapter 5 addresses the dual role of institutional pressures from the external environment and managerial agency (executive leadership) in determining the extent and character of corporate ethics activity, and Chapter 6 looks at how those two kinds of factors influence the development of "window dressing" ethics initiatives versus more serious ethics initiatives.

Part III shifts the focus to explaining individual ethical behavior and the many influences on it. These influences range from issue characteristics, to individual characteristics and commitments, to formal and informal structure, processes, and policies. Chapter 7, "Ethical Decision Making and Conduct in Organizations: Individuals, Issues, and Context" reviews theoretical models of ethical decision making and behavior in organizations and some of the empirical research that has tested those relationships. It addresses a range of successes, failures, and new prospects in the effort to identify factors that influence ethical behavior by organization members (such as age, locus of control, cognitive moral development, ethical issue intensity). Chapter 8, "The Uses and Limits of Formal Organizational Ethics Programs," leaves individual factors behind and looks at questions of how organizations' formal ethics initiatives influence—or fail to influence— individuals' ethical behavior. Chapter 9, "Ethics and the Broader Organizational Context: Ethical Climate and Ethical Culture," combines research from multiple empirical studies into a comprehensive account of successful organizational ethics initiatives, indicating how they need to be deeply ingrained into organizational cultures, and not merely formal initiatives. Chapter 10, "Employees' Fairness Perceptions and Ethics-related Outcomes in Organizations," looks more specifically at questions of how the perceived fairness of organizational practices influences how employees respond to efforts to foster ethical behavior.

The final brief section of the book (not represented in the figure) considers two important issues confronting future empirical business ethics research. Chapter 11, "Methodological Challenges in Empirical Business Ethics Research," considers the often sensitive and difficult methodological questions that arise in conducting empirical research on business ethics and reviews a number of strategies that can be used to deal with these issues. Finally, Chapter 12, "Unfinished Business Ethics: Open Questions for Future Study," provides our reflections on where social scientific business ethics research needs to move in the future if it is to gain stronger theoretical and empirical footing while staying abreast of the changing dynamics of the business world.

References

Ball, G. A., L. K. Treviño, and H. P. Sims. 1994. Just and unjust punishment: Influences on subordinate performance and citizenship. *Academy of Management Journal* 37:299–322.

Barnard, C. I. 1938. *The functions of the executive*. Cambridge, MA: Harvard University Press.

Baumhart S. J., R. C. 1961. How ethical are businessmen? *Harvard Business Review* 39:156–176.

Baumhart S. J., R. C. 1968. *An honest profit: What businessmen say about ethics in business*. New York: Holt, Rinehart, & Winston.

Berle, A. A., and G. Means. 1933. *The modern corporation and private property*. New York: Macmillan Company.

Chatov, R. 1980. What corporate ethics statements say. *California Management Review* 22(4):20–29.

Cochran, P. L., and D. Nigh. 1987. Illegal corporate behavior and the question of moral agency: an empirical examination. In *Research in corporate social performance and policy*, Vol. 9, ed. W. C. Frederick, 73–91. Greenwich, CT: JAI Press.

Donaldson, T., and L. E. Preston. 1995. The stakeholder theory of the corporation: Concepts, evidence, and implications. *Academy of Management Review* 20:65–91.

Greenberg, J. 1990. Employee theft as a reaction to underpayment inequity: the hidden costs of pay cuts. *Journal of Applied Psychology* 75:561–568.

Heermance, E. L. 1924. *Codes of ethics: a handbook*. Burlington, VT: Free Print Co.

Hegarty, W. H., and H. P. Sims. 1978. Some determinants of unethical decision behavior: an experiment. *Journal of Applied Psychology* 62:451–457.

Hegarty, W. H., and H. P. Sims. 1979. Organizational philosophy, policies and objectives related to unethical decision behavior: a laboratory experiment. *Journal of Applied Psychology* 64:331–338.

McClelland, P. D. 1975. *Causal explanation and model building in history, economics and the new economic history*. Ithaca, NY: Cornell University Press.

Miceli, M. P., and J. P. Near. 1992. *Blowing the whistle: The organizational and legal implications for companies and employees*. New York: Lexington Books.

Sharp, F. C., and P. G. Fox. 1937. *Business ethics: studies in fair competition*. New York: Appleton Century.

Smith, A. 1976–1980. *Works and correspondence of Adam Smith*, 7 vols. Oxford: Oxford University Press.

Staw, B. M., and E. Szwajkowski. 1975. The scarcity–munificence component of organizational environments and the commission of illegal acts. *Administrative Science Quarterly* 20:345–355.

Treviño, L. K., and G. A. Ball. 1992. The social implications of punishing unethical behavior: Observers' cognitive and affective reactions. *Journal of Management* 18:751–769.

Waddock, S. A., and S. B. Graves. 1997. The corporate social performance-financial performance link. *Strategic Management Journal* 18:303–320.

White, B. J., and R. Montgomery. 1980. Corporate codes of conduct. *California Management Review* 23:80–87.

PART ONE

Metatheoretical Issues of Normative and Empirical Inquiry in Business Ethics

As noted in the Introduction, most scholarly writing on business ethics has taken an explicitly normative stance. That is, it has focused on questions of what are, or are not, ethically proper practices in various areas of business, such as marketing, finance, accounting, and management. Normative scholarship, however, is not immune to empirical concerns. To evaluate particular business practices, it often is necessary to know in detail how those practices are conducted or what their many outcomes are. Thus, it should be no surprise that scholars who work in largely normative contexts—philosophers, theologians, and others—need sometimes to involve themselves with the work of more empirically minded business scholars. Empirically oriented business scholars also at least implicitly depend on normative thinking as well. Sometimes this may be because they make explicit—if undefended—normative claims, as when a particular empirically based theory is presented as a tool for achieving some allegedly desirable end. In other cases, the dependence on normative views is implicit, occurring insofar as normative concerns drive the choice of focus in a research agenda. For example, we might wonder whether there would have been as much empirical research on the effects of the 1990s' corporate downsizings on surviving employees and surrounding communities had downsizing not been so normatively controversial. That is, if downsizing had all the ethical controversy of, say, corporate decisions regarding how many pens and pencils to buy, would anyone have studied it empirically?

Thus, normative and empirical scholars in business ethics do need to pay at least some attention to each other, but this raises problems. Normative and empirical scholars often reflect very different perspectives, training, and styles of scholarship. Thus, there is much potential for confusion (at best) and mutual suspicion (at worst) because normative and empirical scholars risk holding each other to their own particular standards and expectations. For example, one of us presented the results of one of the empirical studies described in Part II to a group of faculty at a respected university. Following the presentation of this empirical study of corporate ethics programs, a philosopher in the audience claimed that he did not see any connection of the study to business ethics because the study had nothing to do with normative questions of right and wrong. Thus, in Part I of this book, we hope to clarify some of these potential misunderstandings and offer our own account of how normative and empirical inquiry constitute different but related perspectives on business ethics, each with their own values and each with their limitations.

In Chapter 1, we examine in detail the range of issues and practices that generate risks of mutual confusion or suspicion among normative and empirical scholars, concluding that there are real and genuine differences among them that must be treated with care if confusion and suspicion are to be avoided. What does it mean to treat these differences with care? Apart from recognizing the potential pitfalls and thus seeking to avoid them, careful treatment of differences involves thinking systematically about their tenability. That is, are the surface-level differences of practice, outlined in Chapter 1, defensible and sustainable in light of more careful scrutiny of the foundations of both normative and empirical scholarship? Put differently: From a metatheoretical perspective, are the differences noted in Chapter 1 somehow essential to the practices of normative and empirical business ethics, or can they be (or, even, must they be) surmounted in some way? Thus Chapter 2 develops and evaluates three different kinds of metatheoretical understandings of the relationship between normative and empirical business ethics scholarship. In it, we argue that the easy route of ignoring the other field and going one's own way is untenable. Any theoretically deep merging of the two fields, although not impossible, likely would yield a kind of business ethics scholarship very unlike what any of us know now. More realistic, then, might be an approach in which normative and empirical scholars recognize the limitations of their own perspectives, and their at least implicit dependence on each other, in that each provides a partial picture of what is important to know in business ethics, a picture that brackets and holds constant certain elements of the overall picture that are best left to scholars of the opposite type. Chapter 3, then, spells out more of the details of this perspectival position and situates the position in a larger context by relating it to (1) discussions of other divides and dichotomies in research on life in organizations and (2) other attempts explicitly to link normative and empirical concerns regarding the morality of business practices.

ONE

Business Ethics/Business *Ethics*: One Field or Two?

Scene: A conference on business ethics where academics from liberal arts
philosophy departments (business *ethics*) and business schools (*business*
ethics) are gathered to share their past year's work:

> *Business school faculty member*: "These philosophers don't seem to
> know much about business. Their papers are full of mumbo
> jumbo that no one else can understand, least of all business
> managers. What does all of this tell us about management in
> the real world, anyway? I'd like to be a fly on the wall when they
> attempt to deliver these incomprehensible abstractions to the
> local Chamber of Commerce."

> *Philosopher:* "Oh no, a panel discussion by business school faculty on
> employee theft. Someone will probably talk about the relation-
> ship between unauthorized paper clip acquisitions and varia-
> tions in office lighting, holding moonlight constant, of course.
> Big deal! That won't improve anyone's character, nor give the
> genuinely puzzled a guide for moral living. It's no surprise,
> though; they really haven't studied ethics."

This chapter originally was published in 1994 as L. K. Treviño and G. R. Weaver,
"*Business* ethics/business *ethics*: one field or two," *Business Ethics Quarterly* 4(2):113–128. It
was revised slightly for publication in this book.

These vignettes overstate the extent of misunderstanding within the allegedly single, interdisciplinary (DeGeorge 1987a) field of business ethics. Alternative stances toward business ethics, however, should be obvious to anyone familiar with the recent literature (Kahn 1990; Tsalikis and Fritzsche 1989; Stevenson 1989; DeGeorge 1987a, 1987b). Academic business ethics is usually divided into *normative* (that is, prescriptive) and *empirical* (that is, explanatory, descriptive, or predictive) approaches. The former is taken as the province of philosophers and theologians, whereas the latter is considered the domain of management consultants and business school professors. Their different foci, styles, and methods have suggested that the study of business ethics may incorporate not one but two distinct fields (Fleming 1987; Kahn 1990). The surface-level differences between the two approaches may reflect deeper, entrenched metatheoretical assumptions, such as the once commonly accepted fact–value distinction (Hume 1739; Moore 1903; Nagel 1961).

This divided house does not appear to be collapsing, though. Rather, business ethics as a field of study is becoming increasingly well established and institutionalized (DeGeorge 1987a). Unlike other fields where institutionalization involves a shared paradigm (Kuhn 1962), practitioners of "business ethics" from these different domains are guided by different theories, assumptions, and norms (a not necessarily problematic situation), sometimes resulting in misunderstanding or lack of appreciation of each others' work (a presumably problematic situation).

Despite the differences, recent reviews have called for integration of business ethics into a single unified field (Fleming 1987; Kahn 1990). We are concerned, however, that integration is being discussed and attempted without full understanding of its meaning and implications. Thus, we (with backgrounds in philosophy and social science) begin by illuminating the distinctive features of normative business ethics and empirical business ethics that we believe contribute to current misunderstanding (see Table 1.1). Only when key differences are clearly articulated—that is, when we know how we differ—is understanding (and perhaps integration) possible. Our goal in this chapter, in short, is to explicate—rather than critique—the conventional self-image of each side of the normative/empirical debate.

We offer one important caveat before proceeding with the discussion. The empirical and normative approaches are admittedly more complex and less unified than our brief discussion suggests. Philosophy's eclectic nature makes

TABLE 1.1
Normative and Empirical Approaches to Studying Business Ethics

Category	Normative Approach	Empirical Approach
Academic home	Philosophy, theology, liberal arts	Management, social sciences
Language	Evaluative	Descriptive
Definition of ethical behavior	Action that is right, just, fair	Ethically significant choices & decisions, whether right or wrong, good or bad
Underlying assumptions regarding human moral agency	Autonomy & responsibility	More deterministic, with reciprocal causation
Theory: purpose, scope, & application	Prescription & proscription Abstract analysis & critique	Explanation/prediction Concrete & measurable Influence actual behavior
Basis for evaluation of theories	Philosophical reflection on business practice	Empirical study of business practice

any brief attempt to characterize it (or its components, viz., ethics) risky and unsatisfying. The safest characterizations of philosophy are sometimes the most aphoristic, as in Sellars's observation that "the aim of philosophy . . . is to understand how things in the broadest possible sense of the term *hang together* in the broadest possible sense of the term" (1963, 1). The normative approach—in interdisciplinary fashion—draws from philosophy, theology, political and social theory, and other self-consciously critical inquiries. The entire normative task involves not only prescription but also description and analysis. For example, any critique of a corporate practice presumably assumes an accurate description of the practice. Likewise, the application of moral judgments to a corporate or individual entity assumes a conceptual analysis (often called a *metaethical analysis*) to determine the grounds of the judgment in question and its applicability to the subject at hand. Nevertheless, the dominant feature of the normative approach is its emphasis on formulating prescriptive moral judgments (Fleming 1987; Kahn 1990).

Similarly, social science cannot be unidimensionally characterized. In fact, recent debates in organizational science have left the field ideologically divided into multiple schools (Burrell and Morgan 1979) supported by a multitude of possible research methods (Morgan and Smircich 1980). The so-called functionalist paradigm, however, has dominated organizational science (Gioia and Pitre 1990) and the empirical approach to the study of business ethics. It is guided by a presumed natural science model focused on explanation and prediction, rooted in an objective epistemology and metaphysics, and is characterized by a managerial orientation toward stability rather than change (Burrell and Morgan 1979). To simplify the discussion, we present our analysis from the perspective of the dominant paradigm in each area of business ethics—the functionalist paradigm for the empirical approach and the emphasis on formulating prescriptive moral judgments for the normative approach.

ACADEMIC HOME

The underlying assumptions, research questions, and methodologies that guide academic investigations are deeply rooted in the academic home of the investigator. Academics spend years in Ph.D. programs being shaped and socialized to a dominant framework that leads them to make assumptions, to ask certain types of questions, and to search for answers using accepted methodologies. It is arguable that this socialization and training process has profound implications for academics from philosophical and management backgrounds who study business ethics. As a result of their different backgrounds, members of these groups may be suspicious of each other and even may have difficulty thinking of each other as colleagues and peers. Normative business ethicists may consider their peers to be academics from pure liberal arts disciplines (that is, persons not noted for their charitable attitudes toward business), whereas the peer group for business faculty most likely includes other business faculty and perhaps business managers. The latter may be particularly suspicious of "ivory tower" philosophers. The philosophers' negative image can only be bolstered by their reputation for reveling in well-constructed (or well-destructed) but popularly "pointless" arguments (that is, the analytical process is valued over any practical outcome). The social scientists' negative reputation, on the other hand, stems from their insistence on attempting to provide "impoverished" causal explanations for phenomena that, to their philosopher colleagues, are either much more complex affairs or transparently self-explanatory (Brady and Hatch 1990).

Normative Approach

In terms of its academic home, the normative approach is rooted in philosophy and the liberal arts. Philosophical training in ethics focuses attention on questions of what ought to be—how the individual or business ought to behave. The normative approach is clearly and unashamedly value driven (Kurtines, Alvarez, and Azmitia 1990).

Randall and Gibson (1990) complain that most sampled business ethics articles either fail to specify their methodology or use a defective one. This criticism assumes well-defined and widely held methodological canons. As such, this criticism would be misplaced were it directed at philosophically based business ethics. Graduate training in philosophy generally includes nothing like the "research methods" of social science. Contrary to textbook claims, formalized philosophical methods are rare. Even formal logic is more a subject than a tool for philosophy. Although there is methodological self-consciousness in ethics (see the opening chapters of Rawls 1971; Donagan 1977; Gewirth 1978), it tends to be individualized to the task and author at hand. Those few widely received "methodologies" that philosophy occasionally adopts soon become an embarrassment to many, if not all, in the field (as with the logical positivists' philosophy-as-logic-and-meta-science, dominant in the 1930s, and the philosophy-as-analysis-of-ordinary-language methodology of the 1950s and 1960s). One dare not presume to delineate uncontroversially the field or its methods so precisely. More typically, one finds philosophical method described by a small number of heuristic guidelines (for example, Regan 1984).

Philosophers' training often focuses on the metatheoretical issues of other disciplines. It is not unusual for a philosophy book or article to range across topics as diverse as formal models of predator—prey relationships in evolutionary biology and production functions in economics (cf. Rosenberg 1981). This interdisciplinary, metatheoretical focus means that, in selected respects (for example, the history of a field), philosophers may know as much or more about other fields as do the practitioners of those fields. Combined with a general inclination to function as interpreters and critics, this focus does not discourage scholarly imperialism; philosophy often proceeds by unearthing and critiquing arguments and assumptions in ordinary life *and* in the theories of other scholars (not just other philosophers). Thus, out of the philosophical academic home emerge individuals who stand ready to interpret and prescribe business behavior and also critique the work of their social scientist counterparts.

Empirical Approach

The empiricist who studies business ethics is an applied social scientist with training most likely rooted in management or the social sciences (psychology, sociology, anthropology). Mainstream social scientists, trained in the functionalist paradigm, are generally concerned with questions of what *is* rather than what *ought to be*. They assume that the organizational world is "a basically objective one that is 'out there' awaiting impartial exploration and discovery" (Gioia and Pitre 1990, 586). Organizational policies, procedures, and reward systems are seen as capable of influencing the behavior of organizational members. Further, organizational scientists are taught that, as scientists, they should be objective—that science should be value free despite recent challenges to the latter assumption (Kurtines, Alvarez, and Azmitia 1990; Frederick 1986; Miner 1990).

Empiricists answer questions about *what is* by attempting to describe, explain, or predict phenomena in the empirical world utilizing the consensually agreed-on methodologies of their social scientific training: historical analysis, observation, interviews, surveys, and experiments. Research is guided by design criteria that, if followed judiciously, are thought to be capable of testing hypotheses and providing correct answers to specific research questions (Kerlinger 1986). Data are analyzed most frequently by using quantitative statistical methods. Unlike philosophers, social scientists from the functionalist paradigm are uncomfortable ranging into the unknown territory occupied by philosophy and philosophers. They are more likely to let philosophers analyze and criticize each other.

LANGUAGE

Imagine traveling to a distant planet where the inhabitants' language comprises familiar English words. As a visitor, you are delighted at the prospect of being able to communicate with these English-speaking strangers. To your dismay, however, you soon discover that many of their words carry very different definitions. Your well-intended statements about "ethical behavior" are regularly misunderstood, leading to frequent *faux pas*, conflict, and miscommunication. You realize that learning the strangers' language will be even more difficult than learning a totally new language with a different alphabet or a different grammar because you will have to learn new definitions and uses for words you use every day. Even more troublesome is the fact that their word meanings are deeply rooted in cultural assumptions very different from your own.

This scenario is similar to the dilemma facing philosophers and social scientists who study business ethics. Each has independently developed a vocabulary for talking about the phenomenon they study and how they study it. The philosophers' lexicon is quite elaborate, developed based on centuries of philosophical study of ethical questions. Relatively speaking, the social scientist has just begun to develop a vocabulary for asking and answering questions of interest. Because the social scientific study of business ethics is at a relatively early stage of development, its terminology is not necessarily clear. For example, the word *ethical* is often used as an adjective attached to other words, such as *behavior* and *theory*. Consider the following sentence: "Ethical behavior in organizations is a complex phenomenon influenced by individual differences and external influences." For the social scientist, the definition of *ethical behavior* in this sentence does not necessarily mean right, just, or fair behavior. Ethical behavior can represent any behavior of individuals facing ethical decisions. This behavior is complexly determined by a number of influential factors and can be right or wrong, just or unjust, fair or unfair. For example, if an external cause (for example, the organization's reward system) supports attention only to the bottom line, unethical behavior is more likely to result. Thus, the social scientist may use the term *ethical behavior* in a descriptive sense (Freeman and Gilbert 1988) to mean either ethical or unethical behavior, depending on the context. By contrast, note the evaluative meaning of the term *ethical behavior* in the following argument: "Is it correct to say that ethical behavior is 'complex?' We think not. Complexity of human behavior implies difficulty to understand or to recognize. But when a person performs an ethical act, we feel simplicity rather than complexity" (Brady and Hatch 1990, 17). Brady and Hatch use the term *ethical behavior* (as a philosopher would) to mean right action. Whereas philosophers use the term *ethics* to denote the study of proper *and* improper behavior, *ethical behavior* is assumed to mean morally proper behavior. Given this definition of ethical behavior, and certain assumptions about human agency (discussed next), it is not surprising that they then understand ethical behavior to be a simple phenomenon. The social scientist's definition of ethical behavior, however, when linked with totally different assumptions about human agency, suggests an understanding of ethical behavior (meaning ethical *or* unethical action) as complex.

UNDERLYING ASSUMPTIONS: HUMAN AGENCY

The normative and empirical domains invoke radically different explanatory models that rest on distinct and generally unstated underlying assumptions. Assumptions about human agency are particularly relevant to the resultant confusion and misunderstandings. The philosopher believes that ethically significant action is normally autonomous, whereas the social scientist invokes a more deterministic multiple influences perspective.

Normative Approach

The normative approach typically assumes that morally significant actions are performed with autonomy and responsibility. For some (metaphysical libertarians), this assumption entails a fundamental denial that the action can be placed in a causal nexus: "Ethical behavior is not a function of anything other than an individual's free choice" (Brady and Hatch 1990, 15). Although this view may allow for influences on actions, these influences are not determinative of the action (Chisholm 1976; Reid 1788; Thorp 1980; cf. Weaver 1989).

For others (so-called soft determinists), the assumption of autonomy and responsibility suggests that not all causal factors are on equal footing. Autonomous and responsible action results from a particular type of cause (typically one involving the agent's choices, *even* if those choices are themselves determined) (Ayer 1982; Hume 1748; Moore 1912). "For it is not when my action has any cause at all, but only when it has a special sort of cause, that it is reckoned not to be free" (Ayer 1982, 21). Thus, autonomy and responsibility are rendered compatible with causal determinism by distinguishing among types of causal factors; some causal factors rule out autonomy, but others do not. There is no guarantee, however, that the causes discovered by the social scientist will be of the type (for example, choices) the soft determinist requires to preserve autonomy and responsibility. Empirical business ethics is not necessarily committed to explaining responsible and autonomous action in terms of the agent's choices, as opposed to other potential factors.

Apart from concerns about autonomy and responsibility, the actual search for causal conditions of ethical action may appear misplaced in the normative approach. Moral action may seem self-explanatory or self-interpreting in character, needing no additional explanation in causal or nomological terms. Thus, the normative approach may find the explanation of ethical action to lie in the justificatory relationship between the dictates of morality and a person's action rather than in a causal or nomological relationship between the action and its antecedents. The situation is analogous to that of the alleged self-explanatory character of rational action (Dray 1957; Hollis 1977). Causal explanation is thought to be appropriate only for ethical deviance. "We might say that causal models lead us to discover (or make!) *excuses* for ethical failure, but shed very little light upon ethical success" (Brady and Hatch 1990, 17). "Ethical success" approaches self-explanatory status.

Empirical Approach

Social scientists find it difficult to reconcile free will with the social scientist's general assumption that human behavior is lawful and can be predicted and explained (Sappington 1990). Social scientists range from hard determinists (for example, Skinner 1953), who believe that human behavior is completely determined by external factors, to libertarians (for example, Rogers 1959), who believe that people make choices (for example, beliefs and goals) and that these choices, although constrained at times by ability or external barriers, are determined by the individual. Most social scientists, however, would likely categorize themselves with Bandura (1986), who developed a theory of reciprocal causation in which the individual and the environment mutually influence each other. Thus, although most empirically based ethics theories do not eliminate notions of responsibility and autonomy, these social scientific theories emphasize the role of multiple determinants, both internal (for example, locus of control, cognitive moral development) and external to the individual (for example, peers, authority relationships, reward systems). To management researchers, the external determinants (for example, reward systems, codes of conduct) often seem more interesting and useful because they are the factors over which the manager can exercise control. For example, managers can manipulate reward systems and design codes of conduct and training programs to influence subordinate behavior. In sum, in the empirical approach, both *ethical success* and *ethical failure* are viewed as complex phenomena that can be explained by a combination of causal factors. Even whistle blowing, often presumed to be an example of ethical success, is understood by social scientists to be influenced by multiple internal and external causal factors (Near and Miceli 1987). The relative influence of these causal factors is left to be determined through empirical study.

THEORY: PURPOSE, SCOPE, AND APPLICATION

A key difference between the purpose of theory in the philosophical and empirical approaches to business ethics resides in the difference between prescription and description/prediction. Thus, the social scientist may devalue the philosopher's moral judgments because they cannot be understood in empirical terms. They cannot be verified by empirical test or be used to predict or explain behavior. On the other hand, the social scientist's statements about morality are seen to be of little value to the philosopher because they do not address the essential questions of right and wrong. Second, the scope of the normative approach is abstract and general, often more detached from the particulars of actual circumstances than the empirical approach. Finally, normative ethical theory, applied to business ethics, provides tools for analysis and critique, whereas the social science theory, applied to business ethics, provides a basis for understanding and managing human behavior in a complex social world.

Normative Approach

The normative approach includes evaluative, descriptive, and analytical elements. The purpose of normative business ethics is to critique the *real* by reference to the *ideal*. Having understood the actual world, the task is to evaluate its propriety and, sometimes, to prescribe a morally better alternative. Thus, the task includes interpretive description along the lines of history and literary criticism (Kekes 1980, 119). This need not require systematic data collection but rather the search for particularly illuminating cases.

Normative ethical theories create standards by which the propriety of moral beliefs and practices in the business world can be evaluated. Thus, normative ethical theories—for example, Kantianism—play a potential role for which there is no analog in empirical business ethics. What matters to the normative ethicist is not so much the causal antecedents of an action as the instantiation of a moral principle.

Normative business ethics also may engage in a significant amount of conceptual analysis as a prolegomenon to the actual formulation of a prescriptive moral judgment. This metaethical task is exemplified in debates about the ontological status of corporations in relation to attempted attributions of moral responsibility or blameworthiness (for example, "Is a corporation a moral agent?") (Goodpaster 1984). Similar conceptual issues may arise in evaluating attributions of responsibility to organizational officials. Recall, for example, Richard Nixon's attempt to distinguish conceptually between Nixon the *man* and Nixon the *president*, such that the former was admittedly subject to certain legal requirements, whereas the latter was not (cf. Fales 1977).

In terms of scope, modern normative ethical theory typically concerns morality as such, that is, a standard of moral reasoning or action that holds for persons qua persons. "It thus moves at a level of abstraction and generality which detaches its concerns and its formulations from all social particularity" (MacIntyre 1984, 498). For example, Rawls derives his principles of justice by asking what would be chosen by actors ignorant of the particularities of their social conditions and individual psyches (Rawls 1971).

Whereas opinions may differ as to exactly how the principles of morality can be applied to business ethics, it is usually understood that normative ethical theory provides the tools necessary for analysis and informed discussion of ethical issues (Derry and Green 1989). The dominant conception of "applied ethics" (MacIntyre, 1984) contains two elements: (1) context-neutral (that is, putatively universal) ethical theory and (2) context-sensitive discussions of particular ethical issues. Alternatively, however, Derry and Green (1989) distinguish nine approaches to the use of ethical theory in business ethics texts, whereas Toulmin (1981) and Klein (1985) suggest that moral judgments in specific cases are reached largely independently of ethical theory. Theory may provide only after-the-fact legitimacy for contextualized judgments reached in informal (although not thereby nonrational) fashion (Klein 1985). One can at least describe the dominant conception as positing some place for ethical theory in business ethics, even if only a heuristic role. Most textbooks at least mention, if not use, philosophical ethical theories (Derry and Green 1989). Similarly, DeGeorge's (1987b) report on a business college's efforts to improve its business ethics program indicates that ethical theory is thought to play a crucial role. Thus, the dominant conception of business ethics includes normative ethical theory and contextualized studies of business ethics problems and at least the assumption of a connection between the two.

Empirical Approach

Social science theory serves a sense-making purpose in its attempt to make sense of the observable world (Dubin 1976). It provides a conceptual basis for examining regularities and relationships that can lead to generalizations about organizational behavior—to describe, explain, and/or predict specific outcomes of interest to the researcher (Gioia and Pitre 1990; Kerlinger 1986). In contrast to the normative approach, the empirical approach focuses on identifying definable and measurable factors within individual psyches and particular social contexts that influence individual and organizational ethical behavior. One also might argue that an essential purpose of theory in the empirical approach to business ethics is to provide a sound theoretical basis for managing the ethical behavior of individuals and organizations—to provide practical and useful managerial guidance.

Whereas normative business ethics is quite abstract, empirical business ethics is, by definition, concrete. Abstract constructs are expected to be operationally defined so that they can be concretely measured (Kerlinger 1986). Most empirical business ethics researchers study behavior at the individual or organizational level of analysis (Fleming 1987). When applied to business ethics at the individual level of analysis, social science theory is used to explain or predict behaviors such as lying, cheating, stealing, and whistle-blowing. Hypothesized causal factors are derived from the social scientific roots of the investigator. For example, those with roots in psychology have identified individual differences, such as values, locus of control, and cognitive moral development, that are proposed to influence individual managers' reasoning and choices (Treviño and Youngblood 1990;

Weber 1990). Moral psychology (Kohlberg 1969) has provided hypotheses and measurement approaches (Treviño 1992). Sociology has provided theories of differential association (Sutherland and Cressey 1970), hypothesizing that peers and referent others influence unethical behavior (Ferrell and Gresham 1985; Zey-Ferrell and Ferrell 1982). At the organizational level of analysis, researchers have studied ethical climates (Victor and Cullen 1988), culture (Kram, Yeager, and Reed 1989; Pastin 1986), and corporate codes of conduct (Mathews 1987). In addition, variables such as size and resource environments have been studied as correlates of corporate crime (Cochran and Nigh 1987; Staw and Szwajkowski 1975), and corporate reputation (social responsibility) has been associated with firm financial performance (McGuire, Sundgren, and Schneeweis 1988). To the empirical business ethics researcher, the ultimate application of social science theory might be in field experiments that attempt to develop theory-based interventions that can influence actual behavior, such as employee theft (Greenberg 1990). The desired result of such research would be guidance for the development of practical and useful managerial interventions.

THEORY GROUNDS AND EVALUATION

The normative and empirical approaches may be most alike when it comes to the grounds for normative and social science theory but are most different in their guidelines for theory evaluation. One might safely presume that morally significant business practices and their potential conflicts and ambiguities generate much of the theoretical problem set for both approaches to business ethics. Thus, in some sense, both normative and social science theories have an empirical base; however, the normative approach evaluates moral theory based on rational critique, whereas empirical business ethics evaluates social science theory primarily on the basis of its ability to explain or predict organizational behavior.

Normative Approach

Perhaps contrary to the perceptions of social scientists, normative business ethics has an empirical basis (among others) as a source of research questions and in the justification of answers. For the normative business ethicist, business ethics problems are "discovered" through reflection on business practice (perhaps in the light of moral theory). Moreover, actual moral practice functions among the criteria for evaluating moral theories (Regan 1984). For example, were a moral theory to prescribe gratuitous punishment, we would have prima facie grounds for rejecting the theory.

The "method" of ethical theory commonly involves achieving what Rawls (1971, 46–53) calls a reflective equilibrium between theoretical constructions and our considered moral judgments. Everything from "logic and mathematics" to "our knowledge of matters of fact obtained in both common sense and more normal experimental science" to our "reflective, acquired sentiments of moral approval and disapproval" is potentially relevant (Stevenson 1989, 103). Regan (1984) offers the following guidelines for constructing the "ideal moral judgment": seek conceptual clarity and complete information, be rational (that is, avoid logical flaws), be impartial, "be 'cool'" (that is, emotionally calm), and reason on the basis of valid moral principles. Of such principles we are told little, save that, minimally, a valid principle will not conflict with significant numbers of our considered moral beliefs. Regan (1984) also tells his readers how *not* to do business ethics (for example, avoid confusing moral judgments with personal preferences, feelings, popular sentiments, or authoritarian edicts). Beauchamp offers similar directives, emphasizing the analysis and critique of arguments and positions (Beauchamp and Bowie 1988, 13–16). Not all texts, however, offer even heuristic guidelines (cf. Iannone 1989). Moreover, the mere fact of moral disagreement—either within or among cultures—is not in itself held as grounds for doubting the possibility of judging some moral positions as being more correct or well founded than others.

Empirical Approach

To most social scientists, new knowledge is obtained through systematic investigation of relationships and regularities that exist in a concrete social world. This approach has a strong empirical base in the ethical problems and practices of business organizations (for example, employee theft, corporate crime). Theory is built incrementally and deductively, relying on logic and on existing literature and theories about organizational behavior (Whetten 1989). Hypotheses are developed and theory tests are designed to extend existing theory, fill a knowledge gap, or set up tests of competing explanations of the same organizational phenomenon (Gioia and Pitre 1990).

During the initial stages of theory development, logic and reasonableness may be used as a basis for theory evaluation. Ultimately, however, for a social science theory to be considered good, it usually is expected to contribute to the oft-stated goals of prediction and explanation (Dubin 1978). Thus, theory justification is accomplished via the presumed natural science model of empirical confirmation or disconfirmation (Bacharach 1989; Behling 1980) and through the theory's ability to explain behavior or solve problems (Bacharach 1989; Thomas and Tymon 1982). For example, Mackenzie and House (1978) proposed an ideal theory evaluation system, a "recipe for serious scholars" that involves a long-term commitment to theory building. This commitment involves a program of empirical research based on Platt's (1964) concepts of crucial experiments, wherein the scientist attempts to produce counterexamples. In the same spirit, Behling (1980) examined five major objections to the use of ideal natural science criteria for theory evaluation and concluded that, despite the objections, it is the best approach currently available for evaluating social science theory.

Alternative views do exist within the empiricist camp. Thomas and Tymon (1982), for example, suggested that conventional notions of methodological and scientific rigor are deficient as the only guidance mechanisms for theory evaluation because they direct energy away from the relevance or usefulness of research while encouraging research of questionable practical utility. They emphasized the need for theory and research that is relevant to solving real problems. Other practicing organizational scientists have moved farther from the conventional empiricist approach of explanation and prediction based solely on processes of confirmation or disconfirmation. Some have argued, for example, that in reality persuasion is also used to gain theory acceptance (Astley 1985) and that true scientific progress relies on the scientist's commitment to and advocacy of the new theory (Mitroff 1972). Advocacy of one's own theory can be dangerous for the scientist, however; the academic community is likely to label the scientist as a biased and overemotional "crank."

Business ethics theory and research in the empirical tradition have been evaluated along both the confirmation/disconfirmation and explanation/problem-solving dimensions. Fleming (1987) offered examples of criticism from scholars in the business ethics field. Although he calls them "self-criticism" (Fleming 1987, 19), most of the remarks seem more like empiricists' criticisms of the normative approach: "Business ethics research is a strange phenomenon; there is little empirical research; it is mostly writing and reflection. . . ." "Most of the scholarly work is useless. . . . The problem is that businessmen need to know that they are doing ethics in their activities" (Fleming 1987, 19). The normative side (criticizing the empiricists), however, was represented by the following critical remark: "Business researchers are primarily census takers who produce fluff."

In sum, the normative and empirical approaches are in potential conflict regarding theory evaluation insofar as empirical study of ethical behavior reveals a diversity of causal influences on moral beliefs and practices. Theory is evaluated in terms of the extent to which behavior is explained or predicted and management problems are solved. Alternatively, the normative approach evaluates theory on the basis that some moral positions are more correct or well founded than others.

ONE FIELD OR TWO?

Our discussion of the normative and empirical approaches points to a common interest in morally significant business practice (for example, stealing, whistle-blowing, corporate crime). We also have identified numerous sources of confusion and collision, however, suggesting that beyond their common starting point, the two approaches diverge. For example, confusion arises out of differences in language, such as the meaning and usage of the term *ethical behavior*. The potential for collision exists in different underlying assumptions about human agency and the different purposes for theory and criteria for theory evaluation. Focus on these differences suggests that integration attempts may be problematic.

In light of the foregoing analysis, what are we to make of the relationship between empirical and normative business ethics? In particular, how are we to understand the frequent calls for integration? Fleming (1987) reported concern among business ethics scholars that the lack of integration between "the normative and descriptive research methodologies . . . will be dysfunctional for the growth and development of the field" (Fleming 1987, 19). Kahn (1990) represented the normative and contextual approaches as two non-overlapping circles of a Venn diagram and argued that the uncharted *intersection* of the two circles, described as research connecting with business practice, is currently missing. Kahn's map for charting this connective territory was not spelled out with useful detail, however. Further, our earlier analysis suggested that the business ethics field (both normative and empirical) is already grounded in business practice, the primary interest area shared by the two approaches. Thus, these calls for integration fail to provide real guidance regarding the ultimate shape any new form of integration might take or what the process would be for creating it. In sum, we believe that the categories delineated in this chapter provide a basis for understanding the important differences between the two approaches to business ethics and the reasons why calls for integration may go unanswered.

In the next chapter, we explore three levels at which normative and empirical business ethics may relate. First, the normative and empirical approaches may operate in *parallel*, sharing only their concern with certain types of business behavior but self-consciously avoiding any connection between the two approaches to studying them. Second, integration could take the form of a practical *symbiotic* relationship in which the normative and empirical approaches choose to associate in some way for their mutual benefit. The association is a kind of "marriage of convenience," but each approach remains separate and intact, firmly grounded in its own view of the world. Finally, a deeper level of *theoretical hybridization* is a form of integration that would merge the normative and empirical approaches at the substantive theoretical level in a manner that actually would create a new breed of theory. In our in-depth treatment of these three levels, we discuss the problems and prospects of each and of business ethics integration as a whole.

References

Astley, G. 1985. Administrative science as socially constructed truth. *Administrative Science Quarterly* 30:497–513.

Ayer, A. J. 1982. Freedom and necessity. In *Free will*, ed. G. Watson. Oxford: Oxford University Press.

Bacharach, S. B. 1989. Organizational theories: Some criteria for evaluation. *The Academy of Management Review* 14:496–515.

Bandura, A. 1986. *Social foundations of thought and action: A social cognitive theory*. Englewood Cliffs, NJ: Prentice-Hall.

Beauchamp, T. L., and N. E. Bowie. 1988. *Ethical theory in business*. Englewood Cliffs, NJ: Prentice-Hall.

Behling, O. 1980. The case for the natural science model for research in organizational behavior and organization theory. *Academy of Management Review* 5(4):483–490.

Brady, F. N., and M. J. Hatch. 1990. The poverty of causal models in business ethics. Paper presented at the Academy of Management meeting, San Francisco.

Burrell, G., and G. Morgan. 1979. *Sociological paradigms and organizational analysis*. London: Heinemann Educational Books.

Chisholm, R. 1976. *Person and object*. La Salle, IL: Open Court Publishing.

Cochran, P. L., and D. Nigh. 1987. Illegal corporate behavior and the question of moral agency. In *Research in corporate social performance and policy*. Vol. 9. Greenwich, CT: JAI Press, 73–81.

DeGeorge, R. T. 1987a. The status of business ethics: Past and future. *Journal of Business Ethics* 6:201–211.

DeGeorge, R. T. 1987b. Ethical theory for business professors. *Journal of Business Ethics* 6:507–508.

Derry, R., and R. M. Green. 1989. Ethical theory in business ethics: A critical assessment. *Journal of Business Ethics* 8:521–533.

Donagan, A. 1977. *The theory of morality*. Chicago: University of Chicago Press.

Dray, W. 1957. *Law and explanation in history*. Oxford: Oxford University Press.

Dubin, R. 1976. Theory building in applied areas. In *Handbook of industrial and organizational psychology*, ed. M. D. Dunnette, 17–30. Chicago: Rand-McNally.

Dubin, R. 1978. *Theory building*. Revised edition. New York: The Free Press.

Fales, E. 1977. The ontology of social roles. *Philosophy of Social Science* 7:139–161.

Ferrell, O. C., and L. G. Gresham. 1985. A contingency framework for understanding ethical decision making in marketing. *Journal of Marketing* 49:87–96.

Fleming, J. 1987. A survey and critique of business ethics research, 1986. In *Research in corporate social performance and policy*, Vol. 2, ed. W. Frederick, 1–24. Greenwich, CT: JAI Press.

Frederick, W. 1986. Toward CSR[3]: Why ethical analysis is indispensable and unavoidable in corporate affairs. *California Management Review* 28(2):126–155.

Freeman, E., and D. R. Gilbert Jr. 1988. *Corporate Strategy and the Search for Ethics*. Englewood Cliffs, NJ: Prentice-Hall.

Gewirth, A. 1978. *Reason and morality*. Chicago: University of Chicago Press.

Gioia, D. A., and E. Pitre. 1990. Multi-paradigm perspectives on theory building. *Academy of Management Review* 15:584–602.

Goodpaster, T. 1984. The concept of corporate responsibility. In *Just business*, ed. T. Regan, 292–323. New York: Random House.

Greenberg, J. 1990. Employee theft as a reaction to underpayment inequity: The hidden cost of pay cuts. *Journal of Applied Psychology* 75(5):561–568.

Hollis, M. 1977. *Models of man*. Cambridge: Cambridge University Press.

Hume, D. 1739. *A treatise of human nature*. London: John Noon.

Hume, D. 1748. *An enquiry concerning human understanding*. Indianapolis: Hackett Publishing, 1993.

Iannone, A. P. 1989. *Contemporary moral controversies in business*. Oxford: Oxford University Press.

Kahn, W. A. 1990. Toward an agenda for business ethics research. *Academy of Management Review* 15:311–328.

Kekes, J. 1980. *The nature of philosophy*. Totowa, N.J.: Rowman and Littlefield.

Kerlinger, E. 1986. *Foundations of behavioral research*. New York: Holt, Rinehart, and Winston.

Klein, S. 1985. Two views of business ethics: A popular philosophical approach and a value based interdisciplinary one. *Journal of Business Ethics* 4:71–79.

Kohlberg, L. 1969. Stage and sequence: The cognitive–developmental approach to socialization. In *Handbook of socialization theory and research*, ed. D. A. Goslin, 347–480. Chicago: Rand-McNally.

Kram, K. E., P. C. Yeager, and G. E. Reed. 1989. Decisions and dilemmas: The ethical dimension in the corporate context. In *Research in corporate social performance and policy*, vol 11, ed. J. E. Post, 21–54. Greenwich, CT: JAI Press.

Kuhn, T. S. 1962. *The structure of scientific revolutions*. Chicago: University of Chicago Press.

Kurtines, W. M., M. Alvarez, and M. Azmitia. 1990. Science and morality: The role of values in science and the scientific study of moral phenomena. *Psychological Bulletin* 107(3):283–295.

MacIntyre, A. 1984. Does applied ethics rest on a mistake? *The Monist* 67:498–513.

Mackenzie, K. D., and R. House. 1978. Paradigm development in the social sciences: a proposed research strategy. *Academy of Management Review* 3(1):7–22.

Mathews, M. C. 1987. Codes of ethics: Organizational behavior and misbehavior. In *Research in corporate social performance and policy*, Vol. 9, ed. W. C. Frederick and L. Preston, 107–130. Greenwich, CT: JAI Press.

McGuire, J., B. A. Sundgren, and T. Schneeweis. 1988. Corporate social responsibility and firm financial performance. *Academy of Management Journal* 31:854–872.

Miner, J. B. 1990. The role of values in defining the "goodness" of theories in organization science. *Organization Studies* 11(2):161–178.

Mitroff, L. 1972. The myth of objectivity or why science needs a new psychology of science. *Management Science* 18:613–617.

Moore, G. E. 1903. *Principle ethics*. Cambridge: Cambridge University Press.

Moore, G. E. 1912. *Ethics*. New York: Henry Holt & Co.

Morgan, G., and L. Smircich. 1980. The case for qualitative research. *Academy of Management Review* 5:491–500.

Nagel, E. 1961. *The structure of science*. New York: Harcourt, Brace.

Near, J. P., and M. P. Miceli. 1987. Whistle-blowers in organizations. *Research in Organizational Behavior* 9:321–368.

Pastin, M. 1986. *The hard problems of management: Gaining the ethics edge*. San Francisco: Jossey-Bass.

Platt, J. R. 1964. Strong inference. *Science* 146:347–353.

Randall, D. M., and A. M. Gibson. 1990. Methodology in business ethics research: A review and critical assessment. *Journal of Business Ethics* 9:457–471.

Rawls, J. 1971. *A theory of justice*. Cambridge: Harvard University Press.

Regan, T. 1984. *Just business: New introductory essays in business ethics*. New York: Random House.

Reid, T. 1788. *Essays on the active powers of the human mind*. Cambridge: MIT Press, 1969.

Rogers, C. R. 1959. A theory of therapy, personality, and interpersonal relationships, as developed in the client-centered framework. In *Psychology: the study of a science*, Vol. 3, ed. S. Koch. New York: McGraw-Hill.

Rosenberg, A. 1981. *Sociobiology and the preemption of social science*. Baltimore: Johns Hopkins University Press.

Sappington, A. A. 1990. Recent psychological approaches to the free will *versus* determinism issue. *Psychological Bulletin* 108(1):19–29.

Sellars, W. 1963. *Science, perception and reality*. London: Routledge & Kegan Paul.

Skinner, B. F. 1953. *Science and human behavior*. New York: Macmillan.

Staw, B. M., and E. Szwajkowski. 1975. The scarcity–munificence component of organizational environments and the commission of illegal acts. *Administrative Science Quarterly* 20:345–354.

Stevenson, J. T. 1989. Reasonableness in morals. *Journal of Business Ethics* 8:95–107.

Sutherland, E. H., and D. R. Cressey. 1970. *Principles of criminology*. Philadelphia: J. B. Lippincott.

Thomas, K. W., and W. O. Tymon. 1982. Necessary properties of relevant research: Lessons from recent criticisms of the organizational sciences. *Academy of Management Review* 7:345–352.

Thorp, J. 1980. *Free will*. London: Routledge and Kegan Paul.

Toulmin, S. 1981. The tyranny of principles. *The Hastings Center Report* 11(6):31–32.

Treviño, L. K. 1992. Moral reasoning and business ethics; implications for research, education, and management. *Journal of Business Ethics* 11:445–459.

Treviño, L. K., and S. A. Youngblood. 1990. Bad apples in bad barrels: A causal analysis of ethical decision-making behavior. *Journal of Applied Psychology* 75(4):378–385.

Tsalikis, J., and D. J. Fritzsche. 1989. Business ethics: a literature review with a focus on marketing ethics. *Journal of Business Ethics* 8:695–743.

Victor, B., and J. Cullen. 1988. The organizational bases of ethical work climates. *Administrative Science Quarterly* 33:101–125.

Weaver, G. R. 1989. Agent causation and reasons for acting. Paper presented at the American Philosophical Association meeting, Chicago.

Weber, J. 1990. Managers' moral reasoning: Assessing their responses to three moral dilemmas. *Human Relations* 43(7):687–702.

Whetten, D. A. 1989. What constitutes a theoretical contribution? *Academy of Management Review* 14:490–495.

Zey-Ferrell, M., and O. C. Ferrell. 1982. Role set configuration and opportunity as predictors of unethical behavior in organizations. *Human Relations* 35:587–604.

Normative and Empirical Business Ethics: Separation, Marriage of Convenience, or Marriage of Necessity?

In light of the differences and misunderstandings between normative and empirical business ethics research that were identified in Chapter 1, scholars often issue calls for a closer, more integrated relationship between normative and empirical inquiry in business ethics (Fleming 1987; Kahn 1990; Mulligan 1987). Seldom has the nature of the proposed relationship been explicated in detail, however. This chapter outlines three conceptions of the relationship between normative and empirical business ethics, views we characterize as *parallel*, *symbiotic*, and *integrative*. These three positions differ significantly in regard to the possibility, advisability, and intensity of any unifying efforts in business ethics research and theory. They can be illustrated along a continuum ranging from parallelism (no interrelationship at all), through a symbiotic relationship rooted in mutually beneficial pragmatic collaboration, to a theoretical hybridization that fully integrates ostensibly distinct fields.

In contrast to recent calls for a more unified treatment of business ethics, parallelism advocates the separation of empirical and normative inquiry and denies integration of any kind on both conceptual and practical grounds. The other two views in some sense relate normative and empirical inquiry but

This chapter originally was published in 1994 as G. R. Weaver and L. K. Treviño, "Normative and empirical business ethics: Separation, marriage of convenience, or marriage of necessity?" *Business Ethics Quarterly* 4:129–144. It was revised slightly for publication in this book.

differ regarding the type of relation supported (pragmatic collaboration or theoretical hybridization). The symbiotic view supports a surface-level practical relationship in which normative or empirical business ethics rely on each other for guidance in setting agenda or applying the results of their conceptually and methodologically distinct forms of inquiry. For example, symbiosis would occur if empiricists were to focus their theoretical frameworks and investigative lenses on the organizational inducements to insider trading or leveraged buyouts *in response* to moralists' condemnation of such behavior. In a symbiotic relationship, however, the substantive theory, metatheoretical assumptions, and methodology of each approach remain unaltered. By contrast, theoretical integration countenances a deeper merging of *prima facie* distinct forms of inquiry, potentially involving alterations in or unifications of the substantive theory, metatheoretical assumptions, or methodology of each approach. Such a deep level of merger means that the *theoretical content and methods* of multiple fields are altered to produce a single new field of study with its own assumptions, theories, issues, and methods.

This chapter explicates these three positions, summarizes a number of arguments for and against each, and considers their implications for the future of business ethics research. It is intended not as a conclusive answer to questions of integration but as a guide to the issues surrounding alternative views of the feasibility of integration. In pursuing this task, however, we confront an exegetical paradox, for the exposition of one position may assume what another position denies. To claim to explain, much less espouse, the parallelist position presumes the coherence of a normative/empirical distinction, but this distinction is fundamentally incoherent from the standpoint of full theoretical integration. Our rationale for beginning with a distinction rather than with a unity reflects our belief that this is where much research in business ethics currently resides, at least within business colleges and mainstream North American social science.

PARALLEL APPROACHES TO BUSINESS ETHICS

Exposition

The parallelist position espouses the conceptual necessity and practical desirability of the self-conscious separation of normative and empirical inquiry and is something of a staple in mainstream social science methods texts (for example, Kerlinger 1986). For the parallelist, normative and empirical business ethics have in common only a shared concern with certain types of business behavior (for example, employee theft, insider trading). Like parallel lines that point in the same direction but never cross, normative and empirical business ethics are directed toward a common range of phenomena but do not intermingle. From a researcher's standpoint, one engages in either social science or moral inquiry, and there is no substantive or pragmatic connection between the two. An empirical business ethics researcher thus works without taking cues from developments across campus in the philosophy or religion departments and vice versa. Any alteration of either field normally results from factors internal to the field in question, and intellectual life remains relatively tidy.

Rationale

The parallelist position rests on both practical and conceptual arguments. The practical argument takes note of the deeply entrenched stylistic, attitudinal, and methodological differences of normative and empirical inquiry, differences sufficient to make integration difficult at best. For various contextual, procedural, and motivational reasons, efforts of normative and empirical researchers to understand, much less assess, each others' work are likely to generate fundamental misunderstandings or misapplications (see Chapter 1). Thus, for the sake of both fields, the parallelist recommends against crossing disciplinary boundaries.

At a more conceptual level, the entrenchment of a fact/value distinction in most social science (for example, Weber 1949; Kerlinger 1986) and an is/ought distinction in much traditional moral philosophy (for example, Hume 1748; Moore 1903) suggests that the basic concepts of one field forever may appear irrelevant from the standpoint of the other; witness Kerlinger's advice that empirical social science should eschew value-laden concepts, such as democracy (Kerlinger 1986, 21–22) and should avoid purportedly untestable evaluative judgments. Normative and empirical inquiries also often make different *metatheoretical* assumptions, specifically regarding the nature of human action (see Chapter 1; see also Mulligan 1987). Much empirical inquiry at least implicitly assumes a quasi-mechanistic account of human agency, whereas normative theorizing typically assumes some degree of autonomy and responsibility on the part of human agents.

It is common for some organizational researchers—following one possible reading of Thomas Kuhn's work (1962; but cf. Kuhn 1990; Weaver and Gioia 1994 [portions of which appear in Chapter 3 of this volume])—to *assume* a strong conception of the nature and role of metatheoretical frameworks or "paradigms," according to which the foregoing types of metatheoretical differences generate inter-paradigmatic incommensurability (for example, Burrell and Morgan 1979). If the differences of empirical and normative business ethics are united to such a conception of incommensurable paradigms, parallelism becomes a *conceptual necessity*. The different disciplinary frameworks in which empirical and normative business ethics are located allegedly engender necessarily impenetrable barriers to communication and understanding.

An Example of Parallelism

Management research on the punishment of individuals in organizations is dominated by behavioral learning theory perspectives that focus almost exclusively on whether punishment is effective (in the sense of controlling or changing behavior) rather than on whether it is morally proper (Arvey, Davis, and Nelson 1984; Ball 1991; Baron 1990; Baum and Youngblood 1975; Nicholson 1976; Podsakoff, Todor, and Skov 1982). Thus, this literature has a parallelist self-identity. Yet the avoidance of normative issues in managerial punishment research arguably is superficial, for in its focus on effectiveness, management research ultimately rests on normative assumptions. If, for example, the normative rationale for punishment is—as the management literature assumes—to control, change, or deter actions, it is appropriate for empirical inquiry to focus on the effectiveness of punishment as a means or mechanism of control, change, or deterrence. If the normative rationale for punishment were retribution rather than control, empirical inquiry into effectiveness might be entirely beside the point. The very idea of worrying about effectiveness implies a commitment to a normative conception of punishment.

Problems for Parallelism

Apparently parallelist empirical research, then, may not so much avoid normative issues as hide them. By ignoring normative issues, empirical inquiry loses sight of why and for whom it pursues some questions rather than others. Parallelist empirical inquiry risks rendering itself a naive tool for advancing an unquestioned administrative conception of social order and function (Barley, Meyer, and Gash 1988; Sullivan 1983). Empirical inquiry also risks irrelevance, insofar as it ignores relevant topics because of their normative connotations (observe how behaviorist-dominated psychology long ignored issues of moral psychology).

Similarly, the application of normative claims in parallelist fashion can hide a variety of empirical assumptions about how the world works. Self-contained normative inquiry may become too abstract, or too idealistic, to be of any practical value, or it may be applied in counterproductive fashion. In general, *parallelist empirical inquiry risks losing the very legitimacy and independence that empirical purity allegedly would bestow, and parallelist normative inquiry risks irrelevance and self-defeating application.*

Any conceptual argument for parallelism based on the alleged incommensurability of metatheoretical perspective is untenable if it is taken to mean that communication across the normative/empirical dividing line is impossible. Although the incommensurability thesis is commonplace among many organizational researchers (for example, Burrell and Morgan 1979; Gioia and Pitre 1990; Jackson and Carter 1991), serious theoretical and metatheoretical differences need not entail *systematic* communicative failure (Kuhn 1990; Weaver and Gioia 1994). Without support from some kind of incommensurability thesis, however, arguments for parallelism that appeal to institutional, linguistic, or stylistic differences reduce to an embrace of intellectual lethargy and an academicians' version of a "not-invented-here" prejudice. Such differences are rooted more in the historical accidents that led to the present institutionalized norms and organizational and physical structures of academia, and departmentalized research universities are no more immutable features of the societal and intellectual landscape than were the more holistic institutions they began to replace approximately a century ago.

Because intellectual lethargy is unbecoming, because existing disciplinary boundaries are historically contingent in at least some respects, and because there are no systematic difficulties with communication across theoretical and metatheoretical frames, the parallelist espousal of mutual isolation is untenable. Additionally, it generates legitimacy problems for normative inquiry because of irrelevance and for empirical inquiry because of cooptation by an unexamined normative perspective. Consequently, there appear to be good reasons to consider the more openly collaborative symbiotic position.

SYMBIOTIC APPROACHES TO BUSINESS ETHICS

Exposition

The symbiotic position envisions a pragmatic, collaborative relationship between normative and empirical inquiry in which each discipline takes cues from the other regarding such things as the delineation of a research agenda or the applicability of theory. Although the theoretical cores of each approach remain distinct, the fields are admitted to have significant implications and guidance for the conduct and application of each other. In terms of the marital metaphor of our chapter title, normative and empirical inquiry constitute two self-contained individuals who nevertheless engage in an ongoing relationship for their mutual benefit (a marriage of convenience). As in the case of parallelism, the two forms of business ethics inquiry are self-contained by virtue of their differing assumptions, forms of theorizing, and methods, but in symbiosis their work is carried out in communicative fashion. Symbiosis requires a degree of scholarly bilingualism, which in turn requires the elimination of the contextual disciplinary constraints accepted as immutable by the parallelist. Nevertheless, despite intercommunication, the two forms of inquiry remain essentially distinct in their theoretical principles, methodologies, and metatheoretical assumptions.

According to the symbiotic position, information from each type of business ethics inquiry is potentially relevant to the pursuit and application of the other form of inquiry. For example, empirical inquiry may be used in guiding the application of specific moral theories. Normative inquiry, by revealing the moral character of organizational processes, may help to guide the focus of empirical study. Unlike parallelism, symbiosis entails conscious attention to questions of why and for whom empirical inquiry is pursued. Depending on whether an organizational phenomenon is treated as morally proper or improper, empirical research might concentrate on either fostering or eliminating that phenomenon. In sum, symbiotic collaboration allows each approach to business ethics to benefit from the scrutiny of the other while remaining grounded in its own distinct assumptions, theories, and methods.

Rationale

There are two sides, then, to the symbiotic position. One concerns the practical value of a collaborative relationship that avoids the cooptation, irrelevance, and illegitimacy afflicting parallelist approaches to business ethics. Deliberate attention to descriptive, empirical theory can prevent normative researchers from proposing programs of moral improvement, which, however much they embody some noble normative principle, in practice are unfeasible or even likely to undermine moral behavior. Attention to normative theory, in turn, aids empiricists in being self-conscious about the purpose, character, and results of their work.

The other side of the symbiotic view is its insistence on the independence of the theoretical cores of normative and empirical business ethics. Empirical discoveries may limit the applicability but do not compel the rejection of normative theories; the normative principles, after all, are intended to function as ideals, not as descriptions of actual behavior (Treviño 1986). To the normative theorist, limiting the content of normative theory to that which is empirically correct would baptize the moral failings of the *status quo* with moral legitimacy. To the empiricist, empirical theories framed in normative categories would likely prove empirically false, especially if the entire point of normative conception is to stand apart from and critique actual behavior. In this view, normative considerations may direct behavioral inquiry to focus on a particular type of organizational misconduct, but they should not affect empirical inquiry's theories and models of behavior in and by organizations. Symbiosis, in short, affirms a normative/empirical distinction but views communication across that distinction as pragmatically valuable and treats a failure to communicate as intellectually and morally indefensible.

Symbiosis in Practice

Freeman and Gilbert's (1988) work linking corporate strategy and business ethics constitutes one effort to pursue a symbiotic approach to business ethics. Although Freeman and Gilbert's stated agenda is to "infuse corporate strategy with an understanding of values and ethics" (1988, 10), it is important to see what this does and does not include. They use philosophical moral theories to define different approaches to corporate strategy and to unearth and critique the underlying moral assumptions of conventional strategic analysis. Thus, although they reject a naive parallelism and provide conceptual and practical links between normative ethics and business strategy, they remain grounded in a normative/philosophical approach. Even their target generally represents a more rationalistic, normative approach to strategy (for example, Andrews 1980) rather than an empirical, descriptive approach. Their predominant grounding in the normative/philosophical literature can be seen, for example, in their claim that "values explain action" (Freeman and Gilbert 1988, 20). Their defense of this claim appeals to the analytical philosophy of action literature rather than to social psychological research on the relationships among beliefs, attitudes, norms, intentions, and behavior.

In short, although Freeman and Gilbert apply the insights and implications of philosophical inquiry to subject matter usually reserved for management research, their overall approach—and its target—remains normative or philosophical in its overall method and content. Rather than offering some new form of merged empirical/normative theory, Freeman and Gilbert's work functions more as an effort to critique normatively the moral stance of conventional strategic management writings.

The Limits of Symbiosis

Empirical management research may be used to draw limits around the claims of normative inquiry, but an example of that effort will help clarify the difference between symbiosis and deeper forms of theoretical integration. In an effort to use "descriptive research to shed light on prescriptive research," Greenberg and Bies (1992) offer what they term "integrated business ethics" in the form of *empirically based* "challenges to moral philosophy" (1992, 442). Greenberg and Bies criticize utilitarians, for example, for misjudging the behavioral effects of punishment and reward, and they reject Kant's rigorous moral standards on the empirical grounds that people generally view some types of lying as morally acceptable.

There may be a sense in which these empirical claims do constitute "challenges" to "moral philosophy," but, on the symbiotic position, they are not challenges in the sense of *refutations* of normative moral theories. The moralist who insists on holding to these descriptively incorrect positions does not commit some kind of logical blunder. One suspects that Kant knew that most people view some lies as morally acceptable, but the moral theories in part serve to chasten, not pander to, the status quo. His principles might be unrealistically demanding, but impracticality alone does not entail the refutation of a normative theory. Similarly, utilitarianism's alleged problems regarding the behavioral effects of punishment do not *necessarily* invalidate utilitarianism; rather, they may suggest that some other form of application is in order if societal welfare is to be enhanced (cf. Bentham 1789/1970, 14–15).

Such limits on empirical criticisms of normative claims capture the essence of the symbiotic position: Cross-disciplinary criticisms of applicability or focus are permissible, but nothing in such criticism necessarily alters or undermines the substantive content of normative or empirical theory. Empirical evidence alone forces no moralist to give up a normative theory; rather, the moralist can choose between forsaking a general normative principle or delimiting its practical value. Delimiting the practical value of a moral theory may lead to a *pragmatically induced* rejection or modification of a moral theory, but it does not itself entail a *refutation* of the theory. If empirical impracticality is to count as a refutation of a moral theory, it minimally requires an extra argument to the effect that people should not be held to a standard that it is unlikely they could satisfy in normal circumstances. But that argument is itself a form of *moral*, not *empirical*, theorizing.

Problems for Symbiosis

The possibility of pragmatically rooted theory change suggests a difficulty in the symbiotic approach. Although symbiosis would keep intact the separate theoretical cores of normative and empirical inquiry, such separation is difficult in practice. Symbiosis, in short, is always potentially unstable, and, under the right circumstances, can slide into a form of integration that involves pragmatically induced theory change. Such change is not full-fledged theoretical integration; the normative and empirical theories are not merged into some new, unified treatment of business ethics. If one considers the ways in which the categories of one field can be used to frame or structure the inquiries of another, however, it is not clear why or how one should stop short of thinking in terms of a single field of inquiry, rather than two related fields.

THEORETICAL INTEGRATION

Exposition

A maximal form of integration should involve more than a pragmatic, reactive response of one field to another. Rather, it should embody what might be called theoretical *hybridization*: proactively creating a new breed of theory by consciously commingling the cores of two disciplines. In the broader world of psychological, sociological, and political theory, more than a few prominent theorists appear to bridge the normative/empirical chasm by some form of hybridization; at least their works share a resistance to easy classification as either purely normative or purely empirical. In earlier times, de Tocqueville and Marx stand out, and a more current list would include, among others, Giddens's social theory (for example, 1984), Kohlberg's (1969) intentional rejection of the naturalistic fallacy in his moral psychology, Bellah and associates' simultaneous description and critique of individualism in America (1984, 1991), and Etzioni's recent plea for "deontological social science" (1989). It is not just that their descriptive work is motivated by moral commitments (this also holds for symbiosis) but that their descriptions themselves are framed in ineliminably moral categories. Overall, however, the recent history of American social science generally, and management inquiry specifically, does not easily generate examples of intentional hybridization, perhaps because a particular moral outlook has become the taken for granted, and thus unseen, conceptual framework for most such work (cf. Bellah 1983; Sullivan 1983; Sievers 1983). What distinguishes the foregoing authors from the norm is the extent to which they recognize and embrace the incorporation of evaluative claims and categories into their empirical work or, more forcefully, reject the very idea of distinguishing normative and empirical claims.

As the foregoing list of authors should indicate, hybridization may come in diverse forms and to varying degrees. The exact character hybridization might or might not take is a complex issue, dependent on a number of topics both in normative ethics and the philosophy of science that range beyond our current expository focus. For present purposes, however, we believe it is useful to distinguish three varieties of hybridization:

1. *Conceptual importation*, wherein one field invokes the concepts of another in the basic framework of its theorizing. This process already occurs insofar as empirical and normative theories implicitly assume, respectively, particular normative or empirical categorizations of business ethical phenomena. As our earlier comments should indicate, even parallelism in practice cannot avoid this much integration. Conceptual importation is exemplified, for example, in empirical studies of organizational ethical climate (Victor and Cullen 1988) that describe the extent to which organiza-

tional phenomena exhibit normatively delineated characteristics but that neither presume nor deny the propriety of any particular normative stance.

2. *Theoretical reciprocity*, wherein an overall explanatory framework incorporates both empirical and normative theories, and *where the framework's success in providing either an empirical description or normative evaluation of some phenomenon depends, respectively, on its normative or empirical adequacy*. There is, in this case, an intentional interdependence of normative and empirical theories. This is exemplified in Kohlberg's work on moral development, in which the putative moral preferability of a specific cognitive state undergirds an empirical theory of a developmental process toward that state.

3. *Theoretical unity*, according to which the distinction between the normative and the empirical is rejected as methodologically and metatheoretically untenable. This general position can come in diverse forms, ranging from critical social theory (cf. Burrell and Morgan 1979)—in which there is no normatively neutral description of human activity—to naturalistic metaethics, which aims to resolve moral controversy by unapologetically grounding morality in biological or other natural scientific theories (for example, Rosenberg 1990). If some form of theoretical unity is adopted, all other positions—and even, in a sense, our exposition of them—are fundamentally misconceived, for they presume a normative/empirical distinction that in fact does not hold.

Rationale

There would seem to be strong arguments in favor of at least minimal hybridization via *conceptual importation*. The study of business ethics, after all, is the study of *morality in a business context*. Minimally, this means that (1) the organizational scientist who studies business *ethics* must acknowledge and deal with the normative character of moral concepts; and (2) the philosopher who takes on the study of *business* ethics must acknowledge the relevance of the practical business context within which this moral agency occurs. For the empiricist to refrain from invoking such a normative framework is to generate a cognitively impoverished social science. "Without a reference point in the tradition of ethical reflection, the very categories of social thought would be empty. The construction of an entirely new abstract vocabulary [à la Kerlinger] would render the enterprise opaque . . ." (Bellah

1983, 373). To avoid the categories of moral language is to avoid the lived-in world and to lose the meaning of social phenomena.

Theoretical reciprocity rests on the claim that a psychological or sociological investigator cannot just examine evaluatively neutral pieces of behavior but must conceptualize the subject as an agent who acts intentionally in a framework of moral understanding. To describe intentional acts as just, right, or in other categories common even in *empirical* business ethics is to invoke an evaluative moral framework. Moreover, the argument continues, just as part—if not all—of the explanation for why someone accepts a logically correct argument resides in the fact that the argument *is* correct (Carroll 1939), part of the explanation for why one acts morally resides in the fact that the action is morally proper (Kohlberg 1976). Normative theory, in short, helps *explain*, not merely evaluate, psychological processes.

As suggested, *theoretical unity* may have multiple sources, some of which postulate the ultimately normative character of putatively "empirical" claims and others that propose an empirical basis for all defensible normative claims. In either case, there is no longer a fact/value or, more properly, a normative/empirical distinction. Although discussions in the business ethics literature typically challenge the purported neutrality of empirical inquiry, supposedly pure and distinct normative theorizing receives its share of criticism in the philosophical literature. For example, insofar as one accepts the claim that social practices, communities, and relationships help to constitute persons and their ends, one links moral judgment with some degree of sociological description (MacIntyre 1984).

Those unification efforts that instead claim that the putatively empirical is inevitably normative typically have their roots in more interpretive and critical approaches to social inquiry. Such metatheoretical stances postulate that social facts are ultimately inseparable from the interpretive stances of the actors who constitute society. Social facts, in this view, have "no existence independent of the knowledge that agents have about what they do in their day-to-day activities" (Giddens 1984, 26). Insofar as social facts are constructed out of the interpretive understanding of social actors (Berger and Luckman 1967), social facts (for example, the existence of authority) inevitably reflect moral standards and judgments. Where one person "sees" legitimate authority, another may "see" oppressive exploitation, and no appeal to *pure* observable evidence is possible; if social facts are always interpretive, "raw data," were they available, would be fundamentally meaningless. Moreover, because researchers also are social actors, their own work reflects a morally infused interpretation of *their* day-to-day activities. Insofar as the inquirer's interpretation departs from the subjects', social inquiry assumes an essentially critical stance.

Examples of Theoretical Integration

Within empirical business ethics proper, Victor and Cullen (1988) probably come closest to self-conscious theoretical integration by explicitly incorporating three categories borrowed from normative ethical theory (egoism, benevolence, and principle) along with three loci of empirical analysis (individual, local, and cosmopolitan) to develop a typology of organizational ethical climates. Their study represents theoretical integration in its most straightforward form: self-conscious importation of concepts without further normative evaluation or prescription. Victor and Cullen use their normatively rooted typology as the basis for data collection and analysis according to mainstream social science methodology (for example, factor analysis). Their results demonstrate the extent to which empirical data map onto the initial typology and indicate that ethical climates differ among and within organizations.

Minimally, Victor and Cullen's approach enables one to judge the extent to which one or another normative principle is actually practiced and the extent to which there is agreement on a particular principle in practice. In and of itself, this is unlikely to prompt suspicions; a utilitarian, for example, would no doubt find it helpful in making utilitarian calculations to know roughly how many others could be expected to make similar calculations. By using recognizable normative language as a framework within which to develop empirically rooted constructs, Victor and Cullen's social scientific inquiry maintains some degree of normative relevance and independence.

Theoretical Problems with Integration

The direct incorporation of normative categories into empirical work, as in the case of Victor and Cullen's basic form of hybridization, is likely to prompt skepticism arising from the realization that normative principles will never accurately describe the *status quo* because they were never intended to (Brady and Hatch 1992; cf. Treviño 1986). Consequently, this kind of integration always tempts a facile rejection of normative principles and thereby constitutes a danger to the evaluative character and independence of normative theory insisted on in less integrative positions.

A study like Victor and Cullen's, because it uses normative categories, is likely to be more meaningful to people than a study of ethical climate that avoids any normative language, *were such a study even possible*. Nor does Victor and Cullen's study naively assume that one moral theory is preferable because it is most frequently practiced or unacceptable because it is not practiced. Yet the fact that they found emergent categories of moral climate that mixed normative categories usually thought to be in opposition to each other could prompt moralists to reexamine fruitfully some of the traditional conceptualizations of types of normative theories, even though such a discovery in no sense refutes one or another moral theory.

Theoretical integration thus makes for a messier form of social inquiry than is usually countenanced in the business school environment. To many a social scientist, the incorporation of normative commitments and interpretations into empirical social science—or, more strongly, the collapse of any distinction between empirical and normative inquiry—may appear to risk an "anything goes" relativism. Whether or not this is the case depends in part on our understanding of such notions as truth and objectivity, in particular regarding the bases for adjudicating among competing interpretations of social phenomena. Needless to say, according to the generically neopositivist metascience undergirding much North American social science, incorporating normative perspectives or interpretive understanding into empirical inquiry amounts to incorporating arbitrary subjectivity into science. This is so because, by typical empiricist/positivist standards, there can be no moral facts in any ordinary sense. But as our criticism of parallelism indicates, there is a sense in which the incorporation of moral judgments into empirical inquiry already occurs; parallelism merely takes for granted a particular normative framing, which more self-consciously integrative forms of inquiry are willing to question. Moreover, if we reject the positivist assumption that " 'the sciences' and sound knowledge are coextensive" (Laudan 1981, 153–154), it no longer follows that a collapse of a science/nonscience or empirical/normative distinction leads to a relativistic situation in which there are *no* grounds on which to adjudicate among competing claims. Indeed, it may be a traditional overestimation of the sciences that leads to a denigration of other forms of inquiry.

Practical Problems with Integration

If one or more of the possible conceptions of theoretical integration are sustainable, we confront the possibility that business ethics could be a unified field, animated by research that combines empirical and normative inquiry. The distinction between the normative and empirical with which we began in fact becomes untenable in stronger forms of integration and constitutes a merely expositional device to be jettisoned at the first opportunity. Doing so, however, conflicts with the institutionalized self-identities of both disciplines and is likely to lead to charges that too much of value is lost in the process. When theoretical integration is attempted, it is likely subject to hostility and criticism from multiple quarters because, by definition, it breaks more rules and steps on more toes than the run-of-the-mill empirical or normative study that remains within conventional boundaries. Those who believe that existing institutional boundaries should be respected will be quick to defend their institutional territory.

CONCLUSION: PROSPECTS FOR BUSINESS ETHICS INTEGRATION

We have provided an outline of three conceptions of the relationship between normative and empirical business ethics: parallelism, symbiosis, and full theoretical integration or hybridization. We hope this articulation of the nature, rationale, and actual or potential problems of these options will prove useful to those who wish to talk about an "integrated" business ethics in the future. In conclusion, we offer a brief analysis of the prospects each has in the near-term development of business ethics.

Although the *appearance* of parallel inquiry always may be with us because of its entrenchment in the institutionalized norms of academia, we suspect that it will become an ever more tenuous position in actual practice. If concern with business ethics proves to be more than a passing fad, we expect that both business and the public will expect normative theorists to be concerned with the vicissitudes of application and empirical theorists to be self-conscious about the moral purposes of their work. Insofar as business ethics research depends on business and the public for resources and legitimacy, pure parallel inquiry faces increasing difficulty in maintaining its social legitimacy.

Symbiotic inquiry, on the other hand, would seem to have the easiest future, for it provides greater relevance and legitimacy for both normative and empirical inquiry without requiring that the accepted theoretical frameworks and methodologies of either approach be altered or rejected. What it does require, however, is changes in abilities, attitudes, and behaviors on the part of individual researchers and educational and research institutions. In terms of ability, it requires *bilingualism*, the ability of empiricists and moralists to speak each other's language so that communication and understanding can occur. In terms of attitudes, it requires open-mindedness to the very real practical value of input from other approaches so that communication actually occurs. In terms of behavior, it requires ongoing dialogue between the two approaches via the development of research teams drawn from both fields, the sharing of papers across disciplines, and the serious consideration of this input across frontiers. At the same time, it requires a respect for and retention of the unique disciplinary foci that symbiosis demands. Whether or not such retention ultimately is tenable in the face of any long-term pragmatic failures of a field is an open question.

We believe that full theoretical integration faces a more difficult future than does symbiosis because it imposes more significant burdens on the researcher: (1) full-fledged involvement in two fields simultaneously—philosophers and scientists will have to evaluate each others' arguments and methods, not merely read each others' conclusions; (2) the potential challenge of developing a new set of terms, methods, and metatheories; (3) an inevitably long-term research effort; (4) subjecting oneself to simultaneous criticism from more traditional empirical and normative theorists who may fail to grasp or appreciate the character of integrative work. We believe there are few currently in the field who are prepared even to attempt this type of major long-term effort, and those who do may find that they face challenges and criticisms from all fronts. These problems are challenges, not refutations, and so we suggest that judgment as to the feasibility of full-scale integration is best left until after serious efforts at achieving it take place; that is, the possibility and desirability of full-scale integration should be judged by the fruits of serious integrative efforts. Only by such efforts can the character and consequences of full-fledged integrative business ethics be evaluated.

References

Andrews, K. R. 1980. *The concept of corporate strategy*, 2nd ed. Homewood, IL: Richard D. Irwin.

Arvey, R. D., G. A. Davis, and S. M. Nelson. 1984. Use of discipline in an organization: A field study. *Journal of Applied Psychology* 69(3):448–460.

Ball, G. A. 1991. *Outcomes of punishment incidents: The role of subordinate perceptions, individual differences, and leader behavior.* Unpublished doctoral dissertation. The Pennsylvania State University.

Barley, S. R., G. W. Meyer, and D. C. Gash. 1988. Cultures of culture: Academics, practitioners, and the pragmatics of normative control. *Administrative Science Quarterly* 33:24–60.

Baron, R. A. 1990. Countering the effects of destructive criticism: The relative efficacy of four interventions. *Journal of Applied Psychology* 75:235–245.

Baum, J. F., and S. A. Youngblood. 1975. Impact of an organizational control policy on absenteeism, performance, and satisfaction. *Journal of Applied Psychology* 60:688–694.

Bellah, R. 1983. The ethical aims of social inquiry. In *Social science as moral inquiry*, ed. N. Haan, R. Bellah, P. Rabinow, and W. Sullivan, 360–382. New York: Columbia University Press.

Bellah, R. N., R. Madsen, W. M. Sullivan, A. Swidler, and S. M. Tipton. 1984. *Habits of the heart: individualism and commitment in American life*. New York: Harper & Row.

Bellah, R. N., R. Madsen, W. M. Sullivan, A. Swidler, and S. M. Tipton. 1991. *The good society*. New York: Alfred A. Knopf.

Bentham, J. 1789. *An introduction to the principles of morals and legislation*. Ed. J. H. Burns and H. L. A. Hart. London: University of London, The Athlone Press, 1970.

Berger, P., and T. Luckman. 1967. *The social construction of reality*. Garden City, NY: Doubleday.

Brady, F. N., and M. J. Hatch. 1992. General causal models in business ethics: An essay on colliding research traditions. *Journal of Business Ethics* 11:307–315.

Burrell, G., and G. Morgan. 1979. *Sociological paradigms and organizational analysis*. London: Heinemann.

Carroll, L. 1939. What the tortoise said to Achilles. In *The complete works of Lewis Carroll*. New York: Modern Library.

Etzioni, A. 1989. Toward deontological social sciences. *Philosophy of the Social Sciences* 19:145–156.

Fleming, J. 1987. A survey and critique of business ethics research, 1986. In *research in corporate social performance and policy*, Vol. 9, ed. W. Frederick, 1–24. Greenwich, CT: JAI Press.

Freeman, R. E., and D. R. Gilbert. 1988. *Corporate strategy and the search for ethics*. Englewood Cliffs, NJ: Prentice-Hall.

Giddens, A. 1984. *The constitution of society*. Berkeley: University of California Press.

Gioia, D. A., and E. Pitre. 1990. Multiparadigm perspectives on theory building. *Academy of Management Review* 15(4):584–602.

Greenberg, J., and R. Bies. 1992. Establishing the role of empirical studies of organizational justice in philosophical inquiries into business ethics. *Journal of Business Ethics* 11:433–444.

Hume, D. 1748. *An enquiry concerning human understanding*. Indianapolis: Hackett Publishing, 1993.

Jackson, N., and C. Carter. 1991. In defense of paradigm incommensurability. *Organization Studies* 12(1):109–127.

Kahn, W. A. 1990. Toward an agenda for business ethics research. *Academy of Management Review* 15:311–328.

Kerlinger, E. N. 1986. *Foundations of behavioral research*. New York: Holt, Rinehart & Winston.

Kohlberg, L. 1969. Stage and sequence: The cognitive–developmental approach to socialization. In *Handbook of socialization theory and research*, ed. D. A. Goslin, 347–380. Chicago: Rand McNally.

Kohlberg, L. 1976. Moral stages and moralization: The cognitive–developmental approach. In *Moral development and behavior: Theory, research, and social issues*, ed. T. Lickona. New York: Holt, Rinehart & Winston.

Kuhn, T. S. 1962. *The structure of scientific revolutions*. Chicago: University of Chicago Press.

Kuhn, T. S. 1990. Dubbing and redubbing: The vulnerability of rigid designation. In *Minnesota studies in the philosophy of science, Vol.XIV: Scientific theories*, ed. C. Wade Savage, 298–313. Minneapolis: University of Minnesota Press.

Laudan, L. 1981. A problem-solving approach to scientific progress. In *Scientific revolutions*, ed. I. Hacking. Oxford: Oxford University Press.

MacIntyre, A. 1984. Does applied ethics rest on a mistake? *The Monist* 67:498–513.

Moore, G. E. 1903. *Principia ethica*. Cambridge: Cambridge University Press.

Mulligan, T. M., 1987. The two cultures in business education. *Academy of Management Review* 12:593–599.

Nicholson, N. 1976. Management sanctions and absence control. *Human Relations* 19:139–151.

Podsakoff, P., W. Todor, and R. Skov. 1982. Effects of leader contingent and non-contingent reward and punishment behaviors on subordinate performance and satisfaction. *Academy of Management Journal* 25:810–821.

Rosenberg, A. 1990. Moral realism and social science. In *Midwest studies in philosophy*, Vol. XV: *The philosophy of the human sciences*, ed. P. A. French, T. E. Uehling, and H. K. Wettstein. Notre Dame: University of Notre Dame Press.

Sievers, B. 1983. Believing in social science: The ethics and epistemology of public opinion research. In *Social science as moral inquiry*, ed. N. Haan, R. Bellah, P. Rabinow, and W. Sullivan, 320–342. New York: Columbia University Press.

Sullivan, W. M. 1983. Beyond policy science: The social sciences as moral sciences. In *Social science as moral inquiry*, ed. N. Haan, R. Bellah, P. Rabinow, and W. Sullivan, 297–319. New York: Columbia University Press.

Treviño, L. K. 1986. Ethical decision making in organizations: A person-situation interactionist model. *Academy of Management Review* 11:601–617.

Victor, B., and J. Cullen. 1988. The organizational bases of ethical work climates. *Administrative Science Quarterly* 33:101–125.

Weaver, G. R., and D. G. Gioia. 1994. Paradigms lost: Incommensurability *vs.* structurationist inquiry. *Organization Studies* 15:565–590.

Weber, M., 1949. *The methodology of the social sciences*. Glencoe, IL: Free Press.

THREE

Perspectives, Possibilities, and Motives for Integration

Integration of normative and empirical perspectives in business ethics is an example of a larger issue in organization studies generally: how to deal with the competing theoretical positions that pervade the field. For example, closely tied to issues of normative and empirical integration are issues of subjective and objective accounts of organizational phenomena: Should organizations be understood from the evaluative perspective of specific actors, or is there some neutral, value-free third-party perspective from which to view organizational phenomena? In this chapter, we first examine the larger issue of multiple conflicting perspectives in organization studies, of which the normative/empirical divide is an example. We then offer our own way to deal with this apparent conflict and consider efforts by others to do the same. In doing this, we provide a framework for what we do, and do not do, in the remainder of the book. That is, we explain our focus on largely empirical questions without denying the relevance of normative critiques of those empirical efforts.

Portions of this chapter are taken from G. R. Weaver and D. A. Gioia, 1994. "Paradigms lost: Incommensurability vs. structurationist inquiry," *Organization Studies* 15:565–590; and from L. K. Treviño and G. R. Weaver, 1999, "The stakeholder research tradition: Converging theorists, not convergent theory," *Academy of Management Review* 24:222–227; and from "Treviño and Weaver's reply to Jones and Wicks," 1999, *Academy of Management Review* 24:623–624. Both copyright 1999 by the Academy of Management. Reproduced with permission of the Academy of Management in book format via Copyright Clearance Center.

ALTERNATIVE PERSPECTIVES IN ORGANIZATION STUDIES

Organization theorists sometimes argue that the field is divided into multiple paradigms reflecting different theoretical and methodological assumptions. Moreover, attempting to borrow ideas from Kuhn's controversial classic in the sociology of science—*The Structure of Scientific Revolutions* (1962, 1970)—some organizational scholars have claimed that these different "paradigms" of organizational inquiry are incommensurable. *Incommensurability*, as used in this debate, typically is taken to imply that there is no common measure among paradigms of inquiry so that representatives of opposed paradigms "live in different worlds," hold "mutually exclusive" beliefs, use different vocabularies, and so on (Burrell and Morgan 1979; Gioia and Pitré 1990; Jackson and Carter 1991). The "incommensurable paradigms" position tells us, in essence, that we must choose our ontological, epistemological, and methodological options from among the various dichotomies generally thought to affect organizational inquiry, including a dichotomy between description and prescription (along with others, namely, structure versus agency, determinism versus voluntarism, causation versus meaning, holism versus individualism, object versus subject, and so on). If this position is correct, it would seem that the parallelist argument of Chapter 2 is correct and that efforts to integrate normative and empirical inquiry are futile because these two perspectives are so different in their assumptions (see Chapter 1) that they constitute "incommensurable paradigms." As Burrell and Morgan (1979, 25) have put it:

> A synthesis [of paradigms] is not possible, since in their pure forms they [paradigms] are contradictory, being based on at least one set of opposing meta-theoretical assumptions. They are alternatives, in the sense that one can operate in different paradigms sequentially over time, but mutually exclusive, in the sense that one cannot operate in more than one paradigm at any given point in time, since in accepting the assumptions of one, we defy the assumptions of all the others.

One of us has argued extensively elsewhere (Weaver and Gioia 1994) that the popular "incommensurable paradigms" position in organization studies is seriously flawed because it is built on (1) an incomplete reading of the entire incommensurability debate as it originally developed in the history, sociology, and philosophy of science; and (2) a highly debatable philosophical account of language. Regarding the first objection, for example, in the organizational debate, no attention is paid to Kuhn's later revisions and retractions of his early programmatic statements. For example, Kuhn later asserted that "anything that can be said in one language can, with sufficient imagination and effort, be understood by a speaker of another" (1990, 300; see also Kuhn 1983). This is hardly a basis for asserting incommensurable paradigms of inquiry, and yet Kuhn's reasons for rejecting strong forms of incommensurability are rarely addressed by organizational scholars (but cf. Weaver and Gioia 1994). Thus, the idea that different perspectives in organizational inquiry—such as the normative and empirical perspectives on ethics in organizations—are necessarily dichotomous appears more as an institutionalized assumption of the field than as a position rooted in extended scholarly engagement with the issues.

Regarding the second objection, if incommensurability characterized different approaches to understanding organizations, it is not at all clear that we could elaborate how, or even that, various paradigms differ from each other. If incommensurability means that scholars live and work in mutually exclusive "worlds" among which "meaningful communication" is not possible (Jackson and Carter 1991), how would it be possible to understand others, even if only to delineate differences? Again, this situation minimally suggests that "incommensurability" is used in a loose and imprecise sense in the organizational literature. If, however, incommensurable paradigms and Chapter 2's parallelist position are ill founded, how can we grapple in practice with the fact of different frameworks for understanding organizations (and ethics in organizations)?

AVOIDING DICHOTOMIES BY UNDERSTANDING HOW PERSPECTIVES HIGHLIGHT PARTS OF A LARGER PICTURE

One way of thinking about the relationship among different approaches to organizational inquiry can illumine the relationship between normative and empirical inquiry and allow us to proceed in largely empirical fashion without denying the relevance of normative scholarship to empirical inquiry (that is, it is at least a symbiotic position, to use Chapter 2's language). This approach involves adopting the general framework toward inquiry elaborated in Giddens's (1976, 1979, 1984) theory of structuration. The structurational framework we adopt provides a basis for seeing how organizational scholars can invoke different assumptions, pursue different goals, ask different research questions, and use different approaches while still being engaged in a recognizably shared scholarly endeavor. (We hasten to add, however, that we are adapting Giddens's general outlook for our own purposes and do not intend our comments as a formal exposition of Giddens's wide-ranging scholarship.)

The framework offered by structuration theory shows just how the selective bracketing of aspects of social phenomena can occur. In effect, it helps to clarify the relationships among different perspectives by showing just how they constitute perspectives—that is, identifying what they highlight and what they downplay. For example, consider the alleged dichotomy (in organizational research) of human agency and social structure. Social structures, in Giddens's view, "are both constituted 'by' human agency, and yet at the same time are the very 'medium' of this constitution" (1976:121). Thus, at any given time, social structures are synchronically involved in action: They influence actions as constraining and enabling factors. For example, the banking system, *qua* structure, enables one to perform particular financial operations while it also constrains the range of financial actions into which a person might enter at a particular point in time. Human actions, however, are diachronically involved in social structures in that our actions establish or constitute structures; banking systems do not exist except as they are initially created by and thereafter recreated in human actions. If certain individuals were to refrain from performing certain actions and holding to certain beliefs, one could not cash, or even write, a check. Thus, instead of a dichotomy of two "incommensurable" approaches to inquiry, Giddens instead offers a "duality of structure," by which he means "the essential recursiveness of social life, as constituted in social practices: structure is both medium and outcome of the reproduction of practices. Structure enters simultaneously into the constitution of the agent and social practices, and exists in the generating moments of this constitution" (1979, 5). Although "structure has no existence independent of the knowledge that agents have about what they do in their day-to-day activities" (Giddens 1984, 26), those activities take place within an ongoing system of rules, norms, practices, and resources, the characteristics of which are created by and inherited from prior social activity.

Giddens regards the concepts involved in structuration mainly as "sensi-

tizing devices," that is, as ways of thinking about inquiry and the interpretation of research findings (1984, 326). It is in this sense of being a metatheoretical sensitizing device that structuration recommends itself for adequately coming to grips with the diversity of organizational scholarship,
including the diversity of normative and empirical inquiry. A structurational approach is an alternative to the alleged independence and self-
sufficiency of the key concepts that supposedly undergird different
approaches to inquiry. Although a structurational analysis may leave the
day-to-day practices of the different theoretical perspectives largely in
place, it also shows that none of them can claim completeness in and of
themselves. From a structurational perspective, a full understanding of a
society (or organization) needs to consider two viewpoints simultaneously:
(1) a stationary, cross-sectional standpoint, reflecting the rules, resources,
and practices that at any given time influence (without determining) the
actions of agents (e.g., the banking system, in the earlier example); these
rules, resources, and practices constitute the social structures that form the
arena and tools of social action (as when one uses the existence of those
rules, resources, and practices we call "the banking system" not only to cash
a check but even to intend to cash a check); and (2) a dynamic, longitudinal
standpoint, reflecting the way in which by their actions agents intentionally
and unintentionally change the rules and resources of society; although our
actions sometimes recreate existing structures (i.e., rules, practices, and
resources), our actions also sometimes alter them or create new structures.

Structuration's implications for the practice of organizational inquiry can
be seen in the way it resolves "paradigmatic" divides in organization studies.
For example, the determinism/voluntarism divide falls before the realization that although structures constrain and enable action, they also result
from action. Consequently, they can be altered by action—sometimes intentionally, sometimes as the unintended products of intentional action.
Although people's actions are influenced and shaped by structures already in
place, people in turn have an ability to affect those structures. For example,
the existing banking system constrains the types of transactions that can
take place, but it is potentially in the capacity of at least some users to alter or
eliminate the banking system and thereby generate a new and different set of
human activities (e.g., via radical change in government regulatory policy).
Similarly, the causation/meaning distinction falls because meaningful,
intentional phenomena are "causally implicated, in a chronic manner, in

the continuation of day-to-day actions" (Giddens 1984, 345), actions that in turn create or recreate structures. Action is intentional and meaningful, but it is also constrained and enabled by circumstantial factors. As noted, banking systems are intentional phenomena, not mere physical entities; there are no banks unless people intend them to exist and endow them with certain properties. Nonetheless, they have "causal" consequences in that those properties in turn constitute bounds or influences on human action.

The prescription/description divide—the one most pertinent to business ethics research and its concerns for empirical/normative integration—is replaced by the realization that although social inquiry is potentially critical or normative when considered as an extended, historical enterprise, in its structural—functional forms, it may rest content to specify existing institutional orders and their influence on human behavior at a given point in time. To continue the earlier example: scholars can describe the practices of the current banking system; yet they also can specify ways that the system might have been different had human actors made different choices or how it may be altered in the present or future to serve one or another alternative societal purpose.

Any effort, then, to elevate one form of theoretical bracketing (e.g., normative or empirical) above others is shortsighted and presumptuous. Nevertheless, given proper recognition of each approach's particular form of bracketing, each can constitute a legitimate part of a larger scheme. A structurational analysis enables us to let go of the idea of monolithic, impermeable, and imperialistic approaches to organizations while maintaining distinctive and alternative perspectives within organizational inquiry. Applied to business ethics, this means that both normative and empirical theory and research can be seen as legitimate, albeit limited, forms of inquiry. Neither can claim to be exhaustive, and each makes implicit assumptions about the nature and stability of the other, for each typically brackets off the kinds of questions raised by the other.

IMPLICATIONS OF STRUCTURATIONAL APPROACHES

The foregoing structuration-inspired approach offers a way of thinking about the integration of normative and empirical business ethics. Each side of the conventional normative/empirical divide (along with other conventional divides) may be treated in isolation, provided each is understood as a transient or limited perspective within a larger framework of understanding. So empirical research can proceed in its accustomed ways, but without any explicit or implied assumptions that would reach farther than warranted under a structurationist framework. In particular, empirical theorizing must recognize that there is a mutual influence between agency and structure so that any relationships discovered could be different under a normatively different social and cognitive order. Moreover, that new social or cognitive order could be either unintentional in origin or reflect intentional efforts at restructuring according to some normative ideal. Finally, empirical theorizing, because it assumes a particular social and cognitive order, must recognize that it reflects particular normative commitments embedded within that order. For example, conventional empirical research on a topic like work productivity is likely to define productivity from a managerial standpoint rather than from an employee standpoint. Similarly, research on layoffs and downsizing might differ depending on whether we assume a 1990s framework (downsizing as a sign of forward looking, fiscally wise management) or a 1950s framework (downsizing as an indication of failure).

Normative theorizing in turn must recognize that its applicability or feasibility may be limited at any given point in time, although it need not give up the possibility that social and cognitive orders might be restructured to enhance the applicability or feasibility of a particular normative ideal. This limit on applicability is a variant of the "ought implies can" maxim common in much moral philosophy: to hold someone obligated to act in a particular way, to the point that the person deserves reprobation for not acting that way, the person must be able to act that way. No one, for example, can be under an obligation to do what is physically impossible; but what about obligations to do what is economically or commercially impossible under current social conditions? May a business, for example, be excused from concern for particular ethical obligations on grounds that satisfying those obligations is highly risky for the survival of the business and income for its workers and shareholders? In some instances, ethical standards and empirical realities may present straightforward "yes" or "no" answers to questions of this form. If the choice were to allow a business to fail or risk serious physical harm to tens of thousands by eliminating safety-relevant maintenance at an urban chemical factory, most people surely would think it proper to let the business fail, despite the hardship of unemployment for its workers and loss of wealth for investors. Likewise, if the choice were between risking debilitating financial losses for a business (and attendant loss of well-being for its employees) or having the business engage in a wide range of charitable contributions to cultural institutions, it would be difficult for most people to opt for the former.

Many such cases, however, are far from being clear-cut in this fashion because, even though a particular action might not be economically viable under the current social conditions, it might be viable under a different social order. A person's ethical reluctance to exploit public resources (that is, "the commons") for private gain may be economically irrational in a society in which common resources are under no public control because others will continue to exploit those public resources for private gain. If a gatekeeper is put in charge of the commons (for example, a regulatory agency is put in charge of air or water quality), however, that same person's ethically motivated reluctance can lose its disadvantageous character and might even become an economic advantage if it leads to a favorable reputation in the eyes of the gatekeeper. So regarding the normative side of business ethics, we need to say not "ought implies can—right now," but "ought implies could—under some reasonably plausible scenario of social change."

MAINTAINING A BALANCE VERSUS MOVING BEYOND
BRACKETED PERSPECTIVES

Consequently, integration in business ethics involves a balancing act, dealing with an ongoing tension between the empirical specification of what is and the normative specification of what ought to be under current circumstances *or* what could be under other possible circumstances. That is, business ethics inquiry can be symbiotic at a given time, but over longer horizons, it can become more fully integrated (insofar as the social ordering of a particular time is seen as more contingent and as embodying certain evaluative assumptions that are open to change). The nature of this tension can be seen by comparing our position with a recent effort to offer a more integrated account of the relationships and ethical obligations of businesses toward their stakeholders (Jones and Wicks 1999). Jones and Wicks claim to offer a way station on the road to integration, one that requires that (1) normative claims be based in social science reality and (2) empirical theory not be used for normatively improper ends (Jones and Wicks 1999). Although their argument is framed in the terminology of "stakeholder theory," the stakeholder framework clearly involves normative claims about the obligations of organizations to their stakeholders (Donaldson and Preston 1995). Thus, despite the different terminology, it involves the same questions of connections among empirical and normative perspectives that we have been discussing in Part I of this book.

Considering the first of their stipulations, Jones and Wicks argue that normative claims must meet a practicability requirement, according to which any defensible normative claim on an organization must leave it viable, which, for most business organizations, means profitable (1999:214). (Although they grant, in a footnote, that in "rare" cases this requirement may not be sustainable, they do not explain how we are to tell whether we have encountered such a rare situation.) Such a position, however, risks tipping the normative/empirical balance decidedly in the empirical direction, risking normative surrender, just because it overlooks the potential transience of the social and cognitive orders that undergird many empirical regularities. Judgments of practicability, and of the rarity of stakeholders having an interest in company closure or similarly extreme outcomes, involve normatively laden assumptions about broad-ranging, systemic, social questions.

To take two hypothetical extremes for illustration: the practicability standard a normative theory must meet will be very different depending on whether we assume a background of full laissez-faire capitalism or, as an alternative, an extreme welfare state. Employee and community concerns to keep a business going, despite perhaps being exploited by the business, probably are influenced by the extent to which a society provides other forms of social support. So what is rare in laissez-faire capitalism (such as a community demanding that a local employer pursue social goals at high financial risk) is less rare under an extreme welfare state. Put simply: The rarity of stakeholder interests in a business's viability depends on the available alternatives stakeholders face. The processes and frameworks of economic and commercial systems are not brute facts that cannot be altered; people in different legal jurisdictions in the United States, for example, sometimes enjoy (or suffer) different alternatives vis-à-vis the businesses that affect them. So it is important that the normatively significant background assumptions undergirding judgments of practicability not get swept under the rug, so that normative business ethicists will continue to ask not only "what happens if managers behave in certain ways" but also "what happens if managers behave in certain ways under various present *or possible* social conditions (such as a changed legal environment)." True, any reasonably integrated business ethics needs to keep one eye fixed on the managerial world, but it needs the other eye fixed on the broader social factors that set the parameters of that managerial world.

In urging that empirical theory not be used to support normatively improper ends, Jones and Wicks seem to offer the other side of integration: normative limits on empiricism. Their specific empirical target is instrumental claims of the sort that specify how to achieve particular organizational outcomes. Their stipulation presumably would dictate that empirical research may be used (for example) to aid in fostering employee commitment by enhancing organizational justice but may not be used to develop better ways for duping employees into thinking they are treated justly when in fact they are not. It is important to note, however, what is not achieved by this: merely placing normative strictures on the use to which empirical findings are put does not show that normative claims play any theoretical, explanatory role in the empirical research itself; nor does it reveal the normative commitments underlying particular social orders. Rather, normative judgments function merely as limits on what topics may be subjected to empirical research and theorizing. Expressed more specifically, a change in normative position would not change the content of any extant empirical theory; deciding that it is permissible to deceive workers would not alter any empirical theory of organizational justice. The same empirically discovered instrumental techniques either would or would not achieve the now permissible goal. Thus, Jones and Wicks tip the normative/empirical balance toward the empirical side: practicability becomes a clear empirical constraint on normative theory, thus entering into the theorizing process. Normative acceptability is merely a side constraint on empirical research, however, forbidding certain uses of theory but not entering into the construction or assessment of theory itself. Whereas one might want to call this a kind of integration, it is not theoretical integration in the form of reciprocity or unity as discussed in Chapter 2. Nor does it achieve what our structurationist-inspired view does because of the practicability constraint on normative theorizing. There is, in short, little or no recognition that, through human agency, normative ideals can generate changes in empirical realities. In our structurationist viewpoint, any true normative position that is out of harmony with empirical realities (e.g., because it is economically unfeasible) ultimately could gain that harmony if change is brought about in the social order. Empirical realities may influence the applicability of normative judgments, but they also are the outcomes of normatively driven behavior.

INTEGRATION: PRACTICAL PROBLEMS AND MOTIVATIONS

An additional question raised by recent efforts at integration, such as that by Jones and Wicks, concerns the value of the effort. In short, do we really want, or need, a unique, all-encompassing "business ethics theory" that goes beyond our present structurationist outlook (which explains how different outlooks could be seen as limited or bracketed perspectives on a common subject area)? In our metatheoretical account, normative theorizing and empirical research can proceed in their normal fashion, albeit with recognition of their limitations and their potentials for change. Consequently, it is not obvious that there is need for a new, indigenous "business ethics theory" that is necessarily distinct from other normative and social scientific theories that are relevant to understanding the structures and processes that generate ethical or unethical behavior in organizations.

Consider, for example, the multiple recent efforts to develop a "stakeholder theory" of organizations (as opposed to a stakeholder heuristic for examining influences on and impacts of organizations), that is, an account of organizations that offers a central theoretical role to the ethical quality of the relationships between the organization and its various constituents. This area of inquiry is at least closely related to business ethics. Considering efforts to develop *sui generis* stakeholder theories, it appears that the more they are elaborated to gain precision and plausibility, the less they look like distinctively stakeholder theories, as opposed to special case applications of more general, existing organizational science theories, such as those addressing resource dependence, power, conflict and negotiation, legitimacy, etc. For example, Mitchell, Agle, and Wood (1997) relied on a number of these theories to explain organizational–stakeholder relationships (e.g., Jensen and Meckling 1976; Williamson 1975, 1985; Pfeffer 1981). Rowley

(1997) proposed a more complex network theory of stakeholder influences but also relied on a number of established theoretical traditions, including network analysis, resource dependence theory, and institutional theory. In both cases, which we believe *have* advanced our understanding of organization–stakeholder relationships, "stakeholder theory" has added little to the theoretical analysis beyond an umbrella concept and useful heuristic. A similar question applies to Jones and Wicks's proposed "stakeholder theory." Although we do not question its basic claims regarding the instrumental outcomes of various ways of treating an organization's stakeholders, we question whether it constitutes a new, more integrated theory or, rather, an application of existing theories to a new range of questions. Their proposed theory relies heavily on ideas about the role of trust in economic exchange. Much theoretical and empirical work has been conducted on trust between organizations, however, while making no reference to stakeholders or "stakeholder theory" (e.g., Das and Teng 1998; Zaheer and Venkatraman 1995). The more we fill out an empirical stakeholder theory to render it precise and plausible, the more the endeavor appears derivative from other social science theories. In light of this, the energy expended by serious scholars to develop comprehensive stakeholder theories is puzzling.

Returning to efforts to integrate the normative and empirical sides of business ethics, the situation becomes even more problematic. The field is highly diverse, incorporating many, often opposed, normative perspectives and touching on multiple empirical issues. Thus, it is difficult to see how one might hope to achieve more than our bracketed perspectives approach. Practically, scholars working at the boundaries of normative and empirical issues (whether called stakeholder theory, business ethics, or whatever) might well be described as having created something like a research tradition (Laudan 1977, 1981). In contrast to a specific theory about some subject, a research tradition incorporates multiple, varied theories that focus on a general domain of observed or postulated phenomena or related sets of questions or problems. Further, research traditions typically specify not only a subject domain but also may implicitly delineate important questions, basic concepts, and taken-for-granted assumptions. So, for business ethics, questions about honesty in business and the empirically discovered impediments to honesty are "on the table," whereas questions about inventory management and production scheduling typically are not.

Of course, one may try, in various ways, to analyze just what constitutes the theoretical frameworks or stances that make up the shared concepts and concerns of a research tradition. Donaldson and Preston (1995), for example, divide research on organization–stakeholder relationships into three categories: descriptive, instrumental, and normative. Our perspectival account proceeds at an even higher level of abstraction, offering a way of understanding how the empirical and normative elements of business ethics and related subjects (such as stakeholder accounts) fit together. Jones and Wicks's proposed "convergent theory" offers an alternative explication of this fit, one that claims to link normative and empirical theory by requiring that (1) normative theories be empirically practical and that (2) empirical theories be used for normative purposes. If our argument is correct, they do not converge on a theoretical point, but instead they propose teleological side constraints on the otherwise independent theorizing of autonomous theorists. So, rather than generating a *convergent theory*, we see them describing a sociological process of convergence in which theorists contribute to the ongoing development of a research tradition that incorporates theories of different kinds united only by their common concern with a particular class of problems and questions. What unites these diverse theorists is not an integrative (or nearly integrative) theory but a focus on a general domain of interest (e.g., normative and empirical issues in organization–stakeholder relations) (Shapere 1977).

In light of the problems of parsimony and utility attendant to efforts to create new, overarching integrative or would-be integrative theories, we might wonder just why it seems important to researchers to construct integrated theory. After all, there is much about social inquiry to suggest that divergent views will be the norm, especially in light of the often subjective or interpretive nature of social phenomena (e.g., concepts such as welfare or well-being) and because of the role of intentional or unintentional agency in the development, maintenance, and change of social orders. Social phenomena are subject to multiple definitions or interpretations and likewise multiple explanatory influences that themselves will vary in impact as social conditions change. Pragmatic factors play a role in limiting integration as well. In addition to those discussed in Chapter 1, scholars also have noted how some researchers understandably are slow to give up on theoretical perspectives in which they are cognitively or pragmatically deeply invested (Kuhn 1970), whereas societal expectations encourage others to focus on "new and improved" theories in faddish fashion (Abrahamson 1996).

Nevertheless, a range of pragmatic and institutional factors pressures scholars toward some sense of integration or unity (Fabian 2000). The proliferation of theoretical claims and research perspectives makes a field increasingly hard to grasp, or even incoherent, to researchers with limited time and resources. Addressing this kind of issue specifically regarding organization theory, Pfeffer (1993) laments that the theoretical domain "is coming to resemble more of a weed patch than a well-tended garden (616)." Socialization pressures are relevant as well (Fabian 2000). Tension can arise from being socialized into a field of inquiry if (1) it is assumed that some common core unifies scholars into a distinct and identifiable field, while (2) that common core is increasingly difficult to identify. Maintenance of a field as an identifiable institution, in turn, requires that conflict among members fall within certain limits, again suggesting the functional role of certain agreed-on ways of understanding and resulting pressures for an integrative theoretical and methodological framework (Scherer and Dowling 1995).

The dependency of researchers on various forms of external support and institutional legitimacy likewise may encourage efforts at integration and the development of a grand, all-encompassing theory. Normatively oriented scholars in business school environments may need to link their normative concerns to empirical work to enhance their legitimacy in business settings, lest they be perceived as irrelevant idealists. Taken-for-granted conventions about the value of "strong paradigms" also may pressure researchers to look for unity or closure. Multiple authors have pointed out the relatively high prestige of economics (in contrast to the organizational sciences) in the political and corporate worlds and tied that high status to the rational actor model that provides a univocal foundation for so much work in the field (Pfeffer 1993). By contrast, organizational inquiry often displays a pastiche of not-always-consistent theories and findings.

Paradoxically, however, the kind of integration that would move beyond our perspectival approach is unlikely to satisfy these practical and institutional demands for unity. Such full-fledged theoretical unification, as noted in Chapter 2, would need to collapse conventional dichotomies of fact and value, object and subject, and so on in a more aggressive way than our effort to see them as different, bracketed perspectives. Pursuit of such a possibility is a legitimate, and interesting, metatheoretical and theoretical issue and has drawn the attention of some scholars. As Freeman argued (1999, 233), however, such a collapse of conventional dichotomies also calls into question the distinctions among descriptive, instrumental, and normative theories about business ethics and organizations' relationships with stakeholders. Such a collapse of conventional dichotomies is likely to lead to greater rather than less theoretical diversity in the field because there no longer can be a univocal descriptive or instrumental theory that can be screened off from the interpretive influence of different normative perspectives.

Consequently, we are content with the approach we have outlined in the foregoing—one that recognizes the legitimacy of both empirical and normative approaches but which also shows how each provides only a perspective on a large and complex phenomenon. Thus, even though this book is written from a perspective of empirical social science, we do not deny the importance of normative thinking about ethics in organizations or the long-term potential for normative thinking to alter empirical realities. Our bracketed perspectives approach, however, implies that our effort to focus on empirical questions is legitimate as long as we acknowledge that it represents only one limited perspective on the complex phenomenon of ethics in organizations.

References

Abrahamson, E. 1996. Management fashion. *Academy of Management Review* 21:254–285.

Burrell, G., and G. Morgan. 1979. *Sociological paradigms and organizational analysis*. London: Heinemann.

Das, T. K., and B. Teng. 1998. Between trust and control: Developing confidence in partner cooperation in alliances. *Academy of Management Review* 23(3):491–512.

Donaldson, T., and L. E. Preston. 1995. The stakeholder theory of the corporation: Concepts, evidence and implications. *Academy of Management Review* 20(1):65–92.

Fabian, F. H. 2000. Keeping the tension: Pressures to keep the controversy in the management discipline. *Academy of Management Review* 25:350–371.

Freeman, R. E. 1999. Divergent stakeholder theory. *Academy of Management Review* 24:233–237.

Giddens, A. 1976. *New rules for sociological method*. New York: Basic Books.

Giddens, A. 1979. *Central problems in social theory*. Berkeley: University of California Press.

Giddens, A. 1984. *The constitution of society*. Berkeley: University of California Press.

Gioia, D. A., and E. Pitré. 1990. Multiparadigm perspectives on theory building. *Academy of Management Review* 15(4):584–602.

Jackson, N., and P. Carter. 1991. In defence of paradigm incommensurability. *Organization Studies* 12(1):109–127.

Jensen, M. C., and W. H. Meckling. 1976. Theory of the firm: Managerial behavior, agency costs, and ownership structure. *Journal of Financial Economics* 3:305–360.

Jones, T. M., and A. C. Wicks. 1999. Convergent stakeholder theory. *Academy of Management Review* 24:206–221.

Kuhn, T. S. 1962. *The structure of scientific revolutions*, 1st ed. Chicago: University of Chicago Press.

Kuhn, T. S. 1970. *The structure of scientific revolutions*, 2nd ed. Chicago: University of Chicago Press.

Kuhn, T. S. 1983. Response to commentaries. In *PSA 1982*, ed. P. D. Asquith and T. Nickles, 712–716. East Lansing, MI: Philosophy of Science Association.

Kuhn, T. S. 1990. Dubbing and redubbing: The vulnerability of rigid designation. In *Minnesota studies in the philosophy of science*, Vol. XIV: *Scientific theories*, ed. C. Wade Savage, 298–318. Minneapolis: University of Minnesota Press.

Laudan, L. 1977. *Progress and its problems*. Berkeley: University of California Press.

Laudan, L. 1981. A problem-solving approach to scientific progress. In *Scientific revolutions*, ed. I. Hacking, 144–155. Oxford: Oxford University Press.

Mitchell, R. K., B. R. Agle, and D. J. Wood. 1997. Toward a theory of stakeholder identification and salience: Defining the principle of who and what really counts. *Academy of Management Review* 22(4):853–886.

Pfeffer, J. 1981. *Power in organizations*. Marshfield, MA: Pitman.

Pfeffer, J. 1993. Barriers to the advance of organizational science: Paradigm development as a dependent variable. *Academy of Management Review* 18:599–620.

Rowley, T. J. 1997. Moving beyond dyadic ties: A network theory of stakeholder influences. *Academy of Management Review* 22(4):887–910.

Scherer, A. G., and M. J. Dowling. 1995. Towards a reconciliation of the theory-pluralism in strategic management: Incommensurability and the constructivist approach of the Erlangen-School. *Advances in Strategic Management* 12A:195–247.

Shapere, D. 1977. Scientific theories and their domains. In *The structure of scientific theories*, ed. F. Suppe, 518–565. Urbana: University of Illinois Press.

Weaver, G. R., and D. A. Gioia. 1994. Paradigms lost: Incommensurability vs. structurationist inquiry. *Organization Studies* 15(4):565–590.

Williamson, O. 1975. *Markets and hierarchies*. New York: Free Press.

Williamson, O. 1985. *The economic institutions of capitalism*. New York: Free Press.

Wilmott, H. C. 1987. Studying managerial work: A critique and a proposal. *Journal of Management Studies* 24:249–270.

Zaheer, L.G., and N. Venkatraman. 1995. Relational governance as an interorganizational strategy: An empirical test of the role of trust in economic exchange. *Strategic Management Journal* 16:373–393.

PART TWO

The Institutionalization of Organizational Ethics

Having explained how normative and empirical approaches toward ethics in organizations represent bracketed perspectives on the subject matter, we now largely bracket normative issues and focus on the empirical side of business ethics, examining a range of issues and practices as they arise within the current social order (to use Chapter 3's language). Even within empirical studies, there are different perspectives. In Part II, we primarily function as organizational sociologists, paying attention to the structures and practices of organizations vis-à-vis business ethics, rather than to the attitudes and actions of individuals; but we are not concerned with just any ethically significant structures and practices of organizations. Instead, we are concerned specifically with those organizational structures and practices that ostensibly are aimed at fostering ethical behavior by the members of an organization. (Whether these structures actually do result in ethical behavior is a question we leave until Part III.) Large organizations increasingly are introducing formal programs and policies aimed at encouraging legal and ethical behavior on the part of employees, both in the United States and, to a lesser extent, elsewhere. Typically, these are called ethics programs, compliance programs, or ethics and compliance programs. Part II explains the nature and origins of this largely new form of organizational structuring.

Chapter 4 is largely descriptive, briefly examining the recent history of corporate ethics programs and presenting their typical components, and also raising some questions about what might be driving them and what their outcomes might be. Chapters 6 and 7 answer some of these questions.

All three chapters of Part II, to varying degrees, analyze organizational ethics programs in light of the surrounding institutional context of contemporary business organizations. Any organization exists in a context of formal and informal institutions, which, in various ways, shape the organization in question. Much organizational scholarship has focused on the ways in which organizations respond to these institutional pressures. Indeed, a significant portion of this scholarship has focused on phenomena with at least passing relationships to business ethics. For example, previous research has examined how organizations are structured to respond to political and social issues and challenges (Greening and Gray 1994; Meznar and Nigh 1995; Miles 1987); how they respond to pressures to appear socially legitimate (Ashforth and Gibbs 1990; Suchman, 1995); how organizational and contextual factors influence illegal corporate behavior (Baucus and Near 1991); how institutional pressures influence the use and disuse of accounting practices (Covaleski and Dirsmith 1988), medical procedures (Goodrick and Salancik 1996), training programs (Scott and Meyer 1991), and affirmative action policies (Salancik 1979)—just to take a few examples.

External, institutional influences might be formal and explicit, in the fashion of legal requirements. They also might be less formal, or less explicit, as in the case of popular, taken-for-granted assumptions about what good management practice looks like. In either case, organizations are under pressures to satisfy institutional expectations and conventions lest they look out of place (at best) or illegitimate (at worst). Organizations are not entirely at the mercy of institutional pressures, however. Organizational decision makers maintain some degree of latitude, at least in the degree to which they respond to institutional expectations in one way or another (for example, by acquiescence, by resistance). Thus, in Chapters 5 and 6, we examine the influence of both key organizational decision makers, and key elements of the institutional environment, on the introduction of formal corporate ethics programs. Not surprisingly, the resulting picture is not a simple one. Even though both pressures of the external environment and decisions of high-level company executives play roles in the shaping of ethics programs, they play different roles. Although external pressures may have the greatest influence on the introduction of some kind of formal ethics program, management decision making has the greatest role in the way that program is implemented.

In Chapter 5, we find that management decisions are the primary determinants of the kind of behavioral control and influence exhibited by an ethics program. Some ethics programs, for example, are characterized by high levels of overt behavioral control, relying heavily on a profusion of rules, monitoring systems, and disciplinary procedures to prevent unethical behavior. Other organizational ethics programs, however, deemphasize overt behavioral control and instead appeal to employee aspirations to act ethically, encouraging a set of shared ethical commitments without resorting to overt controls. Still other organizations attempt both approaches to varying degrees. We refer to these two approaches as compliance and values control orientations, respectively, and we find that it is management, not external institutional pressures, that primarily determines the control orientation of a formal ethics program. This turns out to be important because, as Part III will show, the choice of control orientation has important implications for the outcomes of any formal ethics program.

Chapter 6 addresses a different aspect of the split between institutional and managerial responsibility for the development of formal ethics programs. Many organizations respond to institutional pressures by creating structures and practices that appear to satisfy external institutional expectations while actually leaving internal, organizational behavior untouched. Such responses constitute a kind of "window dressing," or organizational Potemkin village. Much the same could be true about formal ethics programs. Organizations can do things that appear, on the outside, to be part of an effort to foster ethical behavior, but on the inside those responses have little or no impact. Here again, we see differences in the role of institutional and managerial influences in explaining organizational responses. In particular, we find that external institutional pressures easily can generate the kind of responses that can be reduced to mere "window dressing," whereas responses that are more likely to be deeply ingrained into organizational practices reflect the commitment of top management actually to doing something to foster ethical behavior.

Both these chapters have important public policy implications. Much government policy has been focused on requiring or encouraging organizations to engage in certain formal practices aimed at fostering ethical behavior and legal compliance. Important as those policies may be, however, their reach is limited. The kinds of organizational practices that make a serious difference in ethical and legal behavior are more likely to reflect the commitments and decisions of key organizational decision makers than the influence of legal or other pressures from the institutional environment of business.

References

Ashforth, B. E., and B. W. Gibbs. 1990. The double-edge of organizational legitimation. *Organization Science* 1:177–194.

Baucus, M. S., and J. P. Near. 1991. Can illegal corporate behavior be predicted? An event history analysis. *Academy of Management Journal* 34:9–36.

Covaleski, M. A., and M. W. Dirsmith. 1988. An institutional perspective on the rise, social transformation, and fall of a university budget category. *Administrative Science Quarterly* 33:562–587.

Goodrick, E., and G. R. Salancik. 1996. Organizational discretion in responding to institutional practices: Hospitals and cesarean births. *Administrative Science Quarterly* 41:1–29.

Greening, D. W., and B. Gray. 1994. Testing a model of organizational response to social and political issues. *Academy of Management Journal* 37:467–498.

Meznar, M. B., and D. Nigh. 1995. Buffer or bridge? Environmental and organizational determinants of public affairs activities in American firms. *Academy of Management Journal* 38:975–996.

Miles, R. H. 1987. *Managing the corporate social environment: A grounded theory.* Englewood Cliffs, NJ: Prentice Hall.

Salancik, G. R. 1979. Interorganizational dependence and responsiveness to affirmative action: The case of women and defense contractors. *Academy of Management Journal* 22:375–394.

Scott, W. R., and J. W. Meyer. 1991. The rise of training programs in firms and agencies: An institutional perspective. In *Research in organizational behavior*, Vol. 13, ed. B. M. Staw and L. L. Cummings, 297–326. Greenwich, CT: JAI Press.

Suchman, M. C. 1995. Managing legitimacy: Strategic and institutional approaches. *Academy of Management Review* 20:571–610.

FOUR

Has Business Ethics Come of Age?

A 1986 publication by the Center for Business Ethics posed the question, "Are corporations institutionalizing ethics?" A cynical reader of the time, reflecting on then recent and ongoing scandals in the defense industry and other parts of the business world, might have wondered whether the question referred to efforts by corporations to commit business ethics to an institution, much as one might commit a crazy or demented family member. The question actually referred to whether corporations might be making concern for business ethics an ingrained part of their own structures and practices.

Looking back on that question after fifteen years, we can give a less than clear answer: "yes and no." More precisely, the answer we give depends on how we define the idea of *institutionalizing* business ethics. Institutionalization of a practice or idea can take many shapes. We can, for example, speak of the formal institutions of a society, meaning by that such things as laws, governments, corporations, newspapers, and so on. We also can mean the more informal, taken-for-granted practices and ideas of a society: its manners and morals; familial relationships (or their absence); and the various other norms, practices, ideas, and ideals that help to define a culture, even though they are not explicitly embodied in laws or organizations.

In Part II of the book, we focus on the institutionalization of concern for ethics within business organizations. A flurry of structure and policy creation from the 1980s through the 1990s appears to have embedded concern for ethics into the formal institutions of much of the business world, most clearly in the United States, but also, to some degree, elsewhere. Less clear, however, is the extent to which concern for ethics has become embedded in the informal practices of business organizations—for example, in the ideals managers model for subordinates or in the way difficult choices are sometimes made between ethics and profits. This chapter reviews what is known about what corporations are doing—and not doing—to institutionalize concern for ethics into their formal structures and practices. The remainder of Part II then raises several important questions about this apparent institutionalization of ethics in the corporate world. Chapter 5 explains several key influences on the effort to formally institutionalize business ethics, looking in particular at the role and limits of both the law and the personal ethical standards of managers. Chapter 6, in turn, raises questions about the limits of this formal institutionalization, seeking to explain why the policies and programs of ethics in one organization might be taken rather seriously, whereas in another they might be treated as mere "window dressing." In short, Chapters 4, 5, and 6 explain the "yes and no" answer, considering the ways in which certain approaches to business ethics have become embedded in much of the business world but also the ways in which concern for ethics can be thwarted or limited in scope.

FORMAL CORPORATE ETHICS PROGRAMS

Corporate efforts to address ethics are not entirely new. For example, retailer J. C. Penney Company introduced a company code of conduct in 1913, and enough business codes were in use in the 1920s to warrant compilation into book form (Heermance 1924). Sometimes, though, such "codes of ethics" may have been thinly disguised efforts to discourage careful scrutiny by others (Weaver 1993).

Formal structural attention to ethics in the contemporary business world, however, appears to have originated in the 1980s, in part in response to several high-profile scandals and investigations that, in turn, generated various proposals for the reform and regulation of business practices. Most prominently, the National Commission on Fraudulent Financial Reporting (popularly known as the Treadway Commission), in 1987, issued recommendations for reducing financial fraud. These proposals included the idea that each corporation should adopt a code of conduct and that executives should be attentive to the kinds of signals they send to subordinates about proper and improper behavior. In short, both formal and informal ways of encouraging ethical behavior were proffered by this commission. Meanwhile, a commission appointed in 1986 by President Reagan (the Packard Commission) was charged with investigating fraudulent practices in the defense industry and with developing proposals that would govern the behavior of defense contractors in the future. This proposal, soon widely adopted in defense contracting circles, became known as the Defense Industry Initiative, and it ultimately required companies to adopt various formal policies and programs (for example, codes of ethics and anonymous processes by which employees can report abuses) as a condition of engaging in defense contracting work. These encouragements to formal ethics management programs were further strengthened when, in 1991, the United States Sentencing Commission (USSC) introduced new federal sentencing guidelines for organizational defendants (discussed in more detail in Chapter 5). The USSC guidelines specify base-level fines for various kinds of corporate illegal behavior, but they allow that base fine to be adjusted substantially according to how culpable an organization is in any particular case of illegality. Assessments of culpability are affected by multiple factors under USSC guidelines, but among those factors are considerations of whether an organization has in place appropriate programs and policies that could reasonably be expected to minimize illegal behavior on the part of the organization and its employees. In short, by possessing a formal ethics program that meets contemporary conventions regarding appropriateness and effectiveness, an organization can hope to avoid debilitating fines in the event that illegal actions take place.

Data from several surveys support the idea that contemporary corporate attention to ethics should be dated from the 1980s. Codes of ethics or similar policy documents and statements are probably the easiest and cheapest type of effort to foster, or at least signal, ethical intentions and behavior and thus should serve as an early indication of corporate interest in ethics. Multiple surveys indicate that by the 1990s, well more than 90 percent of large American companies had some kind of ethics code or related policy statement (Center for Business Ethics 1992; Murphy 1995; Weaver, Treviño, and Cochran 1999). Data collected by Weaver, Treviño, and Cochran (1999) from a sample of *Fortune 1000* firms asked when companies adopted their ethics policies. These data indicated that only 20 percent of responding companies adopted their ethics policies before 1976 and that 60 percent had adopted their policies since the mid-1980s—the years of the Treadway Commission, Packard Commission, and revisions in the Federal Sentencing Guidelines. Murphy (1995)—who distinguishes codes of ethics from more succinct ethical credos and values statements—reports similar findings among large American companies. Only 15.5 percent of firms with codes adopted those codes prior to 1973 (along with 22 percent for credos and 8 percent for values statements), and a clear majority of responding firms adopted their various policy statements in the mid-1980s to mid-1990s.

This rapid spread of formal ethics policies and programs through the corporate world during the 1980s and 1990s suggests that a process of institutionalization was at work (DiMaggio and Powell 1983; Meyer and Rowan 1977; Scott 1995). Legal pressures embodied in the USSC guidelines clearly indicate that a somewhat coercive external factor is at work in the promulgation of corporate ethics policies and programs (see Chapters 5 and 6). The 1980s and early 1990s, however, saw noncoercive actors in the business environment highlight the value of corporate attention to ethics. Even though they lack the potentially coercive power of the law, these agencies and organizations do have the capacity to set normative standards for what constitute "up-to-date" business practices. For example, the Conference Board—a high-profile business organization, with high-level executives as its target audience—began to host well-attended annual meetings on ethics during this period. Management consultants—initially through the work of small, independent and nonprofit consultancies, but later through the major consulting and accounting firms—also began to "spread the word" about formal ethics management. Similarly, this period saw academic interest in business ethics grow. Business ethics already had been on the agenda of many philosophy departments, no doubt in part as an effort to maintain relevance (and class enrollments) as the humanities (and humanities faculty positions) began to suffer from increasing careerism and tightening budgets at many colleges and universities in the 1970s and 1980s. The late 1980s and 1990s, however, saw faculty in business schools taking note of business ethics as an area for applied social science research. Not only were scholarly journals that focused on business ethics introduced (such as the *Journal of Business Ethics* in 1982 and *Business Ethics Quarterly* in 1991), but ethics-oriented articles began to appear in mainstream, social scientific management, and business journals (for example, *Academy of Management Review, Administrative Science Quarterly*). Thus, the idea that a corporation should direct formal attention to business ethics was encouraged (to put it mildly) by the government and legitimated by business associations, consultancies, and academics.

Research and theory regarding the influence of environmental factors on management decision making suggest that at some point in this period imitative forces also may have contributed to the spread of ethics programs and policies (that is, mimetic isomorphism) (DiMaggio and Powell 1983). Once a practice is adopted by a substantial number of corporations (especially if they are high-profile corporations), the practice can become taken for granted in the business world, such that executives at other corporations assume they should engage in it also.

With the exception of the work presented in Chapters 5 and 6, however, empirical research has not addressed the origins of and influences on formal ethics programs. This is unfortunate, from a policy standpoint, because there can be important differences between ethics programs introduced (for example) as responses to external pressures and those introduced because senior management is committed to the goal of ethical business behavior. Likewise, without careful empirical study of the origins of ethics programs, it is difficult to know just how effective one or another public policy initiative (such as the USSC guidelines) is in fostering improved corporate behavior.

What is readily available, however, is a picture of the typical elements of formal ethics programs and the extent of their use, and we turn to that issue now. Unless otherwise indicated, our own descriptive data presented subsequently regarding ethics practices are taken from the data collection effort described in detail in Chapters 5 and 6 and reflect practice in large American corporations across most industries as of the middle of the 1990s. We have supplemented our own data with data from other sources, as indicated.

Codes of Ethics and Related Policy Documents

As noted, corporate codes of ethics and similar ethics policy documents and statements come in many forms (Murphy 1995). Regardless of form, however, multiple descriptive studies make it clear that most large corporations have such documents. Most surveys report adoption rates among large companies of greater than 90 percent throughout the 1990s (Center for Business Ethics 1992; Murphy 1995; Weaver, Treviño, and Cochran 1999; results of earlier surveys are reported in Weaver 1993). More recently, 78 percent of employee respondents to the Ethics Resource Center's (ERC) *2000 National Business Ethics Survey* (Joseph 2000) reported that their employers have ethics policy standards. This lower percentage reflects the fact that the ERC surveyed randomly selected individuals regardless of employer, thus including many small businesses with less need and fewer resources for dealing with ethical issues in formal fashion. When the ERC results are restricted to companies with five hundred or more employees, 89 percent of employees report that their employers have formal ethics standards, in keeping with the results of other studies. Interestingly, the ERC data also include nonprofit and governmental organizations and show that such organizations have formal ethics policies at a higher rate (88 percent of nonprofit employees report ethics standards at their place of work, with 95 percent for all government compared with 79 percent for all businesses).

Less clear from any survey data, however, is the specific content of such policies. No studies have analyzed the content of codes in methodologically precise fashion (whether qualitative or quantitative). Weaver's (1993, 54) summary of various surveys of code content, however, suggests that "internal company issues—for example, employee rights and responsibilities—receive more frequent attention than company relations to external parties." Even when ethics policies range more broadly, to consider extraorganizational issues, they also tend to focus on largely tangible, rather than intangible (for example, cultural) impacts and issues (Weaver 1993). Anecdotal evidence from our own interactions with corporate ethics officials suggests, however, that some executives are beginning to wonder whether, and how, they should incorporate more concern for questions of a company's external, or social, responsibilities into their ethics programs and policies. This trend may be a reflection of increasing globalization of the economy, which has brought managers face to face with a range of new issues rooted in diverse cultural and political practices. For example, a newly globalized company may have to grapple with how to introduce concerns for a particular social issue into its American operations, given that such concerns have routinely been a part of its European operations as a matter of political and reputational necessity. (Limited research also indicates that the issues addressed in company codes of ethics vary with cultural and political context (Langlois and Schlegelmilch 1990), although increasingly globalized control in the business world may be reducing the amount of cultural and political variation (but cf. Fligstein and Freeland 1995).

Responsibility for Ethics Policies and Programs

One important transition that has occurred during the recent burst of corporate activity regarding ethics is the spread of dedicated offices devoted to the issue. Whereas it is common for companies to assign responsibility for ethics programs and policies to a specific corporate officer (in our 1994 data, 54 percent did so), it has become increasingly common for companies to designate a specific ethics officer or ethics office that is distinct from other related offices, such as law, audit, and human resources. In our 1994 data, for example, the responsibility for ethics programs and policies was vested in a dedicated ethics officer in 32 percent of responding companies; executives in law departments were responsible in 33 percent of companies, audit in 10 percent, human resources in 9 percent, and the remaining companies assigned responsibility to various other high-level departments, such as corporate secretary. Lest this appear to be a large amount of executive and administrative time being devoted to ethics, consider that 54 percent of companies also reported that the officer formally charged with responsibility for ethics devotes a very small percentage of time to the task (less than 10 percent). Dedicated ethics offices and officers are common (as of mid-2002, the Ethics Officer Association boasts nearly eight hundred individual members representing more than five hundred companies). For many companies, however, ethics remains one among many tasks to which various high-level officers devote some energies. Most dedicated ethics offices (that is, at least two-thirds) were created during the 1990s; whether this practice proceeds to spread, similarly to the earlier spread of codes of ethics, remains to be seen. Introducing an ethics office is considerably more expensive than introducing an ethics code, and there are plenty of precedents for companies vesting responsibility for ethics programs in regular staff functions, such as law or audit. Thus, in the face of competing demands on corporate resources, pressures toward the creation of ethics offices likely will be weaker than those that led to the widespread adoption of codes of ethics.

Another potential issue regarding responsibility for ethics programs and policies involves the practice, by some companies, of outsourcing the task. For example, some companies contract for the use of generic ethics training programs, sometimes provided by means of the Internet. Others contract out the problem-reporting functions of the ethics program so that calls to report problems are taken by an outside party (for example, a private security company). The risks in such approaches are several, however. Will employees perceive such programs as lacking serious commitment on the part of management? Will generic training packages, whether delivered in person or electronically, adequately address the nuances of a company's culture, competitive situation, and labor relations? Some companies may resort to third-party services on the grounds that such services will increase employee confidence in their anonymity when they report problems, but this does not seem to be a straightforward matter. Employees sometimes might fear that vendors of ethics programs and related services could be induced to share information (for a price) as easily as a company employee (for a bonus). Moreover, some companies find ways to encourage anonymity (for example, we know of one company that deliberately keeps its ethics office offsite so that no co-workers will observe an employee opening the ethics office door).

A key issue in assigning responsibility for ethics programs and policies, however, concerns the wisdom of vesting such responsibility in particular functional areas. We have argued elsewhere (Weaver and Treviño 2001) that the prominent use of legal counsel, and the relative disuse of human resource staff, in developing and administering ethics programs is unfortunate. Research on the outcomes of ethics programs (reported in Part III) indicates that employees' reactions to such programs are influenced by their perceptions of how fairly the organization treats them. In short, when the program signals that the company is concerned about the employee, not merely looking to protect the company or its officers from harm, desirable ethics program outcomes (such as reduced unethical behavior) are more likely. The choice of legal or human resources departments as the "home" for a corporate ethics program may send unintended but influential signals to employees regarding the purpose and orientation of the program.

Our own research (presented in Part III to follow) also indicates that ethics programs are more effective when they are closely integrated with other organizational functions. Human resources staff can be crucial in seeing that ethics expectations are integrated into key organizational functions that fall under a human resources department's purview, such as selection, training, compensation, and performance appraisal. Human resources staff can play a crucial role in attracting and selecting employees willing to commit to the organization's values and who are comfortable working in an environment in which ethical issues are discussed openly. The human resources department, more than the legal department, is likely to have the insight and skill for seeing that ethics training moves beyond exercises in learning rules and addresses more informal aspects of the organization's ethical culture (see Chapters 8 and 9). Human resources, through its role in establishing compensation and performance appraisal schemes, can see that ethics is incorporated into such. Because employees' support for ethics programs and policies reflects their perceptions of the organization's fairness toward employees, human resources staff also can have a crucial ethics role in seeing that compensation and appraisal systems accurately reflect the company's value statements. Moreover, employees may perceive that human resources staff members, more than other company managers, are "on their side" and will be respectful of employee concerns. Therefore, ethics programs that include substantial participation by human resources staff are less likely to foster suspicion of unfairness in the eyes of employees (see Chapter 10). Human resource staff involvement in ethics programs should suggest that employees' concerns receive voice and representation in administration of the program.

Policy Training and Dissemination

It is not enough to have a company policy regarding ethics; employees must know what that policy is. The ERC's 2000 data (Joseph 2000) indicate that 55 percent of all employees say their employers provide ethics training (68 percent when restricted to organizations employing five hundred or more people) and, again, higher numbers for nonprofit and government employers. In addition, 48 percent of employees in this survey indicated that their employers have ethics standards, an ethics telephone line or office for seeking advice, and ethics training. Our own data indicate that ethics policy information is widely distributed among the upper reaches of management (approaching 100 percent at some levels) but begins to decline as one examines lower levels of management and nonmanagerial employees. Much the same holds for formal ethics training, with training being offered more frequently to higher levels of management. In short, it appears that corporations typically apportion training and communication regarding ethics in proportion to one's level of responsibility in the organization. Interestingly, the level of responsibility does not necessarily equate to one's potential to do damage to the organization or others; a low-level employee can cause major problems for an organization. (In some cases, the lack of communication and training among operating employees reflects constraints imposed by contracts with organized labor.)

The ERC data (Joseph 2000) do not indicate the frequency of ethics training. Regardless of how training varies by level, our data indicate that training does not occur as frequently as one might think. Taking executive and middle management ranks only, our 1994 data show that in more than 70 percent of reporting companies, ethics training at these ranks occurs at most "every few years." Likewise, regardless of position, at least two-thirds of employees receive some kind of written communications about ethics (for example, a reminder letter about its importance) *not* more than once annually. Employees must deal with the crush of other messages and information, and the portion of time devoted to formal messages and training about ethics remains small. Not only does this risk involve simply not getting the ethics message across, but it also risks undermining whatever part of it is heard and retained because the minuscule attention may be interpreted to mean that top management does not take ethics all that seriously. (The exception, of course, might be when the annual ethics message points out that the chief executive officer (CEO) just fired a senior vice president for violating some aspect of the company's ethics policy.) On a positive note, however, at least some training does seem to have an impact; 87 percent of ERC respondents report that whatever ethics training they get is at least occasionally useful, with higher "usefulness" scores occurring among newer employees. This makes for an interesting contrast when viewed with our data from six years earlier: It is newer employees who find ethics training most useful (ERC data), but it is to the more experienced employees that corporations (middle and senior management) appear to direct the bulk of their ethics training (our data).

Companies are good record keepers about their limited ethics training and communication, however. Most companies (90 percent in our data) require employees to acknowledge receiving the companies' ethics policies either on receipt or on a periodic basis, and almost as many (85 percent) require that employees also acknowledge that they are in compliance with the policy. Whether such acknowledgments are effective in fostering employee awareness of an interest in ethics is unknown. Such recorded acknowledgments provide a company with documentation of ethics dissemination efforts that can be used defensively in legal proceedings or the public relations arena, but they do not necessarily indicate how well employees respond to the message.

Ethics Telephone Question and Reporting Systems

Another highly visible element of formal ethics programs is the implementation of a telephone system that employees can use to raise ethical questions, report actual or potential ethical problems, or both. Our 1994 data showed that just more than half (51 percent) of responding companies had such a telephone line, with calls most typically answered by an ethics office (34 percent), legal department (19 percent), or audit department (18 percent). (Nine percent of companies with telephone lines had calls answered by an external contractor.) Ethics telephone line use varies widely; a quarter of companies in our study reported not more than a single call per month per ten thousand employees, whereas 18 percent reported twenty or more calls per month per ten thousand employees.

Ethics telephone lines are given a variety of labels by the sponsoring corporations, and the labels sometimes suggest management's intentions for the line. Most popular in our study was the use of the term *hotline* to describe the telephone line (57 percent). The largest proportion of telephone lines that were not labeled *hotline* were described with terms suggesting their role in fostering ethical values or giving assistance and counseling to employees (for example, *helpline*). This contrast is congruent with the common distinction between ethics initiatives that are rooted in efforts to control behavior, react to wrongdoing, and ensure legal compliance and initiatives that take a more proactive stance to fostering ethical values and encouraging employees to aspire to high ethical ideals. In the former, the employee is a potentially wayward individual who must be compelled to proper action, whereas in the latter, the employee is a well-intentioned person who needs only to be given the proper tools and advice to reach high ethical ideals. This distinction, and its origins and impacts, are discussed at length in Chapters 5 and 8. For now, note that it is an important distinction, one that affects employees' willingness to cooperate with a company's effort to foster ethical business behavior. In the case of telephone lines, one can question whether lines that suggest efforts to control wayward employees are likely to be used as much as those that suggest they offer help to well-intentioned employees.

Ethics Policy Follow-through and Enforcement

Do companies with ethics policies make efforts to enforce the policy? Are people who violate policies appropriately disciplined? Is consideration of ethical behavior an important part of employees' performance appraisal? Are company responses to ethical problems fair and respectful to all employees? Management's willingness to follow through on ethical issues raised by employees, and to dispense discipline if necessary, forms an important influence on employees' reactions to and support for ethics programs and policies. Company responses to employees' ethical concerns may do much to frame employees' perceptions of ethics programs and their responses to ethics programs. The ERC 2000 survey reports that 58 percent of employees who reported misconduct to their employer were satisfied with the employer's response. Satisfaction rates are much higher in small organizations (fewer than five hundred employees), however, than in large organizations. This finding suggests that satisfactory responses may have more to do with normal managerial concerns and practices and organizational cultures than with the formal ethics programs typical in large companies (although satisfaction could be even lower in large companies without formal programs). Issues of follow-through on ethics problems are important open questions, addressed in detail in later chapters.

Self-assessments of Company Ethics

Do companies make serious efforts to assess the effectiveness of their formal ethics programs? Surely, many informal comparisons take place; various practitioner organizations, such as the Ethics Officer Association, provide multiple opportunities for ethics officers and related staff to meet, often confidentially, and discuss the problems of their work. Although some companies also, in our knowledge, have engaged in large-scale studies of their ethics programs and their outcomes—studies produced either by academics or consultants—such large data collection efforts often involve risks for a company. Specifically, data collected, except under conditions of attorney–client confidentiality, can become evidence against a company in court (say, in the event of a lawsuit concerning a type of unethical or illegal activity). Thus, there are legal disincentives for companies to probe too deeply into the outcomes of ethics programs and their reception among employees. (Obviously, this creates a difficulty for persons who try to study the workings of ethics programs, as we discuss in more detail in Chapter 11.) Our 1994 data indicated that although nearly a quarter of companies made some kind of regular effort to compare their ethical performance with other companies, most seldom did so, and even fewer ever considered asking various external stakeholders (for example, customers) to assess the company's ethical performance.

FORMAL CORPORATE ETHICS PROGRAMS: OPEN QUESTIONS

The foregoing description covers the typical elements included in the ethics initiatives of large American corporations. But just how much should we take this description at face value? As noted at the start of this chapter, formal ethics programs appear to owe at least some of their impetus to external pressures on organizations. Organizations can be quite creative, however, when it comes to finding ways to appear to respond to external expectations while actually conducting "business as usual" on the inside. Memos and wall posters touting the importance of ethics can become a "bad joke" in the eyes of employees, depending on the other messages and influences to which they are subjected.

Leaders' Involvement in Ethics Programs

That not everything is what it seems in the world of corporate ethics programs can be seen from considering the role of top management in such programs. Conventional management wisdom—among both academics and practitioners—highlights the importance of leadership in the effective pursuit of organizational goals. Leaders model key behaviors and attitudes for subordinates, have the capacity to set and interpret organizational goals, and usually are positioned to dispense rewards and punishments in response to the achievement or lack of achievement of goals. Thus, one would expect that if corporate leadership is sincerely committed to a company's espoused ethics goals, there would be some visible sign of leadership support for those goals.

Empirical evidence, however, suggests that this often is not the case. It is not a simple matter of a lack of opportunities. In our 1994 data, 46 percent of officers responsible for ethics had their offices on the same building floor as the company's CEO. However, 66 percent of our respondents—that is, the officers responsible for ethics—indicated that their CEO communicated with them about ethics issues two or fewer times per year. Thirty-two percent of CEOs attended no meetings that focused on ethics, and 30 percent attended one meeting annually that had ethical issues as a primary topic. Forty-nine percent of CEOs sent out company-wide memos about ethics at most once "every few years," and 46 percent did so only annually. Even smaller numbers resorted to recorded audio or video messages to employees about the importance of ethics and the company's ethics program. Given the press of multiple messages and concerns on the typical employee in most large companies, it is easy to suspect that the CEO's rare comments about ethics get "lost in the shuffle." Most employees probably have an unclear idea of just what top management's attitude toward ethics is (cf. Treviño, Hartman, and Brown 2001).

So even though most companies in our study were engaged in one or more of the typical elements of formal ethics programs, it is easy to wonder just how seriously those elements are intended. It is also easy to question whether or not those formal initiatives will receive the kind of informal support (such as CEO support and role modeling) that they may need to gain serious employee attention and commitment. Likewise, we may ask how well formal ethics programs are integrated into and supported by other organizational functions. Does the performance appraisal process support or undermine ethical goals? Are new employees mentored? If so, does the mentoring process explicitly address questions of ethical standards? Issues of leader behavior, integration with other organizational functions, and informal supports for ethics also are likely to be much more important in the as yet largely unstudied area of ethics in small business. After all, most small businesses lack the resources to support formal ethics programs, but they enjoy high levels of personal interaction among leaders and employees and loosely structured, informal ways of organizing—characteristics that could be beneficial or harmful from the standpoint of fostering ethical behavior. These questions of leader influences, integration with other organizational functions, and informal support are addressed in Chapter 6 and Part III of this book.

Cultural Variations

Most available data on and analyses of corporate ethics programs focus on the American context in which these programs originated. Although the use of formal ethics programs has spread beyond the United States, American businesses have been in the forefront when it comes to formalizing the attention to ethical issues (for example, Schlegelmilch 1989). This has not stopped various commentators from urging that non-American and global business adopt typical American practices, such as the use of ethics officers, anonymous telephone reporting lines, and formal codes of ethics (for example, Brothers 1991). Whether this is wise is an open question, however.

To begin, what counts as an important ethical issue varies across cultural and political contexts. A study comparing European and American corporate codes of ethics in the late 1980s found substantial differences in the range of issues addressed (Langlois and Schlegelmilch 1990), with American codes spending considerably more effort in delineating a company's responsibility to its employees (along with the employees' responsibilities to the company). These differences reflect a history of formalized, societally mandated employee involvement in the governance of European businesses (for example, codetermination). When the political and legal systems already include many well-known protections for employees and mandate employee involvement at high levels of organizational decision making, there appears to be less need for company codes of conduct to specify just how companies are to treat employees.

Apart from differences in issues addressed, however, we also can question the wisdom of universal formalization of concern for ethics, or we can at least question the appropriateness of certain types of formal ethics initiatives in different cultural and political settings. An American ethics and compliance officer has observed, for example, that systems for reporting ethical problems and questions need to be culturally sensitive because different societies have varying standards for how one should "raise an issue regarding a fellow employee" (Davids 1999). Even the assumption that concern for ethics requires formal organizational programs and policies is challenged in certain cultural settings. For example, managerial practice in the Philippines has been argued to be sufficiently skeptical of formalization and so strongly inclined toward loosely structured and emotionally involved responses to problems that one should not equate a rejection of formal ethics initiatives with a rejection of ethical behavior (Sison and Palma-Angeles 1997). Ethical behavior might be valued in that business environment, but the means to achieving it may be thought of quite differently. Similarly, typical elements of American formal ethics programs have been argued to reflect American cultural norms, in particular, the individualism of the culture and corresponding tendencies to resolve interpersonal problems through impartial legal and bureaucratic systems (for example, the courts). More collectivistic societies may find other ways of addressing interpersonal and ethical problems, such as through trusted intermediaries in interpersonal friendship networks or by showing less interest in preserving one's individual rights and greater willingness to tolerate the ethical failures of others in one's social group (Weaver 2001). Thus, even though it may be possible to explain, sociologically, the spread of American-style formal ethics programs into non-American business settings (through the influence of Americans and American companies and institutions in the global business environment), it is an open question whether such approaches to ethics are either necessary or sufficient to foster ethical business behavior in all cultural and political settings.

Ethics Programs and Organizational Changes

Finally, we also need to consider how ethics programs fare in the midst of substantial organizational change. This question has two elements. First, we lack any good understanding of how to continue to have a well-functioning ethics program during organizational changes, such as restructurings or mergers. Most discussions of ethics programs have assumed relatively stable background conditions. What happens when those conditions are in turmoil? At least some evidence suggests that such transitions pose serious problems for ethics programs. Data from the ERC 2000 survey (Joseph 2000) indicate that 65 percent of employees in stable organizations who report problems are satisfied with the employer's response, whereas only 43 percent of employees in organizations undergoing major change are satisfied with responses to their reports of problems. Also, employees in situations of change are more likely to suspect that management will see them as troublemakers, rather than good citizens, for reporting problems. (We elaborate these questions further in Chapter 12.)

We also can ask what happens to ethics programs themselves in the midst of radical organizational change. Some kinds of ethics-related organizational programs have become deeply entrenched in the business world. For example, offices and officers devoted to ensuring equal employment opportunities (that is, nondiscrimination) have become a permanent fixture in American business since they were first adopted in the 1960s in response to changes in the legal environment regarding discrimination. Such offices have persisted through both government policy changes and the major corporate restructurings of the late 1980s and early 1990s. Will ethics programs fare as well? The largest growth in corporate ethics programs has occurred in relatively good economic times (that is, the 1980s and 1990s). What will companies do regarding the costs of ethics programs in the midst of economic downturns? How will institutional pressures for ethics programs compare with institutional pressures to restructure, reengineer, or become more "lean and mean"? Answers to these questions depend in part on understanding the sources of existing ethics programs. Insofar as one or more elements of existing programs reflect external pressures rooted in the legal environment, they are likely to stay as long as the legal environment does not radically change. Yet insofar as the current status of ethics programs owes much to managerial choices and economic largesse, their future may be more varied; both managers and economic conditions change over time. To help answer this and other questions raised in this chapter about ethics programs, we turn now to two chapters that explain the influences on the implementation and integration of formal ethics programs.

References

Brothers, T. 1991. *Corporate ethics: Developing new standards of accountability*. New York: The Conference Board.

Center for Business Ethics. 1986. Are corporations institutionalizing ethics? *Journal of Business Ethics* 5:85–91.

Center for Business Ethics. 1992. Instilling ethical values in large corporations. *Journal of Business Ethics* 11:863–867.

Davids, M. 1999. Global standards, local problems. *Journal of Business Strategy* 20:38–46.

DiMaggio, P. J., and W. W. Powell. 1983. The iron cage revisited: Institutional isomorphism and collective rationality in organization fields. *American Sociological Review* 48:147–160.

Fligstein, N., and R. Freeland 1995. Theoretical and comparative perspectives on corporate organization. *Annual Review of Sociology* 21:21–44.

Heermance, E. H. 1924. *Codes of ethics*. Burlington, VT: Free Press Printing Co.

Joseph, J. 2000. *2000 National Business Ethics Survey*, Vol. 1. Washington, DC: Ethics Resource Center.

Langlois, C. C., and B. B. Schlegelmilch. 1990. Do corporate codes of ethics reflect national character? Evidence from Europe and the United States. *Journal of International Business Studies* 21:519–539.

Meyer, J. W., and B. Rowan. 1977. Institutionalized organizations: Formal structure as myth and ceremony. *American Journal of Sociology* 83:340–363.

Murphy, P. E. 1995. Corporate ethics statements: Current status and future prospects. *Journal of Business Ethics* 14:727–740.

Schlegelmilch, B. B. 1989. The ethics gap between Britain and the United Sates: A comparison of the state of business ethics in both countries. *European Management Journal* 7(1):57–64.

Scott, W. R. 1995. *Institutions and organizations*. Thousand Oaks, CA: Sage.

Sison, A. J. G., and A. Palma-Angeles. 1997. Business ethics in the Philippines. *Journal of Business Ethics* 16:1519–1528.

Treviño, L.K., L. P. Hartman, and M. Brown. 2000. Moral person and moral manager: How executives develop a reputation for ethical leadership. *California Management Review* 42(4):128–142.

Weaver, G. R. 1993. Corporate codes of ethics: Purpose, process and content issues. *Business & Society* 32(1):44–58.

Weaver, G. R. 2001. Ethics programs in global business: Culture's role in managing ethics. *Journal of Business Ethics* 30:3–15.

Weaver, G. R., and L. K. Treviño. 2001. The role of human resources in ethics/compliance management: A fairness perspective. *Human Resource Management Review* 11:113–134.

Weaver, G. R., L. K. Treviño, and P. L. Cochran. 1999. Corporate ethics practices in the mid-1990s. *Journal of Business Ethics* 18:282–294.

Corporate Ethics Programs as Control Systems: Influences of Executive Commitment and Environmental Factors

As Chapter 4 has shown, many American businesses have introduced one or more elements of a formal ethics program. Corporate ethics officers now are numerous enough to have their own professional association (the Ethics Officer Association) with members representing over five hundred major corporations and nearly eight hundred individuals. One chief executive officer (CEO) estimated that his company spends one million dollars per year on its ethics and legal compliance programs (Barbakow 1995).

In this chapter, we examine the factors influencing these formal efforts to manage employees' ethical conduct. Academic and practitioner literature often attributes these efforts to governmental pressure (Bureau of National Affairs 1996; Rafalko 1994; United States Sentencing Commission [USSC] 1995; *Wall Street Journal* 1994). This common focus on governmental pressure suggests a narrow and deterministic view of corporate ethics programs. By contrast, we propose a managerial choice perspective (Child 1972, 1997) that highlights the active role of management, both in responding to external pressures and in taking positive action on its own. A managerial choice

This chapter, with minor variations, originally was published in 1999 as G. R. Weaver, L. K. Treviño, and P. L. Cochran, "Corporate ethics programs as control systems: Influences of executive commitment and environmental factors," *Academy of Management Journal* 42:41–57. Copyright 1999 by the Academy of Management. Reproduced with permission of the Academy of Management in book format via the Copyright Clearance Center.

perspective allows for "*pro-action* as well as *re-action*," and recognizes that managers enjoy " 'bounded' autonomy" (Child 1997, 46, 53).

We use survey and archival data from *Fortune 500* companies to examine how formal ethics programs reflect external pressures or top management's own commitment to ethics. First, we use *control theory* to identify specific dimensions over which ethics programs may vary. We then apply our *choice perspective* to propose that both environmental and management factors influence ethics programs' dimensions. We also propose that some dimensions of ethics programs are influenced primarily by *environmental factors*, whereas others are influenced primarily by *management*.

FORMAL ETHICS PROGRAMS AS CONTROL SYSTEMS: SCOPE AND CONTROL ORIENTATION

Formal corporate ethics programs typically include some or all of the following elements: (1) *formal ethics codes*, which articulate a firm's expectations regarding ethics; (2) *ethics committees* charged with developing ethics policies, evaluating company or employee actions, or investigating and adjudicating policy violations; (3) *ethics communication systems* (for example, telephone lines) providing a means for employees to report abuses or obtain guidance; (4) *ethics officers or ombudspersons* charged with coordinating policies, providing ethics education, or investigating allegations; (5) *ethics training programs* aimed at helping employees to recognize and respond to ethical issues; and (6) *disciplinary processes* for unethical behavior. Previous survey research has reported only on the numbers of companies engaging in these activities, without developing constructs that might help explain what these activities represent and the role they play within companies (Berenbeim 1992; Center for Business Ethics 1992). Therefore, we begin by developing a conceptualization of formal ethics programs as a type of organization control system.

Control is a major responsibility of management, and it covers many types of behavior in a company, including ethical conduct and compliance with the law. Formal ethics programs may be conceptualized as organizational control systems aimed at standardizing employee behavior within the domains of ethics and legal compliance. As such, formal ethics control systems have goals similar to those of control systems in general: standardized behavior that allows "stable expectations to be formed by each member of the group as to the behavior of the other members under specified conditions" (Simon 1957, 100).

Ethics Program Scope

Control systems can be characterized in terms of their scope, that is, the degree to which behavioral control is achieved through formalization, specialization, and hierarchy (Bendix 1956; Edwards 1979; Weber 1947). In the case of corporate ethics programs, codes of conduct and other policy documents formalize company values and expectations for ethical behavior. These policies are administered by occupants of specialized positions (for example, corporate and divisional ethics officers, departmental ethics coordinators). Therefore, we define the *scope* of a corporation's ethics program as the number of different ethics program elements included in the formal ethics management effort. In some companies, ethics programs are broad in scope, with multiple elements, including dedicated staff, supporting structures and policies, and extensive employee involvement. In other companies, the scope of ethics management is limited, with little, if any, staff and few supporting structures.

Ethics Program Control Orientation

Control systems also are characterized by their control orientation, that is, the manner in which they standardize behavior. Theorists distinguish between overtly coercive systems that rely on restraints like punishment to achieve behavioral compliance and those systems that aim for member identification with and commitment to organizational goals and values (Adler and Borys 1996; Etzioni 1961; Gouldner 1954; Scott and Meyer 1991; Weber 1947). Similarly, corporate ethics programs can differ in control orientation. Some ethics programs embody a coercive orientation toward control that emphasizes adhering to rules, monitoring employee behavior, and disciplining misconduct. We refer to this as a *compliance-oriented* ethics program (Paine 1994). Corporate ethics programs also may aim to standardize behavior by creating commitment to shared values and by encouraging ethical aspirations (Etzioni 1961; Paine 1994). We refer to formal ethics programs that emphasize support for employees' ethical aspirations and the development of shared values as *values-oriented* programs. Compliance and values orientations need not be mutually exclusive (Paine 1994;

Treviño 1990), however. An organization's ethics program may aim for *both* internalization of values and compliance with rules so that organizational values are not perceived as empty rhetoric (Treviño 1990).

INFLUENCES ON ETHICS PROGRAM SCOPE: ENVIRONMENTAL
FACTORS AND MANAGEMENT COMMITMENT TO ETHICS

Recent research has sought a reconciliation of the once-opposed "determinism" and "choice" positions on organizational structuring (Bourgeois 1984; Hitt and Tyler 1991). For example, Hrebiniak and Joyce (1985) argued that managers might be highly constrained regarding some decisions but free in regard to others. External expectations can be uncertain or in conflict, creating interpretive latitude and opportunities for managerial discretion (DiMaggio 1988; Goodrick and Salancik 1996; Oliver 1991; Powell 1988). In this study, we adopt a managerial choice perspective that sees management as exercising what Child (1997) refers to as "bounded autonomy," such that organizational structures and actions reflect *both* the proactive exercise of managerial discretion and reactions to real or perceived environmental expectations (Dutton and Duncan 1987; Weick 1979).

Environmental Influences on Ethics Program Scope

The institutional environment is a likely influence on formal ethics programs (DiMaggio and Powell 1983; Meyer and Rowan 1977; Scott 1995). Societal institutions often pressure organizations to conform to formal and informal standards of legitimate behavior, and some of these standards are framed in terms of ethical values or explicit expectations for ethical behavior (Suchman 1995). Research typically has cited government agencies, professional and accrediting bodies, and interest groups or other loci of public opinion as having sufficient institutional status to influence business organizations (Elsbach and Sutton 1992; Galaskiewicz 1985; Greening and Gray 1994). Even though the workings of these institutions can be influenced by prior business activity (for example, political lobbying, funding of nonprofit agencies), institutions also generate their own influences on business organizations.

Government. Governmental pressures form a significant element of the institutional environment of business organizations (DiMaggio and Powell

1983; Meyer and Rowan 1977; Miles 1982; Salancik 1979). The USSC guidelines for punishing organizational defendants have been identified as an important influence on formal ethics management (Dalton, Metzger, and Hill 1994; Rafalko 1994). These guidelines, released in 1991, both (1) increased the penalties attached to convictions for illegal corporate behavior and (2) allowed for substantial reductions in penalties for offending companies that had made formal, proactive efforts to control their own ethics and legal compliance (USSC 1994).

The guidelines specify seven requirements for an effective program that are characteristic of control systems (Weber 1947). For example, organizations are expected to develop behavioral policies, assign responsibility to high-level individuals to oversee those policies, communicate the policies, take steps to achieve compliance, and respond to policy violations (USSC 1994). Thus, the USSC guidelines offer strong institutional support for broad-scope ethics programs with staff, codes, training programs, dedicated ethics telephone lines, and disciplinary mechanisms. The sentencing guidelines have not influenced all companies equally, however. In our interactions with senior executives from *Fortune 500* companies, we were surprised by the lack of familiarity with the sentencing guidelines among some of them. Such variation in key decision makers' familiarity with the guidelines should influence whether their organizations implement broad-scope programs consistent with the guidelines' specifications.

HYPOTHESIS 1: The more high-level management is aware of the USSC guidelines, the broader the scope of a company's ethics program.

Media Attention. Shapers of public opinion can spread legitimating and delegitimating accounts of organizations and thus influence the behavior of consumers, interest groups, government agencies, and other institutional actors (Chen and Meindl 1991; Elsbach and Sutton 1992). Media organizations in particular are in a position to exert pressure on organizations by publicizing companies' real or alleged ethical failings (Greening and Gray 1994; Wartick 1992). Companies that have been the target of critical media attention are more likely to develop visible policies and practices in an attempt to restore lost legitimacy or to ward off negative media attention in the future (Ashforth and Gibbs 1990). For example, several apparel marketers and retailers have developed codes and policies regarding their own and suppliers' treatment of employees following media attention to overseas sweatshops (Miller 1997). Thus, media attention directed toward a company's ethical failings is likely to prompt the company to engage in broader scope ethics management.

> HYPOTHESIS 2: The more media attention a company has received for its ethical failures, the broader the scope of the company's ethics program.

Business Standard Setters. Organizations are influenced by high-status "fashion setters" in the business world who set normative standards for a well-designed and well-managed organization (Abrahamson 1996; DiMaggio and Powell 1983; Scott 1995). Formal corporate ethics programs regularly receive endorsements from standard setters, such as the business press and professional associations. For example, the Conference Board, the leading business membership organization targeted toward high-level managers, holds a well-attended annual meeting on business ethics where corporate officers come to learn about ethics management. We have attended many of these meetings, which typically offer (1) favorable descriptions of companies with broad-scope ethics programs; (2) testimonials as to how broad-scope formal ethics programs are an indication of forward-looking management; and (3) how-to-do-it sessions by executives and consultants who have developed corporate ethics initiatives, such as codes of conduct, training programs, and disciplinary and monitoring systems. Given that the Conference Board programs endorse a variety of formal ethics initiatives, we would expect attendees to come away thinking that these initiatives are legitimate and worth implementing.

> HYPOTHESIS 3: A company's presence at Conference Board ethics meetings will lead to the adoption of a broader scope ethics program.

The Influence of Top Management's Commitment on the Scope of the Ethics Program

Executives can act both proactively and reactively (Child 1997), exercising choice in addition to responding to real or perceived external expectations (Child 1972; Hitt and Tyler 1991; Hrebiniak and Joyce 1985; Oliver 1991). An executive's exercise of choice is influenced in part by characteristics of the executive (Finkelstein and Hambrick 1990, 1996; Hambrick and Finkelstein 1987). According to upper-echelon theory (Hambrick and Mason 1984), executives have cognitive frameworks and value commitments that influence organizational outcomes. The value commitments of top executives are particularly important because these officers have the status necessary to influence organizational actions (Finkelstein and Hambrick 1990, 1996). We propose that executives who are strongly committed to ethics will influence their organizations to develop formal ethics programs. This is consistent with the business ethics literature, which stresses the importance of executives' commitment to ethics (Paine 1996).

The point might be illustrated best with an example. Robert Haas, former CEO of Levi Strauss & Company (*Business Week* 1994; Haas 1994; Howard 1990) has been described as wanting the corporation to profit *and* to make the world a better place, and he supports that outlook by requiring that corporate "aspirations" guide all decisions (*Business Week* 1994, 46). As a young adult, Haas marched for civil rights, served in the Peace Corps, served as a White House Fellow in the Johnson administration, and worked as a McKinsey & Co. consultant, where he was known as an environmentalist (Sherman 1997). Haas's ethical commitment appears to have influenced Levi Strauss's development of an aspirations statement, diversity programs, ethics initiatives, and child labor policies for overseas suppliers (Levi Strauss & Company 1997a, 1997b).

If asked, most top managers likely would agree that they are committed to ethics, but commitment to ethics easily can be lost in an environment in which managers are expected to deliver increasing returns to shareholders and to stay ahead of the competition. Executives must decide how to spend their limited time and what messages to send to employees. Many executives' messages to employees focus primarily on meeting "bottom-line" goals. Executives who have a personal commitment to ethics, however, also regularly express concern about how the company's goals are achieved (Haas 1994; Howard 1990), and they communicate concern for the company's nonfinancial obligations (for example, to do the right thing, treat people fairly, and be a good member of society). The top manager who is committed to ethics is also likely to consider an investment in ethics programs, policies, and structures to be an important way to implement and symbolize that commitment.

HYPOTHESIS 4: The more strongly top management is committed to ethics, the broader the scope of a company's ethics program.

Relative Influence of Environment and Top Management's Commitment on Scope

Organizations have little room for exercising managerial discretion if external expectations are clear and means toward those ends are specified (Goodrick and Salancik 1996). Uncertainty in external expectations, however, leaves room for managerial discretion (Covaleski and Dirsmith 1988; DiMaggio 1988; Oliver 1991). The USSC guidelines are clear and specific about the formal ethics program elements that are required if organizations are to benefit from reduced penalties. Thus, under the USSC guidelines, management is *relatively* constrained in choosing the number of ethics program elements to implement (that is, the *scope*). Conference Board meetings also create expectations that companies should engage in broad-scope ethics management because the meetings present companies with broad-scope ethics programs (for example, defense contractors) as exemplars. Media coverage of a firm's ethical failings may not specify particular actions to take, but it does encourage visible organizational responses that symbolize that ethical issues are being addressed (Ashforth and Gibbs 1990; Meyer and Rowan 1977). In response to media attention, a company is likely to adopt multiple ethics program elements to signal clearly its commitment to ethics.

Environmental influences, then, are relatively clear in both the end that is proposed (ethical corporate behavior) and the means that are considered appropriate to achieve that end (broad-scope ethics program structures). Failure to conform to external expectations risks serious consequences for an organization in terms of lost legitimacy, imposition of sanctions, and reduced cooperation from social actors important to organizational survival. Although top management commitment to ethics also should influence ethics program scope, it more easily is subject to negotiation and limitation in the face of other organizational goals and constraints and thus should be a weaker influence on ethics program scope.

HYPOTHESIS 5: Environmental influences will account for more variance in ethics program scope than will top management's commitment to ethics.

INFLUENCES ON ETHICS PROGRAM CONTROL ORIENTATION

Environmental Pressures on Ethics Program Control Orientation

We proposed earlier that environmental factors had a powerful influence on ethics program scope because only a broad-scope ethics program would satisfy relatively clear environmental expectations. Environmental expectations, however, are more ambiguous regarding ethics program control orientation. Conference Board sessions tend to focus on the different types of initiatives (codes, training, hotlines, and so on) that constitute a complete ethics program rather than on recommendations for a particular type of control orientation within those activities. Such initiatives can be either values or compliance oriented. An ethics code, for example, can emphasize shared values, or it can emphasize regulations and the penalties for breaking them. Also, media attention to a company's ethical failings often does not prescribe how to remedy the problem. As long as the company takes action that appears to satisfy societal expectations, the company may enjoy latitude regarding just how it responds. Also, little research exists to support the effectiveness of one ethics program control orientation over another. Thus, environmental pressures that are relatively strong in relation to scope may be weaker when it comes to control orientation (Goodrick and Salancik 1996).

We propose that management's awareness of the USSC guidelines is the only measured environmental factor that will influence ethics program control orientation and that this awareness will influence organizations to adopt a compliance orientation. Clearly, the USSC guidelines are aimed at legal compliance (that is, obeying the rules) and stress the prevention and detection of offenses (USSC 1994, section 8.K). They use compliance-oriented language (referring to "compliance standards and procedures" rather than "ethics programs" [USSC 1994, 1995]). They recommend that companies adopt monitoring, auditing, and reporting systems for detecting illegal conduct. Finally, they stress discipline for employees who violate policies and for managers who fail to detect offenses by others (USSC 1994, section 8.A.1.2). In short, the guidelines foster a control orientation focused on rules, monitoring, and discipline.

HYPOTHESIS 6: The more top management is aware of the USSC guidelines, the more a company's formal ethics program will be compliance oriented.

The Influence of Top Management's Commitment on Ethics Program Control Orientation

Executives who are committed to ethics are likely to encourage a values-oriented approach to ethics management. Managers often project their own attitudes onto others (Mowday 1982), and executives who are committed to ethics may project that outlook onto other organization members. Thus, they will expect organization members to respond to aspirational appeals to "do the right thing" (Treviño 1990). Their goal will be to foster employee identification with and commitment to a set of shared ethical values. For example, the Levi Strauss & Company aspirations statement reflects CEO Haas's concern for people and projects that attitude onto other organization members: *"We all want* a Company that our people are proud of and committed to. . . . We want our people to feel respected, treated fairly, listened to and involved" (Levi Strauss & Company, 1997c; emphasis added). When executives are strongly committed to ethics, ethics programs should be likely to display an orientation that encourages employees to internalize and act on a set of values.

Values and compliance orientations are not mutually exclusive (Paine 1994). Executives who are committed to ethics also will influence their organizations to adopt a compliance orientation. When executives take ethical issues seriously, they recognize the need to support ethical talk with actions. They are attentive to the justice concerns that can arise— specifically, expectations that employees will be held to agreed-on standards and that misconduct will be punished (Lerner 1977; Treviño 1993; Treviño and Ball 1992). This expectation of accountability should include compliance-oriented actions such as discipline for offenses. Thus, whereas environmental factors (USSC requirements) will have a limited influence on ethics program control orientation (encouraging a compliance orientation), we propose that top management commitment will have a more comprehensive impact, affecting both compliance and values orientations.

HYPOTHESIS 7: The more strongly top management is committed to ethics, the more a company's ethics program will be both compliance oriented and values oriented.

Relative Influence of Environment and Top Management's Commitment on Control Orientation

Although the USSC guidelines support a compliance approach toward control, they do not specify how strongly developed this orientation should be, and they do not exclude a complementary values orientation. For example, instead of defining the exact details of an ethics program, the guidelines simply stipulate that companies adopt monitoring, auditing, and disciplinary mechanisms that are "adequate," "reasonable," and "effective" (USSC 1994, section 8.A.1.2). Thus, management retains latitude to determine just how strongly compliance-oriented an ethics program will be and how much the program's compliance aspects will be joined to values-oriented elements. This latitude for management discretion is to be expected given the undeveloped knowledge base for effectiveness in ethics programs. Lack of conventionally accepted means for achieving a desired goal makes it difficult for external actors to specify exactly how organizations should satisfy their expectations, leaving much room for management discretion (Goodrick and Salancik 1996). In these circumstances, executives who are committed to ethics have reasons to pursue specific control orientations and also enjoy the discretion to do so.

HYPOTHESIS 8: Top management's commitment to ethics will account for more variance in ethics program control orientation than will environmental influences.

METHODS

Population and Data Sources

The population studied consisted of all of the Fortune 500 industrial and Fortune 500 service companies listed for 1994. Data were obtained from survey and archival sources, including (1) a mail survey of officers knowledgeable about company ethics practices, (2) registration lists for Conference Board ethics meetings, and (3) a database of article abstracts from twenty-five major U.S. newspapers for 1989 through 1994.

Previous research suggests that for some types of organizational phenomena, a particular high-level corporate officer specializing in that phenomenon provides the most accurate information (Thomas, Clark, and Gioia

1993). We targeted company officials who would be most familiar with any formal efforts their organizations *might* be making to deal specifically with ethics. Using the *National Directory of Corporate Public Affairs*, we telephoned a representative in the public affairs or corporate communications department of each of the one thousand companies to identify the high-ranking officer who could best describe the company's formal ethics activities, if any. The researchers used a common script to ask for the name of "the officer most responsible for dealing with ethics and conduct issues in the company." (If a company did not have a listing in the *National Directory of Corporate Public Affairs*, the call was directed to the company's human resources department.) We framed our query in terms of "ethics and conduct issues" rather than "programs" because we did not expect that all responding companies would have a formal program. Rather, we merely assumed that each company would have someone to whom responsibility for any ethics issues defaulted, but not necessarily someone who supervised a formal ethics program.

We generated a mailing list of individual informants at 990 companies. During late 1994, each informant was sent a questionnaire and up to two follow-up mailings; 254 questionnaires were returned, for a response rate of 26 percent. This response rate is reasonable given the rank of respondents: 57 percent of respondents were vice presidents or higher rank; another 24 percent identified themselves as department heads (Hambrick, Geletkanycz, and Fredrickson 1993). Eighty-six percent of respondents identified their functional area. Of these, only 16 percent were located in separate ethics or compliance departments, 22 percent were in legal departments, 6 percent were in general high-level administration (for example, corporate secretary), 28 percent in human resources, 6 percent in public affairs or corporate communications, 11 percent in audit or other internal control functions, 6 percent in combined legal and corporate secretary functions, and 5 percent in various other departments. Seventy-eight percent were men; respondents' average age was 48 years (standard deviation, or SD = 8.4). The average respondent had been with the company for 15 years (SD = 9.9) and in his or her current position for 5 years (SD = 4.4).

Bias Issues

We conducted conventional tests of response bias by analyzing response rates across the service and industrial classifications in the *Fortune* rankings. Responding companies represented a diverse range of industries (ninety-nine different three-digit standard industrial classification, or SIC, categories; forty-one different two-digit SIC categories). There was no significant difference in response rates between service and industrial companies. Research has considered the impact of financial condition on improper corporate behavior (Baucus and Near 1991; Cochran and Nigh 1987). Therefore, we also measured potential nonresponse bias by comparing responding companies with an approximately equal number of randomly selected nonresponding companies on several financial characteristics (gross revenue, net profit, total assets, return on sales, return on assets), in addition to size as measured by the firm's number of employees. We found no significant differences between responding and nonresponding companies on any financial measures. After removing three large outlier respondents, with 250,000 to 500,000 employees each, we also found no significant difference in size.

It is possible that companies with minimal formal ethics management activities would be less likely to respond. Descriptive statistics indicate, however, that the sample includes wide variance in formal ethics program activity. For example, the median company in ethics program scope (measure described in detail later) has an officer who devotes only 15 percent of his or her time to ethics. The company has a written ethics policy but no ethics telephone line, no ethics or compliance office, no ethics committees, and no ongoing ethics follow-up with employees. Half of our responding companies, then, only did this much or less in regard to addressing ethics issues formally. Thus, the data set incorporates sufficient variance for analyzing the influences driving corporate ethics program characteristics.

Social desirability bias is a risk in any ethics-related study (Fernandes and Randall 1992; Moorman and Podsakoff 1992). We tried to minimize socially desirable responses by ensuring that our survey clearly did not focus on companies' "dirty laundry" or on the effectiveness of company ethics initiatives. Informants were told that the questions concerned formal policies, procedures, and organizational characteristics in an effort to see how companies' ethics activities, if any, vary to fit different organizational situations. We also attempted to minimize bias through the wording of survey items addressing the scope of the ethics program. Many of these items were written in objective, "yes" or "no" fashion (for example, "Does your firm have an ethics committee?"), and nondichotomous items were given multiple descriptive anchors.

Nevertheless, it remains possible that company informants would be self-serving in their responses. Before constructing our questionnaire, however, we completed structured interviews with twenty ethics-responsible officers in a variety of companies. These officers were quite candid about what their companies were *not* doing in regard to ethics and about varying degrees of top management's support for ethics-related activities. This suggested to us that we would receive reasonably realistic reports from these officers. Further, survey respondents were likely not personally "invested" in a particular ethics-oriented role. Only 54 percent of responding companies indicated assigning ethics responsibilities specifically to one officer. More than half of these officers (65 percent) spend no more than 20 percent of their time on ethics-related activities, and only 18 percent show close to full-time commitment to ethics activities (that is, more than 80 percent of the officer's time). For most respondents, ethics activities do not constitute a personal "empire" prompting self-serving responses.

Dependent Variable Measures

Ethics Program Scope. The scope of formal ethics activities was measured using survey items that asked objective questions about the company's ethics structures and activities. These included the presence of a code of ethics or other ethics policy documents, the extent of distribution of those policies to employees, the presence and staff size of special ethics offices and committees, the frequency with which various levels of employees receive ethics-oriented communications and training, and the use of dedicated ethics telephone lines. These items were answered in a yes or no, percentage, or Likert-scale fashion. A composite measure of ethics program scope was formed by summing the z-scores of all the items. Higher scores on the scope measure reflect the presence of more ethics-oriented structures and activities.

Ethics Program Mode of Control. The degree to which values and compliance orientations characterize an ethics program's mode of control was measured according to the reported emphasis in the program on values and aspirations and on monitoring and punishment. For values orientation, four Likert-type items were used that assessed ethics program emphases on (1) encouraging shared values, (2) supporting employee aspirations, (3) communicating company values, and (4) building trust and confidence (for example, "How prominent is the activity of encouraging shared values in

TABLE 5.1
Rotated Factors and Loadings for Ethics Program Control Orientations

Items	Factor 1 Compliance	Factor 2 Values
Employees violating ethics expectations are disciplined	0.87	0.10
Employee failing to abide by policies will be disciplined	0.86	0.11
People not conforming to ethical standards are disciplined	0.76	0.20
Even minor violations of ethical expectations get an employee disciplined	0.66	0.12
Auditing for compliance with law is prominent in company's ethics activities	0.64	0.15
Investigating complaints is prominent in company's ethics activities	0.57	0.17
Ethics activities and policies are oriented toward building trust and confidence	0.04	0.84
Ethics activities and policies are oriented toward communicating the company's values	0.08	0.81
Encouraging shared values is prominent in company's ethics activities	0.24	0.80
Supporting employee goals and aspirations is prominent in company's ethics activities	0.34	0.62
Eigenvalue	4.15	1.78

the firm's overall effort to foster good ethics?" Cronbach's alpha = 0.80). For compliance orientation, six items assessed the prominence of (1) discipline for nonconformity, (2) investigation of complaints, and (3) auditing for compliance (for example, "How prominent is the activity of investigating complaints in the firm's overall effort to foster good ethics?" Cronbach's alpha = 0.84). Factor analysis with varimax rotation resulted in two factors (explaining 59 percent of variance): *compliance orientation* (eigenvalue = 4.15) and *values orientation* (eigenvalue = 1.78) (Table 5.1).

Independent Variable Measures

Awareness of USSC Guidelines. We used three survey items to measure executives' awareness of the USSC guidelines (Cronbach's alpha = 0.88). These five-point Likert-type items queried the extent to which top management meetings and communications addressed the impact of the guidelines and the respondent's knowledge of the guidelines (for example, "High-level managers in this firm have discussed the 1991 U.S. Corporate Sentencing Guidelines"; strongly agree/strongly disagree). Descriptive data for this measure indicate that managers vary in awareness of the guidelines and their requirements (mean = 3.26, SD = 1.17).

Media Attention. We measured media attention to a firm's ethical failings by using the *Newspaper Abstracts* database, covering 25 regional and national newspapers. For each responding company, we summed the number of article abstracts in the database that suggested ethical failure at a company. The period covered ranged from 1989 (the start of the database) through October 1994 (the start of our survey period). Two trained research assistants (each covering about half of responding companies), using the same written guidelines, counted abstracts indicating (1) violation of the law (for example, antitrust, insider trading, discriminatory hiring, fraud, and so on); (2) harm or threat to the public generally or to specific "innocent bystanders" (for example, accusations of poor safety at chemical or nuclear facilities, inattention to safety in aircraft design or maintenance); (3) allegedly ruthless business practices; or (4) suggestions of undisclosed corporate impropriety (for example, the suicide of an officer at a company under investigation). One of the authors repeated the abstract search for 10 percent of the companies evaluated by each research assistant. Using the conservative P-statistic (Light 1971), interrater agreement between one of the authors and one of the research assistants was 71 percent, and it was 70 percent between this author and the other research assistant.

Representation at Conference Board Ethics Meetings. We used conference registration lists to measure a company's representation at the Conference Board's three annual ethics meetings held before administration of our survey (that is, spring of 1992, 1993, and 1994). We considered that a company was represented if one or more of its members appeared on the list for one or more of the three conferences. We did not use the total number of conference attendees from a company so as not to bias the data in favor of companies located close to the New York City conference site. We used a three-year period to allow for the fact that companies might not be able to participate every year.

Top Management's Commitment to Ethics. Measurement of top management's commitment to ethics raised social desirability concerns (Fernandes and Randall 1992). Executives' reports about their *own* ethical commitments would likely be subject to social desirability biases. Our informants would be able to assess how much top management was concerned with ethics by noting the amount of attention paid to ethics in high-level discussions. The attention given to topics in high-level discussions should be an indication of what top management thinks is important. Therefore, we gave informants a list of potential topics of top-management conversation. The potential topics of conversation included items suggesting that executives view ethics as intrinsically valuable (for example, "valuing integrity as much as profits," "doing the right thing," "seeking the good of society;" see Table 5.2), along with other, performance-oriented topics to which one also would expect management to show commitment (for example, finances, strategy, operational problems). We introduced the list by telling informants that we wanted them to assess "the overall business orientation of your firm's top management by [rating] the extent to which various subjects are a topic of conversation for your firm's top management team (i.e., executive vice presidents and higher)." They then saw the list of the various conversation topics, each of which they rated on five-point Likert scales ranging from "never" to "very frequently." The more highly management is rated on items suggesting the intrinsic value of ethics, the more we consider management committed to ethics. The performance items functioned as foils. They were expected to dissuade informants from uncritically giving high rankings to the ethics-related items; for example, the taken-for-granted importance of finances might force ethics out of the highest category.

Principal components factor analysis of eight items assessing management's commitment to ethics generated one factor explaining 55 percent of variance (eigenvalue = 4.44; see Table 5.2). Reliability analysis of the eight items yielded a Cronbach's alpha of 0.88. The mean for these items was 3.43 (SD = 0.75, range = 1 to 5, where 5 denotes very frequent discussion of the topic). By contrast, the mean for the performance foils was 4.56 (SD = 0.52, range = 2.67 to 5.00). This indicates lower and more variable responses for top management's commitment to ethics; respondents in effect were will-

TABLE 5.2

Factor Loadings for

Management Commitment to Ethics

Items	Factor 1 (Commitment to Ethics)
Seeing that justice is done	0.83
Doing the right thing	0.79
Valuing integrity as much as profits	0.76
The company's role in society	0.75
Treating people fairly	0.74
Nonfinancial and nonlegal obligations	0.73
Seeking the good of society	0.71
The importance of self-restraint	0.64
Eigenvalue	4.44

ing to admit that questions of ethics do not receive the same degree of attention from top management as do strategic and financial concerns.

Control Variables. We controlled for the effect of financial performance and company size. We measured financial performance as company return on assets (ROA) relative to industry ROA, defining industries in terms of responding companies' two-digit primary SIC classifications and obtaining data from *Compact Disclosure*. Financial performance was averaged over a three-year period (fiscal year 1992 through fiscal year 1994). Size was measured as total number of employees, using the employee totals provided in the Fortune 500 listings.

Analyses

Because of significant correlations among the dependent variables, we used an omnibus test of significance for the overall model. Canonical correlation analysis of all three dependent variables and all independent and control variables generated a significant overall model (Wilks' lambda = 0.37, $p \leq$ 0.01). We then relied on hierarchical regression to test hypotheses 1 through 4, 6, and 7.

Hypothesis 5 proposed that environmental influences would account for more variance in ethics program scope than would top management's commitment to ethics. The unique contribution to variance explained by a single independent variable can be assessed by noting its squared semipartial correlation. However, we were interested in comparing a single predictor—top management's commitment to ethics—with a *set* of environmental influences. Therefore, we tested hypothesis 5 with usefulness analysis (Darlington 1968). Usefulness analysis reveals the unique contribution of one or more independent variables in predicting a dependent variable's variance. Specifically, it provides the incremental change in explained variance attributable to a set of one or more independent variables beyond the contribution to explained variance of all other variables. The process compares squared multiple correlation coefficients (R^2) associated with each set of predictor variables while removing any variance shared by the predictor(s) in question and the other independent variables. Each set of one or more predictor variables is entered into a hierarchical regression in separate stages and in each possible ordering to show how much variance each set of variables can explain beyond the explanatory capacity of all other variables. At each stage, the amount of incremental variance explained by the newly added set of variables is observed and tested for significance, thus revealing the unique variance (if any) attributable to each set of independent variables.

RESULTS

Table 5.3 reports means, SD, and correlations for all variables. Tables 5.4a, 5.4b, and 5.4c report results of hierarchical regression analyses for each of the dependent variables.

Influences on Ethics Program Scope

The control variables—size and financial performance—accounted for 4 percent of variance in scope (scope equation 1; adjusted R^2 = 0.04, F = 5.44, probability, or $p < 0.01$). The complete model accounted for 32 percent of variance in scope (scope equation 2; adjusted R^2 = 0.32, F = 19.07, $p \leq 0.01$).

Management's awareness of the USSC guidelines was significantly and positively linked to ethics program scope (hypothesis 1; b = 2.42, t = 5.54, $p \leq 0.01$). Media attention to a firm's ethical failures also was significantly and

TABLE 5.3

Descriptive Statistics and Correlations

Variable	Mean	SD	α	1	2	3	4	5	6	7	8
1 Ethics program scope	0.00	8.91		1.00							
2 Compliance orientation	4.05	0.69	0.84	0.23**	1.00						
3 Values orientation	3.94	0.81	0.80	0.26**	0.39**	1.00					
4 Company size	26010	49010		0.20**	0.13	0.12	1.00				
5 Financial performance (3-year industry-weighted return on assets)	1.09	4.93		−0.04	−0.04	−0.05	0.04	1.00			
6 Management awareness of USSC guidelines	3.26	1.17	0.88	0.40**	0.24**	0.15*	0.08	−0.01	1.00		
7 Top management's commitment to ethics	3.43	0.75	0.88	0.25**	0.37**	0.64**	0.11	−0.03	0.12	1.00	
8 Media attention to company's ethical failings	19.65	42.58		0.31**	0.09	0.13*	0.40**	−0.06*	0.14*	0.16*	1.00
9 Company's representation at Conference Board	0.23	0.42		0.37**	0.08	0.06	0.16**	0.01	0.22**	0.04	0.25**

SD, Standard deviation; USSC, United States Sentencing Commission.

N ranges from 242 to 254.

* $p \leq 0.05$ ** $p \leq 0.01$

TABLE 5.4A
Hierarchical Regression Results for Ethics Program Scope

	EQUATION 1			EQUATION 2		
	b	s.e.b.	beta	b	s.e.b.	beta
Constant	−0.57	0.66		−17.39	2.55	
Size of company	0.00**	0.00	0.21**	0.00	0.00	0.07
Financial performance	−0.12	0.12	−0.07	−0.08	0.10	−0.05
Management commitment to ethics				2.20**	0.66	0.19**
Management awareness of USSC guidelines				2.42**	0.44	0.31**
Media attention to company's ethical failings				0.03*	0.01	0.14*
Company presence at Conference Board				5.31**	1.17	0.26**
R^2		0.05			0.34	
Adjusted R^2		0.04			0.32	
F		5.44**			19.07**	
df		2,225			6,221	
ΔR^2					0.30	
$F\ \Delta R^2$					24.74**	

positively related to scope (hypothesis 2; b = 0.03, t = 2.34, $p \leq$ 0.05), as was a company's representation at Conference Board ethics meetings (hypothesis 3; b = 5.31, t = 4.54, $p \leq$ 0.01). Top management's commitment to ethics also was significantly and positively related to ethics program scope (hypothesis 4; b = 2.20, t = 3.31, $p \leq$ 0.01). Thus, hypotheses 1 through 4 were supported.

Management's commitment to ethics and the set of environmental variables (USSC, media attention, and Conference Board representation) each predicted statistically significant variance in scope beyond that accounted for by the other. The set of environmental influences, however, significantly explained 23 percent more variance than was explained by management's

TABLE 5.4B
Hierarchical Regression Results for Compliance Orientation

	EQUATION 1			EQUATION 2		
	b	s.e.b.	beta	b	s.e.b.	beta
Constant	4.01**	0.05		2.62**	0.22	
Size of company	0.00*	0.00	0.13*	0.00	0.00	0.08
Financial performance	0.01	0.01	−0.05	−0.01	0.01	−0.04
Management commitment to ethics				0.30**	0.22	0.32**
Management awareness of USSC guidelines				0.12**	0.04	0.20**
Media attention to company's ethical failings	—	—	—			
Company presence at Conference Board	—	—	—			
R^2		0.02			0.18	
Adjusted R^2		0.01			0.16	
F		2.18			11.91**	
df		2,225			4,223	
ΔR^2					0.16	
$F \Delta R^2$					21.27**	

commitment to ethics; for adding the environmental influences to an equation already containing controls and top management commitment, the change in R^2 = 0.23, F = 25.84, $p \le$ 0.01. By contrast, management's commitment to ethics explained only 3 percent more variance in scope than did environmental influences; for adding management commitment to an equation already containing controls and the three environmental influences, the change in R^2 = 0.03, F = 11.00, $p \le$ 0.01. These results support hypothesis 5. The first column of Table 5.5 summarizes this finding and also provides the unique contribution to explained variance of each of the three environmental variables.

TABLE 5.4C

Hierarchical Regression Results for Values Orientation

	EQUATION 1			EQUATION 2		
	b	*s.e.b.*	*beta*	*b*	*s.e.b.*	*beta*
Constant	3.88**	0.06		1.67**	0.18	
Size of company	0.00*	0.00	.14*	0.00	0.00	0.07
Financial performance	−0.01	0.01	−.06	−0.01	0.01	−0.03
Management commitment to ethics				0.65**	0.05	0.65**
Management awareness of USSC guidelines				—	—	—
Media attention to company's ethical failings				—	—	—
Company presence at Conference Board				—	—	—
R^2		0.02			0.44	
Adjusted R^2		0.01			0.43	
F		2.50			57.46**	
df		2,225			3,224	
ΔR^2					0.41	
$F\ \Delta R^2$					163.74**	

** $p \le .01$ * $p \le .05$

N = 227 (listwise deletion).

USSC, United States Sentencing Commission.

Influences on Ethics Program Control Orientation

The set of control variables showed no significant relationship to an ethics program's compliance orientation (compliance equation 1; adjusted R^2 = 0.01, F = 2.18, not significant, NS). The complete model (compliance equation 2) was significant, explaining 16 percent of variance in compliance ori-

TABLE 5.5

Usefulness Analyses of Environmental Influences and
Management Commitment to Ethics on Explained Variance in Ethics
Program Scope, Compliance Orientation, and Values Orientation [a]

	DEPENDENT VARIABLES		
Independent Variables	*Ethics Program Scope*	*Ethics Program Compliance Orientation*	*Ethics Program Values Orientation*
Top management commitment beyond environmental pressures	0.03**	0.10**	0.38**
Set of all environmental influences beyond top management commitment	0.23**	0.04**	0.01
USSC beyond top management commitment and other environmental pressures	0.09**	0.04**	0.01
Media attention beyond management commitment and other environmental pressures	0.02**	0.00	0.00
Conference Board beyond top management commitment and other environmental pressures	0.06**	0.00	0.00
R^2 (complete model with controls)	0.34**	0.18**	0.44**

USSC, United States Sentencing Commission.

[a] Statistics presented in the table provide the incremental change in R^2 for a given independent variable (or set of independent variables) beyond all other independent and control variables and the significance of that incremental change in R^2.

** $p \leq 0.01$

entation (adjusted R^2 = 0.16, F = 11.91, $p \leq 0.01$). Top management's awareness of the USSC guidelines was significantly and positively related to compliance orientation (hypothesis 6; b = 0.12, t = 3.23, $p \leq 0.01$).

Top management's commitment to ethics was significantly and positively linked to compliance orientation (b = 0.30, t = 5.21, $p \leq 0.01$). Top management's commitment to ethics also was significantly and positively linked to values orientation. The set of controls showed no significant relationship to an ethics program's values orientation (values equation 1; adjusted R^2 = 0.01, F = 2.50, NS). The complete model (values equation 2) was significant, explaining 43 percent of variance in values orientation (adjusted $R^2 = 0.43$, $F = 57.46$, $p \leq 0.01$), with top management's commitment to ethics being positively linked to values orientation ($b = 0.65$, $t = 12.80$, $p \leq 0.01$). Together, these results support hypothesis 7; top management's commitment to ethics influences both compliance and values orientations.

Hypothesis 8 proposed that management's commitment to ethics would play a larger role in predicting ethics program control orientations than would environmental influences. The middle column of Table 5.5 provides results that support hypothesis 8. Each of USSC awareness and management's commitment to ethics explained significant variance in compliance orientation beyond that explained by the other. Management's commitment to ethics, however, explained 10 percent more variance than was explained by USSC awareness ($R^2 = 0.10$, $F = 27.18$, $p \leq 0.01$), whereas USSC awareness explained only 4 percent more variance than was explained by management's commitment ($R^2 = 0.04$, $F = 10.45$, $p \leq 0.01$). No significant relationship was found between compliance orientation and any of the other environmental influences.

We also compared the influence of environmental factors and top management's commitment to ethics on ethics program values orientation. We did this in part to examine hypothesis 8 over both types of control orientation and also because correlational results indicated that USSC awareness and media attention had small but significant relationships with ethics program values orientation (Table 5.3). Results presented in the third column of Table 5.5 show that management's commitment to ethics uniquely and significantly explains a substantial portion of total variance beyond any explained by the set of environmental influences ($R^2 = 0.38$, $F = 149.48$, $p \leq 0.01$), whereas the set of environmental influences does not predict significant variance in values orientation beyond that predicted by management commitment ($R^2 = 0.01$, $F = 1.31$, NS). Top management commitment has a stronger influence on ethics program control orientation than do the measured environmental influences (hypothesis 8).

DISCUSSION

The findings supported our hypotheses that multiple environmental influences (awareness of USSC guidelines, media attention to a firm's ethical problems, representation at Conference Board meetings) and executive commitment to ethics would be associated with ethics program scope. Moreover, the set of environmental influences was associated more strongly with the scope of the ethics program than was executive commitment to ethics. The data also supported our hypotheses related to control orientation of the ethics program. Both management's awareness of the USSC guidelines and top management's commitment to ethics were associated with ethics program compliance orientation, and top management's commitment to ethics was associated with values orientation. Top management's commitment to ethics, however, was related more strongly to a program's control orientation than were environmental influences.

Contributions to the Business Ethics Literature

Conceptualizing Formal Ethics Programs as Control Systems. Normative and theoretical business ethics research often suggested the value of corporate ethics programs (for example, Donaldson and Preston 1995; Jones 1995), but this research either has treated ethics programs in holistic fashion or has focused on individual program elements (for example, codes of conduct). Empirical studies of ethics programs have been limited to atheoretical surveys that treat programs in terms of their separate elements: how many firms have ethics officers, codes, ethics telephone lines, etc. (Berenbeim 1992; Center for Business Ethics 1992). By conceptualizing formal ethics programs in terms of organizational control theory, the study provides a basis for creating theoretically relevant dimensions of ethics programs. Future research can relate these dimensions to outcomes of an ethics program. For example, do broad scope programs lead to greater employee awareness of ethical issues? Does a values orientation lead to less unethical behavior, or is a compliance orientation or a combined compliance/values orientation most effective?

Conceptualizing ethics programs in terms of organizational control systems is consistent with our focus on formal programs; however, we acknowledge that this is a limited view of organizational ethics. We consciously chose not to focus on more informal modes of control, such as informal norms and organizational culture (Ouchi 1980; Wilkins and Ouchi 1983). These more informal modes of control are likely to be important in many organizations, especially in smaller organizations. We also do not claim that ethics programs should be conceptualized exclusively as control systems; ethics programs might play other important roles. For example, ethics programs might play largely symbolic roles that signal organizational legitimacy to external actors without actually influencing employee behavior. Closer to our concern with the control dimensions of ethics programs, they also might be understood as solutions to agency and transaction cost problems (Weaver 1992). We urge future researchers to address these issues.

Finally, our study does not address the ethical propriety of formal ethics programs. Normative theorists may wish to evaluate whether ethics programs of various types operate in ethically proper fashion. Most research in business ethics has taken ethics programs at face value, treating them as ethically proper means by which companies achieve ethical ends. If ethics programs are types of organizational controls, however, it is possible that they, like other controls, can be used for unethical purposes (Braverman 1974).

Environmental Influences, Executive Discretion, and Ethics Program Characteristics. The study also contributes to business ethics research by showing that formal ethics program dimensions reflect multiple influences. Although other streams of organizational study have considered how environmental and managerial factors influence organizational structures and activities, these perspectives have not been used to understand ethics management. Much conventional wisdom assumes, for example, that most firms adopt ethics programs primarily as a response to the USSC guidelines (Rafalko 1994; USSC 1995). Our study provides the first systematic empirical support for this claim, but it also demonstrates that (1) other environmental factors are important and (2) environmental factors have different influences on different dimensions of ethics programs.

Popular (*Business Week* 1994) and academic (Paine 1996; Treviño 1990) writings have stressed the importance of the "tone at the top"—top management's support for ethics-related activities. Our study provides the first systematic empirical support for this proposition by demonstrating that top management's commitment to ethics is associated with program scope and control orientation, but it is particularly important for control orientation. In combination, these findings suggest that environmental factors influence organizations to initiate a broad range of formal ethics-related activities, such as codes, training programs, and telephone lines. Much of the guidance for how programs are implemented comes from the firm's top managers, however, and their commitment to ethics. Thus, management's moral outlook must be viewed as an important influence on an organization's ethical structures and practices (Etzioni 1988; Freeman 1995).

Our findings about the relative influence of environmental factors and executive commitments are consistent with Goodrick and Salancik's (1996) observation that uncertainty in environmental expectations increases managerial discretion. We argued that uncertainty is lower regarding environmental expectations for the scope of an ethics program and higher for ethics program control orientation. Therefore, we expected that top management's commitment to ethics would influence more strongly ethics program control orientation and that ethics program scope would be influenced more by environmental factors. These expectations were supported by the data, thus linking this study of corporate ethics to broader discussions of choice and determinism in organizational structuring.

We believe our finding about the key role of top management is important, but we also acknowledge that more fine-grained analyses of top managers' commitment to ethics will be required in the future. Although executives may be committed to ethics in and of itself, executives also may have more pragmatic, instrumental interests in ethics (Jones 1995). Future research should distinguish different types of top management's commitment to ethics and the consequences of those different commitments.

Study Limitations

Earlier, we addressed the possibility of bias attributable to socially desirable responses to survey items. We also acknowledge the possibility of common methods bias regarding some of the relationships, given that data for dependent variables and some independent variables came from the same survey. We note, however, that at least for measures of ethics program scope, the relatively objective nature of the survey questions should reduce the possibility of bias. We also note that our sample included too few firms in any single industry to allow us to investigate industry effects. Yet industry effects on ethics management certainly are possible and worthy of future study.

Here we focus on questions of alternative causal interpretations. We considered the possibility that environmental factors might influence the development of an ethics program indirectly by influencing top management's commitment to ethics. We reanalyzed our data using LISREL to test this possibility, but we found no support for this kind of mediated relationship.

We also considered the possibility of reverse causality. For example, might ethics program characteristics influence Conference Board attendance? We used attendee lists at the three Conference Board meetings *before* our survey to reduce the possibility of reverse causality. Also, although Conference Board attendees might represent organizations that already have high-scope programs, our observation of the past six meetings does not support this possibility. Conference Board attendees generally represent organizations that are beginning to explore whether and how they might address ethics formally. Once such programs are in place, corporate representatives are likely to join the Ethics Officer Association and attend that organization's meetings, which are oriented toward companies with established programs. Even if companies with established formal ethics programs attend Conference Board ethics meetings, the nature of the program—highlighting all the different things one can do to manage ethics—still is likely to encourage efforts to broaden the scope even of preexisting programs.

We do not believe the presence of an ethics program would contribute to management's awareness of the USSC guidelines. The actual ethics program documents, training programs, and policies we have seen do not refer to the USSC. Further, both theory and practitioner literature point toward awareness of the guidelines as an influence on organizational action.

We also considered whether the existence of an ethics program might influence top management's commitment. It is possible that having a broader-scope ethics program would encourage top managers to talk more about ethics, but we think this is unlikely. Our formal and informal communications with ethics-responsible officers over a period of years suggest that even though a firm may have a broad-scope ethics program, senior management frequently is distant from that program. Descriptive studies of corporate ethics practices also indicate low levels of top management's involvement in ethics programs (Weaver et al. 1999). We also see little reason to believe that having a compliance-oriented program would encourage top management to show more commitment to ethics and even less reason to think a company could develop a values-oriented program without first having executives who are committed to ethics.

Implications for Practice and Public Policy

Many top managers delegate responsibility for ethics management to others (for example, legal counsel). We have listened to ethics-responsible officers' laments about their need for support and commitment from top management. This study supports their concerns. Commitment by top management is important for ethics program scope and control orientation but especially for control orientation. It is the only factor strongly associated with having a program oriented toward shared values. If companies are interested in this type of program, top managers need to communicate and demonstrate their commitment to it. Senior managers need to recognize their central role in the process of managing ethics. Many top managers may not be comfortable having a prominent role in their companies' ethics programs, preferring to leave issues of ethics to legal counsel or human resources managers. Nonetheless, the results of this research suggest that executive commitment to ethics has importance consequences for ethics governance in companies and that managers should take their role seriously.

Finally, suggestions for public policy also follow from our finding that environmental factors and management commitment both influence ethics programs. Policies such as the USSC guidelines provide a strong incentive for firms to develop broad-scope ethics programs so that, if a company is caught in misconduct, it can say that it did all the "right" things. Merely having a broad-scope program, however, may not achieve ultimate public policy goals. Although we do not yet have empirical data to evaluate the effectiveness of one type of ethics program orientation over another, case-based and theoretical research have suggested that values-oriented programs or combined values/compliance programs should be more effective (Paine 1994; Treviño 1990). Our results indicate that the orientation of ethics programs is linked most strongly to high-level management commitment to ethics, not external influences. Policy efforts, then, might be more successful if they focus less on increasing ethics program scope and more on fostering top managers' commitment to ethics. This insight will become even more important in the next chapter, where we consider the role of top management commitment in influencing not only the control orientation of an ethics program but also the extent to which that program is integrated with or disconnected from routine organizational policies and practices.

References

Abrahamson, E. 1996. Management fashion. *Academy of Management Review* 21:254–285.

Adler, P. S., and B. Borys. 1996. Two types of bureaucracy: enabling and coercive. *Administrative Science Quarterly* 41:61–90.

Ashforth, B. E., and B. W. Gibbs. 1990. The double-edge of organizational legitimation. *Organization Science* 1:177–194.

Barbakow, J.C. 1995. The ethics patrol. *Chief Executive* 105:58–61.

Baucus, M. S., and J. P. Near. 1991. Can illegal corporate behavior be predicted? An event history analysis. *Academy of Management Journal* 34:9–36.

Bendix, R. 1956. *Work and authority in industry.* New York: John Wiley & Sons.

Berenbeim, R. 1992. *Corporate ethics practices.* New York: The Conference Board.

Bourgeois, L. J. III. 1984. Strategic management and determinism. *Academy of Management Review* 9:586–596.

Braverman, H. 1974. *Labor and monopoly capital.* New York: Monthly Review Press.

Bureau of National Affairs. 1996. *Prevention of Corporate Liability* 4(4):14–16.

Business Week. 1994. Managing by values. August 1:46–52.

Center for Business Ethics. 1992. Instilling ethical values in large corporations. *Journal of Business Ethics* 11:863–867.

Chen, C. C., and J. R. Meindl. 1991. The construction of leadership images in the popular press: The case of Donald Burr and People Express. *Administrative Science Quarterly* 36:521–555.

Child, J. 1972. Organizational structure, environment, and performance. *Sociology* 6:1–22.

Child, J. 1997. Strategic choice in the analysis of action, structure, organizations and environment: Retrospect and prospect. *Organization Studies* 18:43–76.

Cochran, P. L., and D. Nigh. 1987. Illegal corporate behavior and the question of moral agency: an empirical examination. In *Research in corporate social performance and policy*, Vol. 9, ed. W. C. Frederick, 73–91. Greenwich, CT: JAI Press.

Covaleski, M. A., and M. W. Dirsmith. 1988. An institutional perspective on the rise, social transformation, and fall of a university budget category. *Administrative Science Quarterly* 33:562–587.

Dalton, D. R., M. B. Metzger, and J. W. Hill. 1994. The 'new' U.S. Sentencing Commission guidelines: A wake-up call for corporate America. *Academy of Management Executive* 8(1):7–13.

Darlington, R. B. 1968. Multiple regression in psychological research and practice. *Psychological Bulletin* 69:161–182.

DiMaggio, P. J. 1988. Interest and agency in institutional theory. In *Institutional patterns and organizations: Culture and environment*: ed. L. G. Zucker, 3–22. Cambridge, MA: Ballinger.

DiMaggio, P. J., and W. W. Powell. 1983. The iron cage revisited: Institutional isomorphism and collective rationality in organization fields. *American Sociological Review* 48:147–160.

Donaldson, T., and L. E. Preston. 1995. The stakeholder theory of the corporation: Concepts, evidence, and implications. *Academy of Management Review* 20:65–91.

Dutton, J. E., and R. B. Duncan. 1987. The creation of momentum for change through the process of strategic issue diagnosis. *Strategic Management Journal* 8:279–295.

Edwards, R. 1979. *Contested terrain: The transformation of the workplace in the twentieth century*. New York: Basic Books.

Elsbach, K. D., and R. I. Sutton. 1992. Acquiring organizational legitimacy through illegitimate actions: A marriage of institutional and impression management theories. *Academy of Management Journal* 35:699–738.

Etzioni, A. 1961. *A comparative analysis of complex organizations*. New York: The Free Press.

Etzioni, A. 1988. *The moral dimension*. New York: The Free Press.

Fernandes, M. F., and D. M. Randall. 1992. The nature of social desirability response effects in ethics research. *Business Ethics Quarterly* 2:183–206.

Finkelstein, S., and D. C. Hambrick. 1990. Top-management-team tenure and organizational outcomes: The moderating role of managerial discretion. *Administrative Science Quarterly* 35:484–503.

Finkelstein, S., and D. C. Hambrick. 1996. *Strategic leadership: Top executives and their effects on organizations*. Minneapolis: West Publishing.

Freeman, R. E. 1995. *Presidential address*. Presented at the annual meeting of the Society for Business Ethics, Vancouver, B.C.

Galaskiewicz, J. 1985. Interorganizational relations. *Annual Review of Sociology* 11:281–304.

Goodrick, E., and G. R. Salancik. 1996. Organizational discretion in responding to institutional practices: Hospitals and cesarean births. *Administrative Science Quarterly* 41:1–29.

Gouldner, A. W. 1954. *Patterns of industrial bureaucracy*. New York: The Free Press.

Greening, D. W., and B. Gray. 1994. Testing a model of organizational response to social and political issues. *Academy of Management Journal* 37:467–498.

Haas, R. D. 1994. Ethics in the trenches. *Across the Board* 31(5):12–13.

Hambrick, D. C., and S. Finkelstein. 1987. Managerial discretion: A bridge between polar views of organizational outcomes. In *Research in organizational behavior*, Vol. 9, ed. L. L. Cummings and B. M. Staw, 369–406. Greenwich, CT: JAI Press.

Hambrick, D. C., M. A. Geletkanycz, and J. Fredrickson. 1993. Top executive commitment to the status quo: Some tests of its determinants. *Strategic Management Journal* 14:401–418.

Hambrick, D. C., and P. Mason P. 1984. Upper echelons: The organization as a reflection of its top managers. *Academy of Management Review* 9:193–206.

Hitt, M. A., and B. Tyler. 1991. Strategic decision model: Integrating different perspectives. *Strategic Management Journal* 12:327–351.

Howard, R. 1990. Values make the company: An interview with Robert Haas. *Harvard Business Review* 68(5):132–144.

Hrebiniak, L. G., and W. T. Joyce. 1985. Organizational adaptation: Strategic choice and environmental determinism. *Administrative Science Quarterly* 30:336–349.

Jones, T. M. 1995. Instrumental stakeholder theory: A synthesis of ethics and economics. *Academy of Management Review* 20:404–437.

Lerner, M. J. 1977. The justice motive: Some hypotheses as to its origins and forms. *Journal of Personality* 45:1–52.

Levi Strauss & Co. 1997a. Our culture. http://www.levistrauss.com/hr_culture.html. October 1.

Levi Strauss & Co. 1997b. All about L.S. & Co. http://www.levistrauss.com/all_about.html. October 1.

Levi Strauss & Co. 1997c. Mission, visions, aspirations. http://www.levistrauss.com/lsc_mission.html. October 1.

Light, R. J. 1971. Measures of response agreement for qualitative data: Some generalizations and alternatives. *Psychological Bulletin* 76:365–377.

Meyer, J. W., and B. Rowan. 1977. Institutionalized organizations: Formal structure as myth and ceremony. *American Journal of Sociology* 83:340–363.

Miles, R. H. 1982. *Coffin nails and corporate strategies*. Englewood Cliffs, NJ: Prentice-Hall.

Miller, C. 1997. Marketers weigh effects of sweatshop crackdown. *Marketing News* 31:1,19.

Moorman, R. H., and P. M. Podsakoff. 1992. A meta-analytic review and empirical test of the potential confounding effects of social desirability response sets in organizational behaviour research. *Journal of Occupational and Organizational Psychology* 65:131–149.

Mowday, R. T. 1982. *Employee-organization linkages: The psychology of commitment, absenteeism, and turnover*. New York: Academic Press.

National directory of corporate public affairs. 1994. Washington, DC: Columbia Books.

Oliver, C. 1991. Strategic responses to institutional processes. *Academy of Management Review* 16:145–179.

Ouchi, W. G. 1980. Markets, bureaucracies and clans. *Administrative Science Quarterly* 25:129–41.

Paine, L. S. 1994. Managing for organizational integrity. *Harvard Business Review* 72(2):106–117.

Paine, L. S. 1996. Moral thinking in management: An essential capability. *Business Ethics Quarterly* 6:477–492.

Powell, W. W. 1988. Institutional effects on organizational structure and performance. In *Institutional patterns and organizations*, ed. L. Zucker, 115–136. Cambridge, MA: Ballinger.

Rafalko, R. J. 1994. Remaking the corporation: The 1991 U.S. sentencing guidelines. *Journal of Business Ethics* 13:625–636.

Salancik, G. R. 1979. Interorganizational dependence and responsiveness to affirmative action: The case of women and defense contractors. *Academy of Management Journal* 22:375–394.

Scott, W. R. 1995. *Institutions and organizations*. Thousand Oaks, CA: Sage.

Scott, W. R., and J. M. Meyer. 1991. The rise of training programs in firms and agencies: An institutional perspective. In *Research in organizational behavior*, Vol. 13, ed. B. M. Staw and L. L. Cummings, 297–326. Greenwich, CT: JAI Press.

Sherman, S. 1997. Levi's: As ye sew, so shall ye reap. *Fortune* May 12:104–116.

Simon, H. A. 1957. *Administrative behavior: A study of decision-making processes in administrative organizations*. New York: Macmillan.

Suchman, M. C. 1995. Managing legitimacy: Strategic and institutional approaches. *Academy of Management Review* 20:571–610.

Thomas, J. B., S. M. Clark, and D. A. Gioia. 1993. Strategic sensemaking and organizational performance: Linkages among scanning, interpretation, action and outcomes. *Academy of Management Journal* 36:239–270.

Treviño, L. K. 1990. A cultural perspective on changing and developing organizational ethics. In *Research in organizational change and development*, Vol. 4, ed. R. Woodman and W. Passmore, 195–230. Greenwich, CT: JAI Press.

Treviño, L. K. 1993. The social effects of punishment: A justice perspective. *Academy of Management Review* 17:647–676.

Treviño, L. K., and G. A. Ball. 1992. The social implications of punishing unethical behavior: Observers' cognitive and affective reactions. *Journal of Management* 18:751–769.

United States Sentencing Commission. 1994. *Federal sentencing guidelines manual*. Washington, DC: USSC.

United States Sentencing Commission. 1995. *Corporate crime in America: Strengthening the "good citizen" corporation*. Washington, DC.

Wall Street Journal. 1994. Orange & Rockland hires Robert McGuire for ethics program. October 7:C22.

Wartick, S. L. 1992. The relationship between intense media exposure and change in corporate reputation. *Business and Society* 31(1):33–50.

Weaver, G. R. 1992. Explaining ethical structures: Transaction costs and institutional processes. *Academy of Management Best Papers Proceedings*, pp. 358–362.

Weaver, G. R., L. K. Treviño, and P. L. Cochran. 1999. Corporate ethics practices in the mid-1990s. *Journal of Business Ethics* 18:283–294.

Weber, M. 1947. *The theory of social and economic organization*. Glencoe, IL: The Free Press.

Weick, K. E. 1979. *The social psychology of organizing*. New York: Random House.

Wilkins, A. L., and W. G. Ouchi. 1983. Efficient cultures: Exploring the relationship between culture and organizational performance. *Administrative Science Quarterly* 28:468–481.

Integrated and Decoupled Corporate Social Performance: Management Values, External Pressures, and Corporate Ethics Practices

Chapter 5's analysis of the impetus behind formal ethics programs and their control orientation shows that corporations are subject to multiple pressures to operate in a socially responsible fashion. Some of these influences are external to the company, such as explicit government requirements or more general expectations of social legitimacy (DiMaggio and Powell 1983; Wood 1991). Other influences on socially responsible forms of corporate action are internal to the company, often reflecting the commitments of key managers (Greening and Gray 1994; Miles 1987). Corporations' responses to expectations for responsible behavior often vary (Oliver 1991). In some cases, pressures for social responsibility may generate meaningful changes that are integrated into the regular affairs of the company. In other cases, however, corporate responses to pressures for responsible behavior tend toward "window dressing" in that the responses can be decoupled easily from normal, ongoing organizational activities (Meyer and Rowan 1977).

Our empirical study of Fortune 1000 companies examines how external

This chapter, with minor variations, originally was published in 1999 as G. R. Weaver, L. K. Treviño, and P. L. Cochran, "Integrated and decoupled corporate social performance: Management values, external pressures, and corporate ethics practices," *Academy of Management Journal* 42:539–552. Copyright 1999 by the Academy of Management. Reproduced with permission of the Academy of Management in book format via Copyright Clearance Center.

influences from government, media, and the business community and management commitments to profit making and ethical responsibility work together to determine the integration and decoupling of a specific kind of social performance: formal corporate ethics programs. In this, we build on the analysis reported in Chapter 5, which showed how the scope and control orientations of ethics programs reflect influences from the external institutional environment and from top management's commitment to ethics. In this chapter, however, we consider a broader range of management commitments, and we propose that both external pressures and management's commitments to ethics and to financial and strategic success are responsible for the use of easily decoupled ethics program elements in companies that have ethics programs. We also hypothesize that top management's commitment to ethics is primarily responsible for the use of integrated practices in companies' ethics programs.

CORPORATE ETHICS PROGRAMS: INTEGRATED
AND EASILY DECOUPLED SOCIAL PERFORMANCE

Although corporations can encourage ethical behavior in informal ways (Cohen 1993; Treviño 1990), much effort has been directed toward implementing *formal* programs and policies for guiding ethical behavior in American corporations (Berenbeim 1992; Center for Business Ethics 1992; Weaver, Treviño, and Cochran 1999b). Common elements of corporate ethics programs include training activities, formalized procedures for auditing and evaluating ethical behavior, disciplinary processes for failures to meet ethical expectations, dedicated ethics telephone lines, formal ethics departments and officers, and cross-functional committees for setting and evaluating ethics policies and procedures. Ethics programs ostensibly bring the behavior of organization members into conformity with a shared ethical standard; they constitute a kind of organizational control system that encourages one or both of shared ethical aspirations and compliance with rules (Paine 1994; Weaver and Treviño 1999).

Theory suggests that ethics programs can enhance company performance (Donaldson and Preston 1995; Gatewood and Carroll 1991; Quinn and Jones 1995), usually by bringing an organization's decisions and actions more into conformity with societal ethical expectations. Ethics programs may help to generate legitimacy-enhancing organizational outcomes, a key indicator of corporate social performance (Wartick and Cochran 1985; Wood 1991) and an important contributor to overall organizational success (Ashforth and Gibbs 1990). Ethics programs also can contribute to legitimacy by signaling that the company conforms to societal expectations in its internal organizational processes and structures.

Origins of Corporate Ethics Programs

According to institutional theory (DiMaggio and Powell 1983; Scott 1995), pressures for legitimacy may reside in the explicit demands of societal institutions, such as government agencies (Miles 1987) and the media (Greening and Gray 1994), or in the fact that certain forms of thought or action become taken for granted or infused with intrinsic value (Berger and Luckmann 1967; Selznick 1957). Academic research and practitioner commentary on ethics programs have cited a variety of institutional pressures for ethics programs, including government, media, and fashion-setting members of the business community (Metzger, Dalton, and Hill 1993; United States Sentencing Commission [USSC] 1995; Weaver et al. 1999a).

Treating ethics programs *merely* as legitimacy-preserving responses to external pressures, however, offers an unrealistically constrained view of their origins. Such a view is too deterministic because it ignores the role of managerial choice in organizational decisions (Child 1972, 1997; DiMaggio 1988; Hitt and Tyler 1991). Research on strategic choice suggests that executives' characteristics—including their values and commitments—play an important role in affecting organizational actions (Hambrick and Mason 1984; Hambrick and Finkelstein 1987). Business ethics research also stresses top management's role in influencing organizational ethics practices (Jones 1995; Paine 1996).

Research on corporate social performance grants room for managerial discretion among the factors that influence a company's social performance (Wood 1991). Swanson's theoretical analysis of corporate social performance explicitly argues that management's positive sense of ethical propriety needs to be considered along with more pragmatically focused managerial concerns; some instances of social performance might be instances of "positive duty" rather than merely "negative" efforts to avoid sanctions (Swanson 1995, 48). Managers should be viewed as taking ethical considerations into account in their ordinary, everyday decisions and actions (Freeman 1995). Executives sometimes take a particular stance toward ethics programs because doing so is presumed to enhance or maintain organizational legitimacy and thus contribute to the "bottom line" by securing the support of key institutional actors. Executives' stances toward ethics programs, however, *also* can reflect their own commitment to responsible, ethical behavior as an end in itself. Thus, our study considers the influence of both management's commitment to financial and strategic concerns and management's commitment to ethics on the integration and decoupling of formal corporate ethics programs.

Integrated and Easily Decoupled Ethics Programs

Often a wide gulf can separate line managers and the task-related core of an organization from staff functions developed in response to external pressures (Pfeffer and Salancik 1978). For example, Greening and Gray (1994) observed that some companies' environmental assessment programs influence planning and line management, whereas other companies' programs are decoupled from these everyday organizational activities. *Integrated* structures and policies affect everyday decisions and actions; decisions are made in light of the policy, and persons occupying the specialized structure have the confidence of and regular interaction with other departments and their managers. An integrated structure or policy is likely to be supported by other organizational policies and programs. Thus, managers and employees are held accountable to it, take note of it, and see it as having a valued role in the organization's operations. But not every organizational structure or policy that develops in response to external pressures will be integrated into everyday decisions and actions. Some structures can be decoupled easily. Although with the proper supports they might have an impact on an organization, they also can be marginalized or disconnected from the everyday workings of the organization. Such decoupling is likely to occur when demands of institutional legitimacy appear to conflict with other organizational goals (Meyer and Rowan 1977). An *easily decoupled* structure or policy provides the appearance of conformity to external expectations while making it easy to insulate much of the organization from those expectations. Although the structure or policy exists, it does not guarantee regular interaction with other organizational policies and functions or employee accountability to it.

Easily Decoupled Ethics Practices: Policy Communications.   Ethics programs can vary in the extent to which they are integrated or easily decoupled, even among companies that have ethics codes, telephone lines, ethics officers, and other basic elements of an ethics program. For example, at a major financial services firm, we observed a meeting of about twenty-five middle managers in which the company's general counsel—formally charged with responsibility for ethics and legal compliance issues—distributed copies of several of the company's ethics policy documents to the middle managers. The general counsel inquired about whether the middle managers ever had heard of or seen these policies before. *Every* middle manager denied prior knowledge of the policies. In fact, however, each of them had signed a copy of each policy as a condition of employment. In this organization, even though basic elements of an ethics program were in place, some elements were decoupled from the everyday thinking of ordinary managers. Taken by itself, this company's policy lacks the kind of attributes and support (for example, accountability mechanisms) that encourage salience in the minds of employees.

Easy decoupling seems particularly likely in the case of company efforts to communicate an ethics message to employees through memos, reminders, and policy documents—an ethics program practice among those most commonly used by businesses (Berenbeim 1992; Center for Business Ethics 1992). Employees receive many, sometimes conflicting, communications about what is important in their organizations. Ethics-oriented communications may be presented without any sense that the message is relevant to the responsibilities and goals of individual employees in their particular organizational circumstances. Such personally irrelevant communications are unlikely to trigger attention on the part of employees (Petty and Cacioppo 1986). Therefore, by themselves, memos and reminders about ethics may be perceived by employees as distractions to be skimmed (at best), "filed," and forgotten. In some companies, ethics communications may have an impact because other supporting mechanisms either reinforce or hold employees accountable to the "ethics message." In themselves, however, ethics policy communications are more easily decoupled than are other ethics program practices.

Integrated Ethics Program Practices: Ethics-oriented Performance Appraisal. By contrast, some companies' ethics programs and policies are linked more strongly to everyday organizational activities (Cohen 1993; Metzger, Dalton, and Hill 1993; Weber 1993). Reward systems may reinforce the message of the ethics program (Treviño 1990), especially if ethics concerns are made a part of regular performance appraisals. For example, at a health care products company we examined, one third of *every* manager's annual raise depends on a performance appraisal focused on how well the manager carries out the company's ethical ideals (as evaluated by superiors, peers, and subordinates). Although such an evaluative practice raises questions of subjectivity in appraisal, the practice defines conduct in accordance with ethical values as an identifiable part of employees' expected behavior. Including concern for ethics in performance appraisals creates accountability to and salience for ethical expectations by linking ethics to important personal consequences.

HYPOTHESES

External Influences on Ethics Program Integration and Decoupling

Expectations for legitimacy-enhancing corporate structures and behavior can arise from multiple sources. We focus on explicit pressure from relatively entrenched, influential, and pervasive elements of the external environment: government and the news media (for example, Greening and Gray 1994; Meznar and Nigh 1995; Miles 1987; Wartick 1992). We also consider the influence of standard setters from the business environment on corporate ethics practices (DiMaggio and Powell 1983; Abrahamson 1996).

Government. In 1991, the USSC implemented sentencing guidelines for organizations convicted of violating federal law (USSC 1994). Academic and practitioner observers have credited the guidelines with encouraging the development of corporate ethics programs (Metzger, Dalton, and Hill 1993; USSC 1995). The guidelines offer the prospect of greatly reduced fines and penalties to convicted organizations that can demonstrate formal attempts to guide their own behavior toward legal compliance. Despite their potential impact, the guidelines have not entered the consciousness of all executives equally. For example, the chief counsel at a major bank confided to us that he knew nothing of the guidelines, even though they had been adopted four years earlier. Therefore, we should not be surprised that executives' awareness of the guidelines varies across organizations.

The more key decision makers are aware of the USSC guidelines' stipulations and incentives, the more we should find an organization implementing at least the easily decoupled elements of ethics programs. In part, this is because the guidelines specifically mention easily decoupled practices like policy communication; providing policy communications is a way to "check off" one of the USSC's criteria for proactive efforts to ensure proper behavior. Communications about ethics policy also provide inexpensive but easily documented ways to demonstrate that a company is "doing something" about ethics and legal compliance. Codes of ethics and other formal ethics communications can be distributed to institutional actors, and records can be kept to document how often employees receive these communications. Yet the communications themselves can be decoupled, if necessary, to preserve the autonomy of other aspects of the organization's everyday processes.

> HYPOTHESIS 1: The more a company's top management is aware of the USSC guidelines, the more the company's formal ethics program will incorporate easily decoupled practices (for example, policy communication).

Negative Media Attention. Critical media attention prompts organizations to respond in ways that will preserve or restore their legitimacy (Ashforth and Gibbs 1990; Greening and Gray 1994; Wartick 1992). Corporations may respond to media scrutiny of their ethical failings by adopting one or more elements of a formal ethics program to demonstrate their intentions for future good behavior. For example, recent ethical and legal scandals at the health care firm Columbia/HCA prompted the introduction of a formal ethics office in late 1997, headed by a well-known veteran of the defense fraud cleanup of the 1980s (Pasztor and Lagnado 1997). Negative media attention, however, might not correspond to genuine organizational problems. Moreover, even when a company's failings are real, management's priorities may dictate that the company respond with policies and programs that look good to outside observers but that can be decoupled, if necessary, from the day-to-day activities of the company. Given these possibilities, we expect critical media attention to influence the development of easily decoupled ethics program practices. Something must be done to placate media critics, but because media demands do not necessarily reflect real problems or mesh well with organizational goals, responses are likely to be of the easily decoupled sort.

> HYPOTHESIS 2: The more negative media attention a company receives for real or alleged ethical failures, the more the company's

formal ethics program will incorporate easily decoupled practices (for example, policy communication).

Business Standard Setters. Institutional theory shows that business organizations imitate each other and also are influenced by standard setters who set criteria for good business practice (DiMaggio and Powell 1983; Abrahamson 1996). These standard setters include high-profile consultants, business schools, business publications, and professional and business associations. In regard to setting standards for ethics practices, the Conference Board—a high-profile business association—has been particularly active. The Conference Board's annual ethics meetings typically are attended by several hundred mid- to high-level executives who come to learn about what their organizations might do to encourage ethical behavior. We have attended six recent annual meetings, during which emphasis was given to practices like ethics communications. Thus, we would expect that a company's attendance at Conference Board meetings would encourage it to adopt more extensive efforts to communicate ethics policy to employees. By doing so, the company demonstrates conformity to currently accepted good business practice; but we also expect Conference Board attendance to affect ethics policy communications because such communications can be decoupled easily from other organizational processes. It may be important to insiders and outsiders for a business to look "up-to-date" in regard to currently fashionable business practices, but pressures to look current might not mesh well with an organization's normal practices and day-to-day task-related needs.

HYPOTHESIS 3: A company's presence at Conference Board ethics meetings will be positively associated with the use of easily decoupled practices (for example, policy communication) in the company's formal ethics program.

Management Commitments and Ethics Program: Integration and Decoupling

The fact that ethical behavior can be valued both for its own sake *and* for instrumental, legitimacy-enhancing reasons suggests that management's concern for ethics itself and for strategic, financial, and operational success both should influence ethics program characteristics.

Management's Commitment to Financial and Strategic Performance. Business executives are expected to be committed to the financial, strategic, and operational success of their organizations. Given the business benefits of conformity to institutional pressures (Wood 1991), management's concern for "bottom line" issues entails an instrumental interest in ethics programs. Commitment to financial, strategic, and operational performance should favor those elements of ethics programs that symbolize conformity to institutional pressures while allowing management the possibility of independence from those pressures. Top management's normal commitment to financial success, in short, is likely to encourage the adoption of easily decoupled ethics program practices. Easily decoupled practices signify a concern for ethics—thus contributing to enhanced legitimacy—but if necessary they can be decoupled, thereby maximizing management discretion in pursuit of strategic and financial goals.

> HYPOTHESIS 4: The more a company's top management is committed to financial, strategic, and operational concerns, the more the company's formal ethics program will incorporate easily decoupled practices (for example, policy communication).

Management's Commitment to Ethics. In addition to commitments to typical financial, strategic, and operational concerns, top managers also may be committed to ethics for its own sake (as discussed already). Executives with this kind of outlook periodically are featured in the business press, for example, Robert Haas of Levi Strauss (Haas 1994) or Tom Chappell of Tom's of Maine (McCune 1997). Such executives express concern for integrity, fair treatment of others, and "doing the right thing" for their own sake, not merely for the instrumental benefits of such behavior. This kind of executive commitment to ethics should influence organizational characteristics for several reasons. Other managers—including those who manage ethics programs—may adopt top management's outlook through processes of social learning; top management sets standards for reward and punishment that help to define acceptable behavior (Treviño and Youngblood 1990). The language used by top management helps to create an interpretive framework that can highlight the importance of ethical issues (Baucus and Rechner 1995), and top managers contribute to defining the organizational culture by their own behavior (Treviño 1990). Minimally, such executives are likely to wish to communicate their commitment to ethics through a variety of means. Thus, we should expect such executives to support ethics program communication activities, even though those activities could, in some situations, easily be decoupled.

HYPOTHESIS 5: The more a company's top management is committed to ethics, the more the company's formal ethics program will incorporate easily decoupled practices (for example, policy communication).

We also expect these executives to "follow through" on their commitment to ethics in ways that will capture the attention of employees, holding employees accountable to ethical expectations. They will define ethical roles not only through ethics policy documents, memos, and other communications but also through more deeply embedded organizational activities whose implications are difficult to avoid. Thus, executive commitment to ethics should encourage practices such as the explicit inclusion of ethical concerns into regular employee performance appraisals, as occurred at the health care products firm described earlier. Such practices give the company's ethics policy a more substantive role in the organization. The personal relevance such a practice presents to employees is important for getting employees to focus on the content of the organization's ethical standards (Petty and Cacioppo 1986). Practices like ethics-related performance appraisals integrate ethics expectations into regular organizational activities because they make concern for ethics part of employees' formal role identities and make business ethics relevant to outcomes that are personally important to employees.

HYPOTHESIS 6: The more a company's top management is committed to ethics, the more the company's formal ethics program will incorporate integrated practices (for example, ethics-oriented performance appraisals).

METHODS

Population and Data

We focused our data collection on the Fortune 500 service and 500 industrials (using the 1994 listing). We obtained data from a survey of officers

each company identified as responsible for any ethics practices and programs in the company; a database of American newspaper article abstracts
for 1989 to 1994; and registration lists for Conference Board's ethics meetings. This is the same data set used in our earlier study of ethics program
scope and control orientation (Weaver et al. 1999a; this volume, Chapter 5),
but the present study focuses on a particular subset of the total sample, is
focused on different dependent variables, and uses a different combination of independent variables.

We wanted to get the most accurate perspective possible on the types of
ethics practices companies were using. Thus, we sought to identify the most
informed respondent at each of the one thousand companies (cf. Thomas,
Clark, and Gioia 1993). We used the *National Directory of Corporate Public
Affairs* (1994 edition) to contact the public affairs or corporate communications office of each of the one thousand companies. Using a standard script
for telephone calls, we asked a representative from this office to identify
the "officer most responsible for dealing with ethics and conduct issues in
the company." (If a company was not listed in the *National Directory of
Corporate Public Affairs*, we called the human resources office.) This process
produced a 990-firm mailing list.

In late 1994, each of the 990 officers we identified was sent a survey and
(if necessary) one or two follow-up mailings. We received 254 surveys in
response (26 percent). Given the generally high rank of respondents (57
percent vice presidents or higher), this is an acceptable response rate
(Hambrick, Geletkancyz, and Fredrickson 1993). Average time with present
employer was fifteen years (standard deviation [SD] = 8.4); average time in
present position was 5 years (SD = 4.4).

We did not expect all of these companies to have a formal ethics program.
In some cases, for example, the officer we were able to identify was merely
the one to whom responsibility for ethics and conduct issues defaulted, and
many of the 254 companies in our original sample were engaged in almost
no formal ethics activity. More than a fifth, for example, *at most* had a company code of ethics. Because our questions concerning the integration and
decoupling of ethics programs make sense only in the context of companies
that actually have ethics program elements, we needed to select from among
the respondents those companies that had formal ethics programs. Our survey included five yes/no questions we used to indicate how much a company
was involved in the typical "basics" of formal ethics programs: (1) Does the

company have an official ethics policy? (2) Has the company formally assigned an officer specifically to deal with ethics and conduct issues? (3) Has the company created an ethics committee? (4) Has the company created a specific department to deal with ethics issues? (5) Does the company have a dedicated telephone line for employees to make inquiries or complaints about ethics issues? We summed each company's responses to provide an overall measure of the extent to which the company had adopted the typical basic elements of a formal ethics program (mean = 2.71, SD = 1.32, range = 0 to 5). To ensure that we were examining integration issues in the context of established ethics programs, we limited analyses concerning the integration of ethics programs to the subsample of 128 companies scoring at or above the mean on this index of formal ethics activity.

Nonresponse and Bias Issues

We found no significant difference in response rates for service and industrial companies. Responding companies included ninety-nine different three-digit standard industrial classifications (SICs), indicating that we tapped a wide range of industries. We compared respondents with a roughly equal number of randomly chosen nonrespondents on gross revenue, net profit, total assets, return on sales, and return on assets. No significant differences were found. We also compared respondents and nonrespondents in terms of their size (number of employees). We found no significant differences after removing three large outliers.

Companies with little or no formal ethics activity might be reluctant to respond to a survey about ethics practices. Our interest, however, is in companies that are doing at least "the basics" of formal ethics management. Thus, if largely inactive companies do not respond, that does not affect our results. Even so, as we noted earlier, a fifth of responding companies did little or nothing to manage ethics formally, having at most a company code of ethics but engaging in no other supporting activity. Thus, we do not believe our survey questions precluded responses from companies that are less active in managing ethics.

Biased responses more likely are a concern in regard to individual informants' answers to questions about particular ethics practices. We sought to reduce the potential for socially desirable responses to individual items by indicating that our questionnaire was not focused on companies' successes or failures but on how companies adjust their ethics programs to different circumstances. Also, most of our informants were not full-time ethics officers; rather, they invested only a portion of their energies in ethics-related matters. Thus, most respondents' organizational identity does not depend on ethics-related activities.

Dependent Variable Measures

Easily Decoupled Ethics Practice: Policy Communications. We measured the use of ethics policy communication practices by asking our ethics-responsible informants to assess the frequency that "communications that remind them about ethics and conduct issues" are received by employees at four ranks: (1) high-level management (that is, vice presidents and higher), (2) middle management, (3) low-level management and supervisory personnel, and (4) nonsupervisory employees (clerical, skilled labor, etc.); 5-point Likert scale anchored "not at all," "only at hiring," "every few years," "every year," "two times per year" (Cronbach's alpha = 0.90). We focused on the *frequency* of communications because of our predictions that more external pressure will generate more of these easily decoupled responses. More pressure means companies churn out ethics-related communications more frequently.

Integrated Ethics Practice: Ethics-oriented Performance Appraisals. We measured the use of ethics-oriented performance appraisals with three 5-point Likert items, asking our ethics-responsible informants whether "assessment of ethics is a formal part of performance appraisals," "people get formally evaluated on the ethics of their behavior," and "supervisors are asked to formally assess the ethical performance of their people" (Cronbach's alpha = 0.82).

Independent Variable Measures

Management Awareness of USSC Guidelines. Four five-point Likert items (strongly agree/strongly disagree) assessed managers' awareness of and familiarity with the USSC guidelines (Cronbach's alpha = 0.78). These items measured whether executive meetings and communications discussed the impact of the guidelines, along with the respondent's self-assessed personal familiarity with the guidelines and sense that USSC requirements informed company ethics practices (e.g., "High-level managers in this firm have discussed the 1991 U.S. Sentencing Corporate Guidelines"; "Internal company communications have addressed the impact of the 1991 U.S.

Sentencing Corporate guidelines"; "I am familiar with the 1991 U.S. Sentencing Corporation Guidelines"; "The firm's ethics policies and activities developed in response to the 1991 U.S. Corporate Sentencing Guidelines."). Data indicate variance in awareness among companies in the study (mean = 3.59, SD = 1.03).

Negative Media Attention. We counted newspaper article abstracts appearing in the *Newspaper Abstracts* database from early 1989 (the start of the database) through October 1994 (the start of our survey period). Two research assistants were trained to follow common written guidelines in searching for article abstracts suggesting either (1) violations of law (e.g., discrimination in hiring/firing, fraud, and so on), (2) threat to the general public (for example, safety failures), (3) ruthless or deceptive business practices, or (4) hints of real but undisclosed impropriety (for example, suicide of an executive at a company under government investigation). One of the authors repeated the search for 10 percent of the companies evaluated by each research assistant. Interrater agreement (using the relatively conservative P-statistic (Light 1971)) was 70 percent between the author and one of the assistants and 71 percent with the other assistant.

Presence at Conference Board Ethics Meetings. We measured company attendance at the Conference Board's annual ethics meetings held before the administration of our survey using conference registration lists for 1992, 1993, and 1994. We counted a company as exposed to this standard-setting influence if it appeared on the registration list for one or more of these conferences. We used the three-year period to allow for the fact that such a standard-setting influence may be effective even though companies may not participate every year.

Top Management Commitments. Executives' language is an important element in the social learning process influencing subordinates' behavior and organizational norms (Ford and Ford 1995), and so top management commitments expressed verbally are likely to have an important role in shaping organizational action. We relied on informed observers to report the informal conversation topics focused on by top management. This informant-based method also is advisable because, if asked directly, most executives no doubt would express strong commitment to ethics and to their obvious responsibilities for financial and strategic concerns. Focusing on a behavioral phenomenon like conversation topics and using a third-party observer will remove some of the social pressure attached to questions about deeper commitments. Yet the amount of time executives spend discussing various topics should be a good indication of the concerns to which executives have committed themselves. Moreover, our responding ethics-responsible officers are more likely than other high-level officers to have a realistic view of senior management's attention to ethics than senior management itself; top management commitment to ethics—or its absence—should be salient to ethics-responsible officers.

Our responding ethics-responsible officers were asked to indicate "the overall business orientation of your firm's top management by [rating] the extent to which various subjects are a topic of conversation for your firm's top management team (i.e., executive vice presidents and higher)." Five-point Likert-scale answers ranged from "never" to "very frequently," with higher frequency interpreted by us as a sign of greater concern for and commitment to the topic. We offered respondents a list of possible conversation topics intended to indicate commitment to ethics (for example, "doing the right thing," "seeking the good of society," "treating people fairly," "the company's role in society," "valuing integrity as much as profits") and commitment to financial, strategic, and operational matters (for example, "financial performance," "strategy and planning," "stockholders and investors," "productivity and efficiency"). We avoided any hint of instrumental ("good ethics is good business") thinking in the ethics items, focusing instead on intrinsic concern for ethics. Principal components factor analysis, with varimax rotation, yielded the expected two factors explaining 60 percent of variance (Table 6.1; Cronbach's alpha = 0.85 for ethics, 0.68 for finance/strategy/operations). The lower Cronbach's alpha for financial and strategic commitment likely reflects the diverse range of topics included in the measure.

Control Variables. We controlled for the potential effects of financial performance and size. Financial performance was measured as return on assets relative to industry return on assets over fiscal years 1992 through 1994, defining industry at the two-digit SIC level. On this ratio measure, a firm that is at the mean performance level for its industry scores 1.0. Data were obtained from *Compact Disclosure.* Size was measured as number of employees, with data obtained from the Fortune 500 listings.

TABLE 6.1
Factor Loadings for Top Management Commitments

Items	Factor 1 (Commitment to Ethics)	Factor 2 (Commitment to Finance & Strategy)
Seeking the good of society	0.80	0.10
Doing the right thing	0.79	0.28
Treating people fairly	0.77	0.23
The company's role in society	0.76	0.08
Valuing integrity as much as profits	0.72	0.28
Financial performance	0.07	0.77
Stockholders and investors	0.12	0.73
Strategy and planning	0.28	0.71
Productivity and efficiency	0.23	0.62
Eigenvalue	3.98	1.38

Analyses. We carried out an omnibus test of significance for the overall model in light of the potential for significant correlations among the dependent variables (Wilks lambda = 0.57; F = 5.76; probability, or $p \leq$ 0.01). We then tested hypotheses for each dependent variable in hierarchical regressions, in which controls were entered first as a block, followed by a block with the hypothesized independent variables.

RESULTS

Table 6.2 provides means, SD, and correlations for all variables.

Table 6.3 provides results for influences on the use of communication practices in ethics programs. The control variables did not show a significant relationship to the dependent variable (equation 1; adjusted R^2 = 0.01, F = 0.22, nonsignificant [NS]). The complete model (equation 2) was significant and explained 19 percent of variance (adjusted R^2 = 0.19, F = 4.72, $p \leq$ 0.01). Significant independent variables were top management's concern for financial and strategic matters (t = 1.98, $p \leq$ 0.05), management

TABLE 6.2

Descriptive Statistics and Correlations

Variable	Mean	SD	α	1	2	3	4	5	6	7	8
1 Ethics policy communication (easily decoupled)	4.01	0.82	0.90	1.00							
2 Ethics-oriented performance appraisal (integrated)	2.90	1.05	0.82	0.14	1.00						
3 Top management commitment to financial, strategic & operational concerns	4.55	0.50	0.68	0.23*	0.17	1.00					
4 Top management's commitment to ethics	3.61	0.78	0.85	0.11	0.44**	0.49**	1.00				
5 Management's awareness of USSC guidelines	3.59	1.03	0.78	0.28*	0.15	0.09	0.06	1.00			
6 Media attention to company's ethical failings	30.03	52.92	—	0.22*	0.10	0.19*	0.18*	0.07	1.00		
7 Company's attendance at Conference Board	0.35	0.48	—	0.33*	0.12	−0.03	0.07	0.20*	0.21*	1.00	
8 Size (no. of employees)	33745	58768	—	0.10	0.16	0.05	0.07	−0.03	0.41*	0.12	1.00
9 Financial performance (3-year average, company ROA/industry ROA)	0.97	6.03	—	−0.10	−0.06	−0.06	0.00	0.00	−0.07	0.04	0.03

SD, standard deviation; USSC, United States Sentencing Commission; ROA, Return on Assets.

Usable N ranges from 121 to 128.

$* p \leq .05$ $** p \leq 0.01$

awareness of the USSC guidelines ($t = 2.24$, $p \leq 0.05$), and company attendance at Conference Board ethics meetings ($t = 3.48$, $p \leq 0.01$). Thus, support is provided for hypotheses 1, 3, and 4.

Table 6.3 also offers results for influences on attention to ethics in performance appraisals. The control variables had no significant relationship to the dependent variable (equation 1; adjusted $R^2 = 0.02$, $F = 1.95$, NS). The complete model was significant (equation 2; adjusted $R^2 = 0.24$, $F = 12.26$, $p \leq 0.01$). Top management's commitment to ethics was associated significantly with the use of ethics-oriented performance appraisals ($t = 5.64$, $p \leq 0.01$). This supports hypothesis 6.

DISCUSSION

Corporate responses to expectations for social performance can be decoupled from or strongly integrated with regular organizational activities. This study adds to our understanding of socially responsible corporate processes and outcomes by showing how external expectations of legitimacy and top management's commitments to ethics and to financial, operational, and strategic concerns lead to integrated and easily decoupled forms of corporate social performance.

Major Findings

The results supported most of the hypotheses and the general notion that external factors are more likely to influence the development of easily decoupled ethics program practices, such as ethics policy communications, whereas top management's commitment to ethics is required for more integrated ethics program practices, such as ethics-oriented performance appraisals. Several other aspects of our findings present interesting lessons and questions for our understanding of why corporations resort to easily decoupled or integrated responses to expectations for responsible action and of the relationship between top management's commitment to ethics and its concern for financial and strategic matters.

Easily Decoupled Ethics Program Practices. Top management's awareness of the USSC guidelines was positively associated with ethics policy communications, an easily decoupled practice. Company attendance at Conference Board meetings, where ethics communication practices are endorsed, also was positively associated with the frequent use of ethics policy communica-

TABLE 6.3
Hierarchical Regression Results for Ethics Communications
and Ethics-oriented Performance Appraisal

| | Ethics Communications (easily decoupled) | | | | | |
| | EQUATION 1 | | | EQUATION 2 | | |
Independent Variables	*b*	*s.e.b.*	*beta*	*b*	*s.e.b.*	*beta*
Constant	4.00**	0.09		1.92*	0.67	
Size of company	0.00	0.00	0.11	0.00	0.00	0.05
Financial performance	−0.02	0.01	−0.12	−0.02	0.01	−0.12
Top management's commitment to ethics				−0.04	0.11	−0.04
Top management's commitment to financial, strategic, & operational concerns				0.32*	0.16	0.20*
Management's awareness of USSC guidelines				0.16*	0.07	0.20*
Media attention to company's ethical failings				0.00	0.00	0.06
Company's attendance at Conference Board				0.52**	0.15	0.31**
R^2		0.03			0.24	
Adjusted R^2		0.01			0.19	
F		0.22			4.72**	
df		2,108			7,103	
ΔR^{2a}					0.22	
$F \Delta R^2$					5.85**	

tions. By contrast, negative media attention only showed significant bivariate correlational relationships to ethics policy communications. A significant role in a regression model might have occurred in a larger sample. In the interim, this suggests further study of when, why, and how businesses respond to media attention.

Top management's commitment to financial and strategic concerns also was related significantly to ethics policy communications. Management may see financial and strategic advantage in these easily decoupled ethics pro-

TABLE 6.3 *(continued)*

Ethics-oriented Performance Appraisal (integrated)

EQUATION 1			EQUATION 2			EQUATION 3		
b	*s.e.b.*	*beta*	*b*	*s.e.b.*	*beta*	*b*	*s.e.b.*	*beta*
2.83**	0.12		0.55	0.42		−0.15	0.50	
0.00†	0.00	0.17†	0.00	0.00	0.13	0.00	0.00	0.19
−0.01	0.02	0.07	−0.01	0.01	−0.07	−0.02	0.01	−0.09
			0.65**	0.42	0.47**	0.66**	0.12	0.48**
						0.19*	0.09	0.18*
						0.00	0.00	−0.14
						0.12	0.19	0.06
	0.04			0.26			0.30	
	0.02			0.24			0.26	
	1.95			12.26**			7.51**	
	2,108			3,103			4,106	
				0.22			0.05	
				31.78**			9.96†	

N = 110 (listwise deletion) .

[a] Reported ΔR^2 may include rounding errors.

**$p \leq 0.01$ *$p \leq 0.05$ †$p \leq 0.10$.

gram practices. Interestingly, top management's commitment to ethics itself was not correlated significantly with ethics program communication practices (r = 0.11, NS). This is unexpected in light of our initial argument for hypothesis 5, but it reinforces the more general conclusion that easily decoupled communication practices owe their origins more to their instru-

mental value for dealing with external pressures, whereas integrated practices reflect primarily top management's commitment to ethics. Given the
existence of external pressures for responsible, ethical behavior, companies
simply may be adopting easily decoupled practices irrespective of top management's commitment to ethics.

Integrated Ethics Practices. Our findings support theoretical claims that senior management's personal commitment to ethics is an essential part of
what drives organizations to proactive socially responsible performance
(Jones 1995; Swanson 1995). Although we detected no bivariate correlations
between the use of ethics performance appraisals and any of the tested external pressures, we also conducted exploratory post hoc regression analysis on
these independent variables (Table 6.3, equation 3). A model that includes all
the external pressures as predictors of ethics-oriented performance
appraisal produced a small, marginally significant increase in explained
variance (change in R^2 = 0.05, $p \le$ 0.10). Among the external pressures, only
USSC awareness showed a significant relationship to the use of ethics-oriented performance appraisals. A different analysis, in which we considered
only USSC awareness along with top management's commitment to ethics,
showed a significant but even smaller role for USSC awareness (change in R^2
= 0.03, F = 4.57, $p \le$ 0.05). In other analyses, we varied the order of entry of
top management's commitment to ethics and USSC awareness to assess the
unique contribution to explained variance of each variable (that is, usefulness analysis) (Darlington 1968). Executive commitment to ethics played a
far larger role in explaining the use of ethics-oriented performance appraisal
(21 percent of variance uniquely explained) than did USSC awareness (3 percent of variance uniquely explained). Relatively specific external pressures
for social performance, like the USSC guidelines, may have some influence
on integrated social performance, but that influence remains small compared with top management's commitment to ethics.

Study Limitations

Some of our findings are based on cross-sectional data. Thus, even though
our theory argues for causal relationships between the independent and
dependent variables, we must be careful to consider the possibility of
reverse causality; however, we think this possibility is minimal. In the case
of the USSC guidelines, our experience in examining corporate ethics programs indicates that ethics policies and practices seldom, if ever, make

specific reference to the USSC requirements. Thus, we think it unlikely that the presence of particular ethics program practices would make managers more aware of the guidelines. Data on media attention to companies' ethical failings, and on Conference Board attendance, were drawn from years prior to our survey, and so possibilities of reverse causality do not arise.

Could ethics program practices influence the content of top-management conversation? We find no reason to think so in regard to financial and strategic conversation topics; but might executives be talking about ethics because external pressure has led to creation of an ethics program? We think the possibility is slight. Specifically, our data show that external pressures influenced only easily decoupled ethics program practices. True, such practices may involve periodic formal communiqués from the chief executive officer (CEO) to all employees, but why should these communiqués generate an increase in the ethics content of everyday conversation among senior executives? Theoretically, the most reasonable explanation for the relationship between top management's ethics commitment and an organization's use of ethics-oriented performance appraisals is that the former leads to the latter. This is especially so in light of the fact that ethics-oriented performance appraisal shows no significant correlation to the tested external pressures (Table 6.2). Thus, whereas we grant that reverse causality is a possibility, we think it unlikely.

Our results are based on data obtained from relatively large U.S. companies. Thus, it may not be possible to generalize these findings to smaller companies or to other institutional environments. We also note limits on reliability for our measure of interrater agreement in coding newspaper abstracts (70 percent and 71 percent). This may be due to the sheer volume of abstracts to consider in a study such as this and the often brief or ambiguous content of them. Low reliability (0.68) also may have reduced our ability to detect relationships involving management's commitment to financial, operational, and strategic concerns. Finally, we note that a larger sample size may have shown more or stronger relationships, especially in the regression analysis for the impact of negative media attention on ethics program characteristics.

Implications

The study affirms the importance of distinguishing between easily decoupled and integrated forms of responsible corporate behavior. It also recognizes that a general type of responsible behavior (that is, an ethics program) can embody elements of both and that those elements reflect different external and managerial influences. Researchers investigating the sources of social performance must be careful to delineate the role and limits of institutional pressures and managerial discretion.

Our study shows the importance of directing more attention to executives insofar as they are guided by a sense of "positive duty" (Swanson 1995) toward ethical and socially responsible behavior. Results suggest that efforts to separate matters of ethics and social responsibility from conventional business thinking not only are problematic in theory (Freeman 1995), but they also may fail to do justice to the everyday thought and action of managers. Although much research attention is directed toward showing that socially responsible corporate behavior can contribute to financial success, researchers may do a disservice to managers if they ignore the extent to which managers' decisions also are guided by intrinsic concern for ethics and social responsibility. At many of the companies in our study, executives do talk about ethical responsibilities as part of their everyday work (mean = 3.61), and that focus in turn affects important organizational processes like the design of performance appraisal systems. This outlook also is supported by our bivariate correlational results, which show a significant positive relationship between top management's commitment to ethics and to financial and strategic concerns ($r = 0.49, p \leq 0.01$, Table 6.2). Thus, research should pay more attention to the role of the manager as a moral actor on the corporate stage (Paine 1996) and not assume that most responsible corporate behavior is *only* a matter of satisfying institutional pressures for legitimacy.

Some responses to expectations for socially responsible corporate behavior may be difficult to categorize clearly as integrated or decoupled. In the case of ethics programs, for example, punishment of violators—a practice encouraged by the USSC guidelines—is a case in point. Punishment for ethics violations sometimes can increase the salience of a company's ethics standards and satisfy employees' expectations for justice (Treviño 1992), but punishment also can be carried out in decoupled fashion. An employee may be treated as a scapegoat to be "sacrificed" to public demands that something be done to remedy a company's ethical failings. Punishment in the form of scapegoating may do little to make employees more concerned for ethics and might associate the ethics program with procedural or distributive injustices. To assess more clearly the influences on, and impact of, decoupled and integrated corporate responses to expectations for socially responsible behavior, future research should address the different ways in which integration and decoupling may occur. This affords an opportunity to link research on corporate social performance with areas of organizational inquiry that address the ways organizations respond to external expectations (for example, institutional theory) and the ways observers make sense of organizational actions (for example, research on sense making and on symbolic interaction).

For managers, the study indicates that they hold important, or even primary, responsibility for the integration of responsible corporate processes into the organization's everyday activities. Without a commitment by top management to ethics, a company's ethics practices may be the kind that employees easily can ignore. This also suggests that concern for ethics or other forms of social performance cannot merely be delegated; executive commitment is essential. Thus, if executives are serious about corporate social performance, they may need to rethink their personal role in the corporate social performance equation.

For policy makers, the role of the Conference Board (or similar organizations) is worth noting. New forms of socially responsible corporate behavior may face a legitimacy problem themselves until they are endorsed by high-profile, fashion-setting members of the business community. Government agencies and other institutions are advised to focus their energies on these high-profile organizations in their efforts to encourage responsible corporate behavior. They also clearly need to get the attention and commitment of executives if policy initiatives and public pressures are to generate organizationally integrated responses in the corporate world. This is in keeping with findings of other studies of corporate responses to expectations for social performance, such as work/family initiatives (Kossek, Dass, and DeMarr 1994). When it comes to encouraging responsible corporate behavior, formal public policies may be limited in reach, and the role of executive commitment cannot be ignored. Policy makers, then, need to think more in terms of forming cooperative partnerships with the executives whose commitment will make a crucial difference to the ultimate integration of socially responsible ideals with routine organizational activities.

Of course, even if elements of formal ethics programs are closely integrated with other, routine organizational policies and practices (such as performance appraisals), there remains the possibility that their outcomes might not always be what we would like them to be or that their influence in an organization is affected by a multitude of other factors. So it is not enough to understand the sources of ethics programs and their variations. It is also important to understand how they affect behavior in organizations and how that influence in turn is affected by other organizational phenomena. This is the task of Part III of the book, and we now turn to it.

References

Abrahamson, E. 1996. Management fashion. *Academy of Management Review* 21:254–285.

Ashforth, B. E., and B. W. Gibbs. 1990. The double-edge of organizational legitimation. *Organization Science* 1:177–194.

Baucus, M. S., and P. L. Rechner. 1995. Framing and reframing: A process model of ethical decision making. *International Association for Business and Society 1995 Proceedings*: pp. 2–7.

Berenbeim, R. 1992. *Corporate ethics practices*. New York: The Conference Board.

Berger, P. L., and T. Luckmann. 1967. *The social construction of reality*. New York: Doubleday.

Center for Business Ethics. 1992. Instilling ethical values in large corporations. *Journal of Business Ethics* 11:863–867.

Child, J. 1972. Organizational structure, environment, and performance. *Sociology* 6:1–22.

Child, J. 1997. Strategic choice in the analysis of action, structure, organizations and environment: Retrospect and prospect. *Organization Studies* 18:43–76.

Cohen, D. V. 1993. Creating and maintaining ethical work climates. *Business Ethics Quarterly* 3:343–358.

Darlington, R. B. 1968. Multiple regression in psychological research and practice. *Psychological Bulletin* 69:161–182.

DiMaggio, P. J. 1988. Interest and agency in institutional theory. In *Institutional patterns and organizations: Culture and environment*, ed. L. G. Zucker, 3–32. Cambridge, MA: Ballinger.

DiMaggio, P. J., and W. W. Powell. 1983. The iron cage revisited: Institutional isomorphism and collective rationality in organization fields. *American Sociological Review* 48:147–160.

Donaldson, T., and L. E. Preston. 1995. The stakeholder theory of the corporation: Concepts, evidence, and implications. *Academy of Management Review* 20:65–91.

Ford, J. D., and L. W. Ford. 1995. The role of conversations in producing intentional change in organizations. *Academy of Management Review* 20:541–570.

Freeman, R. E. 1995. Stakeholder thinking: The state of the art. In *Understanding Stakeholder Thinking*, ed. J. Nasi, 35–46. Helsinki: LSR-Publications.

Gatewood, R. D., and A. B. Carroll. 1991. Assessment of ethical performance of organizational members: A conceptual framework. *Academy of Management Review* 16:667–690.

Greening, D. W., and B. Gray. 1994. Testing a model of organizational response to social and political issues. *Academy of Management Journal* 37:467–498.

Haas, R. D. 1994. Ethics in the trenches. *Across the Board* 31(5):12–13.

Hambrick, D. C., and S. Finkelstein. 1987. Managerial discretion: A bridge between polar views of organizational outcomes. *Research in Organizational Behavior* 9:369–406.

Hambrick, D. C., and P. Mason. 1984. Upper echelons: The organization as a reflection of its top managers. *Academy of Management Review* 9:193–206.

Hambrick, D. C., M. A. Geletkanycz, and J. Fredrickson. 1993. Top executive commitment to the status quo: Some tests of its determinants. *Strategic Management Journal* 14:401–418.

Hitt, M. A., and B. Tyler. 1991. Strategic decision models: Integrating different perspectives. *Strategic Management Journal* 12:327–351.

Jones, T. M. 1995. Instrumental stakeholder theory: A synthesis of ethics and economics. *Academy of Management Review* 20:404–437.

Kossek, E. E., P. Dass, and B. DeMarr. 1994. The dominant logic of employer-sponsored work and family initiatives: Human resource managers' institutional role. *Human Relations* 47:1121–1150.

Light, R. J. 1971. Measures of response agreement for qualitative data: Some generalizations and alternatives. *Psychological Bulletin* 76:365–377.

McCune, J. C. 1997. The corporation in the community. *HR Focus* 74(3):12–13.

Metzger, M., D. R. Dalton, and J. W. Hill. 1993. The organization of ethics and the ethics of organization. *Business Ethics Quarterly* 3:27–44.

Meyer, J. W., and B. Rowan. 1977. Institutionalized organizations: Formal structure as myth and ceremony. *American Journal of Sociology* 83:340–363.

Meznar, M. B., and D. Nigh. 1995. Buffer or bridge? Environmental and organizational determinants of public affairs activities in American firms. *Academy of Management Journal* 38:975–996.

Miles, R. H. 1987. *Managing the corporate social environment: A grounded theory*. Englewood Cliffs, NJ: Prentice Hall.

National Directory of Corporate Public Affairs. 1994. Washington, DC: Columbia Books.

Oliver, C. 1991. Strategic responses to institutional processes. *Academy of Management Review* 16:145–179.

Paine, L. S. 1994. Managing for organizational integrity. *Harvard Business Review* 72(2):106–117.

Paine, L. S. 1996. Moral thinking in management: An essential capability. *Business Ethics Quarterly* 6:477–492.

Pasztor, A., and L. Lagnado. 1997. Columbia creates ethics code that's based on self-policing. *Wall Street Journal* November 26:B1.

Petty, R. E., and J. T. Cacioppo. 1986. *Communication and persuasion: Central and peripheral routes to attitude change*. New York: Springer-Verlag.

Pfeffer, J., and G. Salancik. 1978. *The external control of organizations: A resource dependence perspective*. New York: Harper & Row.

Quinn, D. P., and T. M. Jones. 1995. An agent morality view of business policy. *Academy of Management Review* 20:22–42.

Scott, W. R. 1995. *Institutions and organizations*. Thousand Oaks, CA: Sage.

Selznick, P. 1957. *Leadership in administration: A sociological perspective*. New York: Harper and Row.

Swanson, D. L. 1995. Addressing a theoretical problem by reorienting the corporate social performance model. *Academy of Management Review* 20:43–64.

Thomas, J. B., S. M. Clark, and D. A. Gioia. 1993. Strategic sensemaking and organizational performance: Linkages among scanning, interpretation, action, and outcomes. *Academy of Management Journal* 36:239–270.

Treviño, L. K. 1990. A cultural perspective on changing and developing organizational ethics. In *Research in organizational change and development*, Vol. 4, ed. R. Woodman and W. Passmore, 195–230. Greenwich, CT: JAI Press.

Treviño, L. K. 1992. The social effects of punishment: A justice perspective. *Academy of Management Review* 17:647–676.

Treviño, L. K., and S. A. Youngblood. 1990. Bad apples in bad barrels: A causal analysis of ethical decision-making behavior. *Journal of Applied Psychology* 75:378–385.

United States Sentencing Commission. 1995. *Corporate crime in America: Strengthening the "good citizen" corporation*. Washington, DC.

United States Sentencing Commission. 1994. *Federal sentencing guidelines manual*. Washington, DC.

Wartick, S. L. 1992. The relationship between intense media exposure and change in corporate reputation. *Business and Society* 31(1):33–49.

Wartick, S. L., and P. L. Cochran. 1985. The evolution of the corporate social performance model. *Academy of Management Review* 10:758–769.

Weaver, G. R., and L. K. Treviño. 1999. Compliance and values oriented ethics programs: Influences on employees' attitudes and behavior. *Business Ethics Quarterly* 9(2):315–335.

Weaver, G. R., L. K. Treviño, and P. L. Cochran. 1999a. Corporate ethics programs as control systems: Managerial and institutional influences. *Academy of Management Journal* 42:41–57.

Weaver, G. R., L. K. Treviño, and P. L. Cochran. 1999b. Corporate ethics practices in the mid-1990s. *Journal of Business Ethics* 18:283–294.

Weber, J. 1993. Institutionalizing ethics into business organizations. *Business Ethics Quarterly* 3:419–436.

Wood, D.J. 1991. Corporate social performance revisited. *Academy of Management Review* 16:691–718.

PART THREE

Managing Ethical Conduct in Organizations

Part II focused on the move toward institutionalization of ethics management systems in American corporations. The decade of the 1990s saw huge growth in the development of formal systems to manage organizational ethics and legal compliance, such as separate ethics or compliance offices, codes of conduct, communication and training programs, and call-in telephone lines. The emphasis in Part II was on understanding the internal and external forces that have influenced firms to establish different approaches to ethics and compliance management. We conceptualized formal ethics programs as organizational control systems that aim to standardize employee behavior within the realm of ethics and legal compliance. These programs vary in scope (the number of formal elements included in them) and control orientation (compliance-oriented or values-oriented programs). We learned that a firm's approach to ethics and compliance management reflects both proactive exercise of managerial discretion and management's reaction to external pressures. Environmental pressures influence organizations to develop a variety of formal initiatives (program scope); but "how" these programs are implemented depends more on top management's commitment to ethics. We also differentiated ethics and compliance programs as being either integrated or decoupled. Integrated programs are those that affect daily decisions and actions within the organization and hold organization members accountable. Decoupled programs are those that communicate an ethics message that appears to be more "window dressing" than substantive. Integrated programs, like values-based programs, reflect top management's commitment to ethics while decoupled programs reflect management's reaction to external government and normative pressures.

Part III reviews conceptual and empirical work at the individual level of analysis and begins to answer the "so what" question. Do these formal ethics and compliance programs that firms are developing influence employee attitudes and behaviors? Or is the informal ethical context more important? Chapter 7 introduces the individual, issue-related, and contextual factors that are likely to influence ethical decision making and behavior in organizations, both individually and in interaction with organizational context variables. Although individual and issue-related factors are clearly important, one of the most important lessons is that most employees are at the conventional level of cognitive moral development—meaning that they are highly susceptible to influence from peers, significant others, and the context around them. Recognition of that fact provides a basis for understanding the important role played by organizational context.

With regard to the influence of formal programs, Chapter 8 builds on the work in Part II by distinguishing between values-based and compliance-based programs and finds that, although both are useful, values-based programs represent more powerful influences on employees' attitudes and behaviors. In combination, these findings suggest that top management commitment to ethics, which drives the development of values-based programs, has an indirect effect on key employee outcomes.

The findings reviewed in Chapter 8 also begin to suggest the importance of the informal ethical culture in the organization—factors such as ethics program follow-through, perceived fairness, and leadership. These factors are connected to the idea of ethics/compliance program integration discussed above. Once again, top management's personal commitment to ethics seems key. That commitment leads to integrated programs that have the most powerful impact on employee behavior. Interestingly, this research also found that employees' perceptions of senior management's commitment to ethics is highly correlated with their perceptions of their supervisors' commitment to ethics, suggesting that future research should explore the role of ethical leadership at the supervisory level.

Chapter 9 picks up on the importance of organizational context by presenting empirical research that tests the influence of ethical climate and culture factors on employee commitment and observed unethical behavior.

Once again, the most powerful influence is an ethical organizational environment that incorporates "ethics integration" factors, such as norms that are consistent with formal statements, ethical leadership, and supportive reward systems. Chapter 10 takes a different tack by drilling down into the role of employees' fairness perceptions in predicting employees' ethics-related attitudes and behaviors. Building on equity theory, we proposed and found that employees would respond to equitable treatment with commitment to the organization and less unethical behavior. With fairness perceptions, we are moving even farther away from the formal ethics programs discussed in Part II and more in the direction of the informal organizational context. Once again, we find that employees' perceptions of these more informal organizational characteristics are a key influence on ethics-related outcomes.

The resounding message of the work presented in Part III is that employees' ethics-related attitudes and behaviors are powerfully influenced by the organizational context. Most employees are at the conventional level of cognitive moral development and are highly susceptible to external influence. Formal ethics and compliance programs play a role, but that role is clearly not as significant as the role played by the more informal aspects of the organization—program follow-through, leadership, reward systems, fair treatment. When we combine the findings presented in Part II and Part III, we learn that the tone of the informal context is set at the top of the organization by senior executives and then is carried through by leadership and practices at all organizational levels.

SEVEN

Ethical Decision Making and Conduct in Organizations: Individuals, Issues, and Context

In 1986, Treviño (1986, 601) wrote that "the issue of ethical decision making in organizations has received much attention in recent years for a variety of reasons: the post-Watergate atmosphere, mounting public scorn regarding business behavior, and managers' cynicism and internal personal-work values conflicts." Since that time, interest in the topic has increased because of continuing ethical scandals in the political and business arenas; new technologies that trigger novel ethical concerns; and increased public attention to business conduct in a global information environment that quickly spreads news about corruption, inhumane labor practices, and other ethical issues. Further, as indicated in earlier chapters, adoption of the Federal sentencing guidelines in 1991 has made U.S. corporations more aware that they should be managing the ethical and legal decisions of their members. Finally, with flattening hierarchies and decreased supervision, more individuals in organizations are engaged in discretionary decision behavior, which makes individual ethical decision making even more important. This chapter provides an overview of the state of current knowledge in this key area of research, focusing primarily on relationships

Portions of this chapter are taken from the 1998 article by L. K. Treviño, "Ethical decision making in organizations: A person–situation interactionist model," *Academy of Management Journal* 11(3):601–617. Reproduced with permission of the Academy of Management in book format via Copyright Clearance Center.

that have been investigated empirically. We also pose questions that future research will need to address.

An Ethical Decision-making/Behavior Framework

Understanding of ethical decision making and behavior has drawn considerably from moral psychology research. Ethical decision making is thought to involve four sequential subprocesses: (1) moral sensitivity or awareness (recognition that a moral issue exists); (2) moral judgment (deciding that a specific course of action vis-à-vis that issue is morally justifiable); (3) moral motivation (commitment to taking that moral action rather than other actions); and (4) moral character (persisting in moral action despite challenges) (Rest et al. 1999). Most investigations of ethical decision making and behavior in organizations have focused on moral judgment and moral action, although the study of moral sensitivity has grown. The areas of moral motivation and moral character have been neglected, making them ripe for future investigation.

Management research has expanded on moral psychology research by highlighting the important influence of the organizational context on ethical decision making. For example, characteristics of the work, pressures from the immediate job context, and messages sent by the broader ethical climate and culture of an organization influence employees' thoughts and behaviors. Finally, the moral intensity of the issue has been proposed to influence multiple stages of the ethical decision-making process (Jones 1991), as have a variety of individual characteristics, such as locus of control (Rotter 1966) and religiosity (Weaver and Agle, 2002).

We discuss a model of ethical decision-making behavior that builds on models previously proposed by Treviño (1986) and Jones (1991) and that is informed by empirical research findings. The model views ethical decision making in organizations as a multistage phenomenon influenced by multiple variables and their interactions (Flannery and May 2000). It emphasizes the moral recognition, moral judgment, and moral action phases of the process while making suggestions for future study of the moral motivation and moral character phases.

It is important to note that the model we are discussing and most theorizing and research in this area to date assume a kind of linear, orderly sequence in the process of ethical decision making and behavior. Yet we recognize that this is far from certain. Much human behavior takes scripted form in that it is largely automatic, embedded in the routines of life, or triggered by particular contextual clues, and thus devoid of conscious deliberation (stage 2) (Gioia 1992; Gioia and Manz 1985). Ethical behavior may occur in the same way (that is, skipping the deliberative moral judgment stage). For example, an individual's religion may influence ethical behavior by providing behavioral narratives (for example, "the good Samaritan") that can be internalized as behavioral scripts, ready to be implemented given the right contextual triggers (for example, seeing a person in need) (Weaver and Agle 2002). Thus, we discuss this model with the caveat that ethical decision-making processes are often not as neat or linear as the model would appear to suggest.

MORAL RECOGNITION

Moral recognition (also referred to as *ethical* or *moral sensitivity*, or *moral awareness*) represents a key first stage in the ethical decision making process. It represents the moment at which the decision-maker recognizes that "I am facing a moral issue" and presumably sets the stage for moral judgment processes to be engaged. Much empirical research into ethical decision making has provided the decision-maker with a ready-made moral dilemma or has assumed that the decision-maker will recognize that a moral issue exists in a particular situation. Given the ambiguity of many ethical issues, however, awareness of the ethical nature of a situation cannot be taken for granted. If awareness does not exist, moral judgment processes are not likely to be engaged.

Imagine an employee who has just begun to work in the financial services industry. His supervisor has to leave work early and asks that the employee sign the supervisor's name to an important check that must be mailed to a customer that day. The new employee may not recognize the ethical nature of the situation, seeing the situation as a simple request to help the supervisor. His supervisor, however, has asked him to engage in forgery, a serious ethical (and legal) lapse, particularly in the financial services industry, where signatures have special meaning and value. With training or industry experience, the employee would more likely understand why forgery is considered such a serious breach of trust in the financial services industry. Or, if the supervisor asked the employee to "forge" his signature, the ethically loaded word *forgery* would likely trigger ethical concerns. If the employee does recognize the ethical nature of the situation, he or she will be more likely to engage in moral judgment processes that should lead to the conclusion that forging a signature is unethical and wrong (Treviño and Nelson 1999).

Much work on moral sensitivity has been conducted within the context of the dental profession (Baab and Bebeau 1990; Bebeau 1994; Bebeau and Brabeck 1987). This work is important because it has developed measures and methodologies that could be adapted to other contexts. For example, stimulus materials have consisted of video and audio interactions that are shown to respondents who then take on the role of a person in the drama and respond as if they were that person. A scoring manual, developed based on input from practicing professionals, then has been used to measure ethical sensitivity. Research has found that ethical sensitivity is moderately correlated with moral judgment and can be increased through training and experience. The latter finding suggests that specific organizational climate and culture variables may influence ethical sensitivity. For example, moral sensitivity should be higher for employees who attend orientation or ethics training designed to improve ethical issue recognition.

Issue Intensity and Moral Recognition

Jones (1991) proposed that moral issue recognition is influenced by the "moral intensity" of the ethical issue. According to Jones, moral intensity is a construct comprising six dimensions: (1) magnitude of consequences (the amount of harm or benefit that could occur as a result of a decision or action); (2) degree of social consensus (that the issue is ethically problematic); (3) probability of effect (that the harm or benefit will occur); (4) temporal immediacy (how quickly the harm or benefit will occur); (5) proximity (feeling of nearness of the decision maker to the target of the harm or benefit); and (6) concentration of effect (an inverse function of the number of people affected). Social cognition research suggests that high moral intensity issues should increase moral awareness because they gain the decision-maker's attention by being more vivid and salient. Also, decision-makers are more likely to attribute responsibility to the self for high-intensity issues.

In the business context, a number of studies now support the relationship between moral intensity and moral issue recognition, particularly for the magnitude of consequences and social consensus dimensions (for a review, see May and Pauli 2000). As an example, Butterfield and colleagues (Butterfield, Treviño, and Weaver 2000) conducted a study of moral awareness among competitive intelligence professionals. The goal of this research was to understand the factors that trigger moral awareness. Following Jones (1991), they proposed that moral awareness would be influenced by the magnitude of consequences of the issue at hand, by the degree to which consensus exists in the company or industry that the issue is ethically problematic (both moral-intensity dimensions), as well as by whether the issue was framed in moral terms. When moral language is used to frame an issue, it should become more salient because of the typical absence of moral language from business parlance. Use of moral language is also likely to trigger schemas with moral content. In the preceding example, use of the word *forgery* likely would trigger such a schema. Magnitude of consequences, issue framing, and social consensus that the issue is ethically problematic all were found to influence competitive intelligence professionals' moral awareness. Individuals were more likely to recognize the moral nature of a situation when it had the potential for significant negative consequences and when others in the social environment were perceived to see the issue as ethically problematic. In a morally ambiguous situation, framing the issue in moral terms influenced moral awareness. This study was unique in that moral intensity was manipulated in the scenarios and moral awareness was measured qualitatively; respondents to a scenario were asked to list the issues of concern in the scenario, and those were content analyzed for their ethical content. Therefore, the potential for social desirability bias and priming was minimized. In most studies of moral sensitivity, survey respondents are asked directly whether the scenario presents an ethical dilemma, a question that raises social desirability bias and priming concerns.

Insights from research on moral intensity can be helpful in developing ethics education and training programs in business. Such programs could focus explicitly on the moral intensity of situations, encouraging employees to become more aware of the full magnitude of consequences of their decisions (emphasizing the harm that could occur from a particular action) or on issues of proximity (for example, asking the employee to put him- or herself in the role of those affected, such as customers). Such programs, by encouraging employees to talk about ethical issues amongst themselves, also may contribute to a social consensus that an issue is ethically problematic and thereby enhance recognition of the issue when it arises at work.

Important open questions remain regarding moral intensity, and thus moral issue recognition. Prominent among them is the kind of question raised in Part I of this book regarding relationships among normative and empirical theories. As developed by Jones (1991) and used by others, moral intensity is specifically framed in terms of a combined consequentialist and social consensus account of morality. Moral intensity is proposed to be a function of various aspects of the consequences of an action (amount, probability, concentration, immediacy of harm, and proximity of victims) and the extent to which there is a social consensus about the ethical impropriety of the harm; but other considerations might account for moral intensity and sensitivity. For example, suppose a salesperson lies to a customer to get a sale, but, as things turn out, the customer really is better off because of buying this item rather than another. Also, suppose that most people would agree that no harm has been done. According to some normative theories of business ethics, such deception would qualify as unethical, even though it may be difficult to root that unethical quality in either harmful consequences or social consensus. Moreover, some ordinary individuals (i.e., not professional business ethicists) also might view such deception as a moral failure, appealing to general principles regarding the wrongfulness of dishonesty, despite the lack of harmful consequences. How do we account for that kind of moral intensity and moral sensitivity? In short, the way we frame a construct of moral intensity is not necessarily separate from a normative understanding of business ethics. Future research needs to consider the prospects for a broader conception of moral intensity that is able to incorporate more fully other or even multiple normative perspectives (in the integrative mode described in Chapter 2) or the prospects for a more narrowly empirical conception of intensity that is normatively neutral (see the discussion of parallelism or symbiosis in Chapter 2).

In sum, moral issue recognition is thought to be an important first stage in the unfolding ethical decision-making process and is positively associated with moral judgment stage. Moral issue recognition is influenced by characteristics of the issue, such as the moral intensity of the ethical issue and framing of the issue in moral terms. It is also influenced by organizational factors such as social consensus within the organization that the issue is ethically problematic and is likely to be influenced by organizational interventions, such as orientation and training programs. Although work remains to be done regarding issue recognition and issue intensity, the general outlines of the idea are important for understanding the process of ethical decision making and behavior in organizations, especially its earliest stages.

Moral judgment represents the second stage of the ethical decision-making process—the stage at which the individual decides what is the right thing to do regarding a particular ethical issue. The assumption is that the individual has recognized the issue as a "moral issue" and that moral judgment processes now are engaged. Much theory and empirical study of moral judgment have focused on the construct of cognitive moral development introduced by Kohlberg (1969) and modeled after more general developmental theories of Jean Piaget (1932). Kohlberg's original framework underwent much criticism and revision. We begin our discussion of moral judgment by considering Kohlberg's original formulation and various criticisms and amendments to that formulation before turning to more recent research on moral judgment conducted with professional adults by James Rest and colleagues and research conducted by accounting and management scholars. After considering how research on cognitive moral development contributes to our understanding of moral judgment, we discuss other potential influences on moral judgment.

Kohlberg's Theory of Cognitive Moral Development

Kohlberg's theory of cognitive moral development addresses how the cognitive or reasoning processes of ethical decision making become more complex and sophisticated over time. The focus is on the kinds or forms of reasoning an individual uses to justify a moral choice rather than the decision itself. Initially, Kohlberg's theory might appear normatively neutral because it is the form rather than the content of moral reasoning (that is, the way the decision is reached rather than the actual decision) that is the hallmark of different types of moral reasoning. The use of ideas like "development" in Kohlberg's theory implies, however, that some forms of reasoning are better, from a moral stance, than others. In addition, Kohlberg's theory depends on the work of moral philosophers, in particular, R. M. Hare (1952, 1963), whose prescriptivist metaethics claimed to delineate the form reasoning must take if it is to be considered proper moral reasoning, and John Rawls (1971), whose theory of justice envisions proper moral judgment following out of a collective decision-making process carried out in certain ideal, allegedly neutral decision-making conditions. (As critics point out, different forms of moral reasoning are not necessarily content neutral; some forms of reasoning have the potential to rule out certain types of specific conclusions, and judgments of ideal decision-making situations, such as Rawls offers, imply normative stances through their characterization of the ideal.)

Although Kohlberg's theory has gone through multiple iterations, in general, it delineates different types of moral reasoning and proposes transformations from one type to another as persons move from middle childhood to adulthood. His framework proposed three broad categories of moral reasoning, or cognitive moral development, each composed of two more narrowly defined stages. He proposed that individuals pass from stage to stage in an invariant irreversible upward sequence that shifts from simpler to more complex forms of moral reasoning. Based on Piaget's (1932) seminal work on moral development in children, Kohlberg argued that higher stages rely on cognitive operations that are not available at lower stages. Finally, Kohlberg claimed not only that higher stages were normatively "better" than lower but also that those at the highest stage would agree on substantive moral issues (Rest et al. 1999).

In Kohlberg's framework, at stages 1 and 2 (labeled the *preconventional level*), an individual decides what is right based on concrete consequences, particularly obedience to avoid punishment associated with a particular behavior (at stage 1) and getting a "fair deal" in exchange relationships (at stage 2)—a kind of "one hand washes the other" mentality. At stages 3 and 4 (the *conventional level*), right is that which conforms to the expectations of good behavior of the larger society or some segment like a family or peer group—"the way we do things." More specifically, in stage 3, the individual is concerned about fulfilling the expectations of significant others. In stage 4, the individual is capable of taking a somewhat broader perspective. For example, a society's laws become an important determinant of the individual's decisions about what is right and wrong. It is important to note that Kohlberg's research placed most adults in our society at stages 3 or 4, where rules, laws, and the expectations of significant others are paramount. An implication of this is that the large majority of employees in work organizations reason at the conventional level, and thus they rely on rules and leaders to guide them in their thinking about what is right. They are, by definition, looking to others and to the situation to help define what is right and wrong. At stages 5 and 6 (the *principled level*) right is determined more autonomously, being influenced by universal values or principles of justice and rights. Individuals at the principled level are expected to behave consistently with their internally held beliefs (Treviño 1986). According to Kohlberg, however, fewer than twenty percent of American adults ever reach the principled level. In fact, Kohlberg's research found little evidence for stage 5 thinking, and he eventually eliminated stage 6 because of lack of evidence of its existence (Rest et al. 1999).

Criticisms of Kohlberg's Theory. Kohlberg's approach has generated both philosophical/normative and psychological/empirical criticism. On the philosophical/normative side, it has been criticized for its reliance on contestable metaethical and ethical theories (that is, those of Hare and Rawls). In particular, Kohlberg's idea of principled moral reasoning owes much to Rawls's conception of moral decisions taking place behind a "veil of ignorance," requiring that individuals make moral judgments without any knowledge of their actual situation in life. At the risk of summarizing a massive array of critical literature in one sentence, this kind of decision situation is faulted for embodying a conception of the self and justice characteristic of the political and social theory of liberal individualism (MacIntyre 1984; Sandel 1982), which is only one among many conceptions of the self, society, and justice (see Mulhall and Swift 1992 for an extended commentary on this normative debate).

A second important normative critique of Kohlberg lies not so much in a rejection of liberal individualist theories, such as Rawls's, as in a recognition that such theories are limited in scope and thus fail to give due attention to the full range of phenomena and concerns that constitute the moral life (Rest et al. 1999). Rather, theories such as Rawls's are seen as restricted in scope to questions of just social orders, that is, "the basic structure of society" (Rawls 1971, 7). There is much to address in the world of ethics beyond questions of "the basic structure of society," however, and one might reasonably suspect that it is those other questions (for example, "Should I forge the boss's signature to keep this check request moving through the system so that the vendor gets paid on time?") that often characterize people's questions about ethics at work. In response to criticism, Kohlberg himself reduced the scope of his original theory from a consideration of all moral reasoning to a narrow focus on thinking about justice (Kohlberg 1984) and noted that "the moral domain is large and varied, and no one approach to its conceptualization and measurement will exhaust or explain the variance in it" (Kohlberg 1986, 500).

On the psychological/empirical side, the rigid stage progressions proposed by Kohlberg have been criticized. Opposing research, for example, has noted that persons at various ages often display multiple ways of thinking about problems and that novel ways of thinking occur (Siegler 1997). In particular, much research has argued, contrary to Kohlberg, that children are not merely egocentric or deferential to authority in their thinking (for example, Zahn-Waxler et al. 1992; Lapsley 1996). Also subject to criticism has been Kohlberg's emphasis on formal, logically structured models of advanced levels of cognition and on Kohlberg's primary data source regarding the nature of those cognitive processes: verbal self-reports (discussed in more detail later in this chapter). As critics put it, "People know more than they can tell. A distinction is needed between implicit, tacit or intuitive knowledge of a concept and the ability to state explicitly the knowledge one has"(Schweder, Mahaptra, and Miller 1987, 6).

Neo-Kohlbergian Approaches. In light of these criticisms, moral psychologists have developed alternatives to Kohlberg's approach to moral cognition. These alternatives retain the interest in identifying and explaining the nature of different kinds of moral reasoning, but without making normative and psychological claims that are as strong and narrowly defined as Kohlberg's. Most prominently, Rest and colleagues (1999) proposed that moral development involves more gradual and varied upward shifts in the use of and preference for higher levels of thinking in the form of developmental "schemas." In their view, postconventional (that is, higher level) reasoning involves broad appeal to shareable ideals, such as the common good, as well as openness to scrutiny and rational debate, rather than exclusive dependence on a Kantian/Rawlsian type of deontological theory. Thus, their position is more philosophically neutral; it is the willingness to examine or critique one's position, taking others' concerns into account, that constitutes a "higher" level of moral reasoning rather than a willingness to form one's position from the narrowly defined perspective of the liberal individualist, Rawlsian self. Rest and colleagues also offered the concepts of *micromorality* and *macromorality* to suggest that Kohlberg's theory is better at dealing with cognitions related to societal issues that require impartiality, shared ideals, and action based on principle (macromorality) than issues that concern everyday relationships and require the virtues of daily life, such as caring, courtesy, and helpfulness (micromorality). Thus, neo-Kohlbergian approaches preserve the insight that people reason about moral issues in different ways or patterns in varying situations while looking for factors that influence the selection of moral reasoning process and the judgmental and behavioral outcomes of different moral reasoning processes.

Moral Judgment Research Issues and Findings

We now turn from a general discussion of moral development theories to review selected empirical findings relevant to understanding moral judgment processes in organizational settings, beginning with a key methodological issue and moving on to research findings. Although many of the research studies listed were developed out of explicitly Kohlbergian frameworks, we suggest that they be interpreted in light of the modified, neo-Kohlbergian position described earlier.

Methodological Issues: Measuring Moral Development. Kohlberg developed an interview-based method of assessing subjects' cognitive moral development stage; this method is called Standard Issue Scoring. Open-ended interview questions about three hypothetical moral dilemmas were designed to elicit spontaneous reasoning processes (Colby and Kohlberg 1987). This method assumes that interview subjects' verbal productions are indicators of their cognitive processes. It requires substantial training and is time consuming to administer and score. As noted, the interview method is also subject to criticisms that individuals are limited in their ability to report on their own cognitive processes (Nisbett and Wilson 1977) and that such a verbal production task does not account for implicit or tacit knowledge (Shweder, Mahapatra, and Miller 1987).

Weber (1990) developed the Adapted Moral Judgment Interview (AMJI) based on Kohlberg's interview approach. The AMJI poses three dilemmas, one general hypothetical dilemma followed by two business context dilemmas, and asks the respondent to write responses to open-ended questions. Scoring follows a standard scoring guide also developed and validated by Weber.

Kohlberg's students have developed alternative measures that attempt to overcome the limitations of the interview, particularly its time-consuming nature. These include the "sociomoral reflection measure" developed by Gibbs and Widaman (1982) and the "sociomoral reflection objective measure," also developed by Gibbs and colleagues (Gibbs et al. 1984; see Treviño 1992 for a discussion of these instruments). Researchers are also applying discourse processing methods to gain better understanding of moral thinking (Narvaez 1999).

In recent years, however, the most commonly used measure of cognitive moral development has been the Defining Issues Test (DIT; Rest 1979), an objective recognition test that is concerned with how people at multiple developmental levels choose different statements as representing the most important issue in a series of hypothetical moral dilemmas. Major indices assess the relative importance a subject gives to principled moral considerations and provide an overall index of moral judgment development. According to Rest and colleagues, the DIT "began life . . . as a 'quick and dirty' multiple-choice alternative to Kohlberg's time consuming and complicated interview procedure" (Rest et al. 1999, 4). Now that hundreds of studies have validated its reliability and usefulness, however, they represent the DIT as "a device for activating moral schemas" (to the extent that a person has developed them) and for assessing them in terms of importance (Rest et al. 1999, 6). An updated five-dilemma version of the DIT (DIT2) has undergone preliminary testing at the University of Minnesota's Center for Ethical Development and has been found to replicate the original DIT. Research summarized in a book by Rest and Narvaez (1994) suggests that profession-specific DIT-type measures also can be developed that include dilemmas and responses specifically focused within a particular profession.

Gender and Moral Judgment. Carol Gilligan's assertion that males and females differ in cognitive moral development received wide attention when her book, *In a Different Voice*, was published in 1982. Based on her research with girls, Gilligan argued that Kohlberg's focus on justice concerns did not adequately describe female moral development and the tendency of females to focus on care concerns (rather than justice concerns) in their moral reasoning. Research across many samples and contexts, however, has found either no significant differences in male and female moral reasoning or that females score slightly higher than males (see Ford and Richardson 1994; Walker 1984; Rest et al. 1986 for reviews). Similarly, Derry (1987, 1989) found no significant differences in her work comparing the moral reasoning of male and female managers. Nevertheless, researchers continue to think about and probe for gender differences across multiple stages in the ethical decision-making process (see, for example, Ambrose and Schminke 1999 for a review). We agree with Ambrose and Schminke (1999, 468), who state that "substantial research on sex differences in ethics fails to provide a consistent pattern of results. Sometimes men and women differ from one another, sometimes they do not. We believe that the continuation of such research is unlikely to prove fruitful."

National Culture and Moral Judgment. Cross-cultural research based on Kohlberg's interview measure (Snarey 1985) and the DIT (Moon 1985; Rest et al. 1986) has supported the claim that formal types of moral reasoning are universal (Gielen and Markoulis 1994). Similar age and education trends were found across cultures, and Moon (1985) found evidence of postconventional thinking across cultures as well. These findings suggest that moral development theory provides a solid basis for research on cross-cultural business ethics.

External Factors and Moral Judgment. Although moral reasoning is generally thought to improve with age and education, other external factors enter into the equation, including the moral intensity of the issue being faced and the work environment of individuals. Jones (1991) proposed that moral intensity would be associated with higher levels of moral reasoning. Weber (1996) found support for that proposition for the magnitude of consequences (a dimension of moral intensity). Barnett and Valentine (2001) found both magnitude of consequences and social consensus to be associated with judgments that a particular action is unethical. Flannery and May (2000), in a study combining the theory of planned behavior and moral intensity, found that magnitude of consequences influenced ethical decision intentions directly. In addition, magnitude of consequences moderated the influence of attitudes, subjective norms, self-efficacy, ethical climate, and financial cost on ethical decision intentions. These factors influenced managers' thinking less when the magnitude of consequences was high than when it was low. Others, however, have found less support when using other dimensions of moral intensity. Carlson, Kacmar, Wadsworth, and Zivnuska (2001) tested the effects of proximity, concentration of effect, and probability of effect on perceptions of ethicality and found support only for proximity. Additional research will be required to understand fully the influences (direct and interactive) of this complex multidimensional construct.

Beyond the issue itself, the broader work environment seems important. Ponemon and Gabhart (1994) reported on DIT-based moral reasoning research in the accounting profession. The findings of multiple studies raise concern about the moral reasoning of U.S. accountants, especially those at senior levels in public accounting firms. Moral reasoning scores have been found to be lower for accounting students and practitioners compared with other non–business college students, college-educated adults, and professionals (Lampe and Finn 1992). Further, moral reasoning scores were found to be lower for managers and partners in public accounting firms (Ponemon 1988, 1990, 1992; Shaub, 1989) than for those at lower levels in the firm. This finding suggests that socialization processes may select out those with postconventional reasoning abilities or that there is something about the accounting firms or the work itself that depresses moral reasoning over time. Interestingly, the findings were very different for Canadian auditing professionals, suggesting that the educational or socialization processes may be different in Canada. Ponemon and Gabhart (1994) proposed the development of educational strategies in business schools and accounting firms aimed at increasing the moral reasoning capacity of U.S. accountants. They also proposed that U.S. accounting firms should consider adopting rules of conduct that clearly specify ethical strategies, although these should be developed by those with high ethical reasoning skills.

In a similar finding with general managers, Elm and Nichols (1993) found that managers who were older and more experienced reasoned at lower levels than younger, less experienced managers. Given the consistent evidence for positive relationships between cognitive moral development and both age and education, these findings suggest that certain business settings actually may retard moral reasoning, certainly a cause for concern (Treviño 1992). Future research should hypothesize and test characteristics of job and organizational contexts that could influence moral reasoning in a positive or negative direction. For example, based on research by Colby and colleagues (1983), Treviño (1986) proposed that jobs offering opportunities for role taking (taking account of the perspective of others) and responsibility for the resolution of moral dilemmas are more likely to contribute to adult moral development. To our knowledge, this proposition has not yet been tested in business contexts.

Moral reasoning also has been studied in the context of sports (Bredemeier and Shields, 1984), a context relevant to business given that "game" metaphors are often used in business settings. For example, Bredemeier (1985, 1994) found associations between moral reasoning scores and aggressive action tendencies in sports and in daily life. Further, Bredemeier and Shields (1984, 1986a, 1986b, 1986c) found that athletes reason with less maturity in response to sport versus nonsport dilemmas. This is similar to findings that managers reason at lower levels in response to hypothethical business-related dilemmas compared with their reasoning in response to dilemmas from outside the workplace (Weber 1990; Weber and Wasieleski 2001). Additional research will be needed to understand fully the reasons for these context-based differences in moral reasoning. Bredemeier and Shields (1984) hypothesized that the game context (for example, sports) represents a unique sphere that involves cognitive, affective, and value transformations, an effect they labeled *game reasoning.*

If organizations or policy makers wish to support the highest levels of moral reasoning in business, it will be important to understand whether and how the organizational or business contexts instantiate schemas and interpretation systems different from those used in reasoning about the moral dilemmas of daily life. It will also be important to separate contextual effects from selection effects. It is possible that individuals who already think in certain ways select themselves into specific fields of study and types of organizations. For example, research conducted by Frank and colleagues (1993) indicated that students and faculty in economics-related fields, in which a "rationally self-interested" model of human behavior dominates, behaved in more self-interested fashion than students and academics from other fields. Such findings may mean that the self-interested model is learned or that individuals who reason in this manner are attracted to these fields because of their preexisting reasoning styles.

Training and Moral Judgment. A substantial literature on moral education suggests that moral reasoning ability can be improved through cognitive moral development (CMD)-based training interventions. Rest and Narvaez's book (1994) summarizes research from a variety of professional education settings, including business education. They concluded that effective interventions (1) go beyond theory to include direct experience and guided reflection on that experience; (2) use all four components of Rest's model as a guide for developing instruction; (3) are multiunit learning experiences arising at appropriate times in the curriculum; (4) involve learning basic logical and ethical concepts needed to formulate a perspective characterized by openness to critique and the concerns of others. In years of association with business organizations involved in ethics training, however, we have found no evidence of interest in this literature or in CMD-based training tools. Is it possible that U.S. business organizations have little interest in developing the moral judgment of their members? This question raises normative concerns about the goals of ethics training in American business today.

Groups and Group Leadership and Moral Judgment. In organizations, many decisions are made in a group context. Discussing ethical issues in a group setting appears to contribute to individuals' moral judgment, especially if the group's leader is high in CMD. Nichols and Day (1982) and Dukerich and colleagues (1990) found that individual moral reasoning scores increased after consensus-oriented group discussions of DIT dilemmas. Even more interesting was the finding that group performance decreased when less principled individuals were in a leadership role. It either increased or stayed the same when the group's leader was higher in moral reasoning, but more principled individuals were not more likely to emerge as leaders in these groups. Therefore, organizations may need to assign principled individuals to leadership roles if they wish to influence the moral development of group members and the ethical decisions groups make.

MORAL ACTION

Research suggests that moral action is influenced directly by moral judgment, although the relationships are not particularly strong. One can believe that a particular action would be right or wrong, but whether one chooses to act in accordance with that knowledge may depend on a number of personal and situational factors. Some of these factors should have direct effects, whereas others should influence moral action through their inter-action with cognitive moral development. For example, situational factors are more likely to influence the behavior of those individuals who are at the conventional level of CMD. By definition, they are looking outside them-selves for guidance about what is right, what is wrong, and how to behave. The addition of these individual differences and contextual variables should help to increase our ability to predict ethical behavior in organizations beyond the modest relationships found between moral judgment and moral action.

Individual Differences

Treviño (1986) proposed that a number of individual differences should be associated with moral action. We focus on two of those variables here: CMD and locus of control.

Cognitive Moral Development. Kohlberg (1969) argued that higher stages of moral development should be associated with ethical behavior because of the individual's need for consistency between thoughts and behaviors. Hundreds of studies, particularly DIT-based studies, have linked moral reasoning to both positive (for example, helping, whistle blowing, resis-tance to pressure from authority figures), and negative (cheating, stealing) behaviors, with the statistical link estimated to be between 10 and 15 percent (see Treviño 1992; Thoma 1994; Rest and Narvaez 1994). Although not large, the strength of these relationships is similar to that found in other judgment/action research (Ajzen 1988). In a business context, Treviño and Youngblood (1990) found evidence in a laboratory experiment that CMD is related to ethical decision behavior, and Greenberg (in press) found that employees higher in cognitive moral development were less likely to steal. Moral reasoning also has been associated with accounting-related abilities and ethical decisions. For example, experienced auditors with higher DIT scores were better able to detect fraud and financial statement errors (Bernardi 1994). Higher DIT auditors were also more sensitive to client characteristics, such as integrity and competence, both key to discovering fraud and other illegal client behavior. Those with low DIT scores were less likely to identify whistle blowing as a method for disclosing misconduct (Arnold and Ponemon 1991).

Numerous proposals have been made to improve our understanding of the moral reasoning/behavior relationship. For example, Thoma (1994) proposed basing more research on the four-component model because moral reasoning does not tell the complete story. Understanding additional processes that may intervene between moral judgment and action, such as moral motivation, should improve our ability to predict moral action. Thoma (1994) also proposed using a new DIT-based score, the U (or utilizer) score, which "represents an empirical estimate of the agreement between the actual and implied action decisions which, in turn, is viewed as a measure of subjects' reliance on justice reasoning" (p. 205). Research has found that the relationship between moral judgments and action was stronger when the U-score was used.

In sum, CMD theory, as modified by recent research and theory (e.g., Rest et al. 1999) provides a useful theoretical basis for understanding the influences on, and outcomes of, moral reasoning. Most important, we know that moral reasoning is significantly associated with ethical and unethical conduct in the workplace. This work provides a strong foundation for understanding the importance of "managing" ethical conduct in organizations. First, it is clear that most adults are at the conventional level of moral development and therefore require guidance from the organization and significant others (for example, leaders) regarding what is appropriate and inappropriate conduct and why. Therefore, those in positions of authority in organizations bear the responsibility for the ethical frameworks and guidance they create for subordinates; these signal to subordinates what is, and is not, acceptable behavior. Second, it appears that at least some business contexts play a negative role in the moral reasoning of their members, suggesting that characteristics of the work and workplace may be important. For example, managers have been found to reason at a lower level when responding to managerial dilemmas, as opposed to dilemmas from daily life; and more senior managers in multiple types of organizations have been found to reason at lower stages than do employees at lower hierarchical levels. These findings suggest that increasing degrees of enculturation into an organization carry ethical risks. This is particularly problematic in that it is the senior people—those least likely to reason in desirable ways—who are responsible for creating the overall moral climate or framework of the organization. These findings raise important questions for future research.

What are the characteristics of organizational contexts that are associated with lower levels of moral reasoning, and what can be done about them?

Locus of Control. A personality characteristic that has been found to be related to ethical behavior is locus of control (Rotter 1966). Rotter's internal/external scale measures an individual's perception of how much control he or she exerts over the events in life. An *internal* believes that outcomes are the result of his or her own efforts, whereas an *external* believes that life events are beyond control and can be attributed to fate, luck, or destiny. Treviño (1986) proposed that locus of control would moderate the CMD/ethical behavior relationship. Because an internal takes personal responsibility for the consequences of ethical and unethical behavior, an internal should also be more likely to do what she or he thinks is right. An external, on the other hand, is more open to the pressures of the situation and more likely to think that it is beyond his or her capability to act to change the situation. Treviño and Youngblood (1990) found that locus of control influenced ethical decision behavior directly and indirectly through outcome expectancies. In fact, the locus of control/ethical decision behavior relationship was the strongest in the study. Interestingly, no interaction effect was found.

Contextual Factors

In addition to individual differences, the organizational context surrounding an individual should have a strong influence on ethical and unethical behavior. These external factors may have direct effects on decision-making behavior, or they may interact with moral judgment to influence behavior.

Immediate Job Context: Job Pressure. Surveys consistently find that workers feel pressure to act unethically on the job. Persons who are under great time pressure are less likely to pay attention to the needs of others. In effect, moral action takes effort, and in the face of multiple work pressures, that effort is not likely to be expended. Robertson and Rymon (2001) used randomized response techniques to find that when purchasing agents perceived that they were under pressure to perform, they were more likely to engage in deceptive behavior. Pressure should have a stronger impact on those who are lower in CMD. In the research on auditors discussed earlier in this chapter, Ponemon found that, when pressured by time or budget concerns, auditors with low DIT scores were more likely to underreport time (Ponemon 1992).

Immediate Job Context: Role Conflict. Grover (1997) studied a particular type of job pressure: role conflict. He proposed and found that when roles conflict, as they often do in organizations, people experience distress that is resolved by lying to one of the role senders. In a study supporting the interaction between CMD and the situation, Grover (1993) found that individuals closer to the conventional level of CMD were more likely to lie as a result of role conflict. Those at the principled level were not influenced.

Immediate Job Context: Rewards and Punishments. It is axiomatic in psychology that rewards motivate and punishments decrease target behaviors. Moral behavior is no different. Therefore, we would expect ethical and unethical behavior to respond to reinforcement contingencies. A number of studies have found that unethical behavior increases in response to rewards. Hegarty and Sims (1978) found, in a laboratory computer simulation of marketing decisions, that rewarding unethical behavior increased unethical behavior for rewarded subjects. Treviño and Youngblood (1990) found that perceived reward expectancies for unethical behavior increased unethical decisions in an in-basket study. Also, Tenbrunsel (1998) found that when study participants had an incentive to deceive their negotiation partners, they were significantly more likely to do so.

Yet ethical behavior may not respond to rewards in the same manner. Treviño and Youngblood (1990) failed to find that providing vicarious rewards for ethical behavior increased ethical decisions. Qualitative data suggest that subjects did not want to be rewarded for ethical behavior that is expected as part of daily work life. Although people do not expect rewards for doing the right thing, we have also learned that they do not want to feel "punished" for doing so because others get away with misconduct or are rewarded for it (Treviño and Ball 1992).

Influence of Significant Others. Given that most people are at the conventional level of moral development, significant others' beliefs and behavior should be an important influence on their ethical conduct. Differential association theory (Sutherland and Cressey 1970) also suggests that referent others influence deviant behavior. Organizational research supports this notion, finding that a person's perceptions of peers' beliefs predict that individual's ethical behavior, and this relationship is stronger for those peers with whom the individual had intense and frequent contact (Zey-Ferrell and Ferrell 1982; Zey-Ferrell, Weaver, and Ferrell 1979).

This work sets the tone for more recent theorizing that draws on social network analysis to suggest that relationships can influence ethical/unethical behavior in organizational settings (Brass, Butterfield, and Skaggs 1998). Social network theory suggests propositions about the likely targets of unethical conduct in organizations as well as a methodology for predicting how unethical conduct is likely to spread among organization members. This approach has yet to be empirically tested.

An approach related to the influence of referent others and the link between ethical judgment and behavior is the "moral approbation approach" proposed by Jones and Ryan (1997). *Moral approbation* is defined as moral approval from oneself or others. People are thought to desire moral approval from their referent group (Jones and Ryan 1998), and moral approbation is proposed to be related to whether individuals are likely to follow through on what they think is right in an ethical dilemma situation. This approach has also not yet been empirically tested.

Broader External Context: Codes, Climate, and Culture. Treviño (1986, 1990) proposed that the broad ethical culture of an organization would directly influence ethical conduct as well as moderate the cognition/behavior relationship. Again, the moral behavior of employees, especially those at the conventional level of cognitive moral development (most workers), should be influenced by a number of organizational culture variables, such as ethics codes and definitions of authority relationships. The chapters that follow present results from a number of studies (Treviño et al. 1998; 1999; Weaver and Treviño 1999) that have built on and supported these contentions about the important influence of the organizational context on ethical behavior. Context factors that have been studied include the existence and orientation (values-oriented versus compliance-oriented) of formal ethics programs (including codes), employee perceptions of fair treatment, and other aspects of the ethical climate and culture. We will not repeat those findings here, but rather refer to a few additional studies that support this contention as well.

Support for the short- and long-term effects of codes of conduct on ethical behavior in higher education and in the workplace has been found by

McCabe and colleagues (McCabe and Treviño 1993; McCabe, Treviño, and Butterfield 1996). These investigators have conducted research that documented reduced student cheating at honor code institutions (see McCabe, Treviño, and Butterfield, 2001 for a review). Their 1996 study may be of most interest because it found both current and long-term effects of codes on ethical behavior in the workplace. The investigators surveyed alumni of two similar colleges (one with a strong honor code, the other without) who listed business as their occupation. These alumni were asked whether their current organization had an ethics code as well as questions about code implementation and code embeddedness. Social desirability bias was controlled in the statistical analysis. The findings suggested that those currently working in an organization with a code were less likely to self-report unethical behavior. In addition, strength of code implementation had a significant effect. Further, their earlier college honor-code experience interacted with implementation strength of the current organization code to influence self-reported unethical behavior. Unethical conduct was lowest when alumni from the honor-code college currently worked in an organization with a strongly implemented code. This suggests that college honor codes have enduring effects, under certain conditions, and that businesses interested in ethical conduct could benefit by hiring the graduates of honor-code colleges and then strongly implementing an ethics code in their own organization.

Greenberg (in press) conducted a clever field experiment among customer service representatives who worked in offices that either did or did not have a code of ethics. In the experiment, participants were told they would be underpaid for completing a survey after work. They were given the opportunity to steal by offering them a bowl of pennies from which they could take their payment, believing that the amount they took would not be detectable. Those who worked in the code environment were less likely to steal. In addition, those at the conventional level of CMD (as measured by the sociomoral reflection measure (Gibbs, Basinger, and Fuller 1992) were less likely to steal than were those at the preconventional level. Further, a significant interaction effect revealed that, when participants were told that the underpayment had been supplied by the organization (rather than specific managers), level of CMD made little difference in the absence of an ethics code. Where a code existed, however, conventional-level individuals were much less likely to steal than were preconventional individuals.

These studies support the important and complex role played by contextual factors, and they build on earlier research that found that ethics codes influence ethical behavior (for example, Hegarty and Sims 1979), particularly when they are enforced (Laczniak and Inderrieden 1987). Future research should continue to explore these complex relationships, especially aspects of the immediate (e.g., role of supervisors) and broader ethical work context (e.g., role of ethical climate and culture).

EXPLORING THE ROLES OF MORAL MOTIVATION AND MORAL CHARACTER

We stated earlier that moral motivation and moral character have been proposed to be intervening processes between moral judgment and moral action. Few empirical studies have investigated these processes; however, a number of the variables discussed in relation to moral action may influence moral action via motivational processes. For example, locus of control is related to motivation because internals are, by definition, more likely to see the relationship between their actions and outcomes. Similarly, rewards and punishments have clear motivational implications, as does moral approbation. Additional conceptual and empirical work will be required to hypothesize and test the influences of these and other factors on moral motivation and to distinguish that process from moral judgment and action.

Similarly, moral character (defined as "persisting in a moral task" and "having courage") (Rest and Narvaez 1994) has been neglected in both theorizing and empirical research; however, Treviño (1986) proposed an individual difference variable that may be related to moral character. Ego strength is an individual difference construct related to strength of conviction or self-regulating skills. Individuals high on a measure of ego strength are expected to resist impulses and follow their convictions more than those with low-level ego strength. Therefore, they are more likely to follow through on what they think is right. Research has found that self-regulation abilities are associated with morally relevant behavior (cf. Eisenberg 2000). Additional work will be needed to determine whether ego strength is the same as moral character, whether it plays a mediating or moderating role in the ethical decision-making process, and whether the role of other self-regulatory processes needs to be considered.

EXPLORING THE ROLE OF RELIGION

Research on ethical decision making and behavior in organizations has made clear that simple accounts of ethical behavior are untenable. It is not enough to provide people with the right moral principles or theories to follow and expect moral behavior as a result. There are multiple points in the process leading to ethical behavior when failure or diversion can occur. Consider, for example, the case of an individual's religious commitments. Although it might be common to assume that an individual's religion influences ethical behavior, empirical support for that position is mixed at best (Weaver and Agle, 2002). This should not be surprising because religion can influence ethical behavior in a variety of ways, and multiple situational factors can affect the strength of the tie between religion and behavior. Granted, religions usually do provide their adherents with a set of moral guidelines or exemplars; but individuals internalize these guidelines and exemplars to varying degrees. Thus, where one individual may show strong influences of religion in guiding ethical behavior, for another individual, religion may be at best a tangential influence compared with others. For example, the more and deeper a person's relationships with co-workers rather than co-religionists, the more likely the co-workers and organization will influence behavior, in contrast to religious teachings. Even in cases where religion is highly salient to an individual, its salience may be influential in different ways. For one individual, salient religion forms a basis for moral judgment, by application of religiously based ethical principles to the ethical issues faced in life. For another person, salient religion provides a motivation for ethical behavior (for example, perform good deeds to obtain heavenly reward). For yet another, religion serves as a sensitizing device, making the person aware of certain kinds of ethical issues that might otherwise not be noticed. Finally, religion might be practiced by individuals for different reasons. For some persons, it may be practiced as an end in itself, for its intrinsic rewards, whereas for other persons, it may be practiced largely for extrinsic reasons. This difference, in turn, may affect how motivated these individuals are to stand by the ethical claims of their religion in the face of workplace pressures to do otherwise. Consequently, claims that religion does or does not influence ethical decision making and behavior are too simple. Instead, we need to recognize the complexity of these processes and the reasons why religion may or may not be influential.

EXPLORING THE ROLE OF EMOTION

Another limitation of current empirical research is the lack of attention to the role of emotion in our highly cognitive approaches to ethical decision making. This is in keeping with philosophic tradition that has viewed emotions as biasing individuals' thoughts and therefore disrupting rational moral judgment. Philosophers and psychologists more recently suggested that emotions can positively influence moral sensitivity and moral motivation. Eisenberg (2000) reviewed research on emotionality, emotion-related regulation and morally relevant behavior. From this review, we learn that both guilt and shame have been associated with a sense of responsibility and concern that one has violated a moral norm; however, guilt seems to be more highly associated with morality than is shame and more highly associated with empathetic responses. Empathy and positive mood have both been associated with prosocial behavior; negative emotional states appear to interfere with quality cognition generally and moral judgment specifically. Work on the socialization of guilt, shame, and empathy has focused on child development. Therefore, questions about socialization of these emotions in the workplace will need to be addressed by management researchers.

In the business ethics literature, Gaudine and Thorne (2001) outlined a model that proposes the ways in which they believe emotional arousal and positive affect influence multiple stages of the ethical decision-making process. High-quality psychological research is being conducted on the relationship between emotion and moral decision making and behavior. Business ethics researchers also have begun to think about these relationships. Future work that brings the organizational context into consideration should build on this foundation.

CONCLUSION

In this chapter, we have provided an overview of research on individual ethical decision making and behavior in organizational context. We have not attempted to be exhaustive, as others have published exhaustive reviews (e.g., Ford and Richardson 1994; Loe, Ferrell, and Mansfield 2000). Rather, we have painted a picture of the current state of knowledge as we see it. The following chapters offer insight into some of our own research focusing primarily on the role of the ethical context in organizations, from formal ethics programs to less formal aspects of the ethical climate and culture.

References

Ajzen, I. 1988. *Attitudes, personality, and behavior*. Buckingham, UK: Open University Press.

Ambrose, M. L., and M. Schminke. 1999. Sex differences in business ethics: The importance of perceptions. *Journal of Managerial Issues* 11(4):454−474.

Arnold, D., and L. Ponemon. 1991. Internal auditors' perceptions of whistle-blowing and the influence of moral reasoning: An experiment. *Auditing: A Journal of Practice and Theory* Fall:1−15.

Baab, A., and M. J. Bebeau. 1990. The effect of instruction on ethical sensitivity. *Journal of Dental Education* 54(1):44.

Barnett, T., and S. Valentine. 2001. Issue contingencies, ethical environment, and individuals' ethical judgments and behavioral intentions. Paper presented at the national meeting of the Academy of Management, Washington, DC.

Bebeau, M. 1994. Influencing the moral dimension of dental practice. In *Moral development in the professions*, ed. J. Rest and D. Narvaez, 121−146. Hillsdale, N.J.: Erlbaum.

Bebeau, M., and M. M. Brabeck. 1987. Integrating care and justice issues in professional moral education: A gender perspective. *Journal of Moral Education* 16(3):189−203.

Bernardi, R. A. 1994. Fraud detection: The effect of client integrity and competence and auditor cognitive style. *Auditing* 13:68−85.

Brass, D. J., K. D. Butterfield, and B. C. Skaggs. 1998. Relationships and unethical behavior: A social network perspective. *The Academy of Management Review* 23(1):14−31.

Bredemeier, B. J. 1985. Moral reasoning and the perceived legitimacy of intentionally injurious sports acts. *Journal of Sport Psychology* 7:110−124.

Bredemeier, B. J. 1994. Children's moral reasoning and their assertive, aggressive, and submissive tendencies in sport and daily life. *Journal of Sport and Exercise Psychology* 16:1−14.

Bredemeier, B. J., and D. L. Shields. 1984. Divergence in moral reasoning about sport and life. *Sociology of Sport Journal* 1:348−357.

Bredemeier, B. J., and D. L. Shields. 1984. Applied ethics and moral reasoning in sport. In *Moral development in the professions: Psychology and applied ethics*, ed. J. Rest and D. Narvaez, 173−188. Hillsdale, NJ: Erlbaum.

Bredemeier, B. J., and D. L. Shields. 1986a. Athletic aggression: An issue of con-textual morality. *Sociology of Sport Journal* 3:15–28.

Bredemeier, B. J., and D. L. Shields. 1986b. Game reasoning and interactional morality. *Journal of Genetic Psychology* 147:257–275.

Bredemeier, B. J., and D. L. Shields. 1986c. Moral growth among athletes and nonathletes: A comparative analysis. *Journal of Genetic Psychology* 147:7–18.

Butterfield, K., L. K. Treviño, and G. R. Weaver. 2000. Moral awareness in busi-ness organizations: Influences of issue-related and social context factors. *Human Relations* 53(7):981–1018.

Carlson, D. S., K. M. Kacmar, L. L. Wadsworth, and S. Zivnuska. 2001. The impact of moral intensity dimensions on ethical decision making. Paper presented at the meeting of the National Academy of Management, Washington, D.C.

Colby, A., and L. Kohlberg. 1987. *The measurement of moral judgment: Theoretical foundations and research validations, and standard issue scoring manual*, Vols. 1 and 2. Cambridge: Cambridge University Press.

Colby, A., L. Kohlberg, J. C. Gibbs, and M. Lieberman. 1983. A longitudinal study of moral judgment. *Monographs of the Society for Research in Child Development* 48(1–2):1–124.

Derry, R. 1987. Moral reasoning in work-related conflicts. In *Research in Corporate Social Performance and Policy*, Vol. 9. Greenwich, Conn.: JAI Press.

Derry, R. 1989. An empirical study of moral reasoning among managers. *Journal of Business Ethics* 8:855–862.

Dukerich, J. M., M. L. Nichols, D. R. Elm, and D. A. Vollrath. 1990. Moral reason-ing in groups: Leaders make a difference. *Human Relations* 43(5):473–493.

Eisenberg, N. 2000. Emotion, regulation, and moral development. *Annual Review of Psychology* 51:665–697.

Elm, D. R., and M. L. Nichols. 1993. An investigation of the moral reasoning of managers. *Journal of Business Ethics* 12:817–833.

Flannery, B. L., and D. R. May. 2000. Environmental ethical decision making in the U.S. metal-finishing industry. *Academy of Management Journal* 43:642–662.

Ford, R. C., and W. D. Richardson. 1994. Ethical decision-making: A review of the empirical literature. *Journal of Business Ethics* 13(3):206–224.

Frank, R. H., T. Gilovich, and D. T. Regan. 1993. Does studying economics inhibit cooperation? *The Journal of Economic Perspectives* 7(2):159.

Gaudine, A., and L. Thorne, L. 2001. Emotion and ethical decision-making in organizations. *Journal of Business Ethics* 31(2):175–187.

Gibbs, J. C., and K. F. Widaman. 1982. *Social intelligence: Measuring the development of sociomoral reflection*. Englewood Cliffs, NJ: Prentice-Hall.

Gibbs, J., K. D. Arnold, R. L. Morgan, E. S. Schwartz, M. P. Gavaghan, and M. B. Tappan. 1984. Construction and validation of a multiple-choice measure of moral reasoning. *Child Development* 55:527–536.

Gibbs, J. C., K. S. Basinger, and D. Fuller. 1992. *Moral maturity: Measuring the development of sociomoral reflection*. Hillsdale, NJ: Erlbaum.

Gielen, U. P., and D. C. Markoulis. 1994. Preference for principled moral reasoning: A developmental and cross-cultural perspective. In *Cross cultural topics in psychology*, ed. L.L. Adler and U.P. Gielen, 73–87. Westport, CT: Greenwood.

Gilligan, C. 1982. *In a different voice*. Cambridge, MA: Harvard University Press.

Gioia, D. A. 1992. Pinto fires and personal ethics: A script analysis of missed opportunities. *Journal of Business Ethics* 11:379–389.

Gioia, D. A., and C. C. Manz. 1985. Linking cognition and behavior: A script-processing interpretation of vicarious learning. *Academy of Management Review* 10:527–539.

Greenberg, J. (in press). Who stole the money, and when? Individual and situational determinants of employee theft. *Organizational Behavior and Human Decision Processes*.

Grover, S. 1993. Why professionals lie: The impact of professional role conflict on reporting accuracy. *Organizational Behavior and Human Decision Processes* 55:251–272.

Grover, S. 1997. Lying in organizations: Theory, research and future directions. In *Antisocial behavior in organizations*, ed. R. A. Giacolone and J. Greenberg. Thousand Oaks, CA: Sage.

Hare, R. M. 1952. *The language of morals*. Oxford: Oxford University Press.

Hare, R. M. 1963. *Freedom and reason*. Oxford: Oxford University Press.

Hegarty, W. H., and H. P. Sims. 1978. Some determinants of unethical decision behavior: An experiment. *Journal of Applied Psychology* 63(4):451–457.

Hegarty, W. H., and H. P. Sims. 1979. Organizational philosophy, policies, and objectives related to unethical decision behavior. A laboratory experiment. *Journal of Applied Psychology* 64(3):331–338.

Jones, T. M. 1991. Ethical decision making by individuals in organizations: An issue-contingent model. *Academy of Management Review* 16(2):366–395.

Jones, T. M., and L. V. Ryan. 1997. The link between ethical judgment and action in organizations: A moral approbation approach. *Organization Science* 8(6):663–680.

Jones, T. M., and L. V. Ryan. 1998. The effect of organizational forces on individual morality: Judgment, moral approbation, and behavior. *Business Ethics Quarterly* 8(3):431–445.

Kohlberg, L. 1969. Stage and sequence: The cognitive developmental approach to socialization. In *Handbook of socialization theory*, ed. D. A. Goslin, 347–480. Chicago: Rand McNally.

Kohlberg, L. 1984. *Essays on moral development: The psychology of moral development: The nature and validity of moral stages.* San Francisco: Harper & Row.

Kohlberg, L. 1986. A current statement on some theoretical issues. In *Lawrence Kohlberg: Consensus and controversy*, ed. S. Modgil and C. Modgil, 485–546. Philadelphia: Falmer, Lampe & Finn, 1992.

Laczniak, G., and E. J. Inderrieden. 1987. The influence of stated organizational concern upon ethical decision making. *Journal of Business Ethics* 6:297–307.

Lampe, J., and D. Finn. 1992. A model of auditors' ethical decision process. *Auditing: A Journal of Practice and Theory* (Suppl)1–21.

Lapsley, D.K. 1996. *Moral psychology*. Boulder: Westview Press.

Loe, T. W., L. Ferrell, and P. Mansfield. 2000. A review of empirical studies assessing ethical decision making in business. *Journal of Business Ethics* 25:195–204.

MacIntyre, A. *After virtue*. 1984. Notre Dame IN: University of Notre Dame Press.

May, D. R., and K. P. Pauli. 2000. The role of moral intensity in ethical decision making: A review and investigation of moral recognition, evaluation, and intention. Manuscript presented at the meeting of the National Academy of Management, Toronto, August 2000.

McCabe, D., and L. K. Treviño. 1993. Academic dishonesty: Honor codes and other contextual influences. *Journal of Higher Education* 64(5):522–538.

McCabe, D., L. K. Treviño, and K. Butterfield. 1996. The influence of collegiate and corporate codes of conduct on ethics-related behavior in the workplace. *Business Ethics Quarterly* 6:441–460.

McCabe, D., L. K. Treviño, and K. Butterfield. 2001. Cheating in academic institutions: A decade of research. *Ethics and Behavior* 11(3):219–232.

Moon, Y. L. 1985. A review of cross-cultural studies on moral judgment development using the Defining Issues Test. Paper presented at American Educational Research Association annual meeting, Chicago, 1985.

Mulhall, S., and A. Swift. 1992. *Liberals and communitarians*. Oxford: Blackwell.

Narvaez, D. 1999. Using discourse processing methods to study moral thinking. *Educational Psychology Review* 11(4):377–393.

Nichols, M. L., and V. E. Day. 1982. A comparison of moral reasoning of groups and individuals on the "Defining Issues Test." *Academy of Management Journal* 25:201–208.

Nisbett, R. E., and T. D. Wilson. 1977. Telling more than we can know: Verbal reports on mental processes. *Psychological Review* 84(3):231–259.

Piaget, J. 1932. *The moral judgment of the child*. New York: Free Press.

Ponemon, L. 1988. A cognitive-developmental approach to the analysis of certified public accountants' ethical judgments. Unpublished doctoral dissertation, Union College, Schenectady, NY.

Ponemon, L. 1990. Ethical judgments in accounting: A cognitive-developmental perspective. *Critical perspectives on accounting*, 191–215.

Ponemon, L. A. 1992. Ethical reasoning and selection-socialization in accounting. *Accounting, Organizations, and Society* 17(3/4):239–258.

Ponemon, L., and D. R. L. Gabhart. 1994. Ethical reasoning research in the accounting and auditing professions. In *Moral development in the professions: Psychology and applied ethics*, ed. J. Rest and D. Narvaez, 101–119. Hillsdale, NJ: Erlbaum.

Rawls, J. 1971. *A theory of justice*. Cambridge, MA: Harvard University Press.

Rest, J. 1979. *Development in judging moral issues*. Minneapolis: University of Minnesota Press.

Rest, J. R., and Narvaez, D. 1994. *Moral development in the professions: Psychology and applied ethics*. Hillsdale, NJ: Erlbaum.

Rest, J., D. Narvaez, M. J. Bebeau, and S. J. Thoma. 1999. *Postconventional moral thinking: A neo-Kohlbergian approach*. Mahwah, NJ: Erlbaum.

Rest, J., S. J. Thoma, Y. L. Moon, and I. Getz. 1986. Different cultures, sexes, and religions. In *Moral development: Advances in research and theory*, ed. J. Rest, 89–132. New York: Praeger.

Robertson, D. C., and T. Rymon. 2001. Purchasing agents' deceptive behavior: A randomized response technique study. *Business Ethics Quarterly* 11(3):455–479.

Rotter, J. B. 1966. Generalized expectancies for internal versus external control of reinforcement. *Psychological monographs: General and applied*, Vol. 80, p. 609.

Sandel, M. J. 1982. *Liberalism and the limits of justice*. Cambridge: Cambridge University Press.

Schweder, R. A., M. Mahaptra, and J. G. Miller. 1987. Culture and moral development. In *The emergence of morality in young children*, ed. J. Kagan and S. Lamb, 1–83. Chicago: University of Chicago Press.

Shaub, M. 1989. An empirical examination of the determinants of auditors' ethical sensitivity. Unpublished doctoral dissertation. Texas Technological University. Lubbock.

Siegler, R. S. 1997. Concepts and methods for studying cognitive change. In *Change and development: Issues of theory, method, and application*, ed. E. Amsel and K. A. Renninger, 77–98. Mahwah, NJ: Erlbaum.

Snarey, J. 1985. The cross-cultural universality of social-moral development. *Psychological Bulletin* 97(2):202–232.

Sutherland, E., and D. R. Cressey. 1970. *Principles of criminology*, 8th ed. Chicago: Lippincott.

Tenbrunsel, A. E. 1998. Misrepresentation and expectations of misrepresentation in an ethical dilemma: The role of incentives and temptation. *Academy of Management Journal* 41(3):330–339.

Thoma, S. J. 1994. Moral judgment and moral action. In *Moral development in the professions: Psychology and applied ethics*, ed. J. Rest and D. Narzaez, 199–211. Hillsdale, NJ: Erlbaum.

Treviño, L. K. 1986. Ethical decision-making in organizations: A person situation interactionist model. *Academy of Management Review* 11(3):601–617.

Treviño, L. K. 1990. A cultural perspective on changing and developing organizational ethics. In *Research in Organizational Change and Development*, Vol. 4, ed. R. Woodman and W. Passmore, 195–230. Greenwich, CT: JAI Press.

Treviño, L. K. 1992. Moral reasoning and business ethics: Implications for research, education, and management. *Journal of Business Ethics* 11:445–459.

Treviño, L. K., and G. A. Ball. 1992. The social implications of punishing unethical behavior: Observers' cognitive and affective reactions. *Journal of Management* 18:4.

Treviño, L. K., and K. Nelson. 1999. *Managing business ethics: Straight talk about how to do it right*. New York: John Wiley and Sons.

Treviño, L. K., and S. A. Youngblood. 1990. Bad apples in bad barrels: A causal analysis of ethical decision making behavior. *Journal of Applied Psychology* 75(4):378–385.

Treviño, L. K., K. Butterfield, and D. McCabe. 1998. The ethical context in organizations: Influences on employee attitudes and behaviors. *Business Ethics Quarterly* 8(3):447–476.

Treviño, L. K., G. Weaver, D. Gibson, and B. Toffler. 1999. Managing ethics and legal compliance: What works and what hurts. *California Management Review* 41(2):131–151.

Walker, L. 1984. Sex differences in the development of moral reasoning: A critical review. *Child Development* 55:677–691.

Weaver, G. R., and B. Agle. 2002. Religiosity and ethical behavior in organizations: A symbolic interactionist perspective. *Academy of Management Review* 27:77–97.

Weaver, G. R., and L. K. Treviño. 1999. Compliance and values oriented ethics programs: Influences on employees' attitudes and behavior. *Business Ethics Quarterly* 9(2):325–345.

Weber, J. 1990. Managers' moral reasoning: Assessing their responses to three moral dilemmas. *Human Relations* 43:687–702.

Weber, J. 1996. Influences upon managerial moral decision making: Nature of the harm and magnitude of consequences. *Human Relations* 49:1–22.

Weber, J., and D. Wasieleski. 2001. Investigating influences on managers' moral reasoning: The impact of context, personal, and organizational factors. *Business and Society* 40(1):79–111.

Zahn-Waxler, C., M. Radke-Yarrow, E. Wagner, and M. Chapman. 1992. Development of concern for others. *Developmental Psychology* 28:126–136.

Zey-Ferrell, M., and O. C. Ferrell. 1982. Role-set configuration and opportunity as predictors of unethical behavior in organizations. *Human Relations* 35(7):587–604.

Zey-Ferrell, M., K. M. Weaver, and O. C. Ferrell. 1979. Predicting unethical behavior among marketing practitioners. *Human Relations* 32(7):557–569.

EIGHT

The Uses and Limits of Formal Ethics Programs

As we reported in Part II, formal ethics programs have become more common in American corporations. As Part II also made clear, multiple questions can be raised about the outcomes of these programs and about their potential limitations. Do they really reduce unethical behavior in the workplace? Do they generate other positive benefits? Are employees more committed to organizations with ethics programs because they view the organization as somehow more worthy of their support because of its proactive stance toward ethics? Along with consideration of positive benefits, however, it also is important to recognize the potential limitations of formal ethics programs. As Part II indicated, it is possible for formal ethics programs to be marginalized or decoupled from meaningful organizational impacts. Top executives and regular organizational policies and practices may fail to provide the ethics program with the kind of support that it needs to be effective. Some ways to implement ethics programs (for example, narrow compliance or values orientations) may be relatively weak in their impact compared with other, more complex implementations.

In Chapter 7, we provided a review of the various factors likely to in-

Portions of this chapter are adapted from G. R. Weaver and L. K. Treviño, 1999, "Compliance and values oriented ethics programs: Influences on employees' attitudes and behavior," *Business Ethics Quarterly* 9(2):315–335. Reproduced with permission of *Business Ethics Quarterly*. Portions also adapted from L. K. Treviño, G. R. Weaver, D. G. Gibson, and B. L. Toffler, 1999, "Managing ethics and legal compliance: What hurts and what works." Copyright © 1999, by The Regents of the University of California. Reprinted from the *California Management Review*, Vol. 41(2). By permission of The Regents.

fluence organization members to act in ethical or unethical fashion. In this chapter, we look empirically at some of these factors, focusing specifically on the potential for formal ethics programs to influence the behavior of organization members. We begin by building on the distinction between compliance and values ethics program orientations developed in Chapter 5 and empirically consider a range of potential outcomes from those two approaches to ethics initiatives. We then briefly review research that suggests that one of the most obvious elements of efforts to foster ethics in organizations—codes of ethics—might be the least effective in accomplishing anything. This brief review provides grounds for considering a range of organizational factors that can either enhance or undermine any formal effort to foster ethical behavior. So we conclude the chapter by looking more broadly, beyond issues of compliance and values orientations, to a range of organizational processes and characteristics that are at least as important as any formal ethics program in fostering ethical behavior.

COMPLIANCE AND VALUES ORIENTATIONS: INFLUENCES ON EMPLOYEES' ATTITUDES AND BEHAVIOR

Ethics programs attempt to bring some degree of order and predictability to employee behavior. Thus, as argued in Chapter 5, it makes sense to characterize ethics programs as organizational control systems, that is, as systems that aim to create predictability in employee behavior and correspondence between specific employee behaviors and more general organizational goals and expectations.

Control systems have received much analysis in the organizational and sociological literatures, and a number of different dimensions of control systems have been identified. Following the framework adopted for Chapter 5, we focus on the mode by which control systems create order and alignment in the behavior of organization members. Control systems have been distinguished according to whether they create order by coercing behavioral compliance or by generating employee identification with and commitment to collective organizational values (Etzioni 1961; Gouldner 1954; Weber 1947). In the former case, a control system is seen as necessary to bring employee behavior into conformity with organizational requirements—sometimes coercively. In the latter case, organizational goals are assumed to be such that employees can identify with them and thereby act according to them, perhaps because they are consistent with the employees' own needs, goals, or identity (Adler and Borys 1996).

Ethics programs can be characterized in similar terms. Some programs are oriented toward rule compliance and threats of punishment for non-compliance. Other programs emphasize ethical values and the potential for employees to be committed to a set of ethical ideals embodied in the organization. In keeping with Chapter 5, we refer to these two orientations toward control as *compliance orientation* and *values orientation*, respectively. As an example of a compliance orientation, consider our experience in interviewing the ethics-responsible officer at a medium-sized defense contractor. That company's ethics program goals typically were phrased in terms of legal compliance. The program was headed by an attorney, guidelines read like (and referred to) legal statutes and contracts, and communications regarding the guidelines generally took the form of teaching employees the rules with which they were to comply, along with the sanctions for noncompliance. By contrast, an ethics program at a health care products company we visited was defined as a "shared values" program; primarily involved persons from human resources, marketing, and operating backgrounds; and focused more on abstract core ideals, such as "respect" and "responsibility." Moreover, the program director was sensitive to the symbolic impact of a wide range of company actions and policies on employees' ability to commit to the ideals, indicating (for example) his belief that the company's elimination of separate executive dining facilities was important in encouraging employee commitment to the company's ethical ideals. Although penalties were attached to behavior that violated the company's ethical ideals, the program did not focus on explicating those ideals in terms of rules and penalties. Instead, company values were seen as something that people would want to aspire to and as ideals that could be articulated and affirmed in a variety of formal and informal ways.

Values and compliance orientations need not be mutually exclusive. For example, a strong values-based ethics program can coexist with some amount of rules, accountability, and disciplinary mechanisms (Treviño 1990; Weaver, Treviño, and Cochran 1999), as was the case in the health care products company mentioned earlier. Some organizations may develop a program more exclusively values or compliance oriented, whereas others may include aspects of each orientation and attempt to balance the two.

Observers have suggested that these different approaches to ethics management will have different impacts on employee attitudes and behavior. Paine, for example, suggested that compliance approaches alone will do little to generate "moral imagination or commitment" (Paine 1994, 111), in part because they provide a kind of minimalist "don't get caught" motivation. This suggests that these two types of programs may influence different outcomes; a compliance orientation may generate behavioral conformity, whereas a values orientation may generate other outcomes, such as commitment to the organization.

Within a specific organization, employees may perceive different degrees of values and compliance orientations, depending on their immediate organizational context. Even though high-level management may intend to implement an ethics program with a uniform character across the entire organization, that program will be interpreted and implemented by different people in different places. For example, Weber (1995) found that perceptions of ethical climates varied by department within a company. Thus, individual managers' practices, along with specific organizational contexts (for example, sales, auditing, operations) can contribute to differences in ethics program orientation as experienced by employees. In this study, then, we focus on individual employees' perceptions of ethics program orientation in a single company and the link between those perceptions and employee behaviors and attitudes. In the next section, we develop hypotheses concerning these relationships.

Ethics Program Outcomes

Before articulating the theoretical relationships between ethics program orientations and employee outcomes, it is necessary to identify some of the relevant employee outcomes of ethics programs. Practitioners have lamented the lack of attention given to evaluation of the effectiveness of ethics programs. Many firms follow the United States Sentencing Commission (USSC) guidelines' (1994) stipulations for due diligence without identifying desired outcomes from their investment in ethics programs (beyond reduced penalties if they are caught engaging in misconduct) and without systematically evaluating their programs. In this study, we focus on eight presumably desirable outcomes of ethics programs: increased employee awareness of ethical issues, commitment to the organization, employee integrity, willingness to communicate openly about problems, willingness to report an ethics violation to management, improved decision making, willingness to seek advice about ethical issues, and reduced unethical conduct. We recognize that ethics programs might influence other outcomes, including some that may be undesirable from some perspectives (Weaver 1993). Our experience with practicing managers and ethics officers, however, suggests these eight outcomes are among the most salient.

We also develop theory to help us understand the relationships between perceived ethics program orientation and outcomes. For example, why would employees at the health care products company or the defense contractor described earlier act in accord with the ethics/compliance program? Why might they feel committed to the organization or feel free to seek ethical advice? In general, we propose that the outcomes of values-based programs are best understood in terms of research on role identity, perceived organizational support for a set of shared values, and social exchange, whereas the outcomes of compliance-based programs can best be understood in terms of contractual exchange.

Values Orientation: Role Identity and Perceived Organizational Support

If an ethics program encourages a sense of shared values and suggests that the program exists to aid employees in doing their work and achieving their goals, the program can influence employees' role identity and can suggest to employees that they enjoy a high degree of organizational support. Each of these general impacts of a values orientation in turn suggests specific outcomes.

Values Orientation and Role Identity. Widespread attention to shared values, through both formal and informal means, helps to create expectations or norms for appropriate behavior within an organization. According to symbolic interactionist and social identity theories, these expectations define roles for organizational members (Ashforth and Mael 1989; Stryker 1980; Stryker and Serpe 1982). Moreover, because part of a person's sense of self is learned or acquired through interaction with others, these roles constitute an element of one's identity. Interaction with others provides a repertoire of behavioral expectations that contribute to one's sense of self.

Within business organizations, norms obviously exist for profit-oriented, managerial behavior and for a corresponding role identity (or sense of self) as a profit-seeking manager. In an organization with a well-developed, values-oriented ethics program, there will also be forms of social interaction that involve an expectation that employees will aspire to a set of shared ethical values. Consider, for example, the symbolic significance attached to the lack of executive dining facilities at the health care company described earlier; interaction within that organization is structured to suggest that everyone is committed to common values of mutual respect. The focus on shared values, in effect, creates a role identity for employees that specifically incorporates ethical concern and action as components. Even though members of that organization have other role identities (such as that of profit-oriented manager), the significance given to a shared sense of values increases the salience of an employee's ethical identity within the total set of organizational roles (Stryker 1968; Stryker and Serpe 1982). Even if a person has a sense of self that involves a high commitment to ethics in his or her life outside the organization, the focus on values within the organization will increase the salience, and thus influence, of that ethical identity when it otherwise might pale compared with other, job-related identities. This increased salience of one's ethical role identity has cognitive, behavioral, and attitudinal consequences.

Values Orientation and Perceived Organizational Support.   According to social exchange theory (Blau 1964), when one person receives some kind of social (rather than economic) benefit from another, a reciprocal expectation for some kind of return favor is created (Rousseau and Parks 1993). Although much organizational research has focused on social exchanges between leaders and subordinates (for example, Graen and Scandura 1987), recent attention also has been directed to social exchanges between organizations and their members. In particular, research has focused on the idea of perceived organizational support, understood as employees' perceptions that their organization in general "values their contributions and cares for their well-being" (Eisenberger et al. 1986, 501). In short, a perception that the organization supports the employee's goals creates a sense of obligation by an employee to support the organization's goals in return. Perceived organizational support has been related positively to conscientiousness and commitment on the part of employees (Eisenberger, Fasolo, and Davis-LaMastro 1990).

A values-oriented ethics program can be perceived as supporting employees. Instead of focusing solely on the detection and discipline of offenses—suggesting perhaps that employees cannot be trusted or are in some other way ethically incompetent—a values-oriented program suggests that employees already are committed to ethical behavior. The task of the program is to encourage the development of meaningful, shared ethical values within the organization's particular context. In a values-oriented program, emphasis is on activities that aid employees in decision making, provide ethical advice and counseling, and support the development of a consensus about what constitutes good business ethics. Moreover, the focus on *shared* values in such programs suggests that every organization member has the same status vis-à-vis ethics. A strong values orientation, then, supports employee aspirations and suggests that the organization embodies a collective commitment that applies equally to all persons.

Ethical Role Identity, Perceived Organizational Support, and Outcomes. In general, then, we expect that a values oriented ethics program can influence employees through two general processes: (1) by enhancing the salience of the employee's ethical role identity and (2) by creating a greater perception of organizational support that in turn can influence the employee's social exchange relationship with the organization. We expect these general processes to be exemplified in several specific relationships.

Research on roles (McNamara and Blumer 1982) indicates that taking on a role can have cognitive impacts on a person. Values-oriented programs make an employee's ethical role identity more salient, thus enabling employees to recognize and acknowledge more easily the ethical issues they face on the job. In organizations with values-oriented ethics programs, we should find greater levels of employee awareness of, and open concern for, ethical issues. The values orientation of an ethics program, in effect, makes awareness of ethical issues an in-role behavior and should reduce tendencies toward "moral muteness" in which employees keep silent about ethical issues at work (Bird and Waters 1989).

HYPOTHESIS 1: The more employees perceive that an ethics program is values oriented, the more employees will be aware of ethical issues at work.

Ethical organizational role identities also suggest that it is in keeping with an organization's goals for employees to admit uncertainty about the ethics of decisions and to take action to resolve ethical questions. Moreover, the perceived organizational support generated by a values-oriented program means that employees will trust the organization to be concerned for their welfare and to value their presence. Thus, values-oriented programs provide both a role-based motive for raising ethical questions and seeking ethical advice and a social exchange–based sense that advice can be sought without fear of embarrassment or criticism. Thus, values-oriented ethics programs should encourage employees to seek ethical advice.

HYPOTHESIS 2: The more employees perceive that an ethics program is values oriented, the more employees will be willing to seek ethical advice within the organization.

Values-oriented ethics programs also should result in lower levels of unethical behavior within an organization. The nature of the program encourages ethical behavior as part of one's role, and role identities are linked to behavior. Behavior contrary to a salient role, moreover, would generate serious cognitive dissonance (Festinger 1957) and also would violate the terms of the social exchange generated by perceived organizational support.

HYPOTHESIS 3: The more employees perceive that an ethics program is values oriented, the less unethical behavior there will be in the organization.

Previous research has shown positive relationships between perceived organizational support and employee commitment to the organization (Eisenberger, Fasolo, and Davis-LaMastro 1990). The more an organization supports the employee, the stronger a sense of obligation the employee feels toward the organization. Thus, assuming that values-oriented ethics programs do convey a sense of support and respect toward employees, we should find that they generate commitment to the organization; but they also should do this through their influence on employee roles. Most persons probably think of themselves as ethical, at least when they are not "on the job." The more an organization defines ethical behavior as part of employees' role expectations, the less working for the organization is likely to generate conflict between an organizational role (for example, to make a profit) and an extraorganizational role (for example, to be an ethical person). Reduced role conflict typically is associated with reduced stress and greater willingness to stay with an organization. Thus, values-oriented programs are likely to influence employee commitment through their impact on both role identity and perceived organizational support.

HYPOTHESIS 4: The more employees perceive that an ethics program is values oriented, the greater commitment employees will feel toward the organization.

Similarly, the lack of role conflict will allow employees to believe that their integrity is intact. *Integrity* is defined as "wholeness," the ability to believe that one can be the same person and hold the same ethical values at home and at work. As suggested, given the values-oriented program's focus on shared values, the employee should feel less conflict between organizational and extraorganizational roles.

HYPOTHESIS 5: The more employees perceive that an ethics program is values oriented, the more employees will believe that their integrity is intact.

A values-oriented ethics program also can affect the quality of communication processes within organizations. The creation of trust is typical of social exchange processes in general (Blau 1964). The perception of organizational support produced by a values-oriented program in turn should generate more trust between organizations and their members. Therefore, we should expect more open and respectful communication in organizations with values-oriented ethics programs. In particular, we should find greater willingness on the part of employees to deliver "bad news" to supervisors. The sense of support and trust provided by a values-oriented program suggests that there will be fewer fears about "shooting the messenger" of bad news.

HYPOTHESIS 6: The more employees perceive that an ethics program is values oriented, the more employees will believe it is acceptable to deliver "bad news" to superiors.

The trust generated by values-oriented programs, and the more open communication they help encourage, in turn should yield better decision making as a result of the program. Moreover, when ethical awareness is part of employees' role identity, we should find a greater range of potential issues and problems being attended to in decision-making processes; decision processes should take into account a greater array of stakeholder concerns (Freeman 1984). This combination of open and trusting communication, with more attention paid to a broad range of potential issues, should influence employees' perceptions that decision making within the organization is better because of the program.

HYPOTHESIS 7: The more an ethics program displays a values orientation, the more employees will perceive higher quality decision making as a result of the program.

Compliance Orientation: Discipline and Contractual Exchange

The more an ethics program is oriented toward compliance, the more it emphasizes behavioral monitoring and discipline for noncompliance. Neither of these is suggestive of organizational support for employees. If anything, behavioral monitoring suggests distrust of employees. On the other hand, punishment for misconduct may signal that the organization upholds standards of justice and as such may be valued by employees (Treviño 1993). In the absence of other indicators of organizational support, however, employees may see punishment primarily as something to be feared and avoided. The impact of punishment on employees depends on the social context surrounding the punishment, including factors such as the quality of relationships enjoyed by the punished person (Arvey and Ivancevich 1980) and the fairness with which the punishment is carried out (Ball, Treviño, and Sims 1994). All else being equal, we propose that a focus on monitoring and discipline in an ethics program is more likely to engender a contractual employee attitude toward the organization rather than a perception of organizational support and trust or increased salience for one's ethical obligation as an organization member. A compliance-oriented ethics program is more likely to work by threat of coercion and appeal to a more narrow, calculative conception of exchange (Homans 1961). Employees may learn to behave ethically from compliance approaches, but the learning more likely will involve calculation and conditioning rather than role redefinition.

The rules enforced by a compliance program do define expectations for employee behavior, but those rules are imposed from "outside" the employee rather than resulting from values with which all organizational members identify. They constitute a "top-down" imposition, rather than identification and internalization processes. Whatever salience they create for an ethical role identity is created by the fear of discipline for nonconformity. Moreover, the behavioral monitoring characteristic of a compliance orientation signals distrust. Taken together, fear and lack of trust suggest a calculative, self-interested response to the ethics program, one unlikely to enhance organizational commitment or communication.

Compliance-oriented ethics programs nevertheless should have some desired outcomes stemming from employees' calculative responses to them. The experience of punishment for nonconformity and the fear of punishment for anticipated nonconformity together should reduce the amount of unethical behavior in an organization with a compliance-oriented ethics program. Such an orientation also gives employees an incentive to make sure they understand the company's rules. Thus, compliance-oriented programs also should encourage advice seeking by employees. Finally, the threat of discipline for violations of ethics expectations should make ethical issues more salient to employees, heightening their awareness of circumstances that might present risks of ethical failure.

HYPOTHESIS 8: The more employees perceive that an ethics program is compliance oriented, the less unethical behavior there will be in the organization.

HYPOTHESIS 9: The more employees perceive that an ethics program is compliance oriented, the more employees will be willing to seek ethical advice within the organization.

HYPOTHESIS 10: The more employees perceive that an ethics program is compliance oriented, the more employees will be aware of ethical issues at work.

As noted, the existence of rules and punishments for improper behavior can also fulfill employees' expectations for organizational justice (Treviño 1993). People are motivated to seek justice (Lerner 1977), and they expect that organizations to which they belong will support that motivation. Thus, we might expect employees to support a compliance-oriented ethics program by acting as monitors on their own, reporting rule violations to management to see that justice is upheld within the organization. In the absence of perceived organizational support and a role identity that suggests that "watching out" for ethics is part of the job, however, employees may be reluctant to act on the justice motive. Management may not be trusted to protect the whistle blower from retaliation. Without an ethical role identity shared by most employees, co-workers likely will see reporting behavior as "snitching" or "squealing" rather than an exercise of legitimate role obligations. Thus, for a compliance-oriented ethics program to enlist the employee support that justice concerns suggest, it is necessary for the ethics program to also exhibit the kind of values orientation that fosters perceptions of support and a sense of ethical role identity.

> HYPOTHESIS 11: The more employees perceive that an ethics program is both compliance oriented and values oriented, the more employees will be willing to report unethical behavior to management.

METHODS

The data used to test the hypothesized relationships were drawn from a survey of employees in a financial services company. The company supplied a complete list of employee names and addresses for its 17,010 employees. The researchers drew a random sample of two thousand employees for the study; 420 employees responded, for a 21 percent response rate. Surveys were sent directly to employees, along with a letter from the company supporting the research and encouraging employees to participate. Respondents were instructed to return the completed survey directly to the researchers in postage-paid, self-addressed envelopes. Employees were assured of anonymity. There was no identification information on the surveys.

Dependent Variable Measures

All dependent variable scales were developed by the researchers and were based on Likert-type survey items on a five-point scale, anchored by strongly disagree (score of 1) and strongly agree (score of 5), unless otherwise noted. The first dependent variable, *ethical awareness*, represents the extent to which employees are aware of ethical issues at work. This scale consisted of three items with a Cronbach's alpha of 0.74. A sample item is as follows: "If ethics or compliance issues arise here, employees are aware of them." *Employee commitment* to the organization is a seven-item scale adapted from existing scales, including Allen and Meyer's affective commitment measure (1990) and O'Reilly and Chatman's (1986) internalization and identification commitment measures. *Affective commitment* refers to an employee's psychological attachment to the organization because of identification with the organization and its values. *Internalization* refers more specifically to psychological attachment based on congruence between organizational and individual values. *Identification* refers to psychological attachment based on a desire for affiliation. Sample items include statements such as, "I feel attached to this company because of its values," and "Employees in this organization generally represent the organization favorably to outsiders." The scale has a Cronbach's alpha of 0.91.

Employee integrity was measured with a three-item scale with a Cronbach's alpha of 0.72. A sample item is as follows: "I can live by the same values at home and at work." Employees' perception that it is *acceptable to deliver bad news* in the organization is a four-item scale with a Cronbach's alpha of 0.89. A sample item is "Employees here are comfortable delivering bad news to their managers." The likelihood that *employees would report an ethics violation* to management is a six-item scale with a Cronbach's alpha of 0.86. A sample item is as follows: "People in this company would let management know about an ethics or compliance violation by a coworker."

Employees' perceptions that people in the organization *make better decisions because of the ethics/compliance program* was measured using a two-item scale with a Cronbach's alpha of 0.85. A sample item is as follows: "People in this firm make more effective ethical decisions because of the ethics or compliance activities that are in place." Employees' perception that *employees seek ethical advice* consisted of two items with a Cronbach's alpha of 0.87. A sample item is as follows: "When ethical issues arise, employees look for advice within the company."

The extent to which respondents had *observed unethical behavior in the organization* is a thirty-two-item scale adapted from Akaah (1992) and Treviño, Butterfield, and McCabe (1998), with a Cronbach's alpha of 0.95. The scale included a list of thirty-two unethical behaviors (e.g., lying to customers, padding an expense account, giving gifts or favors in exchange for preferential treatment, misusing insider information, and so on). Respondents were asked to report "Over the past year, how often have you observed the following types of behavior in your organization?" The scale was

TABLE 8.1
Pearson Correlations

	Mean	SD	1	2	3	4	5	6	7	8	9
Values orientation	3.38	0.85									
Compliance orientation	3.64	0.73	0.63								
Ethical awareness	3.42	0.76	0.52	0.47							
Employee integrity	4.16	0.81	0.45	0.32	0.43						
Employee commitment	3.64	0.82	0.61	0.45	0.59	0.67					
Acceptable to deliver "bad news"	3.20	0.95	0.53	0.35	0.52	0.56	0.69				
Employees would report violation	3.31	0.77	0.51	0.40	0.67	0.57	0.64	0.70			
Better decision making	3.34	0.89	0.65	0.53	0.68	0.46	0.68	0.60	0.65		
Employees seek advice	3.58	0.90	0.50	0.43	0.61	0.42	0.62	0.55	0.60	0.65	
Observed unethical behavior	1.74	0.58	−0.42	−0.37	−0.44	−0.46	−0.54	−0.44	−0.47	−0.50	−0.40

SD, standard deviation.

All correlations are significant at the $p < 0.01$ level.

anchored by 1 = never, 2 = rarely, 3 = occasionally, 4 = frequently, 5 = very frequently.

Independent Variable Measures

The survey also asked respondents to report on the "orientation of the goals or activities of the ethics/compliance program/policies in place in the organization." These five-point Likert scales, ranging from "not at all" (a score of 1) to "to a very large degree" (a score of 5), were adapted from previous research (Weaver, Treviño, and Cochran 1999).

The *values-based orientation* scale consisted of five items: "counseling employees," "encouraging shared values," "supporting employee goals and aspirations," "evaluating performance in light of company values," and "helping employees make decisions." This scale had a Cronbach's alpha of 0.87. The *compliance-based orientation* scale consisted of three items: "detecting unethical employees," "controlling employee behavior," and "disciplining rule violators." This scale had a Cronbach's alpha of 0.77. Factor analysis of all eight orientation items (not reported here) generated the two expected factors (values and compliance).

RESULTS

Table 8.1 reports means, standard deviations, and correlations for the independent and dependent variables. We conducted a multivariate omnibus test of significance for the complete model, with the eight dependent variables and values-based and compliance-based orientations as the independent variables. The test was significant (Wilks' lambda = 0.216, probability [p] < 0.0001). We then conducted individual regression analyses for each of the dependent variables (see Table 8.2). Because of the exploratory nature of this new area of ethics program research, we regressed each dependent variable on both values and compliance orientations, even in cases where we hypothesized a relationship with only one particular orientation.

For employee awareness of ethical issues, both values and compliance orientations were significant, supporting hypotheses 1 and 10. For employee willingness to seek ethical advice within the organization, both the values-based and compliance-based orientations were significant, supporting hypotheses 2 and 9. For observed unethical behavior, both the val-

TABLE 8.2

Hierarchical Regression Results

	Employees Would Report Violation	Employee Commitment	Employee Integrity	Acceptable to Deliver "Bad News"	Ethical Awareness	Better Decision Making	Employees Seek Advice	Observed Unethical Behavior
Model 1								
Constant B	1.71	1.53	2.77	1.28	1.54	0.75	1.46	2.84
s.e.b.	0.18	0.17	0.19	0.22	0.172	0.18	0.21	0.14
t	9.42**	8.91**	14.30**	5.95**	9.00**	4.15**	7.08**	20.25**
Values B	0.39	0.51	0.35	0.58	0.31	0.51	0.40	-0.21
s.e.b.	0.05	0.05	0.06	0.06	0.05	0.05	0.06	0.04
beta	0.42	0.54	0.38	0.52	0.35	0.50	0.38	-0.32
t	7.29**	10.21**	6.26**	9.21**	6.13**	9.71**	6.65**	-5.23**
Compliance B	0.09	0.11	0.06	-0.01	0.23	0.24	0.22	-0.11
s.e.b.	0.06	0.06	0.07	0.07	0.06	0.06	0.07	0.05
beta	0.08	0.10	0.05	-0.01	0.22	0.20	0.18	-0.14
t	1.37	1.85***	0.89	-0.13	3.88**	3.87**	3.05**	-2.31*
F	56.10**	109.05**	39.02**	69.19**	69.12**	132.86**	66.24**	39.18**
R^2	0.23	0.37	0.17	0.27	0.269	0.42	0.26	0.17
Adjusted R^2	0.23	0.36	0.17	0.27	0.265	0.41	0.26	0.17
df	2,377	2,377	2,377	2,377	2,375	2,371	2,369	2,372

Model 2

Constant B	3.04
s.e.b.	0.53
t	5.70**
Values B	−0.04
s.e.b.	0.17
beta	−0.05
t	−0.28
Compliance B	−0.31
s.e.b.	0.16
beta	−0.29
t	−1.93
Interaction B	0.12
s.e.b.	0.05
beta	0.77
t	2.65**
F	40.34**
R^2	0.24
Adjusted R^2	0.24
d.f.	3, 376
ΔR^2	0.01
$F\,\Delta R^2$	7.04**

$* p < 0.05$ $** p < 0.01$ $*** p < 0.10$ (listwise deletion)

ues-based and compliance-based orientations were significant, supporting hypotheses 3 and 8. For commitment to the organization, only values-based orientation was significant, supporting hypothesis 4. For employee integrity, only values-based orientation was significant, supporting hypothesis 5. For the perception that it is acceptable to deliver "bad news" to superiors, only the values-based orientation was significant, supporting hypothesis 6. For the perception that better decision making results from the ethics program, values-based orientation was significant, supporting hypothesis 7. Regression results also show that compliance orientation is a significant predictor of perceptions of better decision making. For the perception that employees would report an ethical violation to management, the interaction was significant, supporting hypothesis 11.

Study Limitations. We surveyed employees in a single financial services company for this study; however, multiple contextual factors might moderate the way ethics programs are operated and perceived in various companies. Companies vary in environmental pressures that might influence the way ethics programs are operated and perceived (for example, regulatory pressures, industry standards, customer expectations). Companies also bring to the ethics management task their own unique histories and circumstances that can affect how ethics programs function (for example, company cultural norms, labor–management relations, past experience with high-profile ethical scandals). Consequently, we caution against efforts to draw overly general conclusions from this or any other single-company study of ethics programs. For researchers, a study such as this should function as a starting point for additional within- and across-company studies of ethics programs. Research in multiple organizations is needed to determine whether employees in other organizations perceive similar ethics program orientations or whether other firms have orientations that are more heavily compliance or values oriented. Further, it will be important to know whether the associations with outcomes found in this organization are similar in other firms. Managers, consequently, should read this study as a basis for engaging in reflection about how their own companies are managing ethics issues. Results should not be considered a "recipe" for effective ethics management any more than the USSC's requirements should be considered such.

The company we studied would not allow a follow-up to the initial survey.

Therefore, our response rate was a less-than-ideal 21 percent. Comparison of overall demographic data from the firm, however, indicated no response bias across typical demographic categories. For example, the mean age of employees in the company was 36 years; it was 38 years for survey respondents. Mean tenure with the company is seven years for all employees and eight years for respondents. Twenty-eight percent of employees are male, and 29 percent of respondents were male. We also note that common methods bias is a potential problem in any study of employee perceptions and attitudes where all perceptual measures are taken from the same survey. We were interested in employee perceptions of ethics program orientations (rather than "official" descriptions of ethics program orientations), however, and an employee survey was the only way to learn about those.

DISCUSSION

Ethics Program Orientations and Their Outcomes

Corporate ethics/compliance programs can be implemented with varying degrees of emphasis on shared values or behavioral compliance. In the firm that was the focus of this study, employees perceived the company's ethics program to be moderately values based (mean = 3.38) and slightly more compliance based (mean = 3.64). This finding supports the notion that these orientations are not necessarily mutually exclusive but can be found in varying combinations in companies. These means are somewhat lower than the overall means found for the sample of *Fortune 1000* firms in a previous study using related measures (Weaver, Treviño, and Cochran 1999). In that study, which gathered data from corporate officers responsible for ethics instead of from employees, the overall mean for compliance orientation was 4.05, and for values orientation it was 3.94.

All the hypothesized relationships were supported. Employees' perceptions that the company's program is values based were positively associated with employees' awareness of ethics at work, their integrity, their willingness to seek ethical advice, lower observed unethical conduct, commitment to the organization, employees' willingness to deliver bad news to supervisors, and the perception that better decisions are made because of the program. Employees' willingness to report unethical behavior to management was associated with the interaction between a values-based and compliance-based orientation. Perceptions that the company's program is compliance based were associated with lower observed unethical conduct, willingness to seek ethical advice, and employees' awareness of ethical issues at work. Compliance orientation also was significantly linked to employees' perceptions that decision making is better because of the ethics program, although we proposed no hypothesis concerning this relationship. This unexpected finding may reflect a perception by employees that explicit knowledge of rules and expectations renders the decision making task easier.

These findings suggest that the two orientations sometimes work toward the same end. In the company studied, both orientations contribute to reduced unethical behavior, ethical advice seeking, awareness of ethical issues, and perceptions of better decision making. Nonetheless, a perceived values orientation is associated with other important cognitive, attitudinal, and behavioral outcomes (commitment to the organization, integrity, and willingness to deliver bad news) that are not associated with a perceived compliance orientation. Finally, value and compliance orientations sometimes interact. Employees in this company were more likely to say they would report observed unethical conduct if they perceived a combined values and compliance orientation in the ethics program.

To assess better the relative importance of values and compliance orientations in achieving these outcomes, we conducted a usefulness analysis on the two variables. *Usefulness analysis* reveals the unique contribution a particular independent variable makes in explaining a dependent variable, beyond the explanatory contribution made by all other variables. In short, it shows the proportion of variance explained by a particular variable alone. These unique contributions then can be compared to determine which of several variables, taken individually, has the greatest explanatory power. We performed a usefulness analysis to assess the unique contribution that values and compliance orientations make toward explaining all of the outcomes except willingness to report a violation (which reflected an interaction). This involved performing two separate hierarchical regression analyses per dependent variable to show the separate effects of values and compliance orientations. The first analysis initially removes the variance attributable to compliance orientation and then measures the remaining variance uniquely attributable to values orientation. The second analysis reverses the procedure by first removing variance attributable to values orientation and then measuring the remaining variance uniquely attributable

TABLE 8.3
Usefulness Analysis of Effects of Values and Compliance
Orientations on Explained Variance

	Variance Explained by Compliance Orientation Beyond That Explained by Values Orientation	*Variance Explained by Values Orientation Beyond That Explained by Compliance Orientation*
Ethical awareness	0.03	0.07
Employee commitment	0.01	0.18
Employee integrity	0.00	0.09
Acceptable to deliver "bad news"	0.00	0.17
Better decision making	0.02	0.15
Employees seek advice	0.02	0.09
Observed unethical behavior	0.01	0.06

to compliance orientation. Thus, one can compare the ability of each orientation to account uniquely for variance in each measured ethics program outcome. In every case, we found that a values orientation displays greater explanatory capacity, suggesting that it is the more important influence on measured outcomes (Table 8.3).

Values and Compliance Orientations: Finding a Balance

Clearly, it is important to know that both values and compliance orientations are associated with important outcomes of corporate ethics programs. This study's findings generally confirm what has previously been suggested by case-based research and practitioner observations. It goes farther in identifying a number of specific employee outcomes associated with these orientations. The findings also suggest that values and compliance orientations are not simple substitutes for each other. In this company, a perceived values orientation appears to add distinctive and desirable outcomes that are not achieved by a focus on behavioral compliance. Moreover, a values orientation has a larger unique impact on the outcomes.

The discovery of an interaction between values and compliance orientations indicates that the two orientations do not always combine additively in their influences on some ethics program outcomes. In particular, a values orientation appears important to realizing fully the potential benefits of compliance activities such as reporting misconduct. The message of trust and support conveyed by a values orientation may be needed to support such compliance goals. The values orientation may frame the way employees understand the purpose of compliance activities. When a values orientation is strong, compliance activities can be perceived as part of an overall system of support for ethical behavior. Without a strong values orientation, however, compliance activities might be perceived to be part of a system aimed only at detecting misconduct.

For managers, these results show the importance of ethics program orientation. It is not enough simply to "check off" the USSC's recommendations for due diligence in legal compliance. The guidelines have been interpreted to recommend executive oversight, the establishment of a code of conduct, ethics training, a telephone hotline, and discipline for misconduct. Many companies are engaging in these activities; but if employees perceive that they represent merely a compliance orientation, some important outcomes may be unaffected, whereas others might be affected less strongly than they otherwise could be. In the company studied, both values and compliance orientations contribute to employee advice seeking, ethical awareness, better decision making, and reduced unethical behavior; but a values orientation has a larger unique impact on these outcomes. Also, in the company studied, a perceived values orientation provides additional direct benefits that are likely to be important to the long-term goals of any ethics program (such as employee commitment, integrity, and perception that it is acceptable to deliver "bad news"). We expect that most ethics programs would have ethical awareness, employee integrity, and better communication as goals, but only a perceived values orientation was associated with these outcomes. Also, employees are more likely to report misconduct they observe if they perceive both a values orientation and a compliance orientation in the ethics program. Thus, consistent with prior research on ethics programs (Paine 1994), the results of this study suggest that it is not optimal to merely establish and enforce "the rules." Rather, managers need to create a sense of shared values that can help define an ethical role identity for employees and set forth organizational support for employees as an ideal.

Furthermore, because these findings are linked to employee perceptions of ethics program orientation, it is important for managers (and researchers) to consider other contextual factors that might influence employee perceptions of ethics program orientations. For example, the same set of ethics initiatives (such as telephone reporting lines, training) might be located in any of several different functional areas—human resources, general counsel, free-standing ethics office, or others; but the choice of context may influence the perception of program orientation. A location in human resources, for example, may frame the ethics initiatives as more oriented toward values and employee aspirations than a location in the legal department, which might be perceived as oriented more toward rules and compliance. Similarly, persons from different functional backgrounds (for example, law, human resources) may bring to the ethics program different tendencies to think in terms of values- or compliance-oriented activities. The prominence of legal staff in most corporate ethics programs (Weaver, Treviño, and Cochran 1999) is understandable, given the pressures of the USSC's guidelines. Nevertheless, companies may find it useful to consider whether this prominence leads to the perception or reality of an overemphasis on compliance.

For researchers, the study suggests that there is much more to be done to understand the relationships between ethics program characteristics and employee outcomes. In particular, research needs to consider other ways in which values and compliance orientations might interact. Further, where balance between the two orientations is needed, what is the appropriate balance, and how might such balance be achieved? For example, in the case of reporting misconduct, what is the combination of compliance and values orientations that produces the most employee willingness to report observed misconduct?

Research also should consider other possible outcomes of these two approaches to ethics management. We have argued that a values orientation works through its influence on role identity and perceived organizational support and have considered a number of possible outcomes of those processes. This represents a major advance beyond previous work, which, while considering the impact of these two orientations, has not elaborated a theoretically rooted explanation for their impact. Other possible outcomes and theoretical linkages remain unexamined. Perceived organizational support, for example, has been linked to employee innovativeness. Are there, then, respects in which a values orientation encourages a more innovative and ultimately better response to the occasional ethical dilemmas of organizational life?

Looking Beyond Values and Compliance Orientations

The study reported in the foregoing was the first to investigate in detail the relationship between perceived ethics program orientations and employee outcomes in a single company using a large employee survey and quantitative methods. We developed theory and hypotheses based on role theory, identity theory, and exchange theory. As hypothesized, in this company, we found that a perceived values orientation was associated with several employee outcomes, including ethical awareness, employee integrity and commitment, willingness to deliver bad news, the perception that better decisions are made because of the ethics program, ethical advice seeking, and decreased unethical behavior in the organization. A perceived compliance orientation was associated with ethical advice seeking, ethical awareness, perceptions of better decision making, and less observed unethical behavior; however, a perceived values orientation demonstrated a greater unique contribution to each of these outcomes. Finally, employees' willingness to report misconduct was associated with the interaction between the two orientations. Overall, results from this company show that employee perceptions of ethics program orientations are important and that a perceived values orientation is key to most outcomes. Whether this finding can be generalized to all companies, of course, will require additional research of a similar sort.

There is more to organizational ethics than the values and compliance orientation of formal ethics programs, however. As Part II suggested, multiple questions can be raised about the kinds of additional organizational props that formal ethics programs require to be effective. Many ethics programs are large packages of initiatives, occurring in even larger and more complex arrays of organizational phenomena. Taken by themselves, individual ethics program elements may be ineffective or counterproductive; but given appropriate supports, and if these elements are integrated well with other organizational activities, they might have substantial impacts on the overall ethical status of an organization.

The Case of Ethics Codes

For an example of how limited the impact of typical ethics program elements might be in isolation, consider the case of ethics codes. Importance is sometimes attributed to the design of organizational ethics codes (e.g.,

Raiborn and Payne 1990; Molander 1987). One of us conducted an experimental study (Weaver 1995) that considered how variations in the design of ethics codes would influence people's responses to those codes. Company ethics codes often vary in the extent to which they simply describe behavioral expectations or also include justifications for the importance of those expectations. They also vary in whether they include references to sanctions for violations of the code. Communications research and theory suggest that the inclusion of a justification can make any message more relevant to its recipient, thus enhancing recall of the message (Petty and Cacioppo 1986). Theory and research also indicate that the presence of significant consequences for an individual should enhance the relevance and recall of a message (Leventhal 1970; Petty and Cacioppo 1981; Sutton 1982). The experimental study of codes, then, manipulated the presence of rationales and sanctions in a code. It assessed experimental subjects' recall of code content. (It also examined subjects' perceptions of organizational justice because offering explanations for requirements and backing requirements up with consequences are relevant to multiple aspects of organizational justice [Bies and Moag 1986; Greenberg 1990].)

Results of this study offered little support to claims that variations in ethics code design are themselves important. Although the presence of a rationale in codes did show a significant but very small relationship to subjects' procedural justice perceptions, no support was found for the hypothesized relationships of code variations to justice perceptions and subjects' recall of the code. Variations in the content of an ethics code simply might not matter much because a code does not matter much if it is taken in isolation. How does an individual know how seriously to take the code, then, or how to evaluate the intentions behind it or outcomes from obedience and disobedience, without knowing something of the organizational context in which the code is introduced? As the 1995 study noted, it is possible that "at least some ethics code design issues cannot be considered in isolation from an intended organizational context" (Weaver 1995, 379).

The more general lesson from this study, then, is that efforts to assess the impact of ethics programs and their elements need to consider the surrounding organizational context. Verbal and nonverbal cues from top management, for example, can do much to signal the importance or irrelevance of ethics policies and programs. Pressures from immediate supervisors can do much to negate intentions to abide by an ethics policy; the chief executive officer, or CEO, may say ethics is important, but a supervisor can fire an employee for failing to do as directed. Thus, we turn to a larger set of data to assess the relative impact of formal ethics programs and other organizational factors on the ethics-relevant outcomes used in the study described at the start of this chapter.

BEYOND FORMAL PROGRAMS: OTHER INFLUENCES ON ETHICS IN ORGANIZATIONS

In this portion of the chapter, we rely on a larger data set of six companies (including the company studied earlier) to identify influences on ethics-relevant phenomena that stem both from ethics programs and from the wider organizational setting of ethics programs. Methodologically, data were collected the same way as in the results reported in the one-company study reported on here, except that we included data from ten thousand randomly selected employees spread across six companies representing a variety of industry environments (financial services, transportation, utilities, industrial products). Analytically, we present only correlational results from this larger data set (Table 8.4), intending it to be a stimulant to future research rather than the final word on one or another topic or issue. The outcomes under consideration are the same as described and measured in the first study in this chapter. The influences on them are described below and were measured in similar fashion (multi-item, Likert-scale perceptual measures).

Alternative Ethics Program Orientations

Correlational results from this data set are generally supportive of the preceding more detailed findings; both compliance and values orientations matter in generating desirable ethics program outcomes, but a values orientation appears to make a larger difference. Inclusion of other ways in which the orientation or focus of an ethics program can be perceived by employees is noteworthy: the perception that the ethics program is aimed at satisfying expectations of external stakeholders and the perception that the program exists to protect top management from blame for ethical failures or legal problems.

If employees perceive that the ethics program is oriented toward serving the interests of external stakeholders (for example, customers, the community), outcomes are positive, but the relationship is weaker than in the case of values and compliance orientations. More important, we think, is the reaction when employees perceive that the ethics program exists to protect top management from blame. Not surprisingly, where employees perceived that an ethics or compliance program was oriented toward protecting top management from blame, all the important outcomes were significantly more negative. These relationships were particularly strong and negative for commitment to the organization, for the perception that it is acceptable to deliver bad news to management, and that employees would report ethical or legal violations to management. In addition, unethical or illegal behavior was greater, employees were less aware of ethical issues, and employees were less likely to seek advice about ethical concerns. They also did not believe that decision making in the organization was better because of the ethics program. Perhaps the most important message to executives is that this perception that ethics programs exist to "cover" top management failures is real. Employees judge ethics programs by reference to their perceptions of top management's *motives* for implementing an ethics program. If an ethics program is to contribute to beneficial outcomes for all (for example, reduced unethical behavior), it must be something that employees believe to be a sincere attempt to have everyone do what is right rather than just an attempt to create legal "cover" for executives in case of a mishap.

Formal and Informal Ethics/Compliance Program Characteristics

Values and compliance orientations have received attention in the preceding discussion; but, interestingly, other more specific ethics/compliance program and organizational characteristics proved to be more important in our multicompany data set. First, with regard to the program, we asked employees about formal characteristics, including the official policies, procedures, offices, and supporting structures (for example, a telephone hotline). We also asked for employees' perceptions of the more informal ways ethics and compliance concerns are handled every day (for example, how well the company "follows through" on its policies).

Formal Program Characteristics are Relatively Unimportant. All six companies in the study had the "basics" of a comprehensive ethics/compliance program: an ethics/compliance office and officer, a formal code of conduct,

TABLE 8.4

Pearson Correlations (Pairwise deletion) among Ethics and Compliance Management and Outcomes

Ethics and Compliance Management	Unethical Conduct	Ethics Awareness	Advice Seeking	Acceptable to Deliver Bad News	Likely to Report Violations	Employee Commitment	Better Decision Making
Program orientation							
Values	-0.40	0.45	0.49	0.48	0.48	0.59	0.56
Compliance	-0.36	0.41	0.44	0.31	0.41	0.37	0.49
External Stakeholder	-0.18	0.32	0.32	0.26	0.26	0.38	0.39
Protect Top Management	0.34	-0.23	-0.31	-0.43	-0.36	-0.39	-0.27
Formal Program Characteristics							
Code familiarity	-0.08	0.23	0.21	0.11	0.22	0.16	0.27
Refer to code	-0.06	0.20	0.19	0.09	0.18	0.16	0.26
Formal reporting mechanism	-0.32	0.43	0.47	0.39	0.44	0.43	0.54
Ethics in performance appraisal	-0.30	0.44	0.39	0.39	0.37	0.42	0.50

Program follow-through							
Detection of violators	−0.42	0.45	0.49	0.41	0.49	0.44	0.59
Follow-up on reports	−0.48	0.47	0.59	0.54	0.57	0.54	0.60
Consistent policies/actions	−0.56	0.54	0.61	0.55	0.62	0.69	0.67
Ethical culture							
Executive leadership	−0.52	0.54	0.59	0.65	0.60	0.70	0.65
Supervisory leadership	−0.55	0.56	0.59	0.67	0.61	0.66	0.63
Fair treatment	−0.54	0.45	0.55	0.72	0.59	0.76	0.56
Ethics talk	−0.43	0.54	0.58	0.60	0.58	0.61	0.62
Ethics in decisions	−0.41	0.49	0.54	0.52	0.50	0.52	0.58
Ethical behavior rewarded	−0.54	0.47	0.51	0.61	0.59	0.63	0.55
Unethical behavior punished	−0.45	0.41	0.49	0.37	0.49	0.42	0.52
Obedience to authority	0.44	−0.37	−0.45	−0.62	−0.52	−0.58	−0.44
Employee focus	−0.42	0.40	0.46	0.62	0.50	0.67	0.49
Community focus	−0.36	0.39	0.45	0.44	0.42	0.55	0.47
Self-interest focus	0.45	−0.36	−0.40	−0.55	−0.45	−0.57	−0.43

All correlations statistically significant ($p < 0.05$).

and a telephone hotline. So the mere existence of these formal program characteristics did not differentiate among the companies, but employees may be more or less aware of these program characteristics and more or less likely to use them (Badaracco and Webb 1995). Therefore, we asked employees how familiar they were with the code's contents and how frequently they referred to the code for guidance. Interestingly, these factors had little impact on the outcomes, especially unethical conduct. It simply did not matter much whether employees were familiar with or referred frequently to the company's code of conduct.

We also asked employees whether their company has a formal mechanism for raising ethical and legal compliance issues and concerns and whether ethics is a formal part of performance evaluation in the company. Both these program characteristics are more dynamic, suggesting some kind of ongoing attention from the organization, whereas a code can be drafted, distributed, and forgotten. To the extent that employees perceived the company to have a formal mechanism for raising concerns and to make ethics a formal part of performance appraisal, all the outcomes were significantly more positive.

Program Follow-through Is Essential.   With regard to program follow-through, we asked employees whether the company works hard to detect violators, whether the company follows up on ethical concerns raised by employees, and whether there is consistency between ethics/compliance policies and actual organizational practices. Follow-through tells employees that a focus on ethics and legal compliance represents a sincere commitment on the part of management (Toffler 1991).

In our study, to the extent that employees perceived the organization to be following through, all of the outcomes were significantly more positive. Further, employees' perceptions of follow-through were much more important than their perceptions of the formal characteristics. One of the most important influential factors in the study was employees' perception that the company's actions are consistent with its policies. These findings suggest that it is particularly important for employees to perceive that policies are not just "window dressing" and that the company follows words with actions. They also suggest that an approach that goes beyond the establishment of formal programs may be necessary if employees are to be convinced that the organization really means what it says.

Ethical Culture in the Organization

> "Ethics is very broad . . . It doesn't just mean what people typically think of as ethics compliance. There are pieces of ethics that no one would even think of as ethics."

This statement was made by the corporate secretary of a Fortune 500 manufacturing firm, and it suggests that managing ethics in organizations is not just about managing formal ethics and compliance programs. Along these same lines, researchers have suggested that the broader ethical context in an organization—referred to as the *ethical climate and culture*—may be particularly important (Cohen 1993; Toffler 1991; Treviño 1990; Treviño and Nelson 1995; Treviño, Butterfield, and McCabe 1998; Victor and Cullen 1988), perhaps more important than specific ethics/compliance program goals or characteristics.

Ethical culture represents a slice of the overall organizational culture. It combines formal and informal elements that work together to guide employee thought and action in the ethics domain. These elements include leadership, reward systems, perceived fairness, ethics as a topic of conversation in the organization, employee authority structures, and an organizational focus that communicates care for employees and the community rather than self-interest. Although we consider many of these influences in detail in the next chapter, data from Table 8.4 helps to show the rationale for doing so: Elements of an organization's ethical culture have the potential to influence ethical behavior substantially.

Executive and Supervisory Leadership. More than a decade ago, the Business Roundtable report (1988), *Corporate Ethics: A Prime Business Asset*, referred to the crucial role of top management. "To achieve results, the Chief Executive Officer and those around the CEO need to be openly and strongly committed to ethical conduct, and give constant leadership in tending and renewing the values of the organization" (p. 4). Posner and Schmidt (1992, 86) also documented managers' belief that "the behavior of those in charge is the principal determinant of the 'ethical tone'" in their companies.

We were interested in the role of executive leadership because executives play a crucial role in creating, maintaining, and changing ethical culture (Treviño 1990), but we also wanted to investigate the role of supervisory leadership. Leaders at every level serve as role models, and employees have more daily contact with their supervisors than they do with executive leaders. Supervisors are responsible for rewards and punishments, and they are likely to carry the message of how things are really done in the organization. Therefore, in separate sets of questions, we asked employees for their perceptions of both executive and supervisory ethical leadership.

First, it is important to note that employees' perceptions of these two groups were highly related (correlation = 0.78), suggesting that employees do not think differently about supervisors and executive leaders when it comes to attention to ethics and legal compliance. This suggests that if executive leaders value and pay attention to ethics, so do supervisory leaders. Second, leadership was a key ethical culture factor, one of the most important factors in the study. Where employees perceived that supervisors and executives regularly pay attention to ethics, take ethics seriously, and care about ethics and values as much as the bottom line, all the outcomes were significantly more positive. These findings confirmed previous authors' contentions about the importance of executive leadership, but leadership at the supervisory level is equally important. Also, we now understand that employees paint all leaders with the same broad ethical brush. When it comes to ethics, leaders are leaders, and the level (supervisory or executive) does not seem to matter much to employees. If a middle manager puts pressure on subordinates, employees are likely to infer that the pressure is coming from the top.

Fair Treatment of Employees. We also explored a less obvious aspect of ethical culture: employees' perceptions of general fair treatment in the organization. Why should general fair treatment of employees be related to ethics-related outcomes? First, the word *ethics* can mean different things to different people or groups. Kent Druyvesteyn, former ethics officer at General Dynamics, said that when managers say "ethics," employees hear "fairness" (Treviño and Nelson 1995). To most employees, *ethics* means how the organization treats them and their co-workers. This helps to explain why so many calls to ethics hotlines concern human resources issues of fair treatment in hiring, layoffs, performance appraisals, and promotions. Also, recent research has highlighted the importance of fair treatment for ethics-related outcomes, such as employee theft (Greenberg 1990). When employees feel that they are treated unfairly, they are likely to "balance the scales of justice" by engaging in unethical behaviors such as stealing from the organization. Some companies have acknowledged this connection between fair treatment and ethics management. For example, we know of a company that sees the elimination of executive dining rooms and other perks as important to making their ethics programs work. Employees see that rules apply to everyone because every employee, up to the CEO, has to have expense reports signed. "That sends a good message [to employees]. . . . Nobody is above the rules and code of conduct. . . . A high level person could get dismissed if they violated [a rule] as much as another person." Another company pegged executive pay to employee pay because of similar concerns about the implications of fair and consistent employee treatment for ethics management.

It is important to note that the survey questions concerning fair treatment had nothing to do with the ethics/compliance program. Rather, they were general questions that asked whether employees think of the company as fair in terms of rewards and punishments ("Do employees get the rewards and punishments they deserve?"); whether employees are treated fairly in general; and whether supervisors treat employees with courtesy, dignity, and respect. Employees' perception of fair treatment was strongly related to all outcomes and was one of the most influential factors in the study. Of all the influential factors, it had the strongest correlation with employee commitment and with the perception that it is acceptable to deliver bad news to management. We consider fairness issues and their impact on ethics in organizations in more detail in Chapter 10.

Ethics in Discussions and Decisions. We also asked employees whether people in the company talk openly about ethics and values and whether ethics and values are integrated into decisions (including rejecting plans because of ethics and values concerns). One of the ways ethics and values get "baked into" the corporate culture is to make these sorts of discussions the norm (Toffler 1991; Treviño and Nelson 1995). A bad example from our experience goes like this. An oil company employee asked if he could bring an ethical problem to a meeting of divisional presidents. The immediate response was, "If he wants to talk ethics, let him talk to a priest or a psychiatrist. The office is no place for it." The message was as clear as if it had been said explicitly: "We don't talk about ethics. Ethics has no place here." Imagine what employees would think of a formal ethics/compliance program in such an environment.

In our study, perceptions that ethics is talked about and integrated into decision making were important for all outcomes. Open discussion of ethics and values in the company was particularly important, especially for employee commitment, the perception that it is acceptable to deliver bad news, the belief that employees would report an ethics violation, and that decision making is better because of the ethics/compliance program.

Reward Systems that Support Ethical Conduct. Good managers know that people do what is rewarded and avoid doing what is punished. Therefore, an ethical culture should include a reward system that supports ethical conduct (Treviño and Nelson 1995). We asked employees whether ethical behavior is rewarded and unethical behavior is punished in their organizations. Perceptions of both of these dimensions were important for all outcomes; however, employee perceptions that ethical behavior is rewarded were more important than were perceptions that unethical behavior is punished. The sense that ethical behavior is rewarded was particularly important for employees' commitment and their perceptions that it is acceptable to deliver bad news to management and that employees would be likely to report ethical violations.

Unquestioning Obedience to Authority. An ethical organizational culture must emphasize each individual's accountability and responsibility for his or her own actions and an obligation to question authority when something seems wrong. An unethical culture is more likely to require unquestioning obedience to authority: "Just do as I say and don't ask any questions" (Treviño 1990). In fact, in this study we found that where employees perceived an authority structure that expects unquestioning obedience to authority, all outcomes were significantly more negative. Most affected were employee commitment to the organization, willingness to report an ethical or legal violation, and willingness to deliver bad news to management.

Organizational Climate. Organizations can be focused on many things, displaying overall climates oriented toward employee welfare, the needs of external stakeholders such as customers, and so on. Research on ethical climate has found that employees' perceptions of the organization's focus are associated with both unethical behavior and employee commitment (Treviño, Butterfield, and McCabe 1998). In this study, we considered three types of climate: employee focus (where employees perceive an organizational focus on what is best for them and their co-workers); community focus (where employees perceive an organizational focus on what is best for customers and the public); and self-interest focus (where employees perceive that everyone in the organization is simply out for himself or herself).

Where employees perceived the organization to be focused on what is best for employees (employee focus) or customers and the public (community focus), all the outcomes were significantly more positive; however, where employees perceived that people in the organization were mostly out for themselves (self-interest focus), all outcomes were significantly more negative.

Summary of Ethical Culture Findings. As a set, the ethical culture factors emerged as the most important influential factors. Of these factors, leadership, fairness perceptions, the perception that ethics is discussed in the organization, and the perception that ethical behavior is rewarded were the most significant and among the most important factors in the study.

Previous case studies and anecdotal reports have referred to the importance of leadership for organizational ethics, but this large-scale study provides empirical evidence of its importance for ethics/compliance management effectiveness. The findings suggest that leaders at the executive and supervisory level have a key role to play in managing organizational ethics. The marketplace delivers messages daily about the importance of the bottom line. Messages about ethics easily can be lost in an atmosphere that emphasizes global competition and quarterly profits. For example, we have had experience with a highly regulated company that invested significant resources in the development of a "world class" ethics/compliance program. The firm's managers reported, however, that at their monthly two-hour review meetings with the Chief Operating Officer, "We spend 5 minutes on compliance and 115 minutes on profitability. So, you tell me—what matters here?" For outcomes to be most positive, employees must perceive that executives and supervisors care about ethics and values as much as they care about the bottom line, and leaders must demonstrate this commitment every day through words and actions. This important leadership function cannot be delegated to an ethics/compliance officer. Ethics and compliance officers certainly play an important role as they manage formal policies and "keep a finger on" the ethical pulse of the organization. Their policies will not be effective, though, if the officers are not perceived to be part of a leadership team that is working together to maintain a strong and consistent ethical culture in the organization.

Employees' evaluations of fair treatment are also very important. Previous research found that fair treatment can reduce employee theft (Greenberg 1990). This study, however, documents the importance of general fair treatment for a wider variety of specific ethics-related attitudes and behaviors. Of all the factors studied, this was one of the most important in the study, suggesting that employees make a strong connection between general fair treatment and ethics-related outcomes. They will happily support the ethics management efforts of an organization that treats them fairly; but, if they perceive unfair treatment, they are unlikely to help and are more likely to engage in unethical behaviors.

The perception that ethical behavior is rewarded was also one of the most important factors associated with positive outcomes. Although disciplining unethical behavior was important, it was not as important as rewarding ethical conduct. From a practical perspective, it is not easy to reward ethical conduct in organizations. Most ethical conduct is simply expected, and employees do not expect to be rewarded for not cheating on their expense reports or not harassing co-workers. We interpret this finding to mean that it is essential for employees to feel that, over time, people of integrity are the ones who get ahead in the organization—that good guys finish first.

In response to the question of "what hurts" in ethics/compliance management, two culture factors were quite harmful. Outcomes were more negative where employees perceived an expectation of unquestioning obedience to authority and where they perceived a focus on self-interest rather than concern for employees or the community. The negative effects of a focus on self-interest can be seen in the following example. Imagine a financial services company that initiates a values campaign built on respect, trust, and serving the customer. Suppose, however, that the company engages in deceptive sales practices supported by a commission-based reward system that encourages an every-employee-for-himself-or-herself atmosphere. The deceptive sales practices then lead to legal, reputation, and morale problems. Our findings suggest that these problems are linked to an ethical culture that focuses primarily on self-interest. The problems are likely exacerbated by the obvious mismatch between the highly visible values campaign and the reality that self-interest is the true focus of the organization.

Knowledgeable ethics/compliance officers recognize that their job is relatively easy if they work within a highly ethical culture where leaders at all levels take responsibility for communicating a consistent ethics message, where ethics is routinely and openly discussed, where employees feel fairly treated, where ethical employees get the rewards, and where rule violators are punished. On the other hand, their job is virtually impossible if employees perceive a culture in which people are concerned only with themselves, where employees are expected to obey authority without question, where leaders are viewed with cynicism, and employees feel unjustly treated.

Looking Ahead

The lesson of this chapter is twofold: (1) considerations of the design and implementation of formal ethics programs do matter, at least in regard to major features such as control orientations and "protect top management" perceptions; and (2) important as ethics program features sometimes may be, it is at least equally important to consider elements of an organization's ethical culture and climate that are not directly tied to a formal ethics program. Thus, in the next two chapters, we focus on this latter point in two specific ways, first by examining the issue of ethical culture and climate; second, by looking at the role of overall fairness in an organization as a key influence on people's ethical behavior and on their responses to formal organizational ethics initiatives.

References

Adler, P. S., and B. Borys. 1996. Two types of bureaucracy: enabling and coercive. *Administrative Science Quarterly* 41:61–90.

Akaah, I. P. 1992. Social inclusion as a marketing ethics correlate. *Journal of Business Ethics* 11(8):599–608.

Allen, N. J., and J. P. Meyer. 1990. The measurement and antecedents of affective, continuance, and normative commitment to the organization. *Journal of Occupational Psychology* 63:1–18.

Arvey, R. D., and J. M. Ivancevich. 1980. Punishment in organizations: A review, propositions, and research suggestions. *Academy of Management Review* 5:123–132.

Ashforth, B. E., and F. Mael. 1989. Social identity theory and the organization. *Academy of Management Review* 14:20–39.

Badaracco, J. L., and A. P. Webb. 1995. Business ethics: A view from the trenches. *California Management Review* 37:8–28.

Ball, G. A., L. K. Treviño, and H. P. Sims. 1994. Just and unjust punishment: Influences on subordinate performance and citizenship. *Academy of Management Journal* 37:299–322.

Bies, R. J., and J. S. Moag. 1986. Interactional justice: Communications criteria of fairness. In R. Lewicki, B. H. Sheppard, and M. H. Bazerman, (eds.), *Research on Negotiation in Organizations*, vol. 1. Greenwich, CT: JAI Press, 43–55.

Bird, F., and J. Waters. 1989. The moral muteness of managers. *California Management Review* 32(1): 73–88.

Blau, P. M. 1964. *Exchange and power in social life.* New York: Wiley.

Business Roundtable, 1988. *Corporate ethics: A prime business asset.* New York: The Business Roundtable.

Cohen, D. 1993. Creating and maintaining ethical work climates: Anomie in the workplace and implications for managing change. *Business Ethics Quarterly* 3:343–358.

Eisenberger, R., P. Fasolo, and V. Davis-LaMastro. 1990. Perceived organizational support and employee diligence, commitment, and innovation. *Journal of Applied Psychology* 75:51–59.

Eisenberger, R., R. Huntington, S. Hutchison, and D. Sowa. 1986. Perceived organizational support. *Journal of Applied Psychology* 71:500–507.

Etzioni, A. 1961. *A comparative analysis of complex organizations.* New York: Free Press.

Festinger, L. A. 1957. *A theory of cognitive dissonance.* Stanford, CA: Stanford University Press.

Freeman, R. E. 1984. *Strategic management: A stakeholder approach.* Boston: Pitman/Ballinger.

Gouldner, A. W. 1954. *Patterns of industrial bureaucracy.* New York: Free Press.

Graen, G. B. and T. A. Scandura. 1987. Toward a psychology of dyadic organizing. In *Research in organizational behavior,* ed. L. L. Cummings and B. M. Staw, 9:175–208. Greenwich, CT: JAI Press.

Greenberg, J. 1990. Organizational justice: Yesterday, today and tomorrow. *Journal of Management* 15:399–432.

Homans, G. C. 1961. *Social behavior: Its elementary forms.* New York: Harcourt Brace.

Lerner, M. J. 1977. The justice motive: Some hypotheses as to its origins and forms. *Journal of Personality* 45:1–52.

Leventhal, H. 1970. Findings and theory in the study of fear communications. In L. Berkowitz (ed.), *Advances in experimental and social psychology,* vol. 5. New York: Academic Press.

McNamara, J. R., and C. A. Blumer. 1982. Role playing to assess social competence: Ecological validity considerations. *Behavior Modification* 6:510–549.

Molander, E. A. 1987. A paradigm for design, promulgation and enforcement of ethical codes. *Journal of Business Ethics* 6:619–631.

O'Reilly, C., and J. Chatman. 1986. Organizational commitment and psychological attachment: The effects of compliance, identification, and internalization of prosocial behavior. *Journal of Applied Psychology* 71:492–499.

Paine, L. S. 1994. Managing for organizational integrity. *Harvard Business Review* 72:106–117

Petty, R. E., and J. T. Cacioppo. 1981. *Attitudes and persuasion: Classic and contemporary approaches*. Dubuque, IA: Wm. C. Brown.

Petty, R. E., and J. T. Cacioppo. 1986. *Communication and persuasion: Central and peripheral routes to attitude change*. New York: Springer-Verlag.

Posner, B. Z., and W. H. Schmidt. 1992. Values and the American manager: An update updated. *California Management Review* 34(3):80–94.

Raiborn, C. A., and D. Payne. 1990. Corporate codes of conduct: A collective conscience and continuum. *Journal of Business Ethics* 9:879–889.

Rousseau, D. M., and J. M. Parks. 1993. The contracts of individuals and organizations. In *Research in organizational behavior,* ed. L. L. Cummings and B. M. Staw, 15:1–43. Greenwich, CT: JAI Press.

Stryker, S., and R. T. Serpe. 1982. Commitment, identity salience, and role behavior: Theory and research example. In *Personality, roles and social behavior,* ed. W. Ickes and E. S. Knowles, 199–218. New York: Springer-Verlag.

Stryker, S. 1968. Identity salience and role performance: The relevance of symbolic interaction theory for family research. *Journal of Marriage and the Family* 30:558–564.

Stryker, S. 1980. *Symbolic interactionism: A social structural version*. Menlo Park, CA: Benjamin/Cummings.

Sutton, S. R. 1982. Fear-arousing communications: A critical examination of theory and research. In *Social psychology and behavioral medicine*, ed. J. R. Eiser, 303–337. New York: Wiley.

Toffler, B. 1991. *Managers talk ethics: Making tough choices in a competitive business world*. New York: John Wiley & Sons.

Treviño, L. K. 1990. A cultural perspective on changing and developing organizational ethics. *Research in Organizational Change and Development* 4:195–230. Greenwich, CT: JAI Press.

Treviño, L. K., and K. A. Nelson. 1995. *Managing business ethics: Straight talk about how to do it right*. New York: Wiley.

Treviño, L. K. 1993. The social effects of punishment: A justice perspective. *Academy of Management Review* 17:647–676.

Treviño, L. K., K. Butterfield, and D. McCabe. 1998. The ethical context in organizations: Influences on employee attitudes and behaviors. *Business Ethics Quarterly* 8:447–476.

United States Sentencing Commission 1995. *Corporate crime in America: Strengthening the "good citizen" corporation.* Washington, DC.

United States Sentencing Commission, 1994. *Federal sentencing guidelines manual.* Washington, DC.

Victor, B., and J. B. Cullen. 1988. The organizational bases of ethical work climates. *Administrative Science Quarterly* 33:101–125.

Weaver, G. R. 1993. Corporate codes of ethics: Purpose, process and content issues. *Business and Society* 32(1):44–58.

Weaver, G. R. 1995. Does ethics code design matter? Effects of ethics code rationales and sanctions on recipients' justice perceptions and content recall. *Journal of Business Ethics* 14:367–385.

Weaver, G. R., L. K. Treviño, and P. L. Cochran. 1999. Corporate ethics programs as control systems: Influences of executive commitment and environmental factors. *Academy of Management Journal* 42:539–552.

Weber, J. 1995. Influences upon organizational ethical subclimates: A multidepartmental analysis of a single firm. *Organization Science* 6(5):509–523.

Weber, M. 1947. *The theory of social and economic organization.* Glencoe, IL: Free Press.

NINE

Ethics and the Broader Organizational Context: Ethical Climate and Ethical Culture

In Chapter 8, we learned that formal ethics programs can and do influence employees' attitudes and behavior. When employees think about what management expects of them in the ethics arena, however, they do not simply look to the formal ethics program and its elements (such as codes, training programs, and so on). Rather, employees are influenced by messages that emerge from a broad array of management policies, communications, and actions. This chapter reviews the results of research demonstrating the importance of the organization's broad ethical context. In the descriptive business ethics literature, ethical context has been represented primarily by two multidimensional constructs: *ethical climate* (Victor and Cullen 1987, 1988) and *ethical culture* (Treviño 1986, 1990).

ETHICAL CLIMATE

Ethical climate theory and research can be considered a subset of the organizational climate literature. Schneider (1975) argued that there are many types of work climates, one of which Victor and Cullen (1988) labeled *ethi-*

Much of the following chapter is reproduced, with permission, from L. K. Treviño, K. Butterfield, and D. McCabe, 1998, "The ethical context in organizations: Influences on employee attitudes and behaviors," *Business Ethics Quarterly* 8(3):447–476.

cal climate. In his review of the culture/climate literature, Denison (1996, 624) defined *climate* as "rooted in the organization's value system." Climate represents the organization's social environment "in terms of a fixed (and broadly applicable) set of dimensions . . . that are consciously perceived by organizational members."

Victor and Cullen (1988, 101) defined ethical climate as "the prevailing perceptions of typical organizational practices and procedures that have ethical content" or "those aspects of work climate that determine what constitutes ethical behavior at work." They proposed nine ethical climate types based on three major classes of philosophy (egoism, benevolence, and principle) and three loci of analysis (individual, local, and cosmopolitan).

Each of their nine ethical climate types is accompanied by a particular normative expectation (Cullen and Victor 1993). In the *egoistic individual* climate, self-interest is the normative expectation. In the *egoistic local* climate, company interest guides ethical decisions. In the *egoistic cosmopolitan* climate, efficiency is the normative criterion. In the *benevolent individual*, *local*, and *cosmopolitan* climates, the welfare of individuals, groups inside the organization, and those external to the organization (respectively) guides decision. In the *principled individual* climate, people are expected to follow their personal morality. In the *principled local* climate, organizational rules and regulations are the normative criterion. Finally, in the *principled cosmopolitan* climate, external laws and codes guide decisions.

To test empirically for the existence of these nine ethical climate types, Victor and Cullen developed the Ethical Climate Questionnaire (ECQ). Across a series of survey studies, they validated the existence of some, but not all, of the proposed climate types (Cullen and Bronson 1993; Victor and Cullen 1987, 1988). In a key test of their typology (Victor and Cullen 1988), the nine dimensions reduced to five that they labeled caring, law and code, rules, instrumental, and independence. Three of these dimensions (law and code, rules, independence) were consistent with the proposed typology. The others combined items from remaining dimensions. Finally, Victor and Cullen (1987, 1988) found that different ethical climates exist between organizations and that most organizations appear to have a dominant ethical climate type. Building on this work, Weber (1995) found that employees in different departments of a financial institution had different perceptions of the firm's ethical climate because of differences in departmental tasks and stakeholder accountability.

Most important for our purposes, researchers also explored the relationship between ethical climate and attitudinal and behavioral outcomes. Victor and Cullen (1987, 1988) suggested that ethical climates should influence attitudes and behaviors by providing information about the organization and guidance regarding appropriate conduct.

With regard to organizational commitment, Cullen and Victor (1993) argued that, to the extent that people prefer certain types of normative climates, employees should be more committed to organizations with these climate types. Thus, organizational commitment should be higher in organizations with principle- or benevolence-based climates than in organizations with egoism-based climates. Employees may feel more attached to and may identify more with the values of organizations that increase the level of responsibility felt for others and encourage concern for employees and the community (Mowday, Steers, and Porter 1979; Cullen and Victor 1993). In an empirical study, Cullen and Victor (1993) found that perceptions of a benevolent climate were positively related to commitment and perceptions of an egoistic climate were negatively related to commitment.

The relationship between ethical climate and ethical behavior was less clear. Although Wimbush and Shepard (1994) suggested that egoistic climates should be associated with unethical behavior, and principled climates should be associated with ethical behavior, an examination of ethical climate dimensions suggests that most climate types provide little specific behavioral guidance. Only three climate dimensions seem helpful in answering the question, "What should I do?" The *rules* climate says to follow the rules. Assuming that the organization has clear rules guiding behavior in a particular situation, the guidance would be to follow those rules. The *law and code* climate says to follow the law or professional standards. This is obviously helpful in the limited number of situations where the law or professional standards apply. Finally, the *caring* climate says that one should look out for other people, including customers and the public. With regard to empirical support for the ethical climate/conduct relationship, Gaertner (1991) found that a number of ethical climate dimensions influenced ethical decision making indirectly by affecting the decision-making criteria individuals used. Vardi (2001) also found that employees' perceptions of a rules and laws climate were significantly associated with misconduct in a survey study conducted in a metal products company in Israel.

ETHICAL CULTURE

The organizational culture literature views the organization as "both the medium and the outcome of social interaction" (Denison 1996, 635). It also emphasizes broad patterns of underlying values, beliefs, and assumptions; the uniqueness of individual social settings; the evolution of patterns over time; and qualitative research methods. Kopelman, Brief, and Guzzo (1990, 283) point out that the many approaches to the study of culture can be divided into two categories: the phenomenal, "focusing on observable behaviors and artifacts" and the ideational, focusing on underlying shared meanings, symbols, and values. The ethical culture construct as explicated by Treviño (1986, 1990) emphasizes the phenomenal level of culture—the more conscious, overt, and observable manifestations of culture such as structures, systems, and organizational practices rather than the deeper structure of values and assumptions.

Treviño (1986) initially conceptualized the organization's ethical culture as a situational moderator of the relationship between the individual's cognitive moral development stage and ethical or unethical conduct. In that model, culture comprised the organization's normative structure (norms about what is and is not appropriate behavior), referent others' behavior, expectations about obedience to legitimate authority, and the extent to which the organization encourages individuals to take responsibility for the consequences of their actions.

In a subsequent conceptualization, Treviño (1990) further developed the ethical culture construct and proposed direct influences of ethical culture on individual conduct. She defined ethical culture as a subset of organizational culture, representing a multidimensional interplay among various "formal" and "informal" systems of behavioral control that are capable of promoting either ethical or unethical behavior. *Formal cultural systems* include such factors as policies (for example, codes of ethics), leadership, authority structures, reward systems, and training programs. Some of these are related to formal ethics programs (for example, codes, ethics training), whereas others are not (for example, leadership, reward systems, authority structures). *Informal cultural systems* include such factors as peer behavior and ethical norms. To the extent that these formal and informal cultural systems support ethical conduct, individual behavior is expected to be more ethical. For example, ethical conduct should be higher in organizations where leaders and norms encourage and support ethical conduct and where ethical conduct is rewarded and unethical conduct is punished than in organizations without such characteristics.

Underlying the proposed ethical culture/behavior relationship is the assumption that culture can exert a powerful influence on individual behavior. An important characteristic shared by most conceptualizations of organizational culture is the expected relationship between culture and conduct (for a review, see Jelinek, Smircich, and Hersh 1983). Culture helps to establish what is considered legitimate or unacceptable in an organization. Whether defined as an informal organizational control systems (Martin and Siehl 1983; Deal and Kennedy 1982) or an instrument of domination, organizational culture is thought to provide direction for day-to-day behavior. A proposed theoretical relationship between ethical culture and employee attitudes is based on the notion that most people will feel more attached and committed to an organization if they perceive that the organization supports ethical conduct and discourages unethical conduct (Kleiman 1989; Sandroff 1990).

Ethical Climate and Ethical Culture: The Same or Different?

Both ethical *climate* and ethical *culture* refer to aspects of an organization's context that are thought to influence ethical attitudes and ethical behavior. In thinking about how they might be tapping different aspects of the ethical context, it may be helpful to consider the metaphors evoked by the terms *climate* and *culture*. *Climate* suggests meteorological climate and qualities such as temperature, humidity, precipitation, wind, and other atmospheric conditions that can affect individuals (for example, feelings), although it is unclear exactly what the effects will be. By contrast, the word *culture* evokes notions of rules, codes, rewards, leadership, rituals, and stories, sense-making devices that more explicitly guide and shape behavior (cf. Smircich 1983). In this metaphorical sense, ethical climate may characterize organizations in terms of broad normative characteristics and qualities that tell people what kind of organization this is—essentially what the organization values. If so, ethical climate is likely to be associated with attitudes but may influence decision making and behavior only indirectly, as Gaertner found. Ethical culture, on the other hand, characterizes the organization in terms of formal and informal control systems (such as rules, reward systems, and norms) that are aimed more specifically at influencing behavior. Therefore, we may find a stronger relationship between dimensions of ethical culture and ethical conduct. Ethical climate and ethical culture, although somewhat different, are also likely to be related to each other. For example, a culture that supports ethical conduct through codes of conduct is likely to be related to a climate that values rules and laws. To answer questions about the relationship between these constructs and their relationship with attitudes and behaviors, however, both must be included in the same study as has been done here.

METHODS

Sample

The study sample included 1,200 male and female alumni of two private colleges (600 from each college) located in the northeastern United States. They had graduated between five and thirty years before and work in a variety of business occupations, industries, and organizational sizes. Their mean age was 39.7, with a mean of 8.4 years in their present organization and 5.3 years in their current position.

Procedure

Of the 1,200 alumni, 1,179 were successfully mailed a cover letter and a questionnaire measuring personal and organizational characteristics, ethical climate, and ethical culture of their current work organization, attitudes, and behaviors. Completion of the survey was completely voluntary and anonymous; 318 surveys were returned (a 27 percent response rate). Tests for nonresponse bias found no significant differences in the response rate based on the college attended, gender, or age.

Approximately half (154) of the respondents reported that they work in an organization that has an ethics code. Another half (159) reported that their organization does not have a code. Five respondents did not answer the question. The number of respondents from code organizations was somewhat smaller than expected given recent published surveys that have suggested widespread code adoption in business (Center for Business Ethics, 1992; Murphy, 1995). These surveys, however, focused only on the largest American corporations. Because only about half of the respondents completed the portion of the survey (described later herein) related to characteristics of ethics codes, we conducted statistical analyses separately for respondents in code and noncode business settings.

Independent Variable Measures

Where possible, existing measures were used or adapted. Unless otherwise noted, all items were measured using a seven-point Likert scale from "strongly disagree" to "strongly agree" or from "completely false" to "completely true." Cronbach's alpha reliabilities for all measures are reported in Table 9.2.

Ethical Climate. Respondents' perceptions of the ethical climate in their organization were based on the ECQ developed by Victor and Cullen (1987, 1988) and further validated by Cullen and Bronson (1993). Four-item subscales were used to measure the following nine theoretical dimensions of ethical climate: self-interest, company profit, efficiency, friendship, team interest, social responsibility, personal morality, rules and standard operating procedures, and laws and professional codes.

Ethical Culture. Items designed to tap ethical culture were developed for this study based on previous theoretical work (Treviño 1990). Items were developed to measure peer behavior, the extent to which norms support ethical conduct, the extent to which ethical behavior is rewarded, the extent to which unethical behavior is punished, the extent to which organizational leaders act as models of ethical conduct, the extent to which employees are expected to obey authority figures without question, and the extent to which employees report unethical behavior when it occurs.

In addition, Treviño (1990) suggested that formal organizational policies, rules, and statements and their implementation are important aspects of the organizational culture. These generally appear in the form of an organization's ethics code. Respondents were asked whether their current work organization has a code of ethics. "Yes" responses were coded as 1 and no responses were coded as 0. Respondents who currently work for an organization with a code of ethics were asked fourteen additional questions regarding the code's implementation and integration into the organization. Responses to these code-related questions were treated as missing values for respondents in noncode work organizations.

It is possible that some respondents who answered the code existence question in the negative actually work for an organization that has a code tucked away in a file drawer, or that the code exists but is not distributed to employees. We were interested in these employees' knowledge that a code exists so that subsequent code-related questions could be answered. Therefore, in this study, a negative response to the question about the existence of a code represents a lack of knowledge that a code exists rather than a definitive, objective answer to the question.

Dependent Variable Measures

Organizational Commitment. The organizational commitment measure was adapted from O'Reilly and Chatman's (1986) measure of organizational commitment. Items were selected from two dimensions of the three-dimensional commitment measure. The first dimension is "identification," which represents the employee's identification with the attitudes or goals of the organization. Item examples include "I talk up the organization to my friends as a great organization to work for" and "I feel a sense of 'ownership' for this organization rather than being just an employee." The second dimension is a values-based type of commitment that O'Reilly and Chatman (1986) called *internalization*. This dimension reflects the extent to which the employee internalizes the organization's perspectives or characteristics. Item examples include "The reason I prefer this organization to others is because of what it stands for, its values" and "I find that my values and the organization's values are very similar."

Observed Unethical Behavior. A twenty-item scale measuring observed unethical behavior was adapted from Akaah (1992). Subjects were asked to rate the extent to which they observed other members of the organization engaging in a range of unethical behaviors during the past year. We measured "observed" behavior rather than the respondents' self-reported behavior to reduce problems with social desirability bias. We believe that respondents are more likely to report that they observed others' unethical behavior than that they were unethical during the year (despite the anonymity of responses). Items were selected to cover a variety of activities, such as theft (for example, "taking company materials and supplies") or lying ("falsifying time/quality/quantity reports" or "lying to customers").

Control Variable Measures

Job Satisfaction. Cullen and Victor (1993) recommended controlling for job satisfaction in their studies of the influence of ethical climate on commitment. In this study, job satisfaction was measured by a single item: "Generally speaking, I am very satisfied with this job." It was used as a control variable in the regression analyses where organizational commitment was the dependent variable.

Impression Management. Randall and Fernandes (1991) emphasized the importance of controlling for social desirability bias in survey studies of ethical behavior. Therefore, we controlled for social desirability bias in our regression analyses using a fifteen-item measure of subjects' tendency to engage in impression management, adapted from Paulhus (1989).

Statistical Analyses

Relationship Between Ethical Climate and Ethical Culture. To investigate the convergence and divergence of the ethical climate and culture constructs, a principal components factor analysis was conducted on all items from both the ethical climate and ethical culture measures. Then correlational analysis was conducted to determine whether correlations of measures within constructs were higher on average than those between constructs. This would suggest divergence of the two constructs.

Influences of Ethical Climate and Culture on Commitment and Behavior. Because of the existence of multiple dependent variables, omnibus tests (canonical correlation) were conducted for the overall model. These tests were conducted separately for the code sample and for the noncode sample. Given significant omnibus tests, individual regression analyses were then conducted.

The regression analyses also were conducted separately for respondents in code and noncode organizations. For each group (code respondents and noncode respondents), four hierarchical regression analyses were run. Impression management was entered first in all the regressions to control for the potential influence of social desirability on responses. Satisfaction was entered next in regressions where commitment was the dependent variable. Then, because of multicollinearity among climate and culture measures, we conducted two hierarchical regressions for each dependent variable (observed ethical behavior and organizational commitment). In the first regression for each dependent variable, ethical culture dimensions were entered as a block, followed by the ethical climate variables. In the second regression, ethical climate variables were entered as a block, followed by ethical culture. This approach, called *usefulness analysis* (Darlington 1968), has been used in organizational justice research to address similar problems with multicollinearity among the independent variables (Folger and Konovsky 1989). Usefulness analysis uses hierarchical regression to examine an independent variable's contribution to unique variance in the dependent variable beyond the contribution of another independent variable.

RESULTS

Exploratory Factor Analysis of Ethical Climate and Ethical Culture Items

The combined factor analysis revealed ten factors with eigenvalues greater than one. Within these factors, individual items were retained using the criterion of 0.50 (for inclusion in a factor), and items were eliminated if an item's loading was 0.40 or greater for more than one factor. In two cases, an additional item was removed from a factor because the reliability analysis suggested that reliability would be improved by doing so. Table 9.1 shows the remaining ten factors, including items, factor loadings, and eigenvalues. The ten factors were a fourteen-item measure of overall *ethical environment*, which included the degree to which unethical behavior is punished, the degree to which ethical behavior is rewarded, leaders' role modeling, the degree to which the ethics code is effective in promoting ethical behavior, and ethical norms (all derived from ethical culture items written for this study); a six-item measure of *employee-focused climate*; a four-item measure of *community-focused climate*; a three-item measure of *obedience to authority* (derived from culture items); a four-item measure of *code implementation* (derived from culture items); a two-item measure of *self-interest climate*; a four-item measure of *efficiency climate*; a two-item measure of *rules and procedures climate*; a three-item measure of *personal ethics climate*; and a two-item measure of *law and professional codes climate*. Thus, the combined factor analysis resulted in three factors derived from ethical culture items and seven factors derived from ethical climate items, suggesting some differentiation between the ethical climate and culture constructs.

Because the dimensions resulting from this factor analysis differentiated between ethical climate-based variables and ethical culture-based variables, these dimensions were used in subsequent regression analyses with the following exceptions. First, in the regressions of behavior on ethical culture and ethical climate, the item "ethical behavior is the norm in this organization" was deleted from the ethical environment dimension to remove concerns about tautology (similarities between a perceived norm of ethical conduct as an independent variable and observed unethical behavior as the dependent variable). We retained the item in the factor analysis, however, because norms are considered to be an important part of an ethical culture (Treviño 1990). We believe that the item is important and appropriate to include in the construct unless the dependent variable is ethical or unethical conduct. Second, for respondents who work in noncode organizations, three additional code-related items (that these respondents did not answer) were removed from the ethical environment (culture) measure. These are noted with a superscript *b* under Factor 1, Table 9.1. An example is "The ethics code serves as 'window dressing' only in this organization." The reliabilities (Cronbach's alphas) for the full and trimmed ethical environment dimension of ethical culture were identical (0.94).

Correlational Analyses

Correlations, means, standard deviations, and reliabilities for the study variables are displayed separately for the code and noncode samples in Table 9.2. Reliabilities were greater than 0.70 for all variables with the exception of two ethical climate dimensions (personal ethics and rules and procedures).

In the code sample, the ethical environment and code implementation dimensions of ethical culture were each significantly and strongly correlated with all but one of the ethical climate dimensions (personal ethics). The obedience to authority dimension of ethical culture was significantly correlated with the self-interest, efficiency, law and professional codes, employee-focused, and community-focused climates. In the noncode sample, the ethical environment culture dimension was significantly correlated with all ethical climate dimensions. The obedience to authority culture dimension was significantly correlated with all climate dimensions with the

TABLE 9.1

Exploratory Factor Analysis of All Ethical Climate and Ethical Culture Items

Questionnaire Items	FACTOR LOADINGS									
	1	2	3	4	5	6	7	8	9	10
1. Ethical environment										
Management in this organization disciplines unethical behavior when it occurs.	0.80	0.17	0.01	0.02	0.14	0.08	0.04	0.21	0.07	−0.13
Employees in this organization perceive that people who violate the ethics code still get formal organizational rewards.[ab]	0.79	0.13	−0.03	−0.05	0.10	0.09	−0.08	0.04	−0.11	0.17
Penalties for unethical behavior are strictly enforced in this organization.	0.77	0.03	0.09	0.04	0.13	0.12	0.08	0.10	0.05	−0.04
Unethical behavior is punished in this organization.	0.74	0.10	0.01	−0.03	0.04	0.09	0.06	0.11	−0.00	0.13
The top managers of this organization represent high ethical standards.	0.74	0.36	0.22	−0.05	0.10	0.07	0.06	0.20	−0.10	−0.04
People of integrity are rewarded in this organization.	0.65	0.25	0.25	−0.24	0.01	0.10	0.11	−0.07	0.00	0.09
The ethics code serves as "window dressing" only in this organization.[ab]	0.64	0.17	0.21	−0.17	0.04	−0.01	−0.06	−0.09	−0.08	0.34
Top managers of this organization regularly show that they care about ethics.	0.63	0.37	0.30	−0.14	0.12	0.19	0.08	0.14	−0.02	−0.00
Top managers of this organization are models of unethical behavior.	0.64	0.37	0.27	0.00	0.20	0.11	0.08	0.18	−0.14	0.08

Ethical behavior is the norm in this organization.[b]	0.62	0.29	0.26	-0.02	0.08	0.20	0.12	0.11	0.07	-0.06
Top managers of this organization guide decision making in an ethical direction.	0.59	0.27	0.33	-0.23	0.13	0.05	0.16	0.12	-0.06	0.08
The ethics code serves only to maintain the organization's public image.[a, b]	0.57	0.11	0.35	-0.31	0.16	0.18	-0.12	-0.03	0.02	0.00
Ethical behavior is rewarded in this organization.	0.54	0.33	0.26	-0.23	-0.04	0.09	-0.08	-0.13	0.12	0.08
Ethics code requirements are consistent with informal organizational norms.[b]	0.52	0.17	0.18	-0.30	0.06	0.04	-0.01	0.21	0.05	0.10
2. Employee-focused climate										
The most important concern is the good of all people in this organization.	0.27	0.78	0.14	-0.03	0.01	0.18	-0.01	0.06	0.10	-0.06
People are very concerned about what is generally best for employees in this organization.	0.28	0.73	0.27	-0.21	0.00	0.09	-0.02	-0.02	-0.04	0.03
Our major consideration is what is best for everyone in this organization.	0.18	0.71	0.11	-0.07	0.11	0.03	0.10	0.09	0.05	0.03
What is best for each individual is a primary concern in this organization.	0.16	0.68	0.09	-0.02	0.00	-0.05	0.11	-0.04	0.34	0.01
It is expected that each individual is cared for when making decisions here.	0.38	0.63	0.24	-0.13	0.07	0.28	0.01	-0.01	0.07	0.21
In this organization, people look out for each other's good.	0.25	0.59	0.12	-0.13	-0.02	0.29	-0.03	0.07	-0.00	0.34

(Table continues)

TABLE 9.1 (continued)

Questionnaire Items	FACTOR LOADINGS									
	1	2	3	4	5	6	7	8	9	10
3. Community-focused climate.										
The effect of decisions on the customer and the public are a primary concern in this organization.	0.20	0.23	0.83	-0.04	0.12	0.01	0.04	0.10	-0.03	0.08
People in this organization are actively concerned about the customer's, and the public's, interest.	0.27	0.21	0.82	-0.19	-0.03	0.14	0.05	0.06	0.05	0.05
It is expected that you will do what is right for the customer and public.	0.19	0.22	0.76	-0.08	0.13	0.04	-0.03	0.04	0.13	0.14
People in this organization have a strong sense of responsibility to the outside community.	0.21	0.26	0.55	-0.16	0.06	0.37	0.00	0.12	0.01	0.01
4. Obedience to authority										
This organization demands obedience to authority figures, without question.	-0.01	-0.21	0.00	0.80	0.01	-0.11	0.02	-0.03	-0.02	-0.08
People in this organization are expected to do as they're told.	-0.08	-0.05	-0.00	0.70	0.03	-0.07	0.07	0.26	-0.05	-0.03
The boss is always right in this organization.	-0.20	-0.09	-0.17	0.65	-0.12	-0.21	0.15	0.07	0.01	-0.05

5. Code implementation										
Employees are required to acknowledge that they have read and understood the ethics code.	0.15	0.04	−0.03	−0.04	0.80	−0.05	0.08	0.05	−0.05	0.05
The organization has established procedures for employees to ask questions about ethics code requirements.	0.25	−0.01	0.10	−0.13	0.68	0.23	0.08	0.27	−0.10	−0.03
The code of conduct is widely distributed throughout the organization.	0.13	0.17	0.14	0.01	0.65	0.15	−0.08	−0.08	−0.02	0.24
Employees are regularly required to assert that their actions are in compliance with the ethics code.	0.23	0.17	0.23	0.04	0.62	−0.14	0.08	−0.09	0.06	0.02
6. Self-interest climate										
People in this organization are very concerned about what is best for themselves.	−0.25	−0.25	−0.04	0.10	−0.08	−0.69	0.01	0.05	0.01	−0.06
In this organization, people protect their own interests above other considerations.	−0.27	−0.19	−0.27	0.25	−0.00	−0.60	0.14	0.01	0.02	−0.18
7. Efficiency climate										
In this organization, each person is expected above all to work efficiently.	−0.11	0.12	0.02	0.12	0.11	−0.01	0.80	0.09	0.03	0.10
The major responsibility of people in this organization is to consider efficiency first.	−0.03	−0.08	0.02	0.13	0.00	0.00	0.79	−0.23	0.07	−0.02
Efficient solutions to problems are always sought here.	0.36	0.21	0.24	−0.11	0.08	0.01	0.61	0.27	−0.03	−0.04
The most efficient way is always the right way in this organization.	0.13	0.26	−0.07	0.32	0.02	−0.34	0.53	−0.01	0.09	−0.10

(Table continues)

TABLE 9.1 (continued)

Questionnaire Items	FACTOR LOADINGS									
	1	2	3	4	5	6	7	8	9	10
8. Rules and procedures climate										
It is important to follow strictly the organization's rules and procedures.	0.24	0.02	0.05	0.19	0.09	0.04	-0.01	0.75	0.08	0.05
Everyone is expected to stick by company rules and procedures.	0.30	0.13	0.21	-0.07	0.08	-0.09	0.03	0.61	-0.22	0.09
9. Personal ethics climate										
In this organization, people are guided by their own personal ethics.	-0.02	0.02	0.10	-0.20	-0.00	-0.10	0.08	0.13	0.73	0.00
Each person in this organization decides for themselves what is right and wrong	-0.34	0.10	0.03	-0.07	-0.16	-0.09	-0.01	-0.01	0.68	-0.02
The most important concern in this organization is each person's own sense of right and wrong.	0.09	0.27	-0.00	0.09	-0.01	0.22	0.03	-0.25	0.61	-0.01
10. Law and professional codes climate										
In this organization, people are expected to comply with the law and professional standards over and above other considerations.	0.31	-0.03	0.24	-0.21	0.14	0.00	-0.05	0.08	0.16	0.69
In this organization, people are expected to strictly follow legal or professional standards.	0.37	0.27	0.18	-0.27	0.20	-0.12	0.02	0.21	0.02	0.52
Eigenvalues	20.22	4.59	3.51	2.45	2.41	2.06	1.77	1.58	1.57	1.48

[a] Item was reversed.

[b] Item was removed for statistical analyses in noncode sample.

exception of the rules and procedures climate. Therefore, although the factors emerging from the factor analysis differentiated between climate and culture-based items, these dimensions of the ethical context are strongly related to each other. Correlations of the dimensions of ethical culture with those of ethical climate were not lower than correlations of the dimensions of culture and climate with each other, suggesting that the relationships between climate and culture dimensions are more important than the differences between them.

Omnibus Multivariate Tests

Because the study included multiple dependent variables, the omnibus test, canonical correlation, was run for the overall model. Impression management, satisfaction, ethical climate- and ethical culture-based dimensions were the independent variables. Commitment and observed unethical behavior were the dependent variables. This test was run separately for subjects in organizations with and without ethics codes because the regression analyses were conducted separately for these groups. For the code respondents, the multivariate test was statistically significant, Wilk's lambda = 0.187, $F = 11.916$, probability $[p] < 0.0001$. For the noncode respondents, the test was also significant, Wilk's lambda = 0.136, $F = 15.364$, $p < 0.001$. With significant omnibus tests, we proceeded to conduct individual regressions.

Usefulness Analyses—Code Sample—Unethical Conduct

Regression analyses are reported in Table 9.3. All regression analyses controlled for impression management by entering it first in the regression equations. We begin by reporting the findings for unethical conduct in the code sample, with culture dimensions entered first in the hierarchical analysis. With culture entered first, two culture dimensions (ethical environment and obedience to authority) significantly influenced observed unethical behavior (explaining 29 percent of the variance beyond impression management). Ethical climate dimensions were nonsignificant. The stronger the general ethical environment, the less unethical behavior was observed. The higher a focus on strict obedience to authority, the more unethical behavior was observed. Code implementation was not significant.

When ethical climate dimensions were entered first, a single ethical climate dimension (self-interest) was significant (explaining 19 percent of

TABLE 9.2

Summary Statistics

Variables	Mean	SD	Alpha	1	2	3	4	5	6	7	8	9	10	11	12	13
Code Sample[a]																
1. Impression management	3.27	0.84	0.70													
2. Job satisfaction	4.14	1.73	b	0.06												
3. Ethical environment	4.13	1.16	0.94	0.15	0.51											
4. Employee-focused climate	3.23	1.17	0.87	−0.08	0.42	0.63										
5. Community-focused climate	4.46	1.10	0.84	0.06	0.48	0.58	0.52									
6. Obedience to authority	3.07	1.38	0.76	−0.01	−0.33	−0.31	−0.28	−0.28								
7. Code implementation	4.12	1.47	0.75	0.18	0.10	0.44	0.26	0.31	−08							
8. Self-interest	3.54	1.34	0.72	−0.16	−0.36	−0.52	−0.49	−0.44	0.38	−0.18						
9. Efficiency	3.22	1.17	0.76	−0.03	0.02	0.18	0.24	0.15	0.21	0.21	0.10					
10. Rules and procedures	4.36	1.11	0.67	0.13	0.13	0.45	0.23	0.28	0.10	0.33	−0.15	0.18				
11. Personal ethics	3.28	1.06	0.59	−.02	0.08	−.03	0.28	0.11	−0.10	−0.09	−0.06	0.06	−0.15			
12. Law & professional codes	4.95	1.10	0.78	0.10	0.37	0.61	0.35	0.41	−0.32	0.40	−0.27	0.15	0.47	0.06		
13. Unethical behavior	2.11	1.17	0.92	−0.33	−0.36	−0.53	−0.24	−0.36	0.31	−0.31	0.38	−0.05	−0.26	0.03	−0.32	
14. Organizational commitment	4.07	1.50	0.90	0.05	0.66	0.69	0.63	0.68	−0.45	0.26	−0.52	0.11	0.28	0.12	0.51	−0.46

Noncode Sample[c]

	Mean	SD	α	1	2	3	4	5	6	7	8	9	10	11	12
1. Impression management	3.19	0.85	0.70												
2. Job satisfaction	4.06	1.92	[d]	0.14											
3. Ethical environment	3.62	1.36	0.94	0.27	0.59										
4. Employee-focused climate	3.31	1.20	0.86	0.26	0.61	0.72									
5. Community-focused climate	4.42	1.09	0.81	0.24	0.41	0.59	0.45								
6. Obedience to authority	3.08	1.44	0.75	−0.09	−0.31	−0.44	−0.31	−0.42							
7. Self-interest	3.56	1.37	0.74	−0.19	−0.28	−0.53	−0.41	−0.47	0.50						
8. Efficiency	3.18	1.20	0.77	0.05	0.17	0.22	0.24	0.04	0.19	−0.03					
9. Rules and procedures	4.10	1.19	0.66	0.15	0.12	0.29	0.09	0.19	0.15	−0.01	0.29				
10. Personal ethics	3.35	1.04	0.60	0.09	0.37	0.32	0.46	0.28	−0.24	−0.07	−0.03	−0.20			
11. Law & professional codes	4.70	1.10	0.75	0.17	0.33	0.53	0.39	0.47	−0.27	−0.33	0.12	0.29	0.13		
12. Unethical behavior	2.21	1.31	0.94	−0.37	−0.40	−0.58	−0.51	−0.49	0.41	0.49	−0.03	−0.13	−0.29	−0.45	
13. Organizational commitment	3.96	1.57	0.89	0.18	0.71	0.81	0.74	0.61	−0.44	−0.51	0.19	0.16	0.38	0.47	−0.50

[a] $N = 154$; correlations with values of 0.16 and higher are significant at $p < 0.05$.

[b] One-item measure, Cronbach's alpha could not be calculated.

[c] $N = 159$; correlations with values of 0.16 and higher are significant at $p < 0.05$.

[d] One-item measure, Cronbach's alpha could not be calculated.

Note: Noncode results do not include code implementation variable.

the variance beyond impression management). The more the ethical climate was perceived to focus on self-interest, the more respondents reported that they observed unethical behavior. When entered in the second step, culture was also significant (explaining another 13 percent of the variance). Overall ethical environment and obedience to authority were again the significant culture dimensions.

Usefulness Analyses—Code Sample—Organizational Commitment

For organizational commitment, when culture variables were entered first, culture made a significant contribution to the regression model (explaining 23 percent of the variance beyond impression management and satisfaction) (see Table 9.3, part 2). Significant culture variables were once again overall ethical environment and obedience to authority. Climate was also significant (explaining another eight percent of the variance). The climate variables that significantly influenced organizational commitment were employee focus and community focus. Respondents were more highly committed to organizations that were concerned about the welfare of employees and the community. When climate was entered first, the climate step was significant (explaining 28 percent of the variance beyond impression management and satisfaction). Significant variables included employee and community focus (as in the preceding) plus law and professional code climates. Culture was also significant (explaining another 3 percent of the variance). The employee and community focus climate dimensions and the obedience to authority culture dimension remained significant in the final equation.

Usefulness Analyses—Noncode Sample—Unethical Conduct

As explained earlier, the same analyses were run for the subsample of respondents who reported that they worked in noncode organizations. Because these respondents did not answer code-related questions, the code implementation variable was excluded from these analyses and the ethical environment measure was trimmed of code-related items (it nevertheless remained highly reliable, Cronbach's alpha for ethical environment = 0.94). We begin by reporting findings for observed unethical conduct. With culture entered first in the hierarchical regression, culture dimensions (ethical environment and obedience to authority) significantly influenced observed unethical behavior (explaining 29 percent of the variance beyond impression management). This finding is identical to the finding for code organizations. For noncode respondents, however, ethical climate dimensions were also significant, explaining an additional 8 percent of the variance. In the final regression equation, only the law and professional code and self-interest climate dimensions remained. The higher the focus on self-interest, the more respondents reported observing unethical behavior. The higher the focus on law and professional codes, the fewer respondents reported observing unethical behavior.

When ethical climate dimensions were entered first, the same climate dimensions (self-interest and law and professional code) were significant (explaining 36 percent of the variance beyond impression management). The culture step was nonsignificant.

Usefulness Analyses—Noncode Sample— Organizational Commitment

For organizational commitment, when culture variables were entered first, culture was significant (explaining 27 percent of the variance beyond impression management and satisfaction). The significant culture variable was overall ethical environment. The climate step was also significant (explaining another four percent of the variance). The climate variables that significantly influenced organizational commitment were community focus and employee focus.

When climate was entered first, the climate step was significant (explaining 26 percent of the variance beyond impression management and satisfaction). Significant variables included community and employee focus (as in the preceding) plus self-interest. Culture was also significant (explaining another 5 percent of the variance). The employee and community focus climate dimensions and the overall ethical environment culture dimension remained significant in the final equation.

DISCUSSION

In this study, Victor and Cullen's (1987, 1988) and Treviño's (1990) conceptualizations of ethical climate and ethical culture were used to characterize the ethical context of organizations, and both were discussed in terms of potential influences on employees' attitudes and behaviors. This study is

TABLE 9.3
Results of Hierarchical Regression (Usefulness) Analyses

Step	Variables	CODE SUBJECTS			NONCODE SUBJECTS		
		R^2	beta	F	R^2	beta	F

The influence of ethical culture and ethical climate on unethical conduct

Culture entered first

Step	Variables	R^2	beta	F	R^2	beta	F
1.	Control variables	0.11 (0.10)		14.30**	0.13 (0.12)		16.46**
	Impression management		−0.33	14.30**		−0.36	16.46**
2.	Ethical culture	0.29 (0.28)		19.12**	0.29 (0.28)		27.01**
	Impression management		−0.25	11.77**		−0.23	9.09**
	Ethical environment		−0.39	21.01**		−0.43	27.75**
	Code implementation		−0.07	0.78		*a*	*a*
	Obedience to authority		0.23	9.08**		0.21	7.18**
3.	Ethical climate	0.02 (0.00)		0.60	0.08 (0.05)		2.30*
	Impression management		−0.21	7.36**		−0.23	9.86**
	Ethical environment		−0.44	11.88**		−0.12	0.88
	Code implementation		−0.08	0.88		*a*	*a*
	Obedience to authority		0.26	8.15**		0.10	1.14
	Employee-focused climate		0.16	1.78		−0.11	1.03
	Community-focused climate		−0.03	0.11		−0.07	0.62
	Self-interest		0.08	0.62		0.21	5.28*
	Efficiency		−0.01	0.01		−0.03	0.08
	Rules and procedures		−0.10	1.37		0.03	0.13
	Personal ethics		−0.03	0.18		−0.07	0.63
	Law and professional codes		0.12	1.38		−0.20	5.47*

the first investigation to include measures of both constructs in a single study, to factor analyze them together, to investigate the relationships between them, and to examine their relative influences on unethical conduct and organizational commitment.

Ethical Context: The Relationship Between Ethical Climate and Culture

The initial principal components factor analysis (all the ethical climate and ethical culture items) revealed ten ethical context factors. Each of these ten

TABLE 9.3 *(continued)*

Step	Variables	CODE SUBJECTS			NONCODE SUBJECTS		
		R^2	beta	F	R^2	beta	F
Climate entered first							
1.	Control variables	0.11 (0.10)		14.30**	0.13 (0.12)		16.46**
	Impression management		−0.33	14.30**		−0.36	16.46**
2.	Ethical climate	0.19 (0.15)		4.37**	0.36 (0.33)		10.29**
	Impression management		−0.25	9.23**		−0.24	10.44**
	Employee-focused climate		−0.04	0.15		−0.18	3.35
	Community-focused climate		−0.12	1.31		−0.11	1.38
	Self-interest		0.23	5.11*		0.27	10.30**
	Efficiency		0.01	0.01		−0.02	0.04
	Rules and procedures		−0.08	0.75		0.03	0.18
	Personal ethics		0.05	0.40		−0.09	1.01
	Law and professional codes		−0.04	0.15		−0.23	7.71**
3.	Ethical culture	0.13 (0.11)		8.00**	0.01 (0.00)		1.19
	Impression management		−0.21	7.36**		−0.23	9.86**
	Employee-focused climate		0.15	1.78		−0.11	1.03
	Community-focused climate		0.03	0.11		−0.07	0.62
	Self-interest		0.08	0.68		0.21	5.29*
	Efficiency		−0.01	0.01		−0.03	0.08
	Rules and procedures		−0.10	1.37		0.03	0.13
	Personal ethics		−0.03	0.18		−0.07	0.62
	Law and professional codes		0.12	1.38		−0.20	5.47*
	Ethical environment		−0.44	11.87**		−0.12	0.88
	Code implementation		−0.08	0.88	*a*		*a*
	Obedience to authority		0.26	8.15**		0.10	1.14

(Table continues)

TABLE 9.3 *(continued)*

		CODE SUBJECTS			NONCODE SUBJECTS		
Step	Variables	R^2	beta	F	R^2	beta	F

The influence of ethical culture and ethical climate on organizational commitment

Culture entered first

1.	Control variables	0.43 (0.42)		48.90**	0.52 (0.51)		62.93**
	Impression management		0.02	0.10		0.05	0.68
	Satisfaction		0.66	97.39**		0.71	117.82**
2.	Ethical culture	0.23 (0.23)		28.09**	0.24 (0.23)		55.37**
	Impression management		−0.04	0.68		−0.05	1.13
	Satisfaction		0.36	32.33**		0.37	42.46**
	Ethical environment		0.43	38.40**		0.56	87.09**
	Code implementation		0.04	0.54		a	a
	Obedience to authority		−0.23	15.71**		−0.11	4.48*
3.	Ethical climate	0.08 (0.07)		5.51**	0.04 (0.03)		2.71**
	Impression management		−0.01	0.01		−0.07	1.98
	Satisfaction		0.25	17.94**		0.30	26.27**
	Ethical environment		0.14	2.61		0.36	18.54**
	Code implementation		0.00	0.00		a	a
	Obedience to authority		−0.18	9.31**		−0.04	0.62
	Employee-focused climate		0.20	7.56**		0.21	8.43**
	Community-focused climate		0.25	14.87**		0.11	3.82*
	Self-interest		−0.05	0.71		−0.07	1.32
	Efficiency		−0.01	0.01		−0.01	0.08
	Rules and procedures		0.03	0.19		−0.02	0.18
	Personal ethics		−0.02	0.16		0.02	0.15
	Law and professional codes		0.10	2.12		0.03	0.33

factors consisted of items that were derived from either the ethical climate or the ethical culture measures. None of the resulting factors combined items from both the climate and culture measures. Thus, this analysis provided some empirical evidence of differentiation between the ethical climate and ethical culture constructs.

This study also provided further support for the existence of a number of

TABLE 9.3 *(continued)*

Step	Variables	CODE SUBJECTS			NONCODE SUBJECTS		
		R^2	beta	F	R^2	beta	F
Climate entered first							
1.	Control variables	0.43 (0.42)		48.90**	0.52 (0.51)		62.93**
	Impression management		0.02	0.10		0.05	0.68
	Satisfaction		0.66	97.39**		0.71	117.82**
2.	Ethical climate	0.28 (0.27)		17.41**	0.23 (0.22)		14.75**
	Impression management		−0.00	0.00		−0.04	0.77
	Satisfaction		0.29	23.24**		0.34	30.34**
	Employee-focused climate		0.26	13.51**		0.36	25.30**
	Community-focused climate		0.27	17.33**		0.18	8.14**
	Self-interest		−0.12	3.76*		−0.15	7.16**
	Efficiency		−0.03	0.31		0.00	0.00
	Rules and procedures		−0.00	0.02		0.01	0.0e
	Personal ethics		−0.04	0.59		0.05	0.77
	Law and professional codes		0.20	11.22**		0.09	2.42
3.	Ethical culture	0.03 (0.03)		4.18**	0.04 (0.04)		10.32**
	Impression management		−0.00	0.01		−0.07	1.98
	Satisfaction		0.25	17.99**		0.30	26.28**
	Employee-focused climate		0.20	7.56**		0.21	8.43**
	Community-focused climate		0.25	14.87**		0.11	3.82*
	Self-interest		−0.05	0.71		−0.07	1.32
	Efficiency		−0.01	0.01		0.01	0.08
	Rules and procedures		0.03	0.71		−0.02	0.18
	Personal ethics		−0.02	0.16		0.02	0.15
	Law and professional codes		0.10	2.17		0.03	0.33
	Ethical environment		0.14	2.61		0.36	18.54**
	Code implementation		0.00	0.00		[a]	[a]
	Obedience to authority		−0.18	9.31**		−0.04	0.62

[a] Code implementation not entered for noncode subjects.

$* = p < 0.05$ $** = p < 0.01$

Values in parentheses are adjusted R^2s.

ethical climate dimensions. The factor analysis results were generally consistent with previous research findings suggesting that future research can continue to use these measures; however, two of the climate dimensions do not meet conventional reliability standards (0.70) and should be improved.

The study also provided the first reliable scales for the measurement of ethical culture that can be used in future research. A number of the proposed dimensions became part of a single factor we labeled *overall ethical environment*. This factor encompasses ethical leadership, norms, and reward systems that support ethical conduct and (in code organizations) a code of conduct that is consistent with organizational norms. These aspects of ethical culture varied together in the responses and did not turn out to be "separate" culture dimensions as originally proposed. Future investigations that include both culture and climate (as this one did) should use the scales derived from the combined factor analysis (reported in Table 9.1) because the combined analysis removed items that did not discriminate between the two constructs.

The correlational analysis suggested that the factors derived from the ethical climate and ethical culture constructs, although somewhat different, are strongly related. Correlations were particularly high between ethical environment (the main culture-based factor) and employee-focused climate, community-focused climate, law and professional code climate, and self-interest climate (negative correlation).

These results suggest that dimensions of ethical climate and ethical culture are tapping somewhat different aspects of the ethical context of the business organizations represented in this study. Clearly, the ethical culture-derived dimensions are capturing an aspect of the organization's ethical context excluded from the ethical climate construct (for example, leadership and reward systems). As we will see below, this aspect of ethical culture seems important for ethical conduct, especially in code organizations; but the strong relationships between ethical climate and ethical culture-based factors suggest a large degree of overlap and important relationships between these constructs as well. We should not be surprised at a finding suggesting that an organization whose leaders represent high ethical standards and who reward ethical conduct is also an organization that values its employees, its community, and obeying the law. The finding that ethical climate and ethical culture are strongly related is aligned with recent work in the broader organizational climate/culture literature suggesting the close relationship between them (Denison 1996; Pettigrew 1990). A number of researchers are currently using the terms together when talking about creating a particular type of organizational context—for example, one that supports change or success (see, for example, Schneider, Gunnarson, and Niles-Jolly 1990).

Relationship Between Ethical Context and Attitudes/Behaviors

Ethical Context and Ethical Conduct. We proposed that ethical culture would be more strongly associated with ethical conduct than would ethical climate. The empirical results were mixed. Code organizations, where ethical culture-based factors were most strongly associated with observed unethical behavior, provided support for this proposition. In noncode organizations, however, ethical climate factors emerged as better predictors.

In code organizations, when culture dimensions were entered first, climate dimensions did not add significantly to the variance explained by overall ethical environment and obedience to authority. When climate dimensions were entered first, a single climate dimension (self-interest) was significant and positively associated with unethical conduct. When culture was added, the same two ethical culture dimensions as before (overall ethical environment and obedience to authority) added significantly to the variance explained.

In noncode organizations, the results were quite different. When the culture dimensions were entered in the regression equation first, they explained the same amount of variance (29 percent) as they did in the code sample, suggesting that ethical culture influences ethical conduct similarly in the two types of organizations. Two climate dimensions (law and professional code and self-interest) explained an additional 8 percent of the variance. When ethical climate dimensions were entered first, a full 36 percent of the variance was explained, with only self-interest being significant. Culture was nonsignificant. Therefore, in noncode organizations, the key variable was self-interest. To the extent that respondents perceived a focus on self-interested behavior in the organization, they also reported observing more unethical conduct. This finding for self-interest is consistent with Wimbush and Shepard's (1994) prediction that egoistic climates would be associated with unethical conduct. A note of caution in interpreting this finding is in order, however, because it may represent a tautology. To the extent that unethical conduct (for example, lying, cheating, stealing) is defined, to a large degree, as self-interested, it is not surprising to find that respondents who perceive self-interest in their organization will also say that they observe more unethical conduct. With that caution in mind, we believe organizations might find it useful to know that they can survey their employees about self-interest climate and simultaneously learn quite a bit about unethical conduct.

The results for overall ethical environment are consistent with survey research conducted across six firms by Treviño et al. (1999). They found strong relationships between observed unethical conduct and employees' perceptions of the reward system (that ethical behavior is rewarded and unethical behavior is punished), perceptions of the authority structure (whether the context requires unquestioning obedience to authority), and perceptions of ethical leadership (at both the executive and supervisory levels). Unethical conduct was lower where employees perceived a reward system supportive of ethical conduct, an authority structure that does not support unquestioning obedience, and leaders who pay attention to ethics and take it seriously. Interestingly, employees' perceptions of executive and supervisory leadership were highly related (correlation = 0.78), suggesting that employees have similar perceptions of leaders at these two very different organizational levels.

The finding for law and professional codes suggests that a company's more general emphasis on obeying the law and adhering to professional conduct standards is associated with less observed unethical behavior. As suggested earlier, this climate dimension is one of the most behavior-focused in that laws and professional standards are quite specific about behaviors that are acceptable or unacceptable. Future research may want to consider whether an emphasis on laws and professional codes can substitute for a company code, particularly in certain types of organizations, such as professional organizations (such as accounting or law firms) or organizations in highly legalized or regulated industries (such as banking).

It is also important to consider the climate and culture dimensions that did not enter significantly into the regression equations. Four of the seven ethical climate dimensions (employee focus, community focus, personal ethics, efficiency) had no significant association with observed unethical conduct. One of the three ethical culture dimensions (code implementation) did not contribute significantly, which may suggest that a number of aspects of the ethical context are unrelated to conduct, although they may be related to attitudes.

In sum, we found that two ethical culture-based (overall ethical environment and obedience to authority) dimensions were the best overall predictors of unethical conduct, and they operated similarly in code and noncode organizations. A climate focused on self-interest also was associated with unethical conduct in both code and noncode settings but was the most important contextual variable in noncode settings. In noncode settings, a focus on adhering to laws and professional standards also was associated with unethical conduct.

These analyses suggested that the context influenced behavior somewhat differently in code and noncode settings. In code settings, unethical conduct was primarily a function of a behavior-based cultural dimension (overall ethical environment). Observed unethical conduct was lower in a context that encouraged ethical conduct and discouraged unethical conduct through leadership, reward systems, and a meaningful code of conduct. In noncode settings, unethical conduct was primarily a function of an ethical climate dimension (self-interested climate) that was associated with observed unethical behavior. Support for ethical conduct came from a focus on law and professional codes. These findings suggest that researchers and managers may need to think somewhat differently about contextual influences on ethical conduct in code and noncode organizations.

When considering ethical conduct in organizations in general (without the code/noncode distinction), selected dimensions from both the ethical climate and culture constructs are clearly relevant. Therefore, future studies of the relationship between ethical context and unethical conduct should, at a minimum, incorporate the select combination of variables from the original ethical climate and ethical culture constructs that were found to be predictive in this research: overall ethical environment, obedience to authority, self-interest, and law and professional code.

Ethical Context and Organizational Commitment. In this study, we found that measures of ethical climate and ethical culture were almost interchangeable in their ability to predict employee attitudes in both code and noncode organizations, providing organizations with multiple options for influencing organizational commitment. Interestingly, the ethical culture dimensions (overall ethical environment and obedience to authority) associated with ethical conduct also were associated with commitment, making them the most consistently influential study variables. Overall ethical environment was the most consistent culture dimension to be associated with organizational commitment in this study. Similar findings emerged in the six-firm survey study cited earlier (Treviño et al. 1999). Organizational commitment was more positive when employees perceived a reward system supportive of ethical conduct, an authority structure that does not support unquestioning obedience, and leaders who pay attention to ethics and take it seriously.

Two new climate dimensions emerged as significant in relation to organizational commitment. Employee-focused and community-focused climates were the most consistent climate dimensions to be associated with commitment. These employees were more likely to identify and feel a sense of shared values with organizations that supported and rewarded ethical conduct and that emphasized the good of employees, customers, and the public. The finding for employee and community-focused climate was also similar to Cullen and Victor's finding that benevolence-based climates were positively related to commitment. In noncode organizations, self-interest also had a significant (negative) effect on commitment, again similar to Cullen and Victor's (1993) finding regarding egoistic climates. Therefore, a climate focused on self-interest not only appears to promote unethical conduct, but it also has a negative influence on organizational commitment.

Implications for Theory

The findings support the general theory driving this research: that the ethical context of the organization is associated with employee attitudes and behaviors. Questions remain, however, about how best to conceptualize the ethical context of organizations and its relationship with attitudes and behaviors. Cohen (1998) has proposed another way of conceptualizing the ethical context of firms. She defined *moral climate* as "prevailing employee perceptions of organizational signals regarding norms for making decisions with a moral component" (Cohen, 1998:1213). Climate provides a psychological environment of shared perceptions in which certain expected behaviors are more likely to occur. In Cohen's model, cultural processes (e.g., political and technical processes) serve as stimuli that signal managerial expectations for certain types of behavior. Shared interpretations of these cues create a climate that makes certain behaviors more likely. Thus, in the model, cultural processes influence climate, which influences ethical behavior. Ethical behaviors also are influenced by other mediating variables such as individual differences and conditions outside the firm. Cohen's model provides a way to integrate culture and climate into a single model that offers a broader framework for thinking about ethical context and how climate and culture components may be related. Additional research will be needed to explore the relationships among contextual dimensions, attitudes, and behaviors. We believe that theory in this area also can be advanced by conducting inductive qualitative research. Employees could be asked to discuss what drives their ethics-related attitudes and behaviors and specifically to focus on the firm's context. These findings then could be combined with previous theorizing and empirical findings to develop a more complete understanding of ethical context.

Implications for Management

The study findings certainly suggest implications for management. To decrease unethical conduct, an organization should have leaders who encourage and model ethical behavior and reward systems that reward ethical conduct and discipline unethical conduct, an ethics code that is consistent with norms, a focus away from strict obedience to authority and away from self-interest at the expense of other considerations, and a focus on adherence to the law and professional standards when they apply. Some of the management prescriptions are quite clear (for example, to discipline unethical conduct), whereas others raise concerns about common management practices. For example, many organizations base their reward systems almost exclusively on self-interest (for example, commission-only systems). Does this type of reward system produce an ethical climate high on self-interest and a corresponding high level of unethical conduct? Theorizing (Kurland 1996) and media reports about the unethical practices of financial advisers and others suggest that such a relationship can develop. If so, can these reward system pressures be countered by a culture characterized by a strong ethical environment (leadership, codes, norms, and so on)? Or must the reward system be fundamentally changed? Additional research will be needed to answer these questions.

These findings also suggest a number of routes managers can take to obtain the commitment of employees through the ethical context. They can focus on developing a culture that supports ethical conduct and discourages unethical conduct through leadership, reward systems, codes, and norms.

They can focus on developing climates that emphasize the good of employ-ees, customers, and the public rather than self-interest. Even better, they can do all these things. As with prescriptions for decreasing unethical con-duct, many questions remain about the best ways to develop these ethical contexts. Hopefully, future research can answer these questions.

Limitations of the Study

A limitation of the present research is the use of perceptual measures for study variables; this is unavoidable, however, in studies that focus on indi-vidual perceptions of organizational phenomena. In fact, we were very much interested in perceptions. For example, predicting organizational commit-ment from perceptions of the organization's ethical context requires that both be measured through questions based on individual perceptions.

A second limitation involves the potential for social desirability to bias the survey results. Social desirability is particularly problematic when researching sensitive topics such as business ethics (Randall and Fernandes 1991). We addressed this limitation in several ways. First, for unethical behavior, respondents reported on the extent to which they observed others' unethical behavior rather than their own. Social desirability bias would be more likely to influence self-reports of unethical conduct than reports of others' behavior. Second, respondents remained completely anonymous. Randall and Fernandes (1991) suggested that anonymity is an important way to reduce social desirability bias in ethics-related surveys. Third, and per-haps most important, we measured and controlled for social desirability bias in the regression equations by using Paulhus' impression management measure (Paulhus 1989) as Randall and Fernandes recommended. Inspec-tion of the regressions suggests that impression management explained a significant proportion of the variance in the regressions where observed behavior was the dependent variable (11 percent in code organizations and 13 percent in noncode organizations) but not in the commitment regressions.

Third, because this study relied upon cross-sectional survey data, the observed linkages between the independent and dependent variables should be interpreted as correlational and not necessarily causal.

Fourth, the culture measure designed for this study was developed with a bias toward code organizations. This resulted in missing data and the need to conduct separate analyses within the code and noncode subsamples.

Despite the interesting results and insights these analyses produced, future research should refine the ethical culture measure to make it more applicable to both code and noncode organizations. Our findings regarding the number of respondents in code and noncode organizations suggest that previous surveys (that focused almost exclusively on the largest corporations) overestimated the extent to which all business organizations have implemented codes of conduct.

Fifth, this study focused on unethical conduct. Future research may wish to consider the influence of ethical climate and culture on other ethics-related behaviors, such as prosocial behaviors and ethical conduct.

Finally, questions about generalizability remain. The sample for this study included alumni from two colleges who are generally in managerial positions in their organizations. Although we do not expect the relationships between ethical context and attitudes/behaviors to be different for lower-level employees, we cannot be sure that the results can be generalized to all organization members.

CONCLUSION

Our analysis suggests that the ethical climate and ethical culture constructs are tapping somewhat different but strongly related aspects of the ethical context. Several climate and culture-based dimensions were strongly associated with observed unethical conduct and organizational commitment. Employees observed less unethical behavior in, and were clearly more committed to, organizations that supported ethical conduct via cultural systems and that emphasized the good of employees, customers, and the public. The findings suggest that ethical climate and ethical culture are not alternative ways of conceptualizing the ethical context. Rather, both are important because some dimensions are more strongly associated with behavior and others are more strongly associated with commitment. Further, a number of interesting differences were found across code and noncode organizations. Based on the findings presented here, researchers should think carefully about their research questions and the organizations studied in determining which dimensions of the ethical context to include in future investigations. Future research in this area also should ask whether the combination of dimensions emerging from this study captures all relevant dimensions of ethical context or whether there are others (Cohen 1998).

References

Akaah, I. P. 1992. Social inclusion as a marketing ethics correlate. *Journal of Business Ethics* 11(8):599–608.

Center for Business Ethics. 1992. Instilling ethical values in large corporations. *Journal of Business Ethics* 11:863–867.

Cohen, D. 1998. Moral climate in business firms: A conceptual framework for analysis and change. *Journal of Business Ethics* 17(11):1211–1217.

Cullen, J. B., and J. W. Bronson. 1993. The ethical climate questionnaire: An assessment of the development and validity. Paper presented at the Annual Academy of Management Meeting, Atlanta, GA.

Cullen, J. B., and B. Victor. 1993. The effects of ethical climates on organizational commitment: Multilevel analysis. Unpublished manuscript.

Darlington, R. B. 1968. Multiple regression in psychological research. *Psychological Bulletin* 79:161–182.

Deal, T. E., and A. A. Kennedy. 1982. *Corporate cultures*. Reading, MA: Addison-Wesley.

Denison, D. 1996. What is the difference between organizational culture and organizational climate? A native's point of view on a decade of paradigm wars. *Academy of Management Review* 21(3):619–654.

Folger, R., and M. A. Konovsky. 1989. Effects of procedural and distributive justice on reactions to pay raise decisions. *Academy of Management Journal* 32:115–130.

Gaertner, K. 1991. The effect of ethical climate on managers' decisions. In *Morality, rationality and efficiency: New perspectives on socio-economics*. Armonk, N.Y.: M. E. Sharpe.

Jelinek, M., L. Smircich, and P. Hirsh. 1983. Introduction: A code of many colors. *Administrative Science Quarterly* 28:331–338.

Jones, T. M. 1991. Ethical decision making by individuals in organizations: An issue-contingent model. *Academy of Management Review* 16:366–395.

Kleiman, C. 1989. Heading the list of worker wishes isn't more money! Allentown, PA: *The Morning Call* October 2:B10.

Kopelman, R. E., A. P. Brief, and R. A. Guzzo. 1990. The role of climate and culture in productivity. In *Organizational climate and culture*, ed. B. Schneider, 282–318. San Francisco: Jossey-Bass.

Kurland, N. 1996. Trust, accountability, and sales agents' dueling loyalties. *Business Ethics Quarterly* 6(3):289–310.

Martin, J., and C. Siehl. 1983. Organizational culture and counterculture: an uneasy symbiosis. *Organizational Dynamics* Autumn:52−64.

Mowday, R. T., R. M. Steers, and L. Porter. 1979. The measure of organizational commitment. *Journal of Vocational Behavior* 14:224−247.

Murphy, P. E. 1995. Corporate ethics statements: Current status and future prospects. *Journal of Business Ethics* 14:727−740.

O'Reilly, C., and J. Chatman. 1986. Organizational commitment and psychological attachment: The effects of compliance, identification, and internalization on prosocial behavior. *Journal of Applied Psychology* 71:492−499.

Paulhus, D. 1989. Measurement and control of response bias. In *Measures of social psychological attitudes*, ed. J. P. Robinson, P. R. Shaver, and L. Wrightsman. New York: Academic Press.

Pettigrew, A. 1990. Organizational climate and culture: Two constructs in search of a role. In *Organizational climate and culture,* ed. B. Schneider, 413−433. San Francisco: Jossey-Bass.

Randall, D. M., and M. F. Fernandes. 1991. The social desirability bias in ethics research. *Journal of Business Ethics* 10:805−817.

Sandroff, R. 1990. How ethical is American business? *Working Woman Magazine* September:113−116.

Schneider, B. 1975. Organizational climate: An essay. *Personnel Psychology* 28:447−479.

Schneider, B., A. P. Brief, and R. A. Guzzo. 1996. Creating a climate and culture for sustainable organizational change. *Organizational Dynamics* 24(4):7−19.

Smircich, L. 1983. Concepts of culture and organizational analysis. *Administrative Science Quarterly* 28:339−358.

Treviño, L. K. 1986. Ethical decision-making in organizations: A person-situation interactionist model. *Academy of Management Review* 11:601−617.

Treviño, L. K. 1990. A cultural perspective on changing and developing organizational ethics. *Research in Organizational Change and Development* 4:195−230.

Treviño, L. K., G. R. Weaver, D. G. Gibson, and B. L. Toffler. 1999. Managing ethics and legal compliance: What works and what hurts. *California Management Review* 41(2):131−151.

Vardi, Y. 2001. The effects of organizational and ethical climates on misconduct at work. *Journal of Business Ethics* 29(4):325−337.

Victor, B., and J. B. Cullen. 1987. A theory and measure of ethical climate in organizations. In *Research in corporate social performance and policy,* ed. W. C. Frederick, 51−71. Greenwich, CT: JAI Press.

Victor, B., and J. B. Cullen. 1988. The organizational bases of ethical work climates. *Administrative Science Quarterly* 33:101−125.

Weber, J. 1995. Influences upon organizational ethical subclimates: A multi-departmental analysis of a single firm. *Organization Science* 6(5):509–523.

Wimbush, J. C., and J. M. Shepard. 1994. Toward an understanding of ethical climate: Its relationship to ethical behavior and supervisory influence. *Journal of Business Ethics* 13:637–647.

Employees' Fairness Perceptions and Ethics-related Outcomes in Organizations

Chapter 9 focused on the influence of the organization's ethical climate/ culture on employees' ethical conduct and organizational commitment. Since that study was conducted, our work has expanded to include another key influential variable related to the broad organizational context: employees' perceptions of fair treatment in the organization. In the empirical study reported here, we consider how the workings of formal ethics programs are intertwined with employees' perceptions of fairness in organizations. Specifically, we examine the mutually supportive role of employees' perceptions of general organizational fairness and their perceptions of *ethics program follow through*, that is, the extent to which a company takes action to deal with ethical issues employees raise and with violations of the company's formal ethics policies. Both these factors are important influences on ethically significant employee behaviors, such as unethical actions against the organization (theft, vandalism, and other acts) or actions that help the organization achieve ethical goals (for example, reporting unethical behavior to management). Moreover, they are related conceptually: issues of ethics program follow through involve questions of justice. Specifically, whether an organization follows through on espoused ethics policies is an important element of procedural justice in organizations and whether an

Much of the following chapter is reproduced, with permission, from L. K. Treviño and G. R. Weaver, 2001, "Organizational justice and ethics program follow-through: Influences on employees' harmful and helpful behavior," *Business Ethics Quarterly* 11(4):651–671.

organization applies appropriate discipline following violations of ethical standards is an important element of retributive justice.

FAIRNESS PERCEPTIONS AND ETHICAL/UNETHICAL BEHAVIOR

Organizational ethics researchers generally have attributed ethical/unethical conduct to individual differences (Treviño and Youngblood 1990; Weber 1990); issue-related factors, such as the magnitude of an ethical issue's consequences (Jones 1991; Weber 1995); contextual factors, such as ethical climate or ethical culture (Cohen 1993; Treviño, Butterfield, and McCabe, 1998; Victor and Cullen 1988); or the interaction of these factors (Treviño 1986). Until recently (Treviño et al. 1999), organizational fairness, or justice, has not been included as an independent contextual variable in these studies. This is surprising, given that research on organizational ethics and on organizational justice often focus on similar behavioral outcomes. For example, unethical organizational conduct includes a variety of behaviors, many of which may be harmful to the organization (for example, lying, cheating, stealing). Organizational justice research has focused on similar harmful outcomes, such as employee theft (for example, Greenberg 1990) and retaliation (for example, Skarlicki and Folger 1997). Ethics researchers additionally have studied behaviors, such as peer reporting of unethical employee behavior, that can help the organization by alerting management to problems (Treviño and Victor 1992). Justice researchers also have studied employee efforts to help their organizations, such as organizational citizenship behavior (Moorman, Blakely, and Niehoff 1998).

Fairness Perceptions and Employees' Harmful Behavior

Theory provides good reasons to incorporate attention to perceptions of fairness in efforts to understand ethical/unethical behavior in organizations. Justice is a fundamental social expectation that motivates behavior. Van den Bos, Lind, and Wilke (1997) proposed that a broad fairness heuristic guides employees' thinking about their relationship with their organizations, becoming a "pivotal" cognition that influences employees' behavior. As employees think about the extent to which they will commit to and support their organization, they will be concerned about balancing their own interests with the organization's interests. Because it is difficult to engage in exhaustive analyses of decisions about one's relationship with an organization, people resort to decision heuristics in such situations. Perceptions of an organization's overall fairness constitute an important heuristic in making decisions about relationships with an organization. According to the fairness heuristic, if employees perceive just treatment at the hands of their organization, they will be unlikely to see any risk to their own welfare from conforming to organizational expectations, and thus they will be more likely to conform to those expectations. Similarly, they will sense no need to balance the scales of justice by looking for opportunities to improve their own outcomes at the organization's expense.

A well-supported stream of research developed out of equity theory (Adams 1965) indicates that employees will adjust their own behavior to produce what they see as an equitable balance of benefits and burdens at work. According to equity theory, employees who perceive injustices in the workplace will be more likely to look for opportunities to improve their own welfare or status at the organization's expense, or they may retaliate with actions that aim to balance the injustice they perceive. For example, research has found that employees will vandalize (DeMore, Fisher, and Baron 1988) or steal from the organization (Greenberg 1990) to redress perceived injustice. In Greenberg's (1990) field experiment in which employees experienced a pay cut, employee theft was much higher than normal under a condition that was perceived by employees to be unfair. Something like an unwarranted or unexplained pay cut is a relatively specific kind of injustice. In this study, we propose that employees react in similar ways to more general evaluations of organizational injustice, in keeping with the idea that behavior can be motivated by a wide-ranging fairness heuristic (in addition to being motivated by specific instances of injustice) (Van den Bos, Lind, and Wilke 1997). Because employees are less powerful than management, we also propose that these attempts to balance the scales of justice are likely to be covert and indirect, such as stealing from the company, concealing errors, or withholding important information. On the other hand, if employees perceive that their organization treats people fairly, there will be no need to rebalance the scales of justice, and so we should find that this type of harmful unethical conduct is less frequent.

HYPOTHESIS 1: The more employees perceive that their organization is just, the less employees will engage in unethical conduct that harms the organization.

Fairness Perceptions and Employees' Helpful Behavior

Organ (1990) used a social exchange explanation to argue that employees engage in organizational citizenship behavior to reciprocate fair treatment that they receive from their organization. When employees are treated fairly by an organization, they are likely to think about their relationship with the organization in terms of social exchange rather than merely economic exchange. They believe they owe something in return to the organization, and they are motivated to engage in extra role behavior in support of the organization. A variety of studies have reported a significant relationship between perceived fairness and organizational citizenship behavior (Van Dyne, Cummings, and Parks 1995).

Extra-role behavior can be relevant to supporting organizational goals for ethical behavior. Employees might go beyond their normal role requirements and report ethical problems to management rather than, for example, assuming that those are management's problems and keeping silent about them. Reporting problems to management can be conceptualized as a kind of extra-role behavior because, with few exceptions (for example, auditors), attending to and reporting possible ethical problems is not a required in-role task. (We recognize that reporting certain types of illegal or improper behavior may be an in-role behavior imposed by a societal legal system on all citizens or by professional accrediting bodies on their members. The range of unethical behavior we are addressing, however, is much broader than actions that violate specific laws or professional standards.)

Reporting of ethical problems can take several forms. For example, the smooth operation of a business depends on employees' willingness to share information honestly with managers. Managers need information about actual and potential problems in order to make good decisions; but employees often have information that they do not share because of fear of management's response. Bringing an ethical issue to management's attention rarely is an explicit part of an employee's role definition and also can create the embarrassing suggestion that management has not been doing its job well (Dutton and Ashford 1993). Thus, sharing information about ethical problems in the organization constitutes a kind of courageous extra-role citizenship behavior. Reporting problems also can be more formal, as in the formal reporting of ethical or legal problems that takes place through telephone reporting "hotlines" and ethics/compliance offices. In most companies that have such reporting systems, employees are encouraged to report problems they observe, but they are not usually required to do so. Therefore, management must rely on employees' willing cooperation with and participation in these systems.

In summary, employees' perceptions of overall fair treatment should be associated with increased willingness to report problems to management. If employees believe that the organization treats people fairly, they should be more concerned about helping the organization deal with problems that could impede the organization in achieving its goals. Reporting problems will be seen as a matter of reciprocating the organization's fair treatment of employees by being a good organizational citizen.

HYPOTHESIS 2: The more employees perceive that their organization is just, the more willing they will be to report ethical problems to management.

Ethics Program Follow Through, Organizational Justice, and Ethical/Unethical Behavior

Although corporate ethics programs have become widespread in American business, they can be implemented in varying ways. Research indicates that companies adopt ethics programs for multiple reasons and that the implementation details vary with the kinds of influences at work on a company (Weaver, Treviño, and Cochran 1999a). In particular, some companies may adopt largely decoupled approaches to ethics, whereas other companies may adopt ethics program features indicating that the company is serious about following through on ethical concerns, issues, and problems (Weaver, Treviño, and Cochran 1999b). In the former case, the ethics program may be viewed by employees as mere "window dressing" (Treviño et al. 1999) that is disconnected from everyday organizational activities. For example, a company may install reporting systems, but it may not follow up or act on reports of ethical problems. Alternatively, however, a company may make serious efforts to follow up on reports of problems or questions about issues and may engage in appropriate, serious discipline for persons who violate ethical standards.

Employees' perceptions of ethics program follow through can affect their behavior for several reasons, some of which clearly involve issues of justice. First, failure to follow through consistently regarding behavioral expectations can create a sense of procedural injustice. Where follow-through on ethics standards is absent or inconsistent, employees may suspect that the organization does not apply its espoused policies in even-handed, unbiased, predictable fashion. In effect, employees suspect the ethics program of procedural unfairness, and this perception can influence their behavior. For example, a procedural justice study by Friedland, Thibaut, and Walker (1973) found that employees' compliance with rules was influenced by the fairness of surveillance procedures in use (and also by the fairness of the penalties imposed for rule violations—a retributive justice issue). Thus, we propose that unethical conduct is likely to be higher where employees perceive that the organization does not follow through on reports of ethical violations.

Second, where follow-through is lacking, employees' expectations for retributive justice can be violated. In most situations, observers of wrongdoing expect to see the wrongdoer punished and will view such punishment as just because the punishment serves to balance a prior wrong (Hogan and Emler 1981; Treviño 1992). When punishment for an ethical violation does not occur, however, this expectation of retributive justice is violated. Failure to apply appropriate discipline also can be seen as demeaning to or disrespectful of persons who behave ethically, violating their informal expectations of justice (Greenberg 1996). The organization, in this case, does not discriminate between ethical and unethical behavior, and consequently employees who behave in consistently ethical fashion do not find that good behavior receiving the support it deserves. As a result, they will be less inclined to support the organization's ethics policies by behaving ethically themselves and more likely to react against, and seek redress of, the organization's failures of procedural and retributive justice. Therefore, we propose that the more employees perceive that their organization fails to follow through on its espoused ethics policies, the more widespread unethical behavior will be among that organization's employees.

Failure to follow up on reports of unethical behavior and to discipline appropriately should increase unethical behavior for additional reasons. From a strictly behaviorist point of view, there is reduced risk of punishment for wrongdoing in such a situation; so an often effective deterrent is absent. Failure to deal with ethical problems or lapses indicates to employees that "crime might pay," so that self-serving, opportunistic behavior, at the company's expense, is more likely. Social learning theory also shows that when people observe someone being punished for a particular behavior, they will be less likely to engage in that behavior themselves. Likewise, they will be more likely to perform the behavior when they do not see it being punished (Treviño 1992; Walters and Parke 1964). Employees also often are under personal or organizational pressures to act unethically in ways that can harm the organization. If they perceive that the organization's ethics program seriously follows up on and seeks to deter ethical problems and violations, however, unethical behavior should be less common than in organizations where employees perceive that reports of problems are not acted on and that violators of standards are not disciplined appropriately.

Failures to follow through on reported problems and issues and failures to discipline violators also send an important signal to employees about whether the company truly values ethical behavior. When management does not deal with ethical problems or lapses, the inaction about ethics sends a signal that concern for ethics is outside the role identity of people in the organization. Thus, when faced with potential conflicts between ethical standards and other demands (for example, profitability), we should not be surprised if ethics is pushed to the periphery.

HYPOTHESIS 3: The more employees perceive that their organization's ethics program follows through on ethical problems and violations, the less employees will engage in unethical conduct that harms the organization.

Because ethics program follow-through is relevant to perceptions of fairness and justice, it also should influence employees' reporting of ethical problems and failures. Specifically, the multiple forms of unfairness implicit in failures to follow through on ethical standards should reduce employees' willingness to engage in "good citizen" behaviors, such as reporting problems.

Reporting potential problems also is important to people because of the way it reaffirms and protects group values and social cohesion. Much concern with justice in a group or organization stems from the fact that injustices are a threat to the norms and standards, and thus social cohesion, of the group (Durkheim 1964). Persons who are treated unfairly within a group setting will question their status within the group and doubt whether the group values their membership. When employees report potential ethical problems, they are acting to uphold the values that support the cohesiveness of their group and that undergird their place in the group. In short, this kind of justice motive (Lerner 1977) gives people a reason to want to report ethical problems and failures. Whether this motive results in actual reporting behavior will be influenced by employees' perception of whether reports are likely to achieve the valued end (Ilgen, Pritchard, and Nebeker 1981). For example, employees may be bothered by incidents of unethical behavior or concerned about potential ethical failures, but they may fail to act on that concern because they do not expect their action to change anything. When employees see that their organization is serious enough about ethics to take action on their reports of problems, they will be more willing to make such a report.

Employees also may perceive their organization's follow-through efforts as a form of support and protection for employees. As in the case of fair treatment, company follow-through on ethical problems may constitute a form of social exchange in the eyes of employees (Blau 1964). The support and protection they perceive to be provided by the company creates a sense of obligation on the part of employees to aid the organization (Eisenberger, Fasolo, and Davis-LaMastro, 1990; Weaver and Treviño 1999). Thus, when an organization follows through on ethical reports and problems, not only will employees think that their reporting behavior will make a difference (as expectancy theory dictates), but they will feel some degree of obligation to return the organization's support by reporting real or potential ethical problems and failures.

HYPOTHESIS 4: The more employees perceive that their organization's ethics program follows through on ethical problems and violations, the more willing they will be to report ethical problems to management.

INTERACTIONS OF FAIRNESS AND FOLLOW-THROUGH

Thus far, we have proposed that perceptions of organizational fairness influence the extent to which employees act unethically or help their organization by reporting ethical problems. We also proposed that these outcomes will be influenced by the extent to which the organization is perceived to "follow through" when it comes to dealing with ethical issues. In addition to these two hypothesized influences, fairness and follow-through may interact in the way they influence unethical behavior. Specifically, the impact of follow-through on unethical behavior should be greater when employees perceive that the organization generally treats people unfairly. In such situations, employees have a motive to take action against the company in an effort to rebalance the scales of justice in their own minds. In that kind of situation, efforts by the company to follow up on real or potential ethical problems should be more important; when employees have a motive to act unethically, efforts to prevent that behavior are more important and likely to make more of a difference in outcomes. By contrast, when employees perceive fairness in the organization, unethical behavior is less likely, and so ethics program follow-through should have less of an impact in reducing overall levels of unethical behavior.

HYPOTHESIS 5: The impact of ethics program follow-through on unethical conduct in the organization will be lower when employees perceive that their organization is just in general.

We also expect that the impact of ethics program follow-through on reporting behavior will be greater in situations of low organizational justice than in situations where the organization is perceived to treat people fairly in general. Employees can form perceptions of fairness based on ordinary, everyday experiences (for example, "Does my immediate supervisor treat me with respect?") or by reference to the organization's formal policies and procedures (for example, "Does my organization follow through on complaints of unfair treatment?") In the absence of the former (general fairness in the organization), ethics program follow-through becomes a much more important indicator to employees of whether the organization is in any way concerned to uphold ethical standards and norms and to provide an efficacious way for employees to reaffirm and protect those standards and norms. Put differently, when the organization is fair generally, employees may act on their justice motives and report improper behavior, regardless of any particular beliefs or knowledge they have regarding ethics program follow-through. When the only clue employees have regarding the organization's commitment to upholding standards comes from the ethics program itself, perceptions of the program's follow-through should make a larger impact on employee reporting behavior than they otherwise would.

HYPOTHESIS 6: The impact of ethics program follow-through on employee reporting of ethical problems to management will be lower when employees perceive that their organization is just in general.

METHODS

The data used to test the hypothesized relationships were drawn from a larger survey of ethics/compliance management in four companies: a utility, a telecommunications company, and two energy-related companies. Each of these companies had a formal ethics/compliance program in place. Each company supplied the researchers with a list of employees from which we drew a random sample. We negotiated with each company regarding sampling. To have adequate power to conduct statistical analyses within each company, we asked to randomly sample at least 10 percent of employees with a minimum of 500 employees per company (we sampled more employees if the company was willing). In two companies, we drew a random sample of 2,500 employees of approximately 25,000 in one company and 12,000 in the other. For the third company, 600 of the firm's approximately 6,000 employees were surveyed. For the fourth company, 700 of the firm's almost 1,500 employees were surveyed. For all four companies, surveys were sent to employees' homes along with a letter from the company supporting the research and encouraging employees to participate. Respondents returned completed surveys directly to the researchers in stamped, self-addressed envelopes. Respondents were assured of anonymity, and there was no identification information on the surveys. The companies did not allow follow-up surveys, although the researchers requested permission to do so. Overall response rate for the study was 29 percent (31 percent in two of the four companies, 29 percent in one company, and 28 percent in another).

All four companies responded to a request to provide demographic information about the employee population so that we could check for non-response bias. In each company, mean age of survey respondents was almost identical to mean age in the firm. Mean tenure with the firm was almost identical between the sample and population for three of the four companies. In one of the companies, respondents' tenure was somewhat higher than tenure in the employee population (ten years and seven years, respectively). Percentage of male and female employees was almost identical in three of the four firms. In one of the companies, the female response rate was a bit higher than the male response rate: respondents were 32 percent female while the employee population was 29 percent female. These comparisons suggested to us that respondents were generally representative of the populations of these firms.

Dependent Variable Measures

All measures are multi-item scales that were developed by the researchers or adapted from previous research. They were based on Likert-type survey items anchored by strongly disagree (a score of 1) and strongly agree (a score of 5) unless otherwise noted. For each scale, we computed Cronbach's alpha, a measure of the internal consistency or reliability of the scale (that is, the extent to which the items in a scale are all measuring the same construct). For most organizational research, Cronbach's alpha should be between 0.70 and 1.0.

Observed unethical/illegal behavior is a ten-item scale adapted from Akaah (1992) and Treviño, Butterfield, and McCabe (1998). It includes items representing unethical or illegal behaviors that employees might use in reaction to perceived unfair treatment—actions that might harm the organization or increase the employee's inputs. Items are as follows: unauthorized personal use of company materials or services, padding an expense account, taking longer than necessary to do a job, misuse of on-the-job time, concealing errors, falsifying time/quality/quantity reports, calling in sick just to take a day off, lying to supervisors, stealing from the company, and dragging out work to get overtime. For this scale, respondents were asked, "Over the past year, how often have you observed the following types of behavior in your organization? (1 = never, 2 = rarely, 3 = occasionally, 4 = frequently, 5 = very frequently.)" We asked about *observed* unethical behavior to reduce the possibility of social desirability bias, which would likely be more problematic if we asked respondents to report on *their own* unethical conduct. Cronbach's alpha for this eleven-item scale is 0.91.

Reporting of ethical/legal problems was measured by an eight-item scale that included items relating to delivering bad news to management (e.g., "Employees of this firm can deliver bad news to their managers without risking their jobs") and reporting ethics violations (e.g., "I would feel comfortable reporting ethics violations to my manager"). Cronbach's alpha for this scale is 0.88.

Independent Variable Measures

The two independent variable measures—perceptions of general organizational justice and perceptions of ethics program follow through—were Likert-type survey items on a five-point scale, anchored by "strongly disagree" (a score of 1) and "strongly agree" (a score of 5). Because ethics program follow-through is relevant to justice perceptions, we performed a factor analysis of all independent variable items, to ensure that follow-through and organizational justice constituted distinct factors. Factor analysis is a statistical procedure that answers the following question: Are there fewer, more basic variables, underlying a large number of survey items? Factor analysis considers the intercorrelations among the responses to each item (that is, the extent to which they vary with each other) and then determines whether this variation can be allocated across a smaller number of underlying variables called factors. Thus, in the present case, factor analysis serves to determine whether our various individual justice items in fact are measuring two distinct underlying constructs (general justice and ethics program follow-through). As expected, the factor analysis resulted in two unique factors (Table 10.1). The numbers in Table 10.1 represent factor loadings for the items. Items are considered to contribute to a single factor if they load relatively high on that factor (generally 0.40 or higher) and relatively low on other factors (generally less than 0.40). The first factor, general organizational justice evaluations, incorporates nine items, including some written to focus on fair treatment in general (two items—sample: "Generally, employees think of this company as fair"), receiving deserved rewards (distributive justice—five items—samples: "Rewards are allocated fairly in this firm," and "People of integrity get the rewards in this firm"), and being treated respectfully (interactional justice—two items—sample: "Employees can count on being treated with courtesy and respect in this organization"). Cronbach's alpha for this measure is 0.92. The fact that all these items formed one distinct factor, creating a highly reliable scale, is consistent with the existence of a general fairness heuristic in the minds of employees (Van den Bos et al. 1997).

The second factor includes four items that measure the extent to which a company's ethics program is perceived to follow up on reports of ethical problems and respond to ethical lapses with appropriate discipline. Items include the following: "The company follows up on ethical concerns that

TABLE 10.1
Principal Components Factor Analysis for Independent Variables

Item	Factor 1: *General Justice*	Factor 2: *Ethics Program* *Follow-through*
In general, this company treats its employees fairly.	0.81	0.22
Generally employees think of this company as fair.	0.78	0.20
Rewards are allocated fairly in this firm.	0.78	0.14
Employees in this organization are rewarded fairly.	0.83	0.22
In this organization, people get the reward or punishment they deserve.	0.65	0.39
Supervisors in this company treat employees with dignity and respect.	0.72	0.25
Employees can count on being treated with courtesy and respect in this organization.	0.77	0.26
Being consistently ethical helps an employee advance in this firm.	0.64	0.27
People of integrity get the rewards in this firm.	0.64	0.25
If ethics or compliance concerns are reported in this company, action is taken to resolve them.	0.29	0.82
This company follows up on ethical concerns that employees raise.	0.33	0.78
Employees who are caught violating the company's ethics or compliance policies are disciplined.	0.19	0.83
If employees are caught breaking the company's ethics or compliance rules, they are disciplined.	0.21	0.86

employees raise," "if employees are caught breaking the company's ethics or compliance rules, they are disciplined," "if ethics or compliance concerns are reported in this company, action is taken to resolve them," and "employees who are caught violating the company's ethics or compliance policies are disciplined." Cronbach's alpha for these items is 0.88.

RESULTS

Table 10.2 reports means, standard deviations, and correlation coefficients for the independent and dependent variables. The standard deviation is a statistical index that represents the dispersion of values around the mean (or average) and is calculated as the square root of the variance. A correlation characterizes the statistical relationship between two variables. The correlation coefficient represents the magnitude of the relationship (or the degree to which the variables vary together) and the direction (either positive or negative) of the relationship. A perfect positive correlation is represented by +1.0, whereas a perfect negative relationship is represented by -1.0. Correlations also can be tested for statistical significance—or the probability that a relationship occurred by chance alone. Convention in most social science research sets the probability (p) level for tests of statistical significance to be 0.05 or less ($p < 0.05$). Meeting this standard means that the measured relationship is not likely due to chance alone (that is, there is at most a 5 percent probability that the measured relationship is due to chance).

When multiple dependent variables are involved, it is important to test whether differences among their means are likely to have occurred by chance. Therefore, we conducted a multivariate omnibus test of significance for the complete model that included the two dependent variables and the two independent variables. The appropriate statistic for testing the significance of this model is Wilk's lambda. The statistical test was significant at a significance level of $p < 0.05$ (Wilk's lambda = 0.40, $F = 202.83$, $p < 0.0001$), suggesting that the relationships were not due to chance alone, and we could proceed to conduct separate hierarchical regression analyses for each of the dependent variables (see Table 10.3). Hierarchical regression enables us to test the contribution of various independent variables toward overall variation in the phenomenon being explained. In the regression analyses, we entered dummy variables (0, 1) representing the companies in the first step to statistically control for any effects that were due to differences by company. Step two entered the general justice independent variable and the ethics program follow-through independent variable. In the third step, we entered the interaction term (a product of the two independent variables).

For observed unethical conduct, both main effects—perceived fair treatment in general and ethics program follow-through—and the interaction between them were significant. The main effect findings mean that observed

TABLE 10.2

Descriptive Statistics and Intercorrelations

Variable	Mean	SD	1	2	3
General justice	3.12	0.82	—		
Ethics program follow-through	3.46	0.89	0.55	—	
Unethical behavior	2.03	0.82	−0.49	−0.48	—
Willingness to report unethical behavior	3.16	0.79	0.71	0.54	−0.48

SD, standard deviation.

N = 1734, all correlations are statistically significant (p <0.05).

unethical conduct was higher where employees perceived less general fairness (hypothesis 1; t = -13.58, p < 0.01) and less ethics program follow-through (hypothesis 3; t = -11.13, p < 0.01)). The interaction between these variables also was statistically significant, supporting hypothesis 5 (t = 4.713, p < 0.01). Hypothesis 5 proposed that the impact of ethics program follow-through on unethical conduct in the organization would be lower when employees perceive that their organization is just in general. Figure 10.1 provides a plot of the statistical interaction. Unethical behavior is plotted on the vertical axis, with low and high follow-through being plotted on the horizontal axis. The broken line represents a high fairness condition; the solid line represents a low fairness condition. Notice that the broken line (high) has less of a slope than the solid line (low). This means that changing from low follow-through to high follow-through generates a smaller change in unethical behavior in conditions of high perceived general fairness (2.04 - 1.60 = 0.44 change) than in conditions of low perceived general fairness (2.60 - 1.89 = 0.71 change). (High and low conditions for fairness and follow-through were measured at one standard deviation above and below the mean, respectively.)

Perceived fair treatment and ethics program follow-through both were significant predictors of reporting problems to management (hypothesis 2; t = 28.39, p < 0.01; hypothesis 4; t = 10.43, p < 0.01). Their interaction was not a significant predictor of problem reporting, however; hypothesis 6 was not supported.

TABLE 10.3
Hierarchical Regression Results for Influences of General Justice and Ethics Program Follow Through on Observed Unethical Conduct and Reporting Ethical Problems

	Observed Unethical Conduct								
	MODEL 1			MODEL 2			MODEL 3		
Independent Variables	*b*	*s.e.b.*	*beta*[a]	*b*	*s.e.b.*	*beta*	*b*	*s.e.b.*	*beta*
Constant	1.96**	0.03		4.11**	0.08		4.92**	0.19	
Company 2	0.13**	0.04	0.08**	−0.04	0.04	−0.02	−0.02	0.04	−0.01
Company 3	0.05	0.07	0.02	−0.12	0.06	−0.05	−0.10	0.06	−0.04
Company 4	0.24**	0.07	−0.09**	−0.12	0.06	0.04	−0.12*	0.06	−0.04*
General justice				−0.35**	0.03	−0.35**	−0.66**	0.07	−0.66**
Ethics program follow-through				−0.27**	0.02	−0.29**	−0.52**	0.06	−0.56**
General justice × ethics program follow-through							0.09**	0.02	0.52**
R^2		0.01			0.31			0.32	
Adjusted R^2		0.01			0.31			0.32	
F		5.05**			156.42**			135.65**	
df		3,1730			5,1728			6,1727	
ΔR^2			0.01			0.30			0.01
$F \Delta R^2$		5.05**			380.15**			22.22**	

DISCUSSION

A key study finding was the strong relationship between perceived general fair treatment and ethics-related outcomes. Many other studies have found that perceived fairness is important for attitudinal outcomes, such as satisfaction and organizational commitment, and for behavioral outcomes such as employee theft (Greenberg 1990) and retaliation (Skarlicki and Folger 1997). This study's results are consistent with these findings; however, rather than focusing just on theft or retaliation, our observed unethical

TABLE 10.3 *(continued)*

	Reporting Ethical Problems to Management								
	MODEL 1			MODEL 2			MODEL 3		
Independent Variables	*b*	*s.e.b.*	*beta*[a]	*b*	*s.e.b.*	*beta*	*b*	*SE*	*beta*
Constant	3.30**	0.03		0.69**	0.06		0.44**	0.15	
Company 2	−0.14**	0.04	0.09**	0.02	0.03	0.01	0.01	0.03	0.01
Company 3	−0.37**	0.06	−0.15**	−0.05	0.05	−0.02	−0.06	0.05	−0.03
Company 4	−0.38**	0.07	−0.14**	0.09	0.05	0.03	0.09	0.05	0.03
General justice				0.57**	0.02	0.60**	0.67**	0.06	0.70**
Ethics program follow-through				0.20**	0.02	0.22**	0.27**	0.05	0.30**
General justice × ethics program follow-through							−0.03	0.02	−0.163
R^2		0.03			0.55			0.55	
Adjusted R^2		0.03			0.55			0.55	
F		17.96**			417.81**			349.23	
df		3,1730			5,1728			6,1727	
ΔR^2			0.03			0.52			0.00
$F\Delta R^2$		17.96**			986.93**			3.35	

* $p < 0.05$ ** $p < 0.01$ Listwise deletion

b, slope of the regression line or the regression coefficient; SE, standard error of the estimate, or the estimated accuracy of the prediction; beta, standard partial regression coefficient based on the correlations among the multiple independent variables.

behavior-dependent variable included a range of unethical behaviors, all easily covert and typically harmful to the organization. This broader but highly reliable measure is appropriate in part because of the reduced numbers of midlevel supervisory managers in today's downsized organizations (Floyd and Woolridge 1994). Because employees today are more likely to work unsupervised than in the past, they face opportunities for a broad array of unethical behavior directed against the organization. We also focused on general perceptions of justice in the organization rather than on the justice

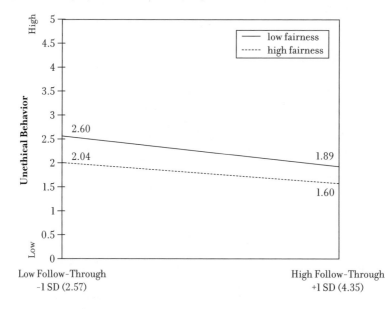

FIGURE 10.1.   Interaction of general fairness and ethics program follow-through

of a specific incident or decision (for example, a pay cut or performance appraisal). We found that a broad spectrum of unethical actions was significantly lower if employees believed that their organization generally treated people fairly.

Previous research indicates that organizations vary in the extent to which they seriously integrate their espoused ethics policies into daily organization life (Weaver, Treviño, and Cochran 1999b). Theoretical arguments suggest that issues of integration raise important justice questions in the eyes of employees (Weaver and Treviño 2001). Given that ethics program follow-through is relevant to the justice of an ethics program, this study affirms that theoretical argument: that follow-through makes an important difference in employees' unethical behavior and in their support of the ethics program by reporting ethical problems. Obviously, following through on actual or suspected ethical failures can serve as a deterrent to unethical behavior. As the data indicate, it also encourages employees to report ethical problems; given the organization's track record in following through on reports of ethical problems, employees can be more confident that their problem reports will be acted on, and thus they will be more likely to actually make such reports (cf. Ilgen et al. 1981). Follow-through also is perceived as important because it is a matter of justice. Ethics programs are likely to make fairness issues particularly salient simply because they call attention to issues of ethics in the organization. We should expect that employees' concerns for fairness will be directed to the ethics program itself, along with the organization generally. If so, the procedural and retributive implications of following through on ethical issues and problems will influence employee behavior. Consistently following through on espoused policies indicates that an organization values procedural justice, and the discipline that comes from following up on ethical failures indicates that retributive justice expectations are taken seriously. Our specific measure included items that, for example, asked whether the company follows up on ethical concerns that employees raise (suggesting attention to procedures) and whether employees caught breaking the company's ethics policies are disciplined (suggesting retributive fairness).

Implications for Research

In recent years, researchers have been carefully parsing justice evaluations into distinctive types (for example, distributive, procedural, interactional). Although highly correlated, these types of justice generally are treated as separate constructs. We followed this line of thinking when we developed our fairness perception measures, developing separate scales for different types of fairness. We conducted a factor analysis of all the independent variable items because we wanted to know whether the different justice constructs would generate separate factors and because we wanted to determine whether elements of ethics program follow-through would be associated with more general issues of justice in organizations. We found that items about fair treatment in general, the fairness of organizational rewards, and treatment of employees with dignity and respect all contributed to a single empirically derived factor measuring employees' perceptions of the overall fairness climate in the organization. At least in the context of a study of ethics-related programs and practices, employees appear to use a broad fairness heuristic (Van den Bos et al. 1997) to judge how well they are being treated. Future research on organizational justice needs to consider the conditions under which employees make fine-grained versus broader-ranging heuristic justice assessments.

We also investigated the effects of perceived justice and injustice on both employee actions that help foster ethical behavior and unethical actions that harm the organization. Previous research has tended to focus on one or the other type of behavior. Our findings suggest that perceived justice not only reduces the extent to which employees engage in covert harmful behaviors but also simultaneously contributes to their discretionary helpful behaviors, such as reporting ethical problems to management. This is in keeping with Greenberg and Scott's observation that "justice may be an important determinant of both prosocial and antisocial organizational behavior" (1996, 149–150). Perceived justice and injustice both arouse individuals to act. Perceived injustice appears to arouse feelings of anger and resentment, leading to covert action aimed at balancing the scales of justice, whereas perceived fairness arouses employees to reciprocate with helpful acts.

The interaction effect we found suggests that business ethics research should focus more attention on how employees' responses to ethics programs represent an interaction of the ethics program with other elements of the organizational context. Although we focused on ethics program follow-through and general justice evaluations, this interaction shows the value of considering other ways in which one or more aspects of ethics programs, and their outcomes, may be influenced by other aspects of the organizational context. The timing of an ethics initiative, vis-à-vis other organizational events, is one such potential contextual factor; the recent history of an organization may frame employees' perceptions of the purpose of any ethics initiative. For example, if an ethics initiative is adopted in the midst of a publicized scandal involving high-level executives, the ethics initiative may be interpreted by employees as a transitory "window dressing" response to that scandal and thus something that employees may ignore, even if the initiative had nothing to do with that scandal. Thus, future research should begin to address contextual influences such as these. Not every contextual factor will matter, of course. In this study, for example, we detected no significant interaction effect for reporting behavior. Overall fairness and ethics program follow-through appear to function independently in regard to reporting behavior.

Implications for Management

The findings seem particularly important when one considers that organizations are competing for the best workers, and more employees work unsupervised in jobs that are less precisely defined. These employees have many opportunities to engage in covert actions that have the potential to subvert or harm the organization and its goals. In addition, because jobs increasingly are less precisely defined, organizations rely on employees not only to comply with organizational rules and decisions, but to contribute to the organization's goals in ways that go beyond role-specified behavior. Because perceived fairness is essential to both types of outcomes, managers need to pay close attention to employees' fairness perceptions. Management may intend that an ethics program operate in a fair manner, with consistent follow-through, but if employees perceive otherwise, unethical behavior and failures to report ethical problems may be more likely.

The results of this study also have implications for ethics/compliance management. Ethics programs generally are administered separately from other human resource programs and practices (Weaver et al. 1999a). Therefore, ethics program administrators have little influence on employees' broader evaluations of organizational justice. Yet it is the broader justice evaluations that had the most powerful separate influence on key outcomes in this study, explaining 30 percent of the variance in observed unethical conduct and 52 percent of the variance in reporting. Further, the interaction of the two types of fairness perceptions was significant for unethical conduct. This suggests that ethics/compliance management should be more tightly coupled with the management of the broader organizational culture to improve employees' perceptions of fairness in the organization in general and in the ethics/compliance program.

In a conceptual paper (Weaver and Treviño 2001), we argued in some detail that increased involvement of human resources departments in corporate ethics management is important. First, human resource departments generally deal with the issues that employees see as ethical issues (for example, fair hiring, promotion, performance appraisal, compensation, restructuring). In fact, ethics officers tell us that more than half the calls to ethics hotlines relate to just these kinds of human resources issues. We argue that perceived fair treatment is closely linked to ethics in employees' minds because of the natural cognitive association between discussions of organizational ethics and information employees hold in memory about justice, fairness, and rights. Further, when the organization focuses on ethics, employees' expectations of fair treatment may rise in parallel. For example, if the organization espouses respect as an ethical value, employees will naturally expect the organization to treat employees with respect in a downsizing initiative. Therefore, although organizational structures may separate ethics management from human resources, employees do not. As a result, we believe it is important that human resources staff and departments be integrally involved in ethics management in the organization as part of a broad organizational effort to support ethics.

Strengths and Limitations of the Research

A strength of this research is that we surveyed randomly selected employees in four organizations, increasing generalizability of the findings. Although we controlled for organization in the regression analyses, one might ask whether the regression models are similar enough across the four organizations to allow us to combine them into a single data set and analyze the data together. We used AMOS, a structural equations modeling program that has the capability to answer this question statistically and determine whether it is reasonable to consider the path coefficients to be the same across companies. (Path coefficients are similar to correlation coefficients and represent the statistical relationship between two variables.) Results indicated that the regression models for each company were similar enough to allow us to combine the data from the four companies into one data set for analysis. (Specifically, we compared an unconstrained model with zero degrees of freedom (allowing the path coefficients to vary) with a constrained model with 18 degrees of freedom (requiring the path coefficients across companies to be the same but the variances and covariances to be unequal). To answer the statistical question, one uses the chi-square statistic and tests the change in it from one model to the other. In this case, we found the chi-square change (19.358) to be nonsignificant, meaning that the models are not statistically different. Further, the model that constrained the path coefficients to be equivalent produced path coefficients that were very similar to the regression coefficients in our regression analyses.)

The potential for social desirability bias and common methods bias remains a limitation. We believed that the variable most sensitive to social desirability bias was the unethical behavior dependent variable. For that reason, we asked how frequently respondents *observed* the behaviors in question over the previous year—not whether or how often they engaged in the behaviors themselves. This focus on others' behavior should have greatly lessened the need for impression management. Respondents also were assured of confidentiality, and they returned their surveys directly to the researchers.

With regard to common methods bias concerns, the fairness items were embedded in a much larger survey of ethics/compliance management. We believe that many of the other survey items would be more obviously tied to ethics-related outcomes than the fairness items that were the basis for this study. In addition, the unethical behavior variable was more objective in that it listed a number of very specific behaviors and asked whether the respondent had observed these in the organization.

CONCLUSION

Many organizations are devoting substantial resources to formal ethics programs in efforts to discourage unethical behavior (Weaver et al. 1999c). This study shows that the success of those efforts will depend in part on whether employees perceive that their organization treats people in a generally fair way. Perceptions of organizational justice not only influence ethical and unethical behavior (as prior justice research has shown), but they also influence employees' willingness to help the organization by reporting ethical problems to management. The extent to which employees perceive that their organization follows through on ethical failures and problems also influences both unethical behavior and the extent to which employees will report problems. Consequently, organizations with formal ethics programs need to focus on the general fairness with which employees are treated and on the extent to which the program follows through on the issues employees bring to it.

References

Adams, J. S. 1965. Inequity in social exchange. In *Advances in experimental social psychology*: Vol. 2, ed. L. Berkowitz, 267–299. New York: Academic Press.

Akaah, I. P. 1992. Social inclusion as a marketing ethics correlate. *Journal of Business Ethics* 11:599–608.

Blau, P. M. 1964. *Exchange and power in social life*. New York: John Wiley & Sons.

Cohen, D. 1993. Creating and maintaining ethical work climates: anomie in the workplace and implications for managing change. *Business Ethics Quarterly* 3(4):343–358.

DeMore, S. W., J. D. Fisher, and R. M. Baron. 1988. The equity-control model as a predictor of vandalism among college students. *Journal of Applied Psychology* 18:80–91.

Durkheim, E. 1964. *The division of labor in society*. Toronto: Collier-Macmillan.

Dutton, J. E., and S. J. Ashford. 1993. Selling issues to top management. *Academy of Management Review* 18:397–430.

Eisenberger, R., P. Fasolo, and V. Davis-LaMastro. 1990. Perceived organizational support and employee diligence, commitment, and innovation. *Journal of Applied Psychology* 75:51–59.

Floyd, S. W., and B. Woolridge. 1994. Dinosaurs or dynamos? Recognizing middle management's strategic role. *Academy of Management Executive* 8(4):47–58.

Friedland, N., J. Thibaut, and L. Walker. 1973. Some determinants of the violation of rules. *Journal of Applied Social Psychology* 3:103–118.

Greenberg, J. 1990. Employee theft as a reaction to underpayment inequity: the hidden costs of pay cuts. *Journal of Applied Psychology* 75:561–568.

Greenberg, J. 1996. *The quest for justice on the job: Essays and experiments*. Thousand Oaks, CA: Sage.

Greenberg, J., and K. S. Scott. 1996. Employee theft as a social exchange process. In *Research in organizational behavior*, ed. B. M. Staw and L. L. Cummings, 18:111–156. Greenwich, CT: JAI Press.

Hogan, R., and N. P. Emler. 1981. Retributive justice. In *The justice motive in social behavior*, ed. M. J. Lerner and S. C. Lerner, 125–143. New York: Plenum Press.

Ilgen, D. R., R. D. Pritchard, and D. M. Nebeker. 1981. Expectancy theory measures: An empirical comparison in an experimental simulation. *Organizational Behavior and Human Performance* 28:189–223.

Jones, T. M. 1991. Ethical decision making by individuals in organizations: An issue-contingent model. *Academy of Management Review* 16:366–395.

Lerner, M. J. 1977. The justice motive: Some hypotheses as to its origins and forms. *Journal of Personality* 45:1–52.

Moorman, R. H., G. L. Blakely, and B. P. Niehoff. 1998. Does perceived organizational support mediate the relationship between procedural justice and organizational citizenship behavior? *Academy of Management Journal* 41:351–357.

Organ, D.W. 1990. The motivational basis of organizational citizenship behavior. In *Research in organizational behavior*, ed. B. M. Staw and L. L. Cummings, 12:43–72. Greenwich, CT: JAI Press.

Skarlicki, D. P., and R. Folger. 1997. Retaliation in the workplace: the roles of distributive, procedural, and interactional justice. *Journal of Applied Psychology* 82:434–443.

Treviño, L. K. 1986. Ethical decision making in organizations: a person-situation interactionist model. *Academy of Management Review* 11:601–617.

Treviño, L. K. 1992. The social effects of punishment in organizations: A justice perspective. *Academy of Management Review* 17:647–676.

Treviño, L. K., and B. Victor. 1992. Peer reporting of unethical behavior: A social context perspective. *Academy of Management Journal* 35:38–64.

Treviño, L. K., and S. A. Youngblood. 1990. Bad apples in bad barrels: A causal analysis of ethical decision-making behavior. *Journal of Applied Psychology* 75:378–385.

Treviño, L. K., K. B. Butterfield, and D. L. McCabe. 1998. The ethical context in organizations: Influences on employee attitudes and behaviors. *Business Ethics Quarterly* 8:447–476.

Treviño, L. K., G. R. Weaver, D. Gibson, and B. L. Toffler. 1999. Managing ethics and legal compliance: What works and what hurts. *California Management Review* 41:131–151.

Van den Bos, K., E. A. Lind, and H. A. M. Wilke. 1997. The psychology of procedural and distributive justice viewed from the perspective of fairness heuristic theory. In *Justice in the workplace*, Vol. 2: *From theory to practice*, ed. R. Cropanzano. Mahwah, NJ: Erlbaum.

Van Dyne, L., L. L. Cummings, and J. M. Parks. 1995. Extra-role behavior: In pursuit of construct and definitional clarity (a bridge over muddied waters). In *Research in organizational behavior*, ed. L. L. Cummings and B. M. Staw, 17:215–285. Greenwich, CT: JAI Press.

Victor, B., and J. Cullen. 1988. The organizational bases of ethical work climates. *Administrative Science Quarterly* 33:101–125.

Walters, R. H., and R. D. Parke. 1964. Influence of response consequences to a social model on resistance to deviation. *Journal of Experimental Child Psychology* 1:269–280.

Weaver, G. R., and L. K. Treviño, L. K. 1999. Compliance and values oriented ethics programs: Influences on employees' attitudes and behavior. *Business Ethics Quarterly* 9:315–336.

Weaver, G. R., and L. K. Treviño. 2001. The role of human resources in ethics/compliance management: A fairness perspective. *Human Resource Management Review* 11:1–22.

Weaver, G. R., L. K. Treviño, and P. L. Cochran. 1999a. Corporate ethics programs as control systems: management and environmental influences. *Academy of Management Journal* 42:41–57.

Weaver, G. R., L. K. Treviño, and P. L. Cochran. 1999b. Integrated and decoupled corporate social performance: Management values, external pressures, and corporate ethics practices. *Academy of Management Journal* 42:539–552.

Weaver, G. R., L. K. Treviño, and P. L. Cochran. 1999c. Corporate ethics practices in the mid-1990s. *Journal of Business Ethics* 18:283–294.

Weber, J. 1990. Managers' moral reasoning: Assessing their responses to three moral dilemmas. *Human Relations* 43:687–702.

Weber, J. 1995. Influences upon organizational ethical subclimates: A multi-departmental analysis of a single firm. *Organization Science* 6(5):509–523.

PART FOUR

Conducting Business Ethics Research in the Future

We began this book by differentiating the social scientific approach to business ethics from the normative approach. From that point of departure, the remainder of the book has focused primarily on the social scientific approach, emphasizing empirical research at the organizational and individual levels of analysis. We believe that individual differences are important, with the most important individual difference being cognitive moral development. Cognitive moral development has implications for the key role played by organizational context because it tells us that most workers are highly susceptible to contextual influences. For that reason, and because we are interested in ethics in organizational context, we focussed our attention primarily on the influence of contextual factors. Our research has answered questions such as the following: What are business organizations doing to manage ethics? Why are they doing it, and to what effect? We have learned that much of what firms are intentionally doing to manage ethics takes the form of formal ethics offices, officers, and programs that can often be divorced or decoupled from important day-to-day activities in the organization. What they actually are accomplishing with regard to ethics has more to do with the less formal aspects of the organizational culture and climate and the "real" ethics messages that are conveyed by how formal programs are implemented in organizational systems and processes, what leaders say and do, and how employees and other stakeholders are treated. We hope that bringing this work together in one place has made a significant contribution to our understanding of business ethics from a social scientific perspective; but this work also makes clear that there is much theoretical and empirical work left to do.

In Chapter 11, we address the knotty methodological issues that face researchers who delve into this sensitive area, and we make recommendations for conducting high-quality empirical research based on our experience and the experience of others. We are the first to acknowledge that conducting high-quality empirical work in organization science is challenging no matter what the topic. Raising questions about organizations' or individuals' ethics presents challenges that those who research less highly charged topics simply do not face. We offer our own insights and the insights of others who have successfully tackled these challenges. We are committed to continuing research in the area, and we encourage others to take up the charge because there is clearly so much more work left to do. We are encouraged by the continuous improvement we have observed in the quality of empirical research in business ethics. More of this work is being published in the best journals in our field, and researchers who identify themselves with a number of organization science subdisciplines (for example, organizational behavior) have taken a keen interest in this and related areas. We would like to see this trend continue with careful qualitative research in underresearched areas and with individual-level and organization-level research that uses all available research tools to best advantage.

In the final chapter, we outline an agenda for future research, suggesting a number of conceptual, empirical, and practical needs. Conceptually, the content domain of business ethics research needs to be mapped more explicitly and relationships among similar constructs made clear. At both the individual and organizational levels, a multitude of topics remain open for exploration, and we have outlined some of the ones we believe to be most important. This belief arises out of our own research, but it also arises out of our interaction with corporate executives who are wrestling with these issues on a daily basis. They have been telling us what they need to know, and we would like to see our own research and that of our colleagues offer them theoretical insight, empirical support for what works and what does not work, and practical suggestions for what they can do to improve ethics management in their organizations.

ELEVEN

Methodological Challenges
in Empirical Business Ethics Research

As the previous chapters no doubt have made clear, researchers who study business ethics face an array of challenging research issues. First, researchers must expect questions about their dependent variable (for example, just what is ethical or unethical behavior on the part of individuals or organizations)? In addition, methodological problems abound, including how to gain access to "real" people and "real" organizations when studying an issue potentially as sensitive as ethical or unethical conduct. Having gained access, how does the researcher address the fact that persons wishing to protect their self-image as ethical individuals or their organization's image are likely to respond to surveys and interview questions in socially desirable fashion? All the social scientists' methods (for example, interviews, surveys, experiments) are available to the business ethics researcher, although these methods often pose unique problems because the topic is ethics. This chapter addresses these issues and offers insights based in part on our own experience conducting business ethics research over the past fifteen years.

Parts of the following chapter are adapted, with permission, from L. K. Treviño, 1992, "Experimental approaches to studying ethical-unethical behavior in organizations," *Business Ethics Quarterly* 2(2):121–136.

DEFINING THE TARGET

Philosophers and other scholars have argued for centuries over theories and definitions of what is ethical and unethical. As Chapters 1 and 2 indicate, a fully integrated theory of ethics in business, combining both normative and empirical perspectives, necessarily involves a commitment on such issues and is not normatively neutral. In pursuit of more modest, empirically oriented understanding of business ethics, however, it is possible to bracket (rather than eliminate) deeper, normative issues. This is because in many organizations and organizational environments, there is a general consensus about a broad class of behaviors thought to be ethical or unethical. Thus, the researcher can work within the confines of that consensus, even while recognizing that from the standpoint of historic debates in normative ethical theory, one or more elements of that consensus remain contestable and that by adopting the conventional consensus, the researcher has made implicit commitments to a specific position in that historic debate. In this, the empirical research exemplifies the symbiotic position described in Chapter 2.

The existence of a general consensus about many business ethics issues helps to explain why, for example, the "disclosure rule" often resonates with people as a useful normative rule of thumb in business ethics. The disclosure rule asks the decision maker, "How would you feel if the action you are contemplating were to be publicized on the front page of a major national newspaper?" Having been raised in society, most of us are familiar with societal standards, and we know whether our actions would be approved or disapproved by a large majority of the people in that society. Although there may be disagreement at the margins regarding what is and is not ethical business conduct, most people agree about a wide range of behaviors that can then be studied. For example, most people in the United States probably would agree that lying to customers about product features, quality, or safety is unethical; that giving bribes or kickbacks to obtain business is unethical; or that forging a signature on a check is unethical. Most large companies have adopted codes of conduct in recent years and, despite some company and industry differences, these codes generally address similar issues with similar standards. As a result, the business ethics researcher can stay very busy focusing on those ethical and unethical behaviors about which there is a large degree of social consensus. This is not to deny that research will be more difficult at the margins of that consensus, where the target (ethical or unethical behavior) becomes much more difficult to deline-eate because debate about propriety is more widespread. Everyone may agree, for example, that theft of a competitor's proprietary information is unethical, but in actual cases they may disagree about just what counts as theft (versus innocent acquisition of such information) (Treviño and Weaver 1997).

Individual-level Issues

In an attempt to measure unethical conduct by individuals, some survey studies have created long lists of unethical behaviors, such as theft, lies, misuse of confidential information (for example, Akaah 1992; Treviño, Butterfield, and McCabe 1998; Treviño, Hartman, and Brown, 2000), ask-ing respondents to rate the extent to which they have engaged in or observed these behaviors over a specified period. The mean of all the behaviors is then used as a dependent variable. Such general measures have been found to be highly reliable, suggesting that a broad "unethical behavior" construct may have meaning in the eyes of organization members and that these behaviors tend to vary together in organizations. Although using any such list may implicitly commit a researcher and research subjects to a particu-lar normative stance, that commitment is not likely to be problematic if it is recognized as a description of what is typically viewed as unethical in a par-ticular social context.

More fine-grained accounts of ethical behavior in business also have been developed, accounts that are more precise than simple lists of multi-ple and diverse forms of ethical or unethical behavior. Robinson and Greenberg (1998) outlined the terms researchers have used to refer to a variety of deviant workplace behaviors. These include antisocial behavior (Giacolone and Greenberg 1997), organizational misbehavior (Vardi and Wiener 1996), workplace aggression (Baron and Neuman 1996), and orga-nizational retaliation behaviors (Skarlicki and Folger 1997), among others. Although these terms refer to intentional counternormative (and generally harmful) behavior directed against organizational stakeholders (internal or external), the definitions also differ in some subtle and not so subtle ways. Therefore, researchers should be clear about the behaviors of interest in their investigations.

In another case, a multidimensional scaling study created a useful typology of deviant workplace behaviors that overlaps significantly (but not completely) with individual-level behaviors generally thought to be unethical (Robinson and Bennett 1995). The authors defined *employee deviance* as "voluntary behavior that violates significant organizational norms and, in doing so, threatens the well-being of the organization, its members or both" (p. 556). The results suggest that these deviant behaviors can be categorized using a minor versus serious dimension and an interpersonal versus organizational dimension, resulting in four categories of employee deviance: personal aggression (including behaviors such as sexual harassment and stealing from co-workers); political deviance (including gossiping, showing favoritism, blaming behaviors); property deviance (including stealing from the company, lying about hours worked, accepting kickbacks, sabotaging); production deviance (including behaviors such as wasting resources, leaving early). The authors suggest that different types of workplace deviance may have different causes and outcomes. Therefore, the development of such typologies can help to advance theorizing in this under-researched area.

When a researcher focuses on a specific type of unethical conduct, even more fine-grained analysis is possible. For example, Greenberg (1996) focused a great deal of his research attention on employee theft; rather than assuming that there is a clear social consensus about what constitutes employee theft, Greenberg's research explores how perceptions of employee theft differ at different organizational levels. In particular, he delves deeply into the definition of employee theft by asking when individuals regard taking company property as theft. His analysis suggested that taking company property is perceived to be theft when the property is taken for personal (rather than company) purposes and when the taking is perceived to be "illegitimate." *Perceived legitimacy* is a complex phenomenon that can be influenced by a variety of impression management tactics used to convince the self and others that the behavior is indeed acceptable. This type of analysis can help future researchers understand how people think about specific types of unethical conduct in organizations. Understanding how workers think about these behaviors can go a long way toward understanding their motivation and behavior.

Less work has been done on the positive side: mapping the content domain of ethical, rather than unethical, behavior. Generally, studies of ethical conduct have treated it as extra-role behavior. For example, researchers typically consider whistle blowing and principled organizational dissent to be ethical behavior, and whistle-blowing behaviors have been used to represent ethical conduct in empirical studies (Treviño and Victor 1992; Treviño and Youngblood 1990). Overlap also exists between organizational citizenship behavior (for example, the altruism dimension) and ethical conduct (Organ 1988); but whether ethical behavior should always be considered extra-role is questionable. Many people may consider it a normal, in-role responsibility. Assigning ethical behavior extra-role status may encourage a sense that it is not normally part of business behavior, whereas empirical studies of managers indicate that many assume ethical behavior to be, in some way, a normal part of their work (Treviño, Hartman, and Brown 2000). The paucity of research on ordinary, in-role ethical behavior may reflect the fact that the kinds of ethical behavior that catch attention are the unusual or dramatic instances, such as whistle blowing, rather than ordinary, everyday "being nice to your co-workers" types of behavior. Ordinary ethical behavior may, in the eyes of most people, be self-explanatory (see Chapter 1), and only deviations from the ordinary generate enough interest to prompt research attention.

Clearly, more work needs to be done to map the content domain of individual ethical and unethical behavior. To the extent that different types of ethical or unethical conduct exist, theory can be developed to understand what motivates each type.

Organizational-level Issues

Similar questions apply to the study of ethical and unethical behavior by organizations in that there are generally accepted paradigm cases of organizational malfeasance (for example, knowingly selling defective products without informing consumers, failing to pay employees for their work) and organizational good behavior (for example, not cheating on corporate taxes). Similarly, there is a broad range of issues where consensus is lacking: environmental actions, advertising practices toward children, political contributions, and others. So, in many respects, the same considerations apply to defining the research target at the organizational level as apply to the individual level. In studying some organizational practices, researchers can bracket normative questions because of the existence of a broad consensus about what is ethical. In regard to other practices, however, researchers may need to consider carefully how perceptions of a practice's propriety themselves are influenced, much the same as Greenberg's work on theft explores how perceptions and definitions of employee theft vary across status levels and situations. For example, company employment practices that look ethical from the senior executive's office may look very different from the factory floor. Researchers focusing on organizational actions need to recognize these differences and account for them in their work either by incorporating these multiple perspectives in their study or by acknowledging a particular normative stance (for example, that the factory floor perspective is, for normative reasons, the right perspective to hold on the issue).

Similar considerations apply specifically to the task of studying corporate ethics programs. Not everything that is identified as an ethics program need be ethical in all its aspects; a company might pursue ethical ends (such as honesty among its salespersons) by unethical means (for example, disproportionate punishment for dishonesty, invasions of salespersons' or customers' privacy). Such questions readily can be applied to the common distinction between compliance- and values-oriented organizational ethics programs. Do strongly compliance-orientated programs in some way violate an employee's rights or fail to show proper respect to employees as moral agents? Do values-oriented programs risk turning into a kind of subtly manipulative system that compromises employees' legitimate autonomy or creates an Orwellian cult-like atmosphere in the workplace? As in the case of individual-level issues, as long as the researcher is working within the confines of a societal consensus about ethical propriety (for example, that it is permissible to dismiss employees for infractions of company standards), normative issues like these can be bracketed. Were the subject of study to be, say, a highly unusual ethics program with cult-like features, it would be more difficult for the researcher to take at face value the ethics of such an "ethics program." The fact that our own research has revealed differences among employees in their perception of what an ethics program is actually about (for example, fostering ethics versus protecting top management; see Chapter 8) suggests that these kinds of questions probably need to be closer to the center of research on organizational ethics than they currently are. Just as Greenberg's research on theft indicates varying perceptions of the ethics of theft at different levels of organizations, so may there be differing perceptions of the nature and ethics of what purport to be ethics programs at different levels of organizations and among different organizational stakeholders.

GAINING ACCESS TO ORGANIZATIONS

One of the most challenging issues facing the business ethics researcher is gaining access to organizations. In our experience, people are more likely to agree to personal interviews than they are to surveys. For example, we have been able to interview high-level executives about such topics as ethics management and executive ethical leadership, but gaining access for the purposes of surveying a broad sample of employees is more difficult. A primary reason is that corporate attorneys usually have to approve these surveys, and they are almost always reluctant to do so. In a key project supported by Arthur Andersen's Ethics and Responsible Business Practices Consulting group (and reported on in Chapter 8), we began with the goal of surveying employees at twenty to thirty firms. We assumed that firms would be interested in participating because the study would be completely free to them (Arthur Andersen was footing the bill), because they would receive valuable information about their own organization (including benchmarking information), and that they would trust Arthur Andersen with the sensitive data. All surveys were to be returned to Arthur Andersen directly. This was to be a landmark study designed to assess influences on ethics program effectiveness. Andersen assigned a seasoned project manager who worked to gain corporate participation, beginning with Andersen's own auditing clients. At the end of a year and a half, only six firms had agreed to participate. When corporate ethics officers were approached, their initial reactions were generally positive. They were delighted that they could learn so much at little or no cost to their firms; but, once attorneys were consulted, the atmosphere changed. Attorneys were concerned about the discoverability of the data in court. For example, we were planning to ask employees questions about the extent to which they had observed a variety of unethical behaviors in their firm (including some illegal behaviors). What if we learned that employees observed racial discrimination or other illegal behaviors in the firm? What if the findings came out in a later court case and it was determined that the firm had not acted on what they had learned? Most firms were not willing to take that chance. Clearly, the current legal environment discourages companies from self-assessment in the area of ethics and legal compliance, making it difficult for business ethics researchers to gain access to organizations, particularly if unethical or illegal conduct is the dependent variable of interest.

What advice can we offer? Obviously, there are firms that will choose to participate in research despite legal concerns. One way to find them is to develop personal trusting relationships with people who have the power to decide to participate in such a study. Their identity will vary from firm to firm, but the person with the clout could be the corporate attorney, the vice president of human resources, or the chief executive officer (CEO). Executives have been known to listen to their attorneys' warnings and go ahead with their plans anyway. Therefore, if the researcher has personal relationships with senior executives, those persons may be helpful in overcoming legal concerns and hurdles. If successful, the researcher should be aware that firms that agree to participate in ethics research likely differ in systematic ways from firms that do not. This is a potential limitation to the generalizability of the research findings and must be acknowledged (Liedtka 1992).

Another potential solution is to be creative about the type of organization studied. The psychological processes underlying ethical attitudes and behaviors may be similar no matter what the organizational context. Similarly, many organizational processes—institutionalization, environmental adaptation, structural differentiation, and others—may be the same in different organizational contexts. For example, as academics, we are all familiar with academic dishonesty and research integrity issues. We may have better luck gaining access to our own organizations than to business firms. Likewise, nonprofit organizations may be as concerned about their social legitimacy as for-profit corporations, and they may take similar steps to ensure that legitimacy. Therefore, it may be possible to learn a great deal about what motivates ethical conduct, how codes of conduct influence behavior, or how formal ethics programs reflect organizational environments by studying these phenomena in academic, nonprofit, or government organizations. Indeed, some of these types of organizations may be open to study of these kinds of questions. Again, the underlying psychological and organizational processes may not be very different, and one can learn a great deal from studying workers in these alternative settings.

A third suggestion is to survey samples that do not require gaining access to particular organizations. Most adults in the United States work for business firms. Therefore, researchers may well be able to answer their research questions by surveying university alumni or by conducting panel surveys that randomly select individuals from a community. None of these methods requires the kind of access discussed previously.

A final suggestion is to consider studying positive ethical behavior rather than unethical behavior. This is in keeping with a relatively new emphasis in psychology on *positive psychology* (for example, Seligman 1990) defined as "the scientific study of ordinary human strengths and virtues," including optimism, resilience, and happiness. Sheldon and King asked, "How can psychologists explain the fact that, despite all the difficulties, the majority of people manage to live lives of dignity and purpose?" (Sheldon and King 2001, 216). Within business ethics research, we could ask similar questions. How can we explain the fact that, despite all of the pressures, most people are ethical at work? The side benefit of asking such questions is that if the dependent variables are honesty and altruism (instead of dishonesty, aggression, or theft), access to organizations may be more attainable.

Designing Research in Business Ethics: Problems and Solutions

As suggested, the entire researcher's tool kit is available to business ethics researchers, but special problems arise because of the uniqueness and sensitivity of the topic. First, unethical conduct is (one hopes) a low-base-rate phenomenon, meaning that it occurs relatively infrequently. Thus, the researcher may have to sample many instances of behavior to observe one instance of unethical behavior. Second, persons engaged in unethical conduct are likely to conceal it. Third, and perhaps most important, evaluation apprehension is likely to plague any attempt to collect valid data on ethical behavior (Rosenberg 1965). Subjects who are aware that the research focuses on ethical behavior may respond in a socially desirable manner, distorting the study results (Babbie 1986; Randall and Fernandes 1990). *Social desirability bias* is the tendency of individuals to respond in a way that minimizes socially undesirable traits and maximizes desirable ones, and it is a challenge that affects most business ethics research, no matter what the method.

Surveys and Social Desirability Response Effects. Surveys are widely used in management research. They have the major advantage of collecting a large amount of data from a large population (Kerlinger 1986); however, surveys rely on self-reported thoughts and behaviors and are therefore particularly vulnerable to response bias (Randall and Fernandes 1991). Randall and Gibson (1990) reviewed thirty years of business ethics research and found that nearly 90 percent of studies relied on self-report questionnaires. They claimed that the validity of these studies is threatened by social desirability bias. In support of this assertion, Randall and Fernandes (1991) found that when respondents reported on their own ethical conduct, they tended to overreport their desirable behaviors and underreport undesirable behaviors. Similarly, in a study of tax evasion behavior, Hessing, Elffers, and Weigel (1988) compared tax evasion data obtained from the government with survey data from taxpayers and found negligible correlations between self-reported tax evasion and actual tax evasion behavior. These findings underscore the difficulty of obtaining accurate self-reports in areas involving sensitive information about unethical or illegal behavior.

Social desirability bias frequently is treated as a personality trait that can be measured and controlled statistically (Fernandes and Randall 1992). Many studies have used the Marlowe–Crowne (M–C) Social Desirability Scale (Crowne and Marlowe 1960); but Paulhus (1984) argued that this scale is flawed because it contains two factors that should be treated as distinct: an impression management factor and a self-deception factor. *Impression management* is directed outward to others and involves the conscious attempt to gain social approval for one's thoughts and actions. *Self-deception* represents an unconscious tendency to see and portray oneself positively. Fernandes and Randall (1992) used both the M–C scale and the Balanced Inventory of Desirable Behaviors (BIDR) developed by Zerbe and Paulhus (1987) in a study of the effects of social desirability bias in business ethics research. They found that social desirability bias had a substantial moderating effect. Self-reported attitudes were influenced even more than self-reported behaviors. More recent business ethics studies that have controlled for social desirability bias (for example, Treviño, Butterfield, and McCabe 1998) found that impression management explained a significant proportion of the variance in regression equations, even where observed rather than self-reported behavior was the dependent variable. Including social desirability measures may present another problem, however. We have found that, because of the sensitivity of the items, business organizations often resist the inclusion of social desirability measures in surveys.

Another way to deal with social desirability bias in surveys is to provide respondents with anonymity, which has been found to reduce the level of social desirability bias somewhat in business ethics research (Fernandes and Randall 1992). Anonymity, however, is likely to have more impact on the impression management aspect of social desirability and less impact on the self-deception aspect. If an individual is inclined toward self-deception, anonymity probably would not make much of a difference (cf. Fernandes and Randall 1992; Paulhus 1984).

Social desirability bias may also be reduced when respondent anonymity is combined with a focus on observed behavior as the dependent variable. Reporting on others' misconduct should be influenced less by the desire to manage impressions than is self-reporting; however, peer reporting is generally seen as counternormative (Treviño and Victor 1992). Individuals concerned about social approval may not wish to be seen as "tattling" on their peers. Therefore, if they are convinced that their responses are anonymous, they may be more likely to respond honestly.

Wimbush and Dalton (1997) recommended two techniques: the unmatched count technique (Raghavarao and Federer 1973; Dalton, Wimbush and Daily 1994) and the randomized response technique (Warner 1965; Dalton, Wimbush, and Daily 1996) to address concerns about socially desirable responding in survey research. Both approaches mask survey responses so that the researcher has no way to know whether any person is admitting to unethical behavior, thereby providing true confidentiality to respondents and encouraging honest responses. We will not attempt to explain the specifics of the techniques here because they are detailed elsewhere (Dalton, Daily, and Wimbush 1997; Dalton and Metzger 1992; Wimbush and Dalton 1997). These approaches, however, produce significantly greater admission of nontrivial employee theft across survey respondents than do conventional survey techniques, and they are particularly useful for determining the base rate of a particular behavior, such as employee theft. Robertson and Rymon (2001) used the randomized response technique to study the deceptive behavior of purchasing agents. They found that purchasing agents are more likely to deceive suppliers when they perceive pressure on them to perform and ethical ambiguity on the part of the firm. These techniques have added useful tools to the ethics researcher's toolkit. Dalton and Metzger (1992) acknowledge that respondents may need to be convinced of the confidentiality of responses. Also, if the researcher is interested in whether any particular person has engaged in unethical conduct, these approaches will not answer that question.

Social desirability bias clearly threatens the validity of the results of any survey that asks respondents to answer questions about sensitive issues.

Therefore, researchers must acknowledge these issues in discussing their methods and attempt to minimize them in their study designs.

Interviews. Liedtka (1992) argues that personal interviews are a highly appropriate methodology for studying individual ethical decision making in organizational context. Interviews can capture the complexities that surround individual thinking in complex organizational situations, and qualitative methodologies can help to develop new knowledge in an area that remains relatively unexplored. Interviews can complement more traditional quantitative methods that may appear more "rigorous" but also may fail to capture real world ambiguities. Interview methods can range from highly structured hypothesis testing approaches to more open-ended dialogues that lend themselves to researcher interpretation and grounded theory development. A vast literature exists to guide researchers embarking on interview-based and other qualitative approaches (for example, Miles and Huberman 1984). Therefore, we limit our focus to the special concerns raised by the application of these methods to business ethics topics.

Like surveys, interview methods face problems of potential socially desirable responding. In one-on-one interviews, it is impossible to offer interviewees anonymity, and guarantees of confidentiality may not be believed. Therefore, the researcher must consider how social desirability bias can be minimized. Options will likely depend on the research question. One possibility may be to ask interviewees to discuss their observations of others rather than their own attitudes and behaviors. For example, in a recent interview study of executive ethical leadership (Treviño, Hartman, and Brown 2000), senior executives were asked to think of and talk about an executive with whom they are familiar who would fit their definition of an ethical leader. In a second part of the interview, they were asked to think of someone who would fit a category between ethical and unethical leadership labeled *ethically neutral leadership*. In each case, interviewees were told not to identify the person to the interviewer. They were to hold the person in mind and use him or her as a reference point when answering the questions, and they were reminded to do this several times during an hour-long interview. The identity of the target person remained completely unknown to the interviewer. This procedure has the benefit of providing a concrete and salient reference point. But, by not identifying the person, the interviewee has no reason to inflate the image of the target.

The validity of interview data may also be questioned because of the interviewee's inability to report accurately on his or her own thought processes (Nisbett and Wilson 1977; Uleman and Bargh 1989). For example, evidence suggests that interviewees do not have a direct understanding of their own moral judgment processes (Rest et al. 1999). Therefore, it is important that the researcher be realistic about the value and limits of interview data. In some cases, interview data are likely best used in the hypothesis-generation phase of research, and they should be corroborated with evidence using other research approaches that are better suited to hypothesis testing. Moreover, in interview-based studies of ethics, the most important insights sometimes may lie in what is *not* said. Interview subjects may withhold information or simply not recognize what the researcher is investigating. For example, in the mid-1990s, we conducted an interview-based study of competitive intelligence practitioners—individuals who gather information on competitors, sometimes by licit means, and other times by questionable means. Our interest was in assessing what factors influenced competitive intelligence collectors sometimes to notice and other times fail to notice potential ethical issues in their work (Treviño and Weaver 1997). If they failed to notice an issue—even after considerable prompting—what were we as researchers to make of that? Their failure to notice the issue seemed important, but as they continued to fail to see it, how could they tell us anything about the issue or their failure to recognize it? Further, how could we capture their silence as data?

Liedtka (1992) recommended a number of techniques for enhancing the validity of retrospective and hypothetical interview reports in the area of business ethics. She proposed the use of " 'hybrid' interview formats that incorporate discussions of interview-selected 'moral dilemmas' (Derry 1987), 'difficult situations,' (Kram, Yeager, and Reed, 1989), or 'problems with ethical components' (Toffler 1986) as central components of the interview. These permit the researcher to ground abstract discussions of values in concrete situations that are directly meaningful to the respondent" (173). They also maximize recall by focusing on salient incidents selected by the respondent, reduce social desirability bias by asking for details, and probe inconsistencies.

Researchers who conduct interviews regarding sensitive topics should also be aware of their ethical responsibilities. For example, discussions of salient ethics-related events can produce emotional reactions that are impossible to predict in advance and that may require emotional support. Also, "informed consent" may have little meaning in an interactive interview context because it is impossible to predict what level of disclosure will be involved in advance (Liedtka 1992).

Experimental Approaches

In experimental research, the investigator develops theory-based hypotheses that are tested by manipulating one or more independent variables while observing variation in the dependent variable (Kerlinger 1986). The two major criteria for evaluating experimental research are *internal* and *external validity* (Campbell and Stanley 1963). When an experiment has internal validity, the experimenter can have confidence in the tested relationships, confidence that x caused y. Laboratory experiments are thought to be highest in internal validity because the investigator can exercise a large degree of control over the experimental conditions. External validity means generalizability. It answers the question of to what population the results can be generalized. Field experiments are thought to be higher in external validity because they are conducted in actual organizations. The settings are generally more complex and realistic than laboratory settings, and the subjects are thought to be more representative of the population under study. Locke (1986) addressed concerns about the generalizability of laboratory experiments by reviewing the literature in a number of heavily researched areas of organizational science and comparing the results of laboratory and field research. For most topics, very similar results were obtained in the laboratory as in the field. Ilgen (1986) concluded that laboratory research is most suitable when (1) the laboratory closely simulates field settings; (2) the laboratory is to be used as a basis for later field research; (3) constraints of time, costs, ethics, or threats to health and safety make field research difficult or impossible; or (4) the aim of the laboratory study is to demonstrate that a particular cause–effect relationship can be obtained (Mook 1983). Despite the usefulness of experimental research, Randall and Gibson (1990) reported that only 6 percent of the studies they reviewed on ethical beliefs and behavior in organizations were experimental. All these consisted of laboratory experiments or simulations. No field experiments were found at the time, and few have been conducted since then.

In the area of ethical decision making, the laboratory researcher can collect data about real decisions (albeit in a simulated setting) rather than self-reports of what an individual thinks or would do. These behaviors may be difficult or inappropriate to observe in the field, or they may occur too infrequently. To be responsive to concerns about external validity, laboratory researchers should attempt to design experiments that set up realistic conditions and use subjects who have substantial work experience. The requirement of realistic experimental conditions often is a problem in existing experimental studies in business ethics. Much research has been done using student samples (see, for example, Weaver 1995). Although such studies can yield useful information, care must be taken to match the study's aims with the subjects' experience and knowledge. Student samples can be useful, provided they have appropriate background and that the study involves procedures and activities regarding which students constitute realistic subjects. Thus, Weaver's student-based experimental study of codes was framed around reactions to a hypothetical code of student conduct (adapted from the code at the student subjects' university). Treviño and Victor (1992) similarly used a student sample in a study of peer reporting of unethical behavior, but it specifically concerned employees in fast food restaurants—a type of employment with which many students could be expected to have experience. Similarly, studies of ethical behavior that focus on issues of cheating and dishonesty can plausibly use student samples, given their experience with the topic. Researchers addressing other questions, for example, ethical issues in major business decisions, need to exercise care in the use of any student samples. The goals of the study need to be carefully delineated to make clear the appropriateness of a student sample.

It may be possible to reduce the probability of evoking socially desirable responses that can distort and invalidate experimental study findings. For example, the experiment can be designed so that the subjects do not know they are being observed. Subjects can be hired for short-term employment rather than being recruited to participate in a research experiment. They can be given a task, the variables of interest manipulated, and the behavior observed, all without the subjects' knowledge. Or the experimenter can provide a cover story, a misleading explanation of the experiment that is designed to be plausible while influencing attitudes and behavior regarding ethics as little as possible (often because the cover story makes no mention of ethics). Further, the manipulation can be embedded within a more complex context to focus the subject's attention away from the phenomenon actually being studied. All these tactics that are designed to reduce social desirability bias are also deceptive, however, and raise ethical concerns that the researcher must consider and address. Human subjects' review committees must be consulted and permission obtained before engaging in any of these types of deception.

Probably the most famous social psychological experiments of all time were conducted by Stanley Milgram in his research program on obedience to authority (1974). Milgram paid recruits from the New Haven, Connecticut, vicinity to participate in a one-hour study of the effects of punishment on learning. The subject played the role of teacher while a confederate played the learner role. The learner was strapped into a chair with an electrode attached at the wrist. The teacher was seated in front of a shock generator and was told to give increasingly severe shocks to the learner each time he failed to provide the correct responses to questions about recalled word pairs. As the shock level intensified, the learner expressed increasing discomfort until he finally announced that he would no longer answer, screamed, and then went silent. When the teacher subject asked the experimenter for guidance, he would receive a scripted response: "Although the shocks may be painful, they are not dangerous. Please continue." If the teacher continued to resist, the experimenter would respond with the following three successive prods: "The experiment requires that you continue"; "it is absolutely essential that you continue"; "you have no other choice, you must go on." If the teacher continued to resist, the experiment was terminated. To the surprise of most observers, the large majority of Milgram's teacher subjects continued the experiment to the end, obeying the experimenter's instructions despite felt and expressed conflict. These research subjects acted as if they were constrained by the situation and its requirements rather than as independent agents who could freely choose to end the experiment.

These experiments provided important new (if discomforting) insights into individual behavior in authority situations. They powerfully demonstrated the difficulty that most people have when told by an authority figure to behave in a way they find objectionable (Kelman and Hamilton 1989). Treviño (1986) suggested that these findings apply to ethical behavior in work settings where authority structures are an accepted part of the work setting. Indeed, research has found that the rate of ethical conduct is higher in settings where employees perceive a culture that requires unquestioning obedience to authority (for example, Treviño, Butterfield, and McCabe 1998; Treviño et al. 1999).

Milgram's experiments have been criticized on ethical grounds. Subjects were deceived, manipulated, and asked to engage in behavior with the potential for long-term negative impact on the subject's self-image (Baumrind 1964). It is quite possible that human subjects review committees would not allow this type of experiment today.

Scenario Studies.   Scenarios or vignettes can be used to test theory about the influences on judgment or decision-making processes in hypothetical situations. The vignettes present subjects with written descriptions of realistic situations and then request responses on a number of rating scales that measure the dependent variable of interest. The vignettes are constructed so that the respondent is presented with concrete, relatively detailed information about the independent variables of interest. This information is systematically varied in different versions of the vignette to which subjects are randomly assigned. As a result, the researcher can determine the influence of different situation characteristics (or combinations of characteristics) on judgments and decisions in hypothetical situations (Alexander and Becker 1978).

Scenarios may be extremely useful vehicles for understanding subjects' judgments in hypothetical ethical decision situations (Weber 1992). For example, Treviño and Victor (1992) used two scenario studies to test the influences of social context conditions on respondents' attitudes toward peer reporting and inclination to report a peer for unethical behavior. They found that role responsibility (the presence or absence of a conduct code requiring peer reporting) influenced the inclination to report a peer in both studies. The interests of group members (the presence or absence of a system that penalizes all members of a group if unethical conduct occurs) influenced the inclination to report a peer in one study only.

In another scenario study aimed at understanding whether moral intensity, issue framing, and social context influence moral awareness (Butterfield, Treviño, and Weaver 2000), competitive intelligence professionals were presented with two realistic competitive intelligence scenarios that presented engaging but morally ambiguous situations. They were told that the research involved "decision making in competitive contexts." No mention was made of ethics in the cover letter or instructions. In the scenarios, the moral intensity, social context information, and framing of the situations were manipulated. Because of concerns about bias, respondents were not asked for their own views. Rather, they were asked to read the scenario and then list the issues *the protagonist in the scenario* would view as important in the scenario. Because the respondent was describing someone else's perspective, there was little if any threat to self-image or moral status. Thus, there was no motivation to manage impressions or provide socially desirable responses. Also, the dependent variable, moral awareness, was open ended and evaluated qualitatively by content analyzing the issues lists generated by the respondents. Respondents were not provided with response options from which to choose. Doing so would have defeated the purpose: to gain insight into whether respondents identify moral issues as important. Listing moral issues among others would have raised serious social desirability concerns (Weber 1992). Allowing respondents to offer their own responses, however, requires the development of valid and reliable coding schemes for those responses.

Clearly, scenario studies are useful for testing the influence of hypothesized variables on subjects' thought and decision processes in hypothetical decision situations. Other methods, however, such as the in-basket exercise discussed subsequently, move in the direction of more closely simulating actual decision making.

The In-basket Exercise. Another experimental approach that has been used to study ethical decision making is the in-basket exercise. This approach is designed to provide more realism than either the traditional laboratory experiment or the scenario study. At the same time, it provides all of the advantages of laboratory experimentation, such as the ability to control variables and to test causal relations.

The in-basket exercise allows the investigator to create a somewhat realistic work setting for decision-making studies (Zedeck 1986). An in-basket simulates the administrative decision-making tasks of a manager's job. Subjects are given a variety of in-basket materials, such as memos and phone messages, and they are asked to play the role of the decision maker, making decisions given the available information. Manipulations, such as information about the organization's policies or reward systems, are embedded in these materials. In-basket exercises have been used effectively in management research, and behavior in properly designed in-basket exercises has been found to correspond to actual on-the-job work performance (Brass and Oldham 1976; Staw and Barsade 1993).

Treviño and Youngblood (1990) conducted an in-basket study to investigate the influences of vicarious reinforcement (reward and punishment) and individual differences on ethical decision-making behavior. Subjects were MBA (master of business administration) students with substantial managerial work experience. In designing the research, the investigators considered demand characteristics and social desirability bias to be major threats to the experiment's internal validity. They worked to reduce these threats in a number of ways. The person who administered the in-basket exercise was unknown to the subjects and was introduced as someone who was simply helping the professors. The experiment was billed as a class-related decision-making exercise rather than a research experiment and an opportunity to learn about in-basket assessment techniques to which students might be exposed in organizations. This explanation provided an ambiguous cover story so that subjects who might suspect an experimental purpose could think of many different hypotheses that would not systematically affect the results. Responses were anonymous. The manipulated variables and the two decisions involving ethical concerns were carefully embedded in the in-basket, which was pretested to ensure that the ethics focus was not apparent. The remaining materials were "fillers" that were included to mask the ethics focus of the study and to contribute to credibility and realism. In an attempt to measure demand characteristics, the first question on a post-exercise questionnaire asked subjects for their perceptions of the purpose of the exercise. Only 6 percent of respondents perceived an ethics focus. The study results suggested that individual differences (locus of control and cognitive moral development) and reward outcome expectancies influenced ethical decision making.

Simulations. The laboratory can most closely approximate field settings through laboratory simulation (McCall and Lombardo 1984). Subjects are placed into a simulated organization where they play organizational roles and make decisions. Variables are controlled and manipulated as they are in the laboratory and dependent variable data are collected, but the researcher gives up the strict control typical of the behavioral laboratory (Fisher 1984). Complex behaviors can be observed as they unfold over time. Anecdotal evidence suggests that managers who participate in simulations take these experiences seriously and rarely step out of role. As with in-basket exercises, manipulated variables can be unobtrusively embedded within the complex context of the simulation, potentially reducing the influence of demand characteristics.

Gaertner (1990) adapted the university edition of the "looking glass" (McCall and Lombardo 1978) simulation to investigate the effect of ethical climate on managers' (experienced MBA students) decision making. Eight memos were added to manipulate perceptions of the company's ethical climate, and two problems requiring ethical decision making also were added. The results suggested that subjects' perceptions of the company's ethical climate contributed to the criteria they used in decision making, which, in turn, contributed to the ethical quality of their decisions.

Field Experiments. Within management, field experiments are often thought to be the most desirable kind of research because generalizability of research findings to the practitioner's world is highly valued and because prediction is often thought to be the social scientist's ultimate goal (Braithwaite 1955; Kaplan 1964). The major problems with field experiments include the difficulty of gaining access to organizations, the inability to observe unethical behavior, the organization's likely resistance to the use of random assignment, and the inability to control the influence of extraneous variables.

Although such field experiments are rare, Greenberg (1990) conducted an impressive field experiment to study the impact of a temporary pay cut on employee theft in several manufacturing plants. Relying on equity theory, Greenberg hypothesized that the pay cut would produce inequity perceptions in employees who would attempt to influence their input–outcome rations by stealing from the company. In accordance with the hypothesis, he found that groups experiencing the pay cut had significantly higher theft rates. Consistent with theories of procedural justice, however, these theft effects were lessened where management provided a sensitive explanation for the pay cut. Because employees were not asked to report their own or others' theft (objective inventory loss data were provided by the organization), this study also avoided any concerns about social desirability bias. It was possible to investigate the influence of a management intervention (the pay cut, management's explanation) without employees' awareness. The impact of other organizational interventions such as codes of conduct, or training interventions, could be similarly evaluated.

Greenberg (1993) complemented the field experiment with laboratory research designed to investigate the processes in more detail. He recruited undergraduate students to participate in a study purported to be about consumers' use of sales catalogs. They were told they would be paid $5.00 for their participation, an amount deemed to be fair by a similar sample. The independent variables were payment (fair versus unfair [some subjects were told they would be paid only $3.00 after all]), interpersonal sensitivity of the explanation (high versus low), and validity of information for determining payment amount (high versus low). At the end of the experiment, the experimenter said that he or she had to go down the hall but left an assortment of coins and bills on the table, suggesting that the subject pay him- or herself the amount owed (either $3.00 or $5.00). The dependent variable, theft, was the amount taken above the amount promised. As in the field study, equity theory was supported. Those who were underpaid stole more. This study was able to demonstrate that the amount of theft was reduced by both the sensitivity and validity of information provided. Subjects were carefully debriefed, and all subjects in the underpayment condition were given supplemental pay so that no subjects were underpaid in the end. These studies provide an excellent example of how field and laboratory experimentation can be used in combination to contribute to knowledge in a highly sensitive area.

Surrogate Measures and Archival Data

Given all these challenges, it is wise to consider the prospects of using surrogate measures and archival data. Often it is reasonably easy to uncover important insights without directly asking potentially sensitive questions about ethics or without asking organizations and their employees anything at all. Sometimes established theories and insights in social science support the use of surrogate measures for phenomena. For example, consider again the study reported on in Chapters 5 and 6. To assess the role of top management's strategic choices on the development of formal ethics programs, we wanted to incorporate a measure of top management's overall commitment to ethics. Of course, we could have asked CEOs or other top managers whether they were committed to ethics, but CEOs are notoriously too busy to respond to surveys. Besides, what CEO would say he or she is not very committed to ethics? So, instead, we chose to rely on a third-party informant, the officer responsible for ethical and legal issues. Would such officers report that their CEOs were not committed to ethics? They might not be quite so blunt, but when we compared commitment measures that were self-reported by those few CEOs who responded and the ethics officers at their companies, the ethics officers gave lower ratings to the CEOs' commitment to ethics. Of course, even then they might be reporting overly optimistic assessments, and, besides, we could not feel content with reports from a relatively small group of companies. So what were we to do? Working on the assumption that, on average, executives will spend time talking about different subjects in proportion to the importance of those subjects to them, we chose to ask our ethics officer respondents to report on the frequency with which various typical managerial issues were items of discussion among top executives. These issues included both typical strategic and operational concerns (for example, strategy and planning, financial performance), along with issues that bore relevance to ethics (for example, doing the right thing, treating people fairly). Not only were we able to get a sense of top management's concern for ethics, but we were able to do so in a context that, we hoped, would discourage biased responding. After all, respondents were also being asked to rate conversational frequencies for issues like financial performance.

Other, even less obtrusive surrogates are conceivable. In Chapter 4, for example, we reported on the proximity of a company's CEOs' offices to the offices of their ethics responsible officers. Our assumption in this case is that the greater the proximity, the more the executive team in general has ready access to, and actual concern for, questions of ethics in the organization.

Our studies reported in Chapters 5 and 6 also assessed the influence of external forces in the institutional environment on top management decision making. We could have tried to ask executives questions as to why they introduced their ethics programs. Again, socially desirable responses are likely. Which executive would not say, "We did it because we care about ethics"? Instead, we asked our respondents to report on the extent to which the top executive team is familiar with and has talked about the United States Sentencing Commission (USSC) guidelines, on the assumption that the more familiar executives are with the guidelines, the more likely they will bring their companies' policy into line with the guidelines.

We also assessed the influence of external, institutional influences by obtaining attendance lists from high-profile industry meetings focused on ethics (for example, Conference Board meetings). These archival data provided us with a more objective account of a company's exposure to external influences favoring the development of ethics programs. As a result of this multipronged data collection effort, using both surrogate and archival data, we were in a position to assess more accurately the role of top management's own commitments in the creation of ethics programs compared with environmental influences on ethics structures and programs.

Media reports and legal records provide seemingly attractive archival sources of information about ethics in organizations. Newspapers often report ethical failures of organizations and their employees and sometimes also report on efforts at improvement, such as the introduction of ethics programs. Legal records provide evidence of a subset of corporate actions that have a strong overlap with unethical corporate behavior: illegal corporate behavior, or behavior that, although legal, results in a civil suit. These sources raise several important difficulties, however, that require great care in their use.

First, there are issues of properly interpreting these reports. Just what kind of newspaper report counts as evidence of unethical behavior—reports that hint at ethical failure or that raise allegations? Or reports that provide conclusive documentation? Any of these might be appropriate, depending on the research question. It may, for instance, be sufficient to consider allegations if one is studying a company's responses to perceptions of ethical illegitimacy. For example, the research reported in Chapters 5 and 6 was focused on ethics programs in part as a means of maintaining a company's societal legitimacy in response to suspicions of ethical impropriety. Given that research question, both proven and alleged improprieties were relevant. On the other hand, in studying responses to actual problems internal to the company, a higher standard of evidence probably is in order. Legal records provide similar difficult choices. Does one consider only criminal convictions and civil suits a company lost? Or are cases of acquittal still relevant indications of a potential role for legal pressures on a company's structuring decisions? Moreover, is it actually appropriate to use legal records as a surrogate for something like unethical behavior? After all, some companies may be very good at hiding rampant unethical behavior, in which case legal records would be very misleading. So, again, the use of the archival measure depends on the research question: as indications of what is actually occurring in companies, legal records may be inaccurate, but as indications of the kind of external pressures a company is subjected to, they may indeed provide reasonable measures.

Even if one agrees about the kind of incidents and records that are appropriate, they must be read, interpreted, and recorded by researchers. Often this is a large task, requiring multiple researchers to be involved, and thus raises issues of consistency in interpretation. Even if only one researcher is involved, there remain issues of consistency across time. Consequently, it is important to pay attention to good methodological standards for qualitative analyses (cf. Miles and Huberman 1984), including the use of other researchers to check on at least a sampling of the primary researchers' interpretation and coding of various reports and documents.

It may be tempting to try to avoid the work and uncertainties of the interpretation and coding process for archival data by simply relying on computerized counts of key words and phrases. To do so, however, is not necessarily better or more precise than other methods and can lead to inaccurate findings. For example, our own research into newspaper reports of corporate unethical actions and legal problems turned up many article headlines with references to lawsuits in the title. On examining the details of the articles, however, it became clear that most of these articles actually dealt with lawsuits over rather common business disputes (for example, about product delivery delays or involving disputes with shareholders) that in most cases should not be counted as ethical failures on the part of the company. Thus, it would not have been a good indication of a company's ethical status, or legal problems relevant to the creation of ethics programs, simply to count the number of headlines mentioning lawsuits. What mattered was the content, and, in this case, accurate assessment of the content required that researchers actually read the article or an abstract of the article.

Another example of the problems of interpreting archival data arises in connection with the use of various published indices and ratings of corporations, such as the rating systems invoked by socially responsible investment funds or published rankings in business magazines. Any such index or rating system relies on criteria that, although they sound relevant to ethics (for example, reputation, most admired) nevertheless raise multiple normative questions. Most obviously, one can ask why certain ranking criteria should be used rather than others—for example, why rate tobacco companies lower than gambling companies? Do all arms sales count against a company? Or just some? If just some, which ones? In addition, even if the criteria are clear, who assesses how well particular companies fit the criteria? Are company data sources used? Are external evaluators used? If so, who evaluates the evaluators? Because most such ranking systems and indices use multiple measures, how are different criteria combined into a single ranking? How many tobacco sales, for example, does it take to equal a certain amount of weapons sales? Or how many tobacco sales equate to particular kinds of labor practices, either good or bad? In short, although indices may be tempting archival data points, care is required in their use (cf. Waddock and Graves 1997 for a good example of the use of such indices).

Questions arise yet again when one finds that archival measures and field data do not mesh. In the case of the study reported in Chapters 5 and 6, we collected archival data about media coverage of company's ethical failings. We also asked our respondents a set of questions probing the respondent's own assessment of the extent to which the company had been subject to negative media scrutiny over ethical problems. These two different measures were not well correlated with each other, forcing us to choose between our own interpretation of media problems and our respondents' interpretations (whatever they might be). In the interest of avoiding common methods biases in our study, and also because we knew what our interpretive standards were, we relied on archival data. Different research questions and research designs, however, might suggest another course of action.

Researchers often will need to be creative in developing archival and surrogate measures. For example, in one of our studies we initially needed to contact each of the Fortune 1000 companies to find out who the company's "ethics responsible officer" was. We did this by calling each company's corporate communications or corporate public affairs office. In many cases, we received an answer right away, but, in some cases, it took minutes or even days for someone to find out who the appropriate officer was. In one case, the person answering the company telephone turned to co-workers in the room to ask, "Do we have anyone in the company responsible for ethics?" We then heard a hearty round of laughter on the part of the co-workers. Were we engaged in a study of the effectiveness of company ethics programs, we could have systematically timed the delay in answering such a seemingly simple question on the assumption that, in most companies, a more effective and active ethics program will generate quicker responses to such questions.

Research Support and Funding

The study reported in Chapters 5 and 6 has an interesting origin: it was funded by a temporary entity called the Ethics in Business Research Fund, which was created using money that several major accounting firms were forced to pay as a penalty for illegal behavior. We are not suggesting that every instance of illegal business behavior is a potential gain for researchers because we have seen few other examples like this. We mention it to highlight the broad and creative stance that researchers will need to take to find financial support for business ethics research. Funding for ethics research is, in our experience, "hit and miss." There is no predictable, steady pipeline for such research, as is enjoyed by fields in science and engineering or even some other applied social science and organizational fields. In our own experience, it pays (that is, pays for research) if scholars build a wide-ranging network of contacts because business ethics research funding can be transient and can arise from multiple and varied sources. We heard about the Ethics in Business Research Fund only because a distant acquaintance who was chief financial officer of a modest-sized company saw a small notice of the fund in an accounting practitioners' magazine and brought it to our attention. In another case, a board member of a practitioner organization, who also had some academic interests, heard one of us speak on ethics at an academic conference and approached us regarding a possible study. Thus, unfortunately, gaining support for ethics research often is a matter of being in the right place at the right time. This, in turn, means being proactive and seeking out potential sources of funding and presenting ideas for research, even if the funding source traditionally has not supported ethics research. Proposals for ethics research may be met with skepticism: What is there to study? How could it possibly be studied? Is this simply going to criticize our company? How will this be relevant to managers? Thus, successful funding of empirical research in ethics will need to present examples of successful and valuable research and repeatedly will need to make a strong case for the value, feasibility, and methodological rigor of such research. Empirical business ethics research does not enjoy a ready list of willing contributors.

CONCLUSION

There is much work yet to be accomplished if we are to increase our understanding of ethics in organizations. We will need to conceptualize more fully the phenomena under study, that is, ethics at both the organizational and individual levels. We will also need to think carefully about gaining access to appropriate samples and designing both qualitative and quantitative studies that increase understanding while answering research questions in a reliable and valid manner. Using diverse but complementary methods and data sources within a particular research stream can be a useful approach, especially in an underresearched area. For example, the researcher can begin with a qualitative interview study that attempts to understand how people think about a particular topic. Such studies usually generate hypotheses that then can be tested using more traditional survey or experimental methods. In all cases, care must be taken to avoid or at least control for social desirability bias in respondents and subjects and interpretive failures on the part of researchers. This chapter discussed a number of successful methods and techniques that have been used, and it is hoped that future researchers will add to this tool kit. Finally, business ethics research frequently raises its own challenging ethical issues about the conduct of research, such as the use of deceptive practices, that must be anticipated and addressed.

References

Akaah, I. P. 1992. Social inclusion as a marketing ethics correlate. *Journal of Business Ethics* 11(8):599–608.

Alexander, C., and H. Becker. 1978. The use of vignettes in survey research. *Public Opinion Quarterly* 42:93–104.

Babbie, E. 1986. *The practice of social research*, 4th ed. Belmont, CA: Wadsworth.

Baron, R. A., and J. H. Neuman. 1996. Workplace violence and workplace aggression: Evidence on their relative frequency and potential causes. *Aggressive Behavior* 22:161–173.

Baumrind, D. 1964. Some thoughts on ethics of research: After reading Milgram's "Behavioral study of obedience." *American Psychologist* 19:421–423.

Braithwaite, R. 1955. *Scientific explanation*. Cambridge: Cambridge University Press.

Brass, D. J., and G. R. Oldham. 1976. Validating an in-basket test using an alternative set of leadership scoring dimensions. *Journal of Applied Psychology* 61:652–657.

Butterfield, K., L. K. Treviño, and G. R. Weaver. 2000. Moral awareness in business organizations: Influences of issue-related and social context factors. *Human Relations* 53(7):981–1018.

Campbell, J. P., and J. Stanley. 1963. *Experimental and quasi-experimental designs for research*. Chicago: Rand McNally.

Crowne, D. P., and D. Marlowe. 1960. A new scale of social desirability independent of psychopathology. *Journal of Consulting Psychology* 24:349–354.

Dalton, D.R., and M. B. Metzger. 1992. Towards candor, cooperation, and privacy
in applied business ethics. *Business Ethics Quarterly* 2:207–221.

Dalton, D. R., C. M. Daily, and J. C. Wimbush. 1997. Collecting "sensitive" data in
business ethics research: A case for the unmatched count technique (UCT).
Journal of Business Ethics 16:1049–1057.

Dalton, D. R., J. M. Wimbush, and C. M. Daily. 1994. Using the unmatched count
techniques (UCT) to estimate base r. *Personnel Psychology* 47(4):817–828.

Dalton, D.R., J. M. Wimbush, and C. M. Daily. 1996. Candor, privacy and "legal
immunity" in business ethics research: An empirical assessment of the randomized response technique. *Business Ethics Quarterly* 6:87–99.

Derry, R. 1987. Moral reasoning in work-related conflicts. In *Research in corporate
social performance and policy*, ed. W. Frederick, 25–50. Greenwich, CT: JAI
Press.

Fernandes, M. F., and D. M. Randall. 1992. The nature of social desirability
response effects in ethics research. *Business Ethics Quarterly* 2(2):183–205.

Fisher, C. D. 1984. Laboratory experimentation. In *Method and analysis in organizational research*, ed. T. Bateman and G. Ferris, 169–185. Reston, VA: Reston
Publishing Co.

Gaertner, K. 1990. The effect of ethical climate on managers' decisions. In *Morality, rationality, and efficiency: Perspectives on socioeconomics*, ed. R. M. Coughlin.
Armonk, NY: M. E. Sharpe.

Giacolone, R. A., and Greenberg, J. 1997. *Antisocial behavior in organizations*.
Thousand Oaks, CA: Sage.

Greenberg, J. 1990. Employee theft as a reaction to underpayment inequity: The
hidden cost of pay cuts. *Journal of Applied Psychology* 75:561–568.

Greenberg, J. 1993. Stealing in the name of justice: Informational and interpersonal moderators of theft reactions to underpayment inequity. *Organizational
Behavior and Human Decision Processes* 54:81–103.

Greenberg, J. 1996. *The quest for justice on the job: Essays and experiments*. Thousand
Oaks, CA: Sage.

Greenberg, J. 1998. The cognitive geometry of employee theft: Negotiating the
line between taking and stealing. In *Dysfunctional behavior in organizations*, Vol.
2: *Nonviolent behaviors in organizations*, ed. R. W. Griffin, A. O'Leary-Kelly, and
J. Collins. Greenwich, CT: JAI Press.

Hessing, D. J., H. Elffers, and R. W. Weigel. 1988. Exploring the limits of self-
reports and reasoned action: An investigation of the psychology of tax evasion
behavior. *Journal of Personality and Social Psychology* 54:405–413.

Ilgen, D. R. 1986. Laboratory research: A question of when, not if. In *Generalizing from laboratory to field setting*, ed. E. A. Locke, 257–267. Lexington, MA: Lexington Books.

Kaplan, A. 1964. *The conduct of inquiry*. San Francisco: Chandler.

Kelman, H. C., and V. L. Hamilton. 1989. *Crimes of obedience*. New Haven: Yale University Press.

Kerlinger, F. N. 1986. *Foundations of behavioral research*. 3d ed. New York: CBS College Publishing.

Kram, K., P. Yeager, and G. Reed. 1989. Decisions and dilemmas: The ethical dimension in the corporate context. In *Research in corporate social performance and policy*, ed. J. Post, 21–54. Greenwich, CT: JAI Press.

Liedtka, J. M. 1992. Exploring ethical issues using personal interviews. *Business Ethics Quarterly* 2:161–181.

Locke, E. A. 1986. *Generalizing from laboratory to field settings*. Lexington, MA: Lexington Books.

McCall, M. W., and M. Lombardo. 1978. Looking Glass, Inc.: An organizational simulation. Technical Report No. 12, Greensboro, NC: Center for Creative Leadership.

McCall, M. W., and M. Lombardo. 1984. Using simulation for leadership and management research: Through the looking glass. In *Method and analysis in organizational research*, ed. T. S. Bateman and G. R. Ferris, 201–221. Reston, VA: Reston Publishing Co.

Miles, M. B., and A. M. Huberman. 1984. *Qualitative data analysis: A sourcebook of new methods*. Beverly Hills, Calif.: Sage.

Milgram, S. 1974. *Obedience to authority: An experimental view*. New York: Harper & Row.

Mook, D. G. 1983. In defense of external invalidity. *American Psychologist* 38:379–387.

Nisbett, R. E., and T. D. Wilson. 1977. Telling more than we can know: Verbal reports on mental processes. *Psychological Review* 84:231–259.

Organ, D. W. 1988. *Organizational citizenship behavior: The good soldier syndrome*. Lexington, MA: Lexington Books.

Paulhus, D. L. 1984. Two-component models of socially desirable responding. *Journal of Personality and Social Psychology* 46:598–609.

Raghavarao, D., and W. T. Federer. 1973. Application of the BIB designs as an alternative to the randomized response method in survey sampling. Number BU-490-M in the Mimeo Series of the Biometrics Unit. Cornell University.

Randall, D. M., and M. F. Fernandes. 1991. The social desirability response bias in ethics research. *Journal of Business Ethics* 10:805–817.

Randall, D. M., and A. M. Gibson. 1990. Methodology in business ethics research: A review and critical assessment. *Journal of Business Ethics* 9(6):457–472.

Rest, J., D. Narvaez, M. J. Bebeau, and S. J. Thoma. 1999. *Postconventional moral thinking: A neo-Kohlbergian approach*. Mahwah, N.J.: Erlbaum.

Robertson, D. C., and T. Rymon. 2001. Purchasing agents' deceptive behavior: A randomized response technique study. *Business Ethics Quarterly* 11(3):455–479.

Robinson, S. L., and R. B. Bennett. 1995. A typology of deviant workplace behaviors: A multi-dimensional scaling study. *Academy of Management Journal* 38:555–572.

Robinson, S. L., and J. Greenberg. 1998. Employees behaving badly: Dimensions, determinants and dilemmas in the study of workplace deviance. In *Trends in organizational behavior*, Vol. 5, ed. D. M. Rousseau and C. Cooper. New York: John Wiley & Sons.

Rosenberg, M. J. 1965. When dissonance fails: On eliminating evaluation apprehension from attitude measurement. *Journal of Personality and Social Psychology* 1:28–42.

Seligman, M. 1990. *Learned optimism*. New York: Knopf.

Sheldon, K. M., and L. King. 2001. Why positive psychology is necessary. *American Psychologist* 56:216–217.

Skarlicki, D. P., and R. Folger. 1997. Retaliation in the workplace: The roles of distributive, procedural and interactional justice. *Journal of Applied Psychology* 82:416–425.

Staw, B. M., and S. G. Barsade. 1993. Affect and managerial performance: A test of the sadder-but-wiser vs. happier-and-smarter hypotheses. *Administrative Science Quarterly* 38:304–331.

Toffler, B. L. 1986. *Tough choices: Managers talk ethics*. New York: John Wiley & Sons.

Treviño, L. K. 1986. Ethical decision making in organizations: A person–situation interactionist model. *Academy of Management Review* 11(3):601–617.

Treviño, L. K., and V. B. Victor. 1992. Peer reporting of unethical behavior: A social context perspective. *Academy of Management Journal* 35:38–64.

Treviño, L. K., and G. R. Weaver. 1997. Ethical issues in competitive intelligence practice: Consensus, conflicts and challenges. *Competitive Intelligence Review* 8(1):61–72.

Treviño, L. K., and S. A. Youngblood. 1990. Bad apples in bad barrels: A causal analysis of ethical decision making behavior. *Journal of Applied Psychology* 75:378–385.

Treviño, L. K., K. Butterfield, and D. McCabe. 1998. The ethical context in organizations: Influences on employee attitudes and behaviors. *Business Ethics Quarterly* 8(3):447–476.

Treviño, L. K., L. P. Hartman, and M. Brown. 2000. Moral person and moral manager: How executives develop a reputation for ethical leadership. *California Management Review* 42(4):128—142.

Treviño, L. K., G. Weaver, D. Gibson, and B.L. Toffler. 1999. Managing ethics and legal compliance: What works and what hurts. *California Management Review* 41(2):131—151.

Uleman, J. S., and Bargh, J.A. 1989. *Unintended thought*. New York: Guilford.

Vardi Y., and Y. Wiener. 1996. Misbehavior in organizations: A motivational framework. *Organization Science* 7:151—165.

Waddock, S. A., and S. B. Graves. 1997. The corporate social performance-financial performance link. *Strategic Management Journal* 18:303—319.

Warner, S. L. 1965. RR: A survey technique for eliminating evasive answer bias. *Journal of the American Statistical Association* 60:63—69.

Weaver, G. R. 1995. Does ethics code design matter? Effects of ethics code rationales and sanctions on recipients' justice perceptions and content recall. *Journal of Business Ethics* 15(5): 367—385.

Weber, J. 1992. Scenarios in business ethics research: Review, critical assessment, and recommendations. *Business Ethics Quarterly* 2:137—160.

Wimbush, J. C., and D. R. Dalton. 1997. Base rate for employee theft: Convergence of multiple methods. *Journal of Applied Psychology* 82:756—763.

Zedeck, S. 1986. A process analysis of the assessment center method. In *Research in organizational behavior*, ed. B. M. Staw and L. L. Cummings, 8:269—296. New York: JAI Press.

Zerbe, W., and D. Paulhus. 1987. Socially desirable responding in organizational behavior: A reconception. *Academy of Management Review* 12:250—264.

Unfinished Business Ethics:
Open Questions for Future Study

One need not look beyond news headlines to see that there is much unfinished business in the area of business ethics. Despite several decades of
fairly high-profile attention devoted to business ethics during the late
twentieth century—including the studies and programs described earlier in
this book—the twenty-first century already has featured not just the largest
bankruptcy filing in American history (Enron), but one that appears directly
linked to ethical improprieties on the part of the company and its auditors.
Thus, we titled this chapter "Unfinished Business Ethics" because, despite
significant advances, we have become quite aware of the unfinished agenda
for business ethics research. This agenda will likely always be unfinished
because the landscape surrounding business ethics is vast, complex, and
highly dynamic. Changes in technology, culture, politics, demographics,
and other areas of life, for example, globalization, workforce diversity, and
so on, continue to challenge organizations by creating new ethical issues
and questions and by forcing new ways to manage with those issues.
Consider how the U.S. Sentencing Commission (USSC) Guidelines for
Corporations altered the context surrounding American business in late
1991. Largely as a result of that contextual shift, most large American corporations now have codes of conduct and varying levels of formal and informal systems to manage ethics and legal compliance. Most of the development of ethics programs occurred during times of economic prosperity. It

remains to be seen whether difficult economic conditions will influence organizations' ongoing commitment to these programs.

Ongoing change in the context surrounding organizations continues with the attention nongovernmental organizations (NGOs) now command because of the rapid dissemination of information via the Internet and other means. Matters that once concerned a limited internal or local audience now can be the subject of widespread public scrutiny. Both conceptual and empirical scholarship will be needed to help management understand and cope with such changes. In this chapter, we identify some of the conceptual challenges facing business ethics researchers and follow that discussion by suggesting areas of research that remain much in need of empirical investigation.

Conceptual Challenges

As we suggested in previous chapters, improvements will be needed in conceptualizing key phenomena in business ethics. That includes wrestling with the complex relationships between normative and empirical business ethics (Part I of this book). It will also mean carefully mapping the content domains at both the individual and organizational levels and clearly defining the concepts of interest.

At a general level, for example, questions remain to be answered regarding what our focus should be when we study ethical and unethical individual and organizational conduct. We also should consider how these constructs relate to others currently being studied in other areas of organizational inquiry. At the individual level, books and articles are being written about deviant, antisocial, aggressive, and counterproductive behavior as well as citizenship behavior and specific types of conduct, such as theft or whistle-blowing behavior. Are these, or are they not, part of the domain of business ethics research? And what can business ethics research learn or adopt from these studies?

At the organizational level, questions remain about the relationships among social responsibility, corporate reputation, corporate citizenship, corporate philanthropy, and corporate crime, and what any or all of these have to do with business ethics. For example, business ethics has generally been treated as a mostly internal organizational issue related to managing the behavior of one's employees, whereas corporate social performance has been considered more of an issue of relationships with external stakeholders, such as the community. There is clear overlap between the two, however, at both theoretical and practical levels. Theories of ethical behavior and corporate social responsibility often share common normative concerns and frameworks and even common roots in organization theories. (For example, our study of decoupled ethics initiatives in Chapter 6 treated them as a type of corporate social performance.) At a practical level, what is the relationship between individuals involved in corporate functions (such as ethics and compliance) and public affairs, two areas that are tripping over each other more and more in organizations? What are the theoretical and practical implications of separating or integrating these areas of research and organizational activity?

In the same way, we may question the relationship, if any, between business ethics and corporate philanthropy and other corporate reputation-building activities. Initial reports of the immense Enron bankruptcy have been accompanied by stories of management's largesse in the Houston community. As a result, the company was considered a model corporate citizen, but the corporation's concurrent ethical lapses would suggest no relationship, or perhaps even an inverse relationship, between philanthropy and ethics. Is it possible that companies engaged in unethical business practices use philanthropy as a way to manage their reputations? These relationships are not well understood, either theoretically or empirically.

These latter questions relate to issues of corporate structure and the way business ethics fits into a broader conceptual and organizational framework. Corporations are struggling to determine the appropriate relationships among their ethics and compliance offices, public affairs offices, corporate philanthropy offices, audit functions, and so on, and how all of this relates to corporate strategy and performance. Theoretically, what do these functions share and how are they different? Should all the functions listed in the foregoing operate under a single umbrella in organizations? If not, which ones should be aligned and which ones separated? If separated, how should they be linked? What should reporting and communication relationships be like? As corporate ethics functions have matured, some corporations are experimenting with decentralizing the function. This is in keeping with the current management "mantra" that preaches the value of reduced hierarchy and decentralization of authority. Yet, something tells us that there are theoretical reasons why "ethics" may need to be managed from the top and center of organizations to be successful. Research will be needed to investigate that question.

Questions also arise concerning just what do we mean by *success* in the management of business ethics? What does it mean to be an ethical company, and how would one measure that? One of the major challenges of studying business ethics is that success is often evidenced, in a more negative sense, by the "absence" of unethical or illegal conduct; but empirical researchers generally wish to account for increases in some phenomenon. It is difficult to explain variance in something that is absent (for example, illegal behavior). One can study decreases in unethical or illegal conduct over time, but that requires longitudinal research that is rare in organizational science and particularly challenging in this sensitive area. Also, even if the dependent variable of interest declines from one year to the next, it is difficult to attribute that decline to a single management structure or action when so many phenomena are constantly changing in organizations.

This kind of issue is easy to notice in a practical context. From a practical perspective, ethics officers have had to decide whether more calls to their ethics hotlines, for example, indicate success or failure of their programs. On the one hand, such calls indicate that employees are aware of ethical issues and asking for advice. On the other hand, they also may indicate that substantial problems do exist. Will structures and programs to manage business ethics always be necessary, or should ethics offices and officers be working to put themselves "out of business"? Would that be an indicator of success? Is it possible to imagine a large organization in which ethics is so ingrained in the broader organizational culture that no separate programs or structures are necessary to keep it alive? At what point would we say that such a culture has been achieved? Researchers need to think carefully about the meaning of success and will need to be on the lookout for opportunities to investigate it in longitudinal studies.

Levels of analysis issues are also important, as they are in all areas of organization science. By definition, management researchers are concerned with the complex interplay between individuals, groups, organizations, and their broader environments; but business ethics researchers have not yet considered these issues in a systematic manner. Our own work has hinted at relationships across levels of analysis, but many questions remain. For example, how does executive ethical leadership translate into supervisory ethical leadership and ultimately influence employee behavior? How does the values transmission process operate across levels in the organization?

Finally, does ethics management require the development of its own unique theories, or can we adequately understand ethical behavior at the individual and organizational level by relying on existing theories? One could argue that existing theory is sufficient. After all, ethical behavior is just a particular kind of behavior, and many theories exist to help us understand behavior in organization settings. At the individual level, existing psychological and social psychological theories already have proven to be enormously helpful. Much of what we now know about ethical conduct in organizations has relied on theories developed by others, such as cognitive moral development (Kohlberg 1969), planned behavior (Ajzen 1991), social learning theory (Bandura 1986), role conflict (Gross, Mason, and McEachern 1958), reinforcement (Skinner 1953), organizational justice (Greenberg 1996), and social cognition (Fiske and Taylor 1991) just to name a few. At the macrolevel, business ethics researchers have successfully called on control theory (Etzioni 1961), institutional theory (DiMaggio and Powell 1983), and resource dependence theory (Pfeffer 1981) to predict relationships. With such theoretical richness available, why develop new theory? The reason is that because some believe that effective research on business ethics requires integration of the normative with the social scientific. For example, Jones and Wicks (1999) developed what they termed a convergent stakeholder theory that moves stakeholder research toward theoretical integration. We have argued (Treviño and Weaver 1999; Chapter 3, this book), however, that the stakeholder approach is not a theory at all, but rather a research tradition within which researchers with an interest in organizational–stakeholder relations apply a variety of extant theories to their research questions. In our view, applying extant theories is likely to be more successful because truly integrative theories are extremely rare (for example, Kohlberg 1969) and, when they do exist, tend to please no one and are subject to criticism from all sides (Modgil and Modgil 1986).

This is not to deny, however, the potential value of coming full circle and raising questions about the normative propriety of various efforts to manage ethical behavior. To date, little, if any, attention has been devoted to analyzing the ethical quality of ethics programs themselves. Most such programs have been developed in light of a mix of social scientific findings, intuitive judgments of propriety, legal directives, and the constraints imposed by the operational and financial situations of organizations. The ethical status of the outcome of such programs has mostly been taken for granted; our own studies, for example, mostly assume the ethical propriety of ethics programs; but serious questions can be raised regarding the ethics of ethics programs. Do anonymous reporting systems, for example, violate individuals' rights to confront accusers? Similarly, at what point do efforts to foster proper behavior become exercises of unjustifiable cognitive or behavioral influence? According to some ethical theories (Kantian views, for example), behavior that is coerced is, in important respects, behavior that ultimately cannot be viewed as ethical behavior. So, even though prospects for fully integrative normative and empirical approaches to business ethics are daunting, this is not to deny that there is much room for empirically informed normative critiques of both existing practice and the recommendations implicit or explicit in current empirical research.

Empirical Challenges

In addition to the conceptual challenges outlined herein, the need remains for ongoing quality empirical work. In the next sections, we suggest just some of the many areas of organizational- and individual-level business ethics research that are in need of investigation.

Organizational-level Topics. At the macrolevel, we need to understand better the extent to which formal systems for managing ethics and legal compliance have become institutionalized elements of the modern corporation versus a more tenuous fad or fashion (Abrahamson 1996). Difficult financial times often make staff functions the target of cost-cutting measures. Therefore, the time may be ripe for attempts to understand the factors that contribute to whether the ethics/compliance function is considered to be peripheral or integral to the business. Our own work suggests that senior executives' personal commitment to ethics plays a role (Weaver, Treviño, and Cochran 1999a, 1999b), but other factors are also likely to be involved.

We also need additional work aimed at further understanding the internal and external influences on the scope, orientation, and integration of formal ethics and compliance programs. For example, industry environments provide an important, but underresearched normative context. The defense contracting industry has been involved, for many years, in formal efforts to foster ethical behavior and legal compliance known as the Defense Industry Initiative (DII). This initiative resulted from defense industry contracting scandals and spawned the development of the earliest compliance programs that ultimately became the model for subsequent programs in other industries. Is this model, developed for a highly regulated industry such as defense, appropriate for less regulated industries? What industry characteristics do and should influence ethics or compliance program characteristics? Have we identified the most important characteristics, or are there others we should be studying?

Another relevant question may relate to how organizations learn from each other in this arena. For example, in a type of avoidance learning, organizations may pay particular attention and learn what *not* to do from firms that get caught engaging in misconduct. Are firms more likely to pay attention to such news when they identify with the organization involved— when it is similar in size or industry? When does such attention turn to action, and what kinds of actions are precipitated? Alternatively, under what circumstances is learning a more positive type of social learning? For example, Merck Corporation is widely known in the business ethics community for its unusual decision to develop and then donate a medicinal cure for a parasite-based ailment afflicting people in many developing countries. The parasite causes blindness ("river blindness"), and Merck committed to providing and distributing a cure for free and forever to people who suffer from the disease. Since that time, a number of other pharmaceutical firms have followed suit, donating their own drugs in a similar fashion. How strong are the various contextual processes that encourage organizations to imitate each other regarding ethical issues, how might they work, and what factors might inhibit this kind of diffusion of ethical innovations? Do external members of boards of directors play a role in the development and spread of ethics initiatives? How powerful is the influence of professional organizations (for example, the Ethics Officer Association) in spreading ethics innovations? Can social network studies (Rowley 1997) and social contagion theories help us to understand how organizations learn about and adopt new attitudes and behaviors in the ethics arena?

Given the amount of structural change occurring in today's business organizations, it will be important to understand better how such changes influence ethics and compliance programs and vice versa. For example, are ethics and values considered in merger and acquisition discussions? To what extent do they influence whether a deal is made or not made? Once such agreements exist, how do or should organizations manage the process of integrating distinct ethics or compliance programs? Culture clashes often are blamed for the failure of corporate "marriages" that look good on paper (for example, Daimler Chrysler). How do differences in the "ethical cultures" of organizations figure into these clashes? We know ethics officers who are currently wrestling with these issues or who fear having to do so in the future. What kind of guidance can business ethics researchers provide to them?

Nongovernmental organizations (NGOs) are growing in importance as a result of advances in information technology and information dissemination. For example, a small organization such as Transparency International has garnered enormous attention because of its publication of its annual Corruption Index, which ranks countries in terms of corrupt business practice. An increasing number of indices are being published that rank companies based on a variety of criteria, including their ethical and social performance. How are businesses reacting to this kind of attention, which is so difficult to anticipate and predict?

Globalization presents unique challenges to business ethics researchers and managers. How does one manage business ethics when the targets of management action represent multiple cultures, histories, and varying value priorities? Although we know quite a bit about values differences across national cultures due to work by Hofstede (1980) and others, more research is needed to understand how those value differences affect the management of business ethics. Beliefs about what is and is not ethical may not differ as much across cultures as does common business practice. For example, in many countries, bribery is a common practice, but that does not mean that bribery is considered to be ethical in those environments. Therefore, foreign nationals in such environments may accept organizational rules against paying bribes. On the other hand, nepotism is a common practice in collectivist cultures, where it also is considered to be ethical, whereas it is thought to be unethical in the United States. In the case of nepotism, a U.S.-based firm may have to change its rules to accommodate the values of its more collectivist organization members (Donaldson, 1996). An understanding of history also may be required. Ethics managers who have proposed implementing ethics hotlines in Europe have learned quickly that Europeans react negatively to such attempts that immediately revive bitter World War II and Soviet-era memories. Thus, managers require a complex understanding of the differences that exist across cultures and the implications of these differences for the effective management of business ethics across borders. Thus, not only do questions of ethical differences arise in global contexts, but also differences regarding how organizations can foster ethical behavior in light of varying cultural norms for organizational structuring and management (Weaver 2001).

The foregoing questions highlight the need for interdisciplinary study of ethics in organizations. Interdisciplinary study obviously is needed when dealing with efforts to meld normative and empirical insights and theories, but it is needed in other ways as well. A good understanding of organizational ethics in a global context likely will require the insights of scholars from management, cross-cultural psychology, cultural anthropology, and history. Similar, though less obvious, concerns hold for efforts to link the study of organizational ethics with the close relations noted earlier in this section (for example, studies of corporate social responsibility and organizational justice). Even though they are related topics, researchers in some of those areas may not attend to work done in another of those areas, such that the various subfields of organizational inquiry develop along independent trajectories with independent norms for what constitutes an interesting study, and different taken-for-granted methodological and theoretical positions. Thus, as in the case of normative and empirical inquiry, scholars will need to work to overcome these disciplinary (or subdisciplinary) barriers if many important questions about ethics in organizations are to be answered.

Microlevel Challenges. At the microlevel, additional work will be required to develop and test a fuller, more complex model of individual ethical decision making and behavior. Even the relatively simple model proposed by Treviño (1986) has not been tested fully. For example, characteristics of work, such as opportunities for role taking and resolution of moral conflict, that were proposed to influence the stage of moral development have not been studied empirically. Also, to our knowledge, individual differences such as field dependence and ego strength that were proposed to moderate the cognitive moral development/ethical behavior relationship have not been investigated. Further, we now know that the 1986 model was incomplete. It did not include the influence of moral intensity of the issue, added by Jones (1991), or other proposed stages in the ethical decision-making process, such as moral sensitivity, moral motivation, and moral character, that derive from Rest's (1986) work. Jones's moral intensity model has inspired a significant amount of empirical research, but most of that work has been aimed at the moral recognition and moral judgment stages of the ethical decision-making process. More research is needed to determine whether the moral intensity of issues influences the other stages (for example, moral motivation, moral character) and to document the dimensionality of the moral intensity construct. Recent research has suggested that two dimensions of that construct may be most important: magnitude of consequences and social consensus (Butterfield, Treviño, and Weaver 2000; May and Pauli 2000). As noted in Chapter 7, however, the construct also may need to be expanded beyond its current focus on utilitarian and social consensus standards of ethical behavior.

Current models of ethical decision-making behavior also focus primarily on ethical judgment and ethical action, neglecting moral awareness, recognition or sensitivity, moral motivation, and moral character. Therefore, future research will need to test more complex models. Among the additional complexities to be considered, however, is the question of whether unethical behavior and ethical behavior always ensue from the same general kind of process. People are capable of committing both right and wrong acts, often in close temporal proximity or even at the same time. Might the factors that collectively influence a person to act ethically differ not just in degree of influence, but in kind, from those that influence a person to act unethically? Emotional empathy, for example, may play an important role in determining a person's choice among several ethically acceptable courses of action but might play no role, or a different kind of role, in leading people to unethical behavior. Are the cognitive processes that lead to ethical judgments qualitatively different from the ones that lead to unethical judgments? In short, is there one model of ethical behavior, or are there multiple models for ethical and unethical behavior or for different categories of ethical behaviors (for example, do ethical decision processes about workplace matters mirror ethical decision processes about family matters)?

We should also recognize that current ethical decision-making and behavior models are highly cognitive in nature. This is not surprising given their roots in the cognitive moral development tradition. Even Jones's model relies heavily on social cognition theory (Fiske and Taylor 1991) for its predictions, another cognitive approach; however, emotion or affect is likely to play a larger role than it has been given credit for in the past. Ethical decision making is not as cold and calculating as these models suggest. Positive emotions, such as joy, pride, and hope, and negative emotions, such as anxiety, guilt, and fear, are likely to play a significant role in these processes and may be associated with multiple stages of the ethical decision-making process. Affect is receiving significant attention in the organizational behavior literature, and that work should find applicability in the business ethics arena.

Fairness and trust are also important topics of research within organizational behavior. These literatures offer significant opportunities for application to business ethics research. Greenberg (1990) has contributed significantly with his research on employee theft and distributive and procedural justice reactions to a pay cut. We also have begun to incorporate fairness considerations into our theoretical and empirical work (Treviño et al. 1999; Treviño and Weaver 2001; Weaver and Treviño 2001). The trust literature has potential to be applied as well, particularly as it relates to trust in one's supervisor and how that might impact relevant outcomes.

The role of fairness and trust leads to considerations of the importance of leadership. Leadership is one of the most heavily investigated areas within organizational behavior, and anecdotes about ethical leaders are common. Yet it is surprising to find how little systematic research attention has been paid to the ethical dimension(s) of leadership, particularly at the supervisory level. Supervisors are the persons who translate organizational values into day-to-day action. Therefore, it will be important to understand better what employees look for in supervisors and executives, from an ethics perspective, and how those qualities and behaviors influence important employee outcomes.

Demographic diversity is increasing in American society and in organizations. Therefore, it is appropriate to ask whether different demographic groups, like different cultures, have different values or behavioral norms that would require alternative approaches to ethics management. First, we need to know whether relevant values actually differ among these demographic groups. If they do, we should investigate whether different ethics management approaches will be needed; and, for all groups, we should be asking what the goals of ethics management should be. Should organizations be aiming for simple compliance with organizational values? Should they be shooting for identification or even internalization of the organization's values? Or should the goal be increasing the cognitive moral development of organizational members so that their independent decisions will be more ethical? What are the implications of these varied goals for ethics management and for subsequent employee attitudes and behaviors?

Along with demographic changes in the workforce, ethics scholars need to attend to the impact of technological change on organizations on the management of ethical issues within organizations. New organizational technologies have the potential to change the nature of relationships among organization members in terms of the frequency with which and depth to which those relationships are developed. New technologies also have the potential to change the time frame within which organizational decisions and behavior occur. Thus, technology can change how social learning processes create particular organizational stances toward ethics or alter the extent to which employees experience pressures to make ethical compromises or simply not to think about ethical issues. If empathy, for example, is an important affective element of ethical issue recognition or decision making, how will it be affected by the development of "virtual" workplaces? Thus, although much research has been done in various fields on ethical issues generated by new technologies, research also is needed that looks at how new technologies change the way more traditional questions of ethics arise and are dealt with in organizations.

More research also is required on the impact of a variety of specific ethics initiatives, such as codes, communications, hotlines, and training. Codes of conduct have received the most attention thus far (for example, Greenberg, in press; McCabe, Treviño, and Butterfield 1996; Treviño et al. 1999; Weaver 1993), and we have learned that codes do have an impact, although that impact depends on code implementation and follow-through. More work will be required to understand these limitations better. We have seen very little, if any, research on the outcomes of other ethics initiatives. For example, business organizations are investing substantial sums in ethics training. Such training varies widely in its goals, instructors, and methods, and it is rarely evaluated beyond asking participants about their satisfaction with the training experience. What are the relevant goals of ethics training? Do they include raising ethical awareness, rules comprehension, attitude change, ethical decision-making ability, moral judgment development? What type of training is most likely to accomplish each of these goals? How often should ethics training be repeated for it to be effective? Is ethics training more effective when conducted by external consultants, internal trainers, managers, or first-line supervisors? Is ethics training more effective if it occurs in a particular type of ethical environment? These are just a few of the questions that need to be systematically studied.

Along the same lines, many questions remain about the implementation and effects of values- versus compliance-oriented ethics programs. Our own research (Treviño et al. 1999; Weaver and Treviño 1999) is based on employees' perceptions of a program's orientation; but more fine-grained analysis of what constitutes a values-based or compliance-based program is needed. How are values best communicated? How are the values and compliance portions of these programs best combined?

Finally, little research has addressed the potential underside of efforts to manage organizational ethics. Typically, formal ethics programs are taken at face value by researchers and practitioners, as means (however flawed) toward promoting ethical behavior. But are there respects in which they might do the opposite? Are there respects in which they might be experienced as alienating or oppressive by employees, with corresponding reductions in the kinds of valued outcomes one would normally expect from an ethics program? Our own research on ethics program orientations indicates that there can be different outcomes from different program orientations, but we considered only the kinds of outcomes usually expected to develop out of ethics programs. What other counterintuitive, surprising, or unethical results might stem from various efforts to foster ethics in organizations?

Practical Issues. The paucity of funding for business ethics research remains a serious issue that may limit the quality of future research. Yet, with all of the business ethics centers that exist at colleges and universities, the potential exists to address this problem. Many of these centers have focused their attention on hosting conferences. In our view, the field needs fewer conferences and more high-quality research. We encourage these centers to consider redirecting at least some of their resources in the direction of funding high quality research, including doctoral dissertations.

CONCLUSION

We have identified a number of conceptual and empirical issues that can keep business ethics researchers busy for years to come. We probably have neglected to mention many more. If substantial progress is to be made in the study of business ethics, carefully designed high-quality research will be needed. We believe that understanding of business ethics can be advanced significantly if researchers engage in more grounded theory building, using rigorous qualitative research techniques. Such investigations are particularly needed in areas that are under-researched, such as understanding the role of affect in ethical decision making, the ethical dimensions of leadership, or what organizations pay attention to in their environments. Even where theories already exist, qualitative investigations may help to enhance them. For example, theories of ethical climate and culture probably could be enhanced by asking organization members what they look for and to what they pay attention. When theory testing is the goal, research needs to move beyond single respondent surveys that are likely to suffer from single source and common methods bias. More laboratory and field experiments are needed, but of course these need to take careful account of the very real ethical issues that arise when conducting research in such a sensitive area.

References

Abrahamson, E. 1996. Management fashion. *Academy of Management Review* 21(1):254–286.

Ajzen, I. 1991. The theory of planned behavior. *Organizational Behavior and Human Decision Processes* 50:179–211.

Bandura, A. 1986. *Social foundations of thought and action: a social cognitive theory*. Englewood Cliffs, NJ: Prentice-Hall.

Butterfield, K., L. K. Treviño, and G. R. Weaver. 2000. Moral awareness in business organizations: Influences of issue-related and social context factors. *Human Relations* 53(7):981–1018.

DiMaggio, P. J., and W. W. Powell. 1983. The iron cage revisited: Institutional isomorphism and collective rationality in organizational fields. *American Sociological Review* 48:147–160.

Donaldson, T. 1996. Values in tension: ethics away from home. *Harvard Business Review* September–October:48–62.

Etzioni, A. 1961. *A comparative analysis of complex organizations*. New York: Free Press.

Fiske, S. T., and S. E. Taylor. 1991. *Social cognition*, 2nd ed. New York: McGraw-Hill.

Greenberg, J. 1990. Employee theft as a reaction to underpayment inequity: The hidden costs of pay cuts. *Journal of Applied Psychology* 62:451–457.

Greenberg, J. 1996. *The quest for justice on the job: Essays and experiments*. Thousand Oaks, CA: Sage.

Greenberg, J. (in press). Who stole the money, and when? Individual and situational determinants of employee theft. *Organizational Behavior and Human Decision Processes*.

Gross, N., W. S. Mason, and A. W. McEachern. 1958. *Explorations in role analysis*. New York: John Wiley & Sons.

Hofstede, G. 1980. *Culture's consequences: International differences in work-related values*. Beverly Hills, Calif.: Sage Publications.

Jones, T. M. 1991. Ethical decision making by individuals in organizations: An issue-contingent model. *Academy of Management Review* 16(2):366–395.

Jones, T. M. and A. C. Wicks. 1999. Convergent stakeholder theory. *Academy of Management Review* 24:206–221.

Kohlberg, L. 1969. Stage and sequence: The cognitive developmental approach to socialization. In *Handbook of socialization theory*, ed. D. A. Goslin, 347–480. Chicago: Rand McNally.

May, D. R., and K. P. Pauli. 2000. The role of moral intensity in ethical decision making: A review and investigation of moral recognition, evaluation, and intention. Paper presented at the National Academy of Management meeting.

McCabe, D., L. K. Treviño, and K. Butterfield, K. 1996. The influence of collegiate and corporate codes of conduct on ethics-related behavior in the workplace. *Business Ethics Quarterly* 6:441–460.

Modgil, S., and C. Modgil, C., eds. 1986. *Lawrence Kohlberg: Consensus and controversy*. Philadelphia: Falmer.

Pfeffer, J. 1981. *Power in organizations*. Marshfield, Mass.: Pitman.

Rest, J. 1986. *Moral development: Advances in research and theory*. New York: Praeger.

Rowley, T. J. 1997. Moving beyond dyadic ties: A network theory of stakeholder influences. *Academy of Management Review* 22(4):887–911.

Skinner, B. F. 1953. *Science and human behavior*. New York: Macmillan.

Treviño, L. K. 1986. Ethical decision-making in organizations: A person situation interactionist model. *Academy of Management Review* 11(3):601–617

Treviño, L. K., and G. R. Weaver. 1999. The stakeholder research tradition: Converging theorists, not convergent theory. *Academy of Management Review* 24:222–227.

Treviño, L. K., and G. R. Weaver. 2001. Organizational justice and ethics program follow through: Influences on employees' helpful and harmful behavior. *Business Ethics Quarterly* 11:651–671.

Treviño, L. K., K. Butterfield, and D. McCabe. 1998. The ethical context in organizations: Influences on employee attitudes and behaviors. *Business Ethics Quarterly* 8(3):447–476.

Treviño, L. K., G. Weaver, D. Gibson, and B. Toffler. 1999. Managing ethics and legal compliance: What works and what hurts. *California Management Review* 41(2):131–151.

Weaver, G. R. 1993. Corporate codes of ethics: Purpose, process and content issues. *Business and Society* 32(1):44–58.

Weaver, G. R. 2001. Ethics programs in global businesses: Culture's role in managing ethics. *Journal of Business Ethics* 30(1):3–15.

Weaver, G. R., and L. K. Treviño. 1999. Compliance and values oriented ethics programs: Influences on employees' attitudes and behavior. *Business Ethics Quarterly* 9(2):325–345.

Weaver, G. R., and L. K. Treviño. 2001. The role of human resources in ethics/compliance management: a fairness perspective. *Human Resource Management Review* 11:1–22.

Weaver, G. R., L. K. Treviño, and P. Cochran. 1999a. Integrated and decoupled corporate social performance: Management commitments, external pressures, and corporate ethics practices. *Academy of Management Journal* 42:539–552.

Weaver, G. R., L. K. Treviño, and P. Cochran. 1999b. Corporate ethics programs as control systems: Influences of executive commitment and environmental factors. *Academy of Management Journal* 42(1):41–57.

Index

cognitive moral development and, 174–77
internal and external locus-of-control
    perceptions and, 177, 181
job pressure and, 177–78
moral approbation and, 179–81
peer influences on, 178–79
rewards and punishment and, 178
role conflict and, 178
moral approbation, effect on moral behavior,
    179
moral character, influences on, 181–83
moral education, effective tools for, 173–74
moral facts, and theoretical integration, 41
moral intensity
    dimensions of, 162–64
    effect of, on level of moral reasoning, 171–72
    need for broader conception of, 164, 336
moral judgment. *See also* ethical decision
    making
age and, 171–72
Canadian versus U.S. comparison on, 172
context-based differences in, 173
explanation of, 165
external factors and, 171–73
gender and, 170–71
in group contexts, 174
group leadership and, 174
job design and, 173
managers' age and tenure and, 172
national culture and, 171
organizational rank and, 172
probability and, 172
proposals for future research on, 172–73,
    176–77
proximity and, 172
work environment and, 172
moral motivation
emotion and, 183
influences on, 181–83
moral muteness, of employees, 197
moral psychology, in work of Adam Smith, xv
moral reasoning. *See also* ethical decision
    making; moral judgment
in business and nonbusiness contexts, 173
relationship between aggressive action
    tendencies and, 173
moral recognition

emotion and, 183
explanation of, 160
importance of ethics talk for, 163–64
issue framing and, 163
measures of, 162
moral intensity and, 162–65
organizational culture and training as
    correlates of, 162–65
moral sensitivity. *See* moral recognition
moral theory. *See* ethical theory; normative
    ethical theories
multidimensional scaling, 299
multivariate omnibus test, explanation of, 280

Narvaez, D., 170–71, 174
National Business Ethics Survey (2000), 76, 79–
    80, 82, 86
National Commission on Fraudulent
    Financial Reporting (Treadway
    Commission), recommendations of, 72
National Directory of Corporate Public Affairs
    (Columbia Books), 100, 134
naturalism, xiii
natural science model
critiques of, 21
as a model for the social sciences, 10, 21
Newspaper Abstracts (computer database), 104,
    137
Nichols, M. L., 174
noncoercive actors, influence on organiza-
    tional ethics, 74–75
nonresponse bias, 101, 135, 304
normative/empirical distinction. *See* empiri-
    cal research; normative scholarship;
    theoretical integration
normative ethical theories. *See also* ethical
    theory; normative scholarship
application of, in parallelist fashion, 32
explanation of, 16–18
explanatory role of, 39
normative principles as ideals, 34–36, 40, 54
normative scholarship. *See also* ethical theory;
    normative ethical theories; philosophy
academic home of, 10–11
of Adam Smith, xv
application of ethical theory in, 17–18
causation and autonomy in, 14–15